THE CHRISTIAN IMAGINATION

THE CHRISTIAN

IMAGINATION

Theology and the Origins of Race

Willie James Jennings

Yale

UNIVERSITY PRESS

New Haven & London

Set in Electra and Trajan types by Tseng Information Systems, Inc.,
Printed in the United States of America by Sheridan Books, Ann Arbor, Michigan.

The Library of Congress has cataloged the hardcover edition as follows:

Jennings, Willie James, 1961–
The Christian imagination : theology and the origins of race / Willie James Jennings.
p. cm.
Includes bibliographical references (p.) and index.

ISBN 978-0-300-15211-1 (hardcover : alk. paper)
1. Race—Religious aspects—Christianity. I. Title.
BT734.2.J46 2010
270.089—dc22
2009040203

ISBN 978-0-300-17136-5

A catalogue record for this book is available from the British Library.

This paper meets the requirements of ANSI/NISO Z39.48-1992 (Permanence of Paper).
10 9 8 7 6 5 4 3

For Mary and Ivory,
who while they picked cotton,
feet touching the soil,
dreamed of a different world

CONTENTS

Acknowledgments

Many colleagues heard, read, and provided helpful comments on portions of this book. The first group to do so were the scholars of the Afro-Scholars consultation, Alexis Abernethy, Henry Allen, Rhae-Ann Brooker, Venessa Brown, Denise Isom, Randal Jelks, Brenda King, Michelle Loyd-Paige, A. G. Miller, Edward Miller, Isaac M. T. Mwase, Barbara Omolade, William Pannell, Yolanda Pierce, Charsie Sawyer, and Donn Charles Thomas. I am also thankful for encouraging advice from the late Dr. Kwame Bediako and Dr. Gillian Bediako. At Duke University Divinity School, I enjoy the support of a beautiful faculty. I want to thank Esther Acolaste, Emmanuel Katongole, Richard Payne, W. C. Turner, Tonya Armstrong, and Tammy Williams for the wonderful conversations that fueled the fire of this book. I am also thankful to Richard Lischer, Amy Laura Hall, Richard Payne, and Greg Jones for taking the time to read the whole manuscript, which was originally well over five hundred pages! I want to offer special thanks to the Rev. Dr. J. Kameron Carter, who continues to be a wonderful conversation partner for me as I have been working out the ideas presented here. I also want to thank the members of the De-colonial Cosmopolitanism workshop organized by the esteemed Walter Mignolo. They are Costas Douzinas, Emma Perez, Bruce Lawrence, Siba N. Grovogui, Nelson Maldonado-Torres, Richard Rosa, Oscar Guardiola-Rivera, Eunice Sahle, Erdem Denk, Ramon Grosfóguel, William D. Hart, and Ebrahim Moosa. They offered helpful responses to my presentation of some of the ideas in this book. A very special word of appreciation goes to three individuals whose editorial work made this text far better than it would have been otherwise and reminded me of the deepest lesson of writing: clarity is sister to profundity. Anne Weston, formerly the editorial assistant at Duke University Divinity School, worked closely with me to meet every deadline and was an unwavering supporter of the project. I will forever sing her praises and call her blessed. Working with her and offering wonderful help were my research assistants, Sameer Yadav and Tommy Givens. I thank them for their good work. Jennifer Banks of Yale University Press is simply brilliant, capturing in almost every editorial comment exactly what I was attempting to say. Working with Jennifer has been pure joy. I am also very appreciative of the work of Lawrence Kenney, senior manuscript editor at Yale University Press. His comments on the text were always helpful.

I am extremely thankful for my family, who supported me in ways extravagant, humbling, and completely undeserved. I am deeply appreciative of my life partner, Joanne Browne Jennings, my marvelous daughters, Njeri Ariel and Safiya Eliana Simone, and my mother-in-love, Elise Browne. They are magnificent. I take great honor in being known first as Joanne's husband and the father of Njeri and Safiya. Their unwavering support, probing questions, and considerable humor kept my intellectual feet from slipping and my heart from sinking. They reminded me for whom I write and aspire to be a helpful theological voice. This book is dedicated not only to them but finally to my parents, Mary and Ivory Jennings Sr., who taught me to see the world with Christian eyes.

THE CHRISTIAN IMAGINATION

INTRODUCTION

Mary, my mother, taught me to respect the dirt. Like many black women from the South, she knew the earth like she knew her own soul. I came along late. I was the last of her eleven children, born not of the South but of the North, the fruit of the great migration when black folks wearied of the Jim Crow South and, in search of work, pointed their hopes toward northern cities and replanted their lives in colder air.[1] So I was born in Grand Rapids, Michigan, and found myself each spring with my mother, Mary, in her garden in the backyard.

There near the soil Mary deepened my understanding of her life, her history, and her hopes. My mother and my father, Ivory Jennings, were both magnificent storytellers. They told stories the way water cascades over Niagara Falls or runs down the Mississippi, stories that encompassed larger or smaller fragments of people, places, jokes, incidents, sayings, sermons, arguments, clothing, foods, meals, body parts, and prayers. I could never take in all those stories. I had to simply let them wash over me, again and again, until I was able to locate myself in the stream of their historical consciousness. Yet running through their amazing stories were several themes. Like large, immovable rocks that shaped the contours of the water's flow, these themes carried the keys for understanding every story.

Foremost was Jesus. Ivory and Mary loved Jesus. To say they were devout Christians is simply too pale a descriptor. A far more accurate characterization would be, "There were Ivory, Mary, and Jesus." Woven into the fabric of their lives was the God-man Jesus, who, rather than simply serving as an indicator of their orthodoxy, became the very shape of their stories. The stories of Jesus and Israel were so tightly woven into the stories my parents told of themselves, their lives in the South and in the North and then with their youngest children in the North, that it took me years to separate the biblical figures from extended family members, biblical sinners from the sinners all around us, and biblical places of pain from their places of pain. I was never able to separate biblical hopes from their real hopes. They knew the Bible, but, far more important, they knew the world through the Bible.

Ivory and Mary also channeled what Toni Morrison so eloquently called "the hurt of the hurt world," the knowledge of the deepest struggles and contradictions of black folks living among white folks.[2] My mother was one of those black women who carry intimate knowledge of slave voices. As a little girl she lived with her grandmother, a former slave. She also knew from her own experiences the lives of poor folks in the South who picked cotton, got cheated for their backbreaking labor, and worked diligently to stay out of harm's way with whites. The experience of agricultural labor, life in the dirt, also brought her into a contradictory but very intimate relationship with the land itself.

My parents loved the soil, the earth, the outside, and in their garden I saw the freedom they felt with it. The garden announced to them and the world that they were absolutely free to be themselves. My mother was a small woman with very muscular hands formed in the crucible of picking, pulling, holding, and hauling. She had a strong back, and when she bent over to touch the earth you could sense her power. She moved through her garden like it was an extension of her body. While in her garden, momma loved to talk about the Native American side of the family, her mother looking and her grandmother being part Cherokee.[3] She had irrefutable evidence for this native lineage, but I could rarely follow all the names, places, and events, especially as I was more content with observing how she worked the plants and the dirt with such brilliant efficiency. I was more interested in the corn, tomatoes, potatoes, beans, blackberries, carrots, and other gifts she brought forth from the earth. It was while she and I were in the garden that they came upon us.

To reach the garden in the backyard, you had to walk up the long driveway of our house and cross a gravel area and then walk across some grass. From the garden you could hear anyone walking across the gravel, the sound of pebbles crunching announcing their presence. But on one memorable occasion, I did not hear them. All I heard was the sound of feet moving through grass, and as I turned I saw two white men walking toward us. I knew my mother was at the farthest end of the garden, and I wanted to alert her. But that was unnecessary. I don't know how she knew or how she moved so quickly, but as I turned to find her with my eyes she was already positioning her body in front of mine. Her actions were ancient and modern—a mother moving her body in front of her child in the presence of strangers, a black woman placing her body between the body of her tender young son and the bodies of white men.

"Hello," they said, "I am ＿＿＿ and this is ＿＿＿. We are from First Christian Reformed Church down the street." They went on to ask my mother her name, which she told them in her regal southern voice: "I am Mary Jennings." She did not tell them my name. This was for my protection my mother would say. White men should not know the names of young black boys, as such knowledge would never be used for my good. The older man proceeded to talk about their church, the activities they had for kids, and what they were hoping to do in the neighborhood. He talked for a long time and quite formally, like he was giving a rehearsed speech. The younger man stood looking around nervously. After what seemed to me hours, the younger man showed his impatience with his fellow missionary's speech and bent down to speak to me. This was an odd gesture, I thought, not only because it too seemed rehearsed but also because it seemed inappropriate. I was about twelve years old, and when he bent down he was facing my navel. His words and verbal gestures were equally misplaced. He talked to me like I was a kindergartener or someone with little intelligence: What was my name, what school did I go to, did I like school? Does any twelve year old like school?

The strangeness of this event lay not only in their appearance in our backyard but also in the obliviousness of these men as to whom they were addressing—Mary Jennings, one of the pillars of New Hope Missionary Baptist Church. I thought it incredibly odd that they never once asked her if she went to church, if she was a Christian, or even if she believed in God. Mary and her twin sister, Martha, were about as close to their scriptural counterparts as you could get. Without fail they were in their customary seats in church every Sunday, and you could calibrate almost every activity of the church by and around them or us, their children. In addition, every Sunday they would visit every single person on the sick and shut-in list. The depth and complexities of Mary's faith were unfathomable, as unfathomable as the blindness of these men to our Christian lives.

My mother finally interrupted the speech of this would-be neighborhood missionary with the words, "I am already a Christian. I believe in Jesus and I attend New Hope Missionary Baptist church, where Rev. J. V. Williams is the pastor." I don't remember his exact reply to my mother's declaration of identity, but he kept talking for quite a few more wasted minutes. Finally they gave her some literature and left. I remember this event because it underscored an inexplicable strangeness embedded in the Christianity I lived and observed. Experiences like these fueled a question that has grown in hermeneutic force for me: Why did they not know us? They should have known us very well.

The church they were from—down the street—was not simply any church. It was First Christian Reformed Church, a mother church of the Christian Reformed denomination, a denomination that has its spiritual roots in the theology of John Calvin, its ethnic roots in the Netherlands, and the branches of its consciousness shaped by the historical contours of American immigrant life. Our house at 717 Franklin Street was about two hundred yards from where that beautifully majestic church stood. I knew the church grounds very well because they had the nicest basketball court in the neighborhood. The court stood at the end of the large church parking lot, and that was where I planted, in John Edgar Wideman's beautiful characterization of every aspiring basketball player's beginning, my "hoop roots."[4] Unlike Wideman, however, I never harbored any illusions of being a serious basketball player because I was too short and too slow and had a pitiful jump shot. But what I lacked in talent I made up for in effort. So usually if you were looking for me and I wasn't riding my stingray bike, playing with my best buddies, Kevin and Troy, or running with my nephew Jonathan in the neighborhood, I was, along with many other black boys and young men, in that parking lot playing basketball. And every Sunday, we drove back and forth past that church and that court heading to New Hope.

Why did these men not know me, not know Mary and Ivory, and not know the multitude of other black Christians who filled the neighborhood that surrounded that church? I am not asking why they weren't familiar with us, and I am certainly not asking about the logistics of their missional operations. The foreignness and formality of their speech in our backyard signaled a wider and deeper order of not knowing, of not sensing, of not imagining. The most common way to narrate this historical reality of Western Christianity displayed in my backyard is to speak of different Christianities, white and black, or different cultural expressions of Christianity, (European) immigrant and (African) slave, or even of a sinful division by faith formed from the historical realities of slavery. However, such narratives draw away too quickly from the strangeness displayed at the edge of my mother's garden. In the small space of a backyard I witnessed a Christianity familiar to most of us, enclosed in racial and cultural difference, inconsequentially related to its geography, often imaginatively detached from its surroundings of both people and spaces, but one yet bound to compelling gestures of connection, belonging, and invitation. Here, however, we were operating out of a history of relations that exposed a distorted relational imagination.

There is within Christianity a breathtakingly powerful way to imagine and enact the social, to imagine and enact connection and belonging. I could sense that power not only in the courageous yet wooden display of those neighborhood missionaries but also in the beauty and ease of my mother as she worked the ground, the earth. Though very different, their gestures drew from a crucial aspect of Christian existence and Christian desire buried inside the more mundane sense of what it means to be a Christian. In order to understand this I need to tell you another story. Years later I found myself a student at the very college founded by that church and that denomination, Calvin College. By the time I arrived at Calvin College I was sure I was called to be a minister. My road to this self-revelation was quite rocky, not because I resisted my intense Christian upbringing but because very early I emerged as a precocious provocateur of the poor pastor of my church, the Reverend J. V. Williams. I questioned everything and brought those questions to Reverend Williams, who had no earthly idea how to answer any serious theological inquiry. My questions and questioning were as constant and long as a Michigan winter, and my youthful patience as short as its summer heat waves. Needless to say, I did not endear myself to the pastor. This meant that I lacked the usual (for most black Baptist young men) fatherly mentoring of a young minister by their pastor.

I think he realized that such mentoring would have in fact been wasted on me, not only because of my thorn-in-the-flesh constant queries but also because I represented a generation of postmigration black children who tore large rips in the garments of racial and denominational identity we dutifully wore out of respect for our elders. He was so right to be suspicious of us. We were poised to imagine our belonging in ways unanticipated by our parents and grandparents who had fled the hateful South. But those imaginative possibilities desperately needed guidance. They needed theological voices that would have drawn us beyond the cultural nationalism, or the conservative theo-political ideologies, or the crass materialism that would beckon in the coming decades.

So it was that I found myself as a student at Calvin College being asked to preach in chapel. It was a last-minute invitation, the scheduled speaker having reported he would not be available for the program. The irony of this occasion was that it served as the site of my trial sermon. Here this son of Mary did not preach his first words among his own people, in the womb of the black church, but at the Dutch Reformed School, shaped in the austere aesthetic of John Calvin. I remember the text, Galatians 2: 20, but not the sermon. I was glad when it ended. But something strange happened afterward.

As people milled around, gathering up books and book bags to return to class, I noticed moving toward me a line of my professors, about five of them. Anyone who has been around Dutch Reformed professors (especially theology professors) would never accuse them of being given to exaggerated displays of emotion. Their classroom demeanor matched the orderly presentation of the buildings and the grounds: clear, precise, thoughtful. But as they approached me, I remember vividly how each reached for my hand, some clasping it with both their hands, others hugging me, all looking into my eyes with eyes that exposed fatherly love and appreciation. They each said in their moment of touching me,

"Willie, thank you for the Word of God." I knew their words were standard and proper responses to sermons heard in Reformed churches with histories much older than I, that young black man. But their gestures spoke something even more ancient, of a sense of connection and belonging and of a freedom to claim, to embrace, to make familiar one who is not. After chapel, we returned to class, where they assumed their proper pedagogical form, but the stark contrast between that moment and the theologically informed Christian education I was receiving was now overwhelming. Nothing else in my formal theological education corroborated that moment. Indeed it juts out as a moment of clarity regarding the deeper reality of theology and theological identity hidden beneath historical tragic developments.

I could narrate this story as a moment of Freudian transference built on a psychological replacement, Dutch professors in the place of a black Baptist pastor; or I could invoke current sensibilities and narrate this as an aspect of the psychic exchanges common inside of colonized subjectivity. I mouthed words, I performed rationalities conducive to the further production of knowledge and self-knowledge within certain white Western regimes of identity formation and was rewarded for it with displays of approval. However, such accounts sound like jazz musicians who have not learned to hear the intricacies of standard classic jazz tunes and subsequently can neither play what they hear nor hear what they play. I am not dismissing such narrative possibilities, but more is going on than these narrations can see. On that day in that space, I saw and felt what I had seen in my mother's garden and in the many hospital rooms she visited in pastoral care and in the few snatches of time when someone's actions move them toward a depth of intimacy both unanticipated and startling. It was the exercise of an imaginative capacity to redefine the social, to claim, to embrace, to join, to desire. Yet it is precisely the episodic character of this capacity among Christians that indicates something deeply, painfully amiss.

This book attempts to narrate exactly what is missing, what thwarts the deepest reality of the Christian social imagination. Indeed, I argue here that Christianity in the Western world lives and moves within a diseased social imagination. I think most Christians sense that something about Christians' social imaginations is ill, but the analyses of this condition often don't get to the heart of the constellation of generative forces that have rendered people's social performances of the Christian life collectively anemic. Those shortsighted analyses suffer on the one side from unfamiliarity with the deep theological architecture that patterned early modern visions of peoples, places, and societies and therefore lack the sense of what was turned horribly wrong theologically. And on the other side, Christian theology now operates inside this diseased social imagination without the ability to discern how its intellectual and pedagogical performances reflect and fuel the problem, further crippling the communities it serves. That is, theology lacks the ability to see the profound connections between an embrace by very different people in the chapel and theological meditations articulated in the classroom, between connecting to the earth, to strangers, and to the possibilities of identities formed and reformed precisely in and through such actions.

This inability is not due to conceptual gaps in the history of Christian thought, nor is it due to incoherence in doctrinal logics, nor should it be attributed to any number of intellectual problems and challenges arising with the Enlightenment. One must look more deliberatively at the soil in which the modern theological imagination grew and where it continues to find its deeper social nutrients. One crucial site where I have watched the display of this interrupted social imagination is in the theological academy. As student, professor, and academic dean, I have watched with a sense of melancholy the formation process of Christian intellectuals. I watched what at first I took to be a cultural and social clumsiness that seems bound to what the sociologist Pierre Bourdieu calls "the scholastic disposition."[5] Later I realized that what I was witnessing was not a social clumsiness at all but a highly refined process of socialization. I watched a complex process of disassociation and dislocation that was connected to the prescribed habits of mind for those who would do scholarly theological work.

This process of disassociation and dislocation I watched was not the theory/practice split in conceptual work, or the split between the classical and practical disciplines, or the separation of the church from the academy, or a split between orthodox and orthopraxis; neither can it be characterized through the arguments regnant in the tired debates about the nature, purposes, and values of abstract thinking versus situated thinking and all the permutations of that conflict. This process touches on these matters. What I observed in the theological academy was fundamentally the resistance of theologians to think *theologically* about their identities. It was the negation of a Christian intellectual posture reflective of the central trajectory of the incarnate life of the Son of God, who took on the life of the creature, a life of joining, belonging, connection, and intimacy. Such a posture would inevitably present the likelihood of transformations not only of ways of thinking but of ways of life that require the presence of the risks and vulnerabilities associated with being in the social, cultural, economic, and political position to be transformed.

The social vision that holds court in the theological academy imagines its intellectual world from the commanding heights of various social economies: cultural, political, and scholastic. I don't mean that scholars in the theological academy think they are in charge of the academic or political worlds. I mean that the regulative character of their intellectual posture created through the cultivated capacities to clarify, categorize, define, explain, interpret, and so forth eclipses its fluid, adaptable, even morph-able character. This eclipse is not due to the emergence of a new intellectual style but points to a history in which the Christian theological imagination was woven into processes of colonial dominance. Other peoples and their ways of life had to adapt, become fluid, even morph into the colonial order of things, and such a situation drew Christianity and its theologians inside habits of mind and life that internalized and normalized that order of things.

Adaptability, fluidity, formation, and reformation of being were heavily weighted on the side of indigenes as their requirement for survival. As Christianity developed both in the old world of Europe and in the new worlds of the Americas, Asia, and Africa, it was no longer able to feel this tragic imbalance. Indeed, it is as though Christianity, wherever it went in the modern colonies, inverted its sense of hospitality. It claimed to be the host, the owner of the spaces it entered, and demanded native peoples enter its cultural logics, its ways of being in the world, and its conceptualities. Thus the persistent preoccupations of the modern theological academy with various enlightenment problems bound up in such matters as answering the intellectual threat of atheism, reasserting the importance of orthodoxy, engaging in new forms of the conservative-liberal debate, determining how one should read sacred texts, or the obsessive labeling and positioning of theological trends (for example, Barthian, *ressourcement*, liberationist, postliberal, radical orthodoxy, feminist, womanist, postcolonial) not only display the continuing encasement in racial logics and agency, but also reflect the deep pedagogical sensory deprivation of this horrific imbalance. Western Christian intellectuals still imagine the world from the commanding heights.

My claim here would seem to fly in the face of a number of theologians and philosophers who believe that societies have now entered a post-Christian or post-establishment Christian reality in the Western world in which the easy alignment of Protestantism with the quasi-religious sensibilities of the nation-state has vanished. Whatever the claimed cause of this situation for the church in the modern "post-Christendom" world, the conclusion is the same: Western Christians are a minority, an exilic people in a strange land.[6] While the old Anglo-Saxon Protestant hegemony may be over, such readings of the reality of Christian existence in the West are painfully superficial. They bypass the deeper realities of Western Christian sensibilities, identities, and habits of mind which continue to channel patterns of colonialist dominance.

At one level these are the historical commanding heights imagined by Western, white, male identities, but at another level these are ways of being in the world that resist the realities of submission, desire, and transformation. A Christianity born of such realities but historically formed to resist them has yielded a form of religious life that thwarts its deepest instincts of intimacy. That intimacy should by now have given Christians a faith that understands its own deep wisdom and power of joining, mixing, merging, and being changed by multiple ways of life to witness a God who surprises us by love of differences and draws us to new capacities to imagine their reconciliation. Instead, the intimacy that marks Christian history is a painful one, one in which the joining often meant oppression, violence, and death, if not of bodies then most certainly of ways of life, forms of language, and visions of the world. What happened to the original trajectory of intimacy?

In this book, I want to answer that question by telling the story of modern Christianity's diseased social imagination. It was not my intent to write a history of the problem. This book is not a historical account that moves through all the complex realities of churches and colonialist nations, indigenes and slaves, land and commodity forms, racial formation and social imagination, nation and ecclesial dispute, all from the fifteenth century through the twentieth. Such a multivolume project would be a welcome addition to what I have done here. But as a theologian, my goal has been to paint a portrait of a theological problem in order to suggest a way forward. In order to arrive at my goal I take the reader on a journey into the lives of several people who may seem completely unrelated. These are people from diverse places and times who are drawn into my circle of concern first because they are Christians attempting to live as Christians at various times in the colonialist moment. But, more important, they illumine aspects of the problem in profound ways.

They are neither the progenitors of the problem nor its triggers. They represent microcosms of the great transformation. What I am doing is working like a film director. Rather than telling the story of a devastating flood by reviewing its meteorological antecedents or tracking the rise of the water or focusing on the flow patterns of the water (the buildings it topples, the crops it destroys), I focus on the person trapped on the roof with no place to go, the woman in a shelter with her children waiting for word on missing relatives, a dog desperately trying to swim to a spot of land to rest. Thus the majority of the chapters build around various peoples and their approach to their new situation in the newfound worlds. Yet a central argument and a theological position flow through the text.

At this point, however, I simply want to invite readers into my exploration of the Christian capacity for intimacy and why Christians have been so unable to enter fully into this marvelous gift given by God's Son to the world. I could speak of this gift in terms of reconciliation. But I have purposely stayed away from the theological language of reconciliation because of its terrible misuse in Western Christianity and its tormented deployment in so many theological systems and projects. The concept of reconciliation is not irretrievable, but I am convinced that before we theologians can interpret the depths of the divine action of reconciliation we must first articulate the profound deformities of Christian intimacy and identity in modernity. Until we do, all theological discussions of reconciliation will be exactly what they tend to be: (a) ideological tools for facilitating the negotiations of power; or (b) socially exhausted idealist claims masquerading as serious theological accounts. In truth, it is not at all clear that most Christians are ready to imagine reconciliation.

The smaller steps I take in this book are to outline specific things that changed and in so doing brought us to the present moment. Understanding these changes involves considering concepts, Christian doctrines, and events together that to my knowledge have not been thought of together. To draw these things together I have attempted to listen quietly and patiently to voices rarely heard by theologians and to ask questions about things only now entering the horizon of theological reflection, questions of race, space, place, geography, and identity and of the theological significance of Native American identities and Jewish–Gentile identity in relation to black–white racial identity as well as the importance of translation, literacy, and language. I draw attention to all of these matters in this book, but I must warn that the journey I take here will be different, and the turns should not be anticipated but followed and only at the end should readers decide whether this was a sure route and a good destination.

This book is a work of Christian theology, although it may not seem so to those readers steeped in Christian theological discourse. Admittedly, this text does not enter into extensive conversation with Western or Eastern theologians of the past. It is not in that sense an exercise in retrieval and comparison. However, it does enter into sustained theological analysis of particular Christian performances in order to capture the social condition of Christianity itself. This act of analysis is coupled with an act of retrieval in which I attempt a recalibration of a theological trajectory in order to posit a new vision for theology itself. In effect, I am attempting to do theology in a different modality—theological analysis of theology's social performances—in hopes of articulating a vision more faithful to the God whose incarnate life established and establishes the contours, character, and content of Christian theology.

This work also joins the growing conversation regarding the possibilities of a truly cosmopolitan citizenship. Such a world citizenship imagines cultural transactions that signal the emergence of people whose sense of agency and belonging breaks open not only geopolitical and nationalist confines but also the strictures of ethnic and racial identities. This is indeed a noble dream even if it is a moving target given the conceptual confusions and political struggles around multicultural discourse. Yet I hope to intervene helpfully in this conversation by returning precisely to the question of the constitution of such a people and such a citizenship. However, rather than building the hope of a cosmopolitanism from the soil of an imagined democratic spirit, I seek a deeper soil. That deeper rich soil is not easily unearthed. It is surely not resident at the surface levels of Christianity and ecclesial existence today. Yet Christianity marks the spot where, if noble dream joins hands with God-inspired hope and presses with great impatience against the insularities of life, for example, national, cultural, ethnic, economic, sexual, and racial, seeking the deeper ground upon which to seed a new way of belonging and living together, then we will find together not simply a new ground, not simply a new seed, but a life already prepared and offered to us.

Part I

DISPLACEMENT

Zurara's Tears

At dawn on August 8, 1444, Infante Henrique—Prince Henry of Portugal, the Navigator—sat on horseback at the port of Lagos patiently awaiting the disembarkation of cargo that had arrived from Cape Blanco. Spectators assembled to witness the portentous ritual that was about to occur. People from town and countryside lined the streets and crowded together on boats, all hoping to catch sight of this sign of Portugal's arrival as a world power. The day before this staged event, Lançarote de Freitas, the man who had led the very successful expedition in search of this cargo, had suggested to his lord, Prince Henry, that it be taken from the ship and herded to a suitable place for auction and distribution.

Lançarote's suggestion pleased the Infante. The place of auction and distribution would be a field just outside the city gates. The early-morning unloading time, also suggested by Lançarote, would catch the cargo during a lull in their lament. His rationale for these suggestions arose from the source of the lament: "Because of the long time we have been at sea as well as for the great sorrow that you must consider they have at heart, at seeing themselves away from the land of their birth, and placed in captivity, without having any understanding of what their end is to be."[1] Carefully planned and perfectly executed, the disembarkation and movement from port to field, from hostile sea to Portuguese interior, had the effect Prince Henry desired. These actions announced boldly that under his leadership Portugal would stand beside the Muslims, Valencians, Catalans, and Genoese as peoples with power over black flesh. They now emerged as bearers of black gold, slave traders.[2]

This event did not mark the first time slaves had appeared at the port of Lagos. The newness of the event lay in the number of slaves, 235, in their place of origin, parts of Africa theretofore unvisited by the Portuguese, and, most important, in the ritual that surrounded their sale. This ritual was deeply Christian, Christian in ways that were obvious to those who looked on that day and in ways that are probably even more obvious to people today. Once the slaves arrived at the field, Prince Henry, following his deepest Christian instincts, ordered a tithe be given to God through the church. Two black boys were given, one to the principal church in Lagos and another to the Franciscan convent on Cape Saint Vincent. This act of praise and thanksgiving to God for allowing Portugal's successful entrance into maritime power also served to justify the royal rhetoric by which Prince Henry claimed his motivation was the salvation of the soul of the heathen.[3]

The immediate focus in this story, however, is not the famed Prince Henry the Navigator, although he is a central actor and, as will become apparent later in this chapter, an incredibly important part of my concern. Nor is the immediate focus the African slaves, though they are the point of the matter. The immediate focus is the person who was charged to record, narrate, and interpret this ritual, Henry's royal chronicler, Gomes Eanes de Azurara (or Zurara). It was Zurara who pronounced the moods and motivations of royalty. It was Zurara who set in texts the theological vision Prince Henry performed by his actions. Zurara did not share in Henry's power, but he shared the stage with Henry, and in that sense he manifested his own power, the power of the storyteller. Zurara might be described accurately as a pre-Enlightenment historian, but that would be a soulless description. Zurara was a Christian intellectual at the dawn of the age of European colonialism, charged with offering the only real account of official history, a theological account.

At this time in the history of late medieval Christendom all accounts of events, royal or common, were theological accounts; that is, Christian accounts. Zurara, however, draws one's attention precisely because of what begins to happen to theological vision and Christian voice at this moment in history. He was not an official theologian of the church. Born in the ever-widening echo of Thomas Aquinas's thinking on the church and well before the epic-making theologians of Salamanca and Alcalá, Gomes Eanes (as he signed his name) did not rub shoulders with the keenest theological minds of the time, although he received enviable scholastic training. He was apprenticed to his predecessor as chronicler, Fernão Lopes, and given complete access to the library of the royal court, one of the strongest collections in Europe. There Zurara followed a Renaissance pattern of reading, both in scope and character. He read much—from Christian Scripture to theology to philosophy to astrology (science), from Aristotle to Dante to Averroes to Augustine, Aquinas, and Peter Lombard to medieval epics and romances. This serious intellectual work prepared him to assume the mantle laid down by Lopes.[4]

Zurara's ascension to the position of royal chronicler implied no small secretarial post. In addition to being the chronicler, he was in charge of the royal library and all its records. He had also been appointed a commander in the elite military Order of Christ, in which the vows of celibacy, poverty, and obedience structured the ordered existence of nobles, knights, and squires, an order under the leadership of Prince Henry himself. Zurara writes as one seated next to power, and from that position he wrote the important accounts of the Navigator's successes. His *Chronicle of the Capture of Ceuta* (1450) and his *Chronicle of the Deeds of Arms Involved in the Conquest of Guinea* (1457) remain crucial narratives of a founding moment in Christendom's colonialism.[5]

Zurara narrates this ritual of slave capture and auction on August 8, 1444, in his Guinean chronicle, showing himself to be a royal chronicler in beautiful form, telling the story of Portugal's rise by means of the chivalric genius of Prince Henry, the bravado of his loyal men, and the divine blessing of God. One could call this narrative royal religious ideology or pious propaganda, but by the time modern readers arrive at his account of this moment they see something different, even prophetic. As Zurara describes the event planned by Prince Henry and his assistant Lançarote, the triumphal coherence of his narrative starts to crack open. It is the only time in the entire chronicle that he set a chapter in a penitent prayer:

> O, Thou heavenly Father—who with thy powerful hand, without alteration of thy divine essence, governest all the infinite company of thy Holy City, and controllest all the revolutions of higher worlds, divided into nine spheres, making the duration of ages long or short according as it pleaseth Thee—I pray Thee that my tears may not wrong my conscience; for it is not their religion but their humanity that maketh mine to weep in pity for their sufferings. And if the brute animals, with their bestial feelings, by a natural instinct understand the suffering of their own kind, what wouldst Thou have my human nature to do on seeing before my eyes that miserable company, and remembering that they too are of the generation of the sons of Adam?[6]

Zurara has not changed. This is still the story of Prince Henry. But at this moment the story of Portugal and its leader has been displaced by the suffering presence of these Africans. The power of Zurara's description draws life from the pathos of these slaves. He invokes the idea of divine providence, of which he is a firm believer, and as he does so he locates a question that will from this time forward shadow this doctrinal theme: How should I understand the suffering of these

Africans?[7] Even when not speaking of Africans, every articulation of providence by colonial masters and their subjects will carry the echo of Zurara's question. Zurara recognizes their humanity, their common ancestry with Adam. One should not, however, read moral disgust into his words. Zurara asks God in this prayer to grant him access to the divine design to help him interpret this clear sign of God-ordained Portuguese preeminence over black flesh. He seeks from God the kind of interpretation that would ease his conscience and make the event unfolding in front of him more morally palatable. His question seeds a problem of theodicy born out of the colonialist question bound to the colonialist project.

The irony that this question is posed in a Christian prayer that grasps the divine immutability must not go unnoticed. The idea of divine immutability anchors humans in the actions of a God who does not repent, change, or get caught by surprise but who works out without failure the divine will in space and time. That idea, even with the Scholastic incrustations of Zurara's time, still carried the strong flavor of intimacy and trust in a God who is faithful and loving, even if mysterious. It makes sense that Zurara invokes it in the context of prayer. To do so exhibits his spiritual schooling in the Psalms, which show that the proper questioning of God should indeed take place inside prayer to God. Divine immutability rightly understood holds humans and their questioning of God inside knowledge of a loving and faithful God who hears their pained inquiries. The problem here is that Zurara will put divine immutability to strange new use. He employs providence, making it work at the slave auction. He then offers the famous account that has often been partially quoted:[8]

> On the next day, which was the 8th of the month of August, very early in the morning, by reason of the heat, the seamen began to make ready their boats, and to take out those captives, and carry them on shore, as they were commanded. And these, placed all together in that field, were a marvelous sight; for amongst them were some white enough, fair to look upon, and well proportioned; others were less white like mulattoes; others again were as black as Ethiops [Ethiopians], and so ugly, both in features and in body, as almost to appear (to those who saw them) the images of a lower hemisphere. But what heart could be so hard as not to be pierced with piteous feeling to see that company? For some kept their heads low and their faces bathed in tears, looking one upon another; others stood groaning very dolorously, looking up to the height of heaven, fixing their eyes upon it, crying out loudly, as if asking help of the Father of Nature; others struck their faces with the palms of their hands, throwing themselves at full length upon the ground; others made their lamentations in the manner of a dirge, after the custom of their country. And though

we could not understand the words of their language, the sound of it right well accorded with the measure of their sadness.[9]

Few places in the chronicle touch the intricacy of this account. Zurura slows the story down to give us sight of this suffering as well as to express a racial calculation. He goes through the differences in flesh and spirit, body and beauty that will become an abiding scale of existence:

> But to increase their sufferings still more, there now arrived those who had charge of the division of the captives, and who began to separate one from another, in order to make an equal partition of the fifths; and then was it needful to part fathers from sons, husbands from wives, brothers from brothers. No respect was shown either to friends or relations, but each fell where his lot took him. O powerful fortune, that with thy wheels doest and undoest, compassing the matters of this world as pleaseth thee, do thou at least put before the eyes of that miserable race some understanding of matters to come; that they may receive some consolation in the midst of their great sorrow. And you who are so busy in making that division of the captives, look with pity upon so much misery; and see how they cling one to the other, so that you can hardly separate them. And who could finish that partition without very great toil? For as often as they had placed them in one part the sons, seeing their fathers in another, rose with great energy and rushed over to them; the mothers clasped their other children in their arms, and threw themselves flat on the ground with them; receiving blows with little pity for their own flesh, if only they might not be torn from them. And so troublously they finished the partition.[10]

Zurara ends this chapter and this important episode in the chronicle with Prince Henry bringing a holy coherence to the whole matter:

> The Infante was there, mounted upon a powerful steed, and accompanied by his retinue, making distribution of his favours, as a man who sought to gain but small treasure from his share; for of the forty-six souls that fell to him as his fifth, he made a very speedy partition of these for his chief riches lay in his purpose; for he reflected with great pleasure upon the salvation of those souls that before were lost. And certainly his expectation was not in vain; for, as we said before, as soon as they understood our language they turned Christians with very little ado; and I who put together this history into this volume, saw in the town of Lagos boys and girls (the children and grandchildren of those first captives, born in this land) as good and true Christians as if they had directly descended, from the beginnings of the dispensation of Christ, from those who were first baptized.[11]

Zurara deploys a rhetorical strategy of containment, holding slave suffering inside a Christian story that will be recycled by countless theologians and intellectuals of every colonialist nation. The *telos* and the denouement of the event
will be enacted as an order of salvation, an *ordo salutis*—African captivity leads
to African salvation and to black bodies that show the disciplining power of the
faith. Zurara clearly intends the text to be read in this way. But his narrative inadvertently exposes a deeper point of coherence that betrays his idealized vision of
Prince Henry. That point of coherence counteracts his placement of the Infante
and his actions as the point of salvific coherence. The deeper point of coherence
is the suffering Christ image, the paradigmatic image of suffering carried in the
body of Jesus of Nazareth. Zurara's rhetoric moves inexplicably near biblical allu-
sions and accounts of Jesus' suffering: "Therefore, to consecrate the people by his
own blood, Jesus also suffered outside the gate. Let us then go to him outside the
camp, bearing the stigma that he bore" (Hebrews 13:12–13 NEB).

Zurara wrote a passion narrative, one that reads the gestures of slave suffering
inside the suffering of the Christ.[12] The christological architecture his words fall
into is inescapable, words tracing out the actual frame of Jesus' own march of
suffering, separation, and death. Both Jesus and the slaves suffer outside the city
gates. Outside the city gate for Jesus meant suffering in a place designated by
the Roman state for displaying its considerable power over bodies. The parallel
with the slaves is remarkable. They too stand outside the city gates and mark the
orchestration of the Portuguese state over their lives. This christological architecture of the sale of slaves like the Christ event signifies a similar instrumentality,
a similar use of the body for the sake of the state. As Zurara articulates the exercise of church and state power over bodies he echoes some of the deepest realities of Jesus' agony and in effect triggers misapprehension and reversal similar
to those found in the condemnation of Jesus. The innocent suffer the penalty of
the guilty. Like Jesus, these peoples of distant lands are brought to a place where
a crucifying identity, slave identity, will be forever fastened like a cross to their
bodies: "They brought Jesus to the place called Golgotha, which means 'Place
of a Skull,' and they offered him drugged wine, but he did not take it. Then they
fastened him to the cross" (Mark 15:22–24a NEB).

The crucifixion portrays Christ's powerlessness, a powerlessness shared by
the chronicler, who is helpless to do anything other than remember the scene
and tell the story. Zurara places himself in his story in the position of one who
watches helplessly as horror unfolds. His position in the chronicle does not align
with the positions of Pilate and the women who wept at the suffering of Jesus
of Nazareth. Zurara takes a position like that of the writers of Matthew, Mark,
Luke, and John, who recall Jesus' torture-induced agony. His language here does

not claim a connection between the two agonies, of slave and savior. But his language cannot prevent it. Jesus prostrated on the ground at Gethsemane and contorted on the cross personifies tribulation through his groans, tears, and loud cries, his eyes steadfastly on heaven seeking paternal consolation. In comparison, slave flesh throws itself to the ground, groans, fixes its eyes on heaven, and cries loudly, "as if asking help of the Father of Nature." Holy body and slave body act the same, but Zurara will not allow himself to see a Jesus-like cry of dereliction in the slaves' cries. That would be to see too much. The Father of Nature will not be fully identified with the Father of Jesus Christ. But Zurara comes close to it. He joins two forms of indecipherability, the screams of Jesus and the screams of the slaves. The words of the slaves expose a chasm between perception and right interpretation. In like manner the following passage from Mark's gospel shows Christ's words being misunderstood. Those pitiful words mark for the hearers their inability to join perceived pain to true interpretation: "At midday a darkness fell over the whole land, which lasted till three in the afternoon; and at three Jesus cried aloud, 'Eloï, Eloï, lema sabachthani?' which means 'My God, my God, why have you forsaken me?' Hearing this, some of the bystanders said, 'Listen! He is calling Elijah.' Then Jesus gave a loud cry and died" (Mark 15:33–34, 37 NEB)."

While the listeners in this passage misinterpret Christ's words Mark does not. Yet in Zurara's narrative neither listener nor writer can translate the words uttered by this soon-to-be chattel. The action of church and state power, however, was not thwarted by linguistic boundaries. The languages of the newly formed slaves required no hope of a Pentecostal miracle, no need to pray for interpretation, because the imperial reflex on display captured strange tongues and drowned them in the familiar sound of Portuguese. Indeed, one may discern an evil prophecy created and soon to be fulfilled in this burial of native tongues beneath the loud sound of Portuguese: The languages of the enslaved will be bound to the languages of the Europeans, as peasant to royalty, as the lesser to the greater. Unknown tongues will be overcome not by a surprising linguistic act of God, but by the energies of market and nation-state.

Another crucial parallel between these two narratives is the central role of death. Christ takes on death to overcome it, while slaves are bound to death by being killed and through its use as a threat in order to subdue them. This is a reversal of the reversal, a christological deformation. That is, the body of Jesus will ultimately indicate the victory of God over death, but in this horrific scene the African's body indicates the ultimate victory of death. The holy use of Jesus' body—the one who became a slave to die as a sinner for humankind—parallels the separation of slaves into lots for Portuguese servitude. Echoing the merciless beating of Jesus, mothers are beaten, Zurara observes, "with little pity for their own flesh," as they cling hopelessly to their children, attempting to prevent the tearing away. At the end, all that remains is the dividing of the slaves into equal lots, just as all that was left was the dividing of the Savior's garments. What Mark writes, "They shared out his clothes, casting lots to decide what each should have," reveals the telos of the captured body, consumption (Mark 15:24b NEB).

Prince Henry emerges from this segment of the chronicle as the stabilizing focal point, moving the reader out of the chaos of this first auction. His powerful presence overcomes the screams, cries, beatings, and noise of the captives as well as the horrified cries of some of the onlookers. He will lead them into the light of salvation for untold generations. Yet Zurara gave too much in this story. It will not all fit easily into the account. From this point forward this account haunts his constant justification of the slave trade—we, the Portuguese, will save them. They will become Christians. Yet inadvertently, in telling the story of Portugal's rise, Zurara joins the slave body to the body of Jesus. He would not have done this on purpose, as he seems unaware of the immense tragedy of the moment he has entered. But Zurara also reveals he is not innocent. He knows—behold the man! Zurara prays, he cries, he speaks to those who do the dirty work of mutilating the black body.

The christological pattern of his narrative illumines the cosmic horror of this moment and also helps the reader recognize the unfolding of a catastrophic theological tragedy. Long before one would give this event a sterile, lifeless label such as "one of the beginning moments of the Atlantic slave trade," something more urgent and more life altering is taking place in the Christian world, namely, the auctioning of bodies without regard to any form of human connection. This act is carried out inside Christian society, as part of the *communitas fidelium*. This auction will draw ritual power from Christianity itself while mangling the narratives it evokes, establishing a distorted pattern of displacement.

Christianity will assimilate this pattern of displacement. Not just slave bodies, but *displaced* slave bodies, will come to represent a natural state. From this position they will be relocated into Christian identity. The backdrop of their existence will be, from this moment forward, the market. Zurara narrates this horror of displacement within a strange new soteriological orientation. Divine immutability yields Christian character—an unchanging God wills to create Christians out of slaves and slaves out of those black bodies that will someday, the Portuguese hope, claim to be Christian.

Slave society was not the new reality appearing here. Zurara understood enough Scripture, Christian tradition, and ecclesial and state polities to articulate a hermeneutics of forced servitude. The new creation here begins with Zurara's simple articulation of racial difference: "And these, placed all together in that field, were a marvelous sight; for amongst them were some white enough, fair to look upon, and well proportioned; others were less white like mulattoes; others again were as black as Ethiops [Ethiopians], and so ugly, both in features and in body, as almost to appear (to those who saw them) the images of a lower hemisphere."[13] Through comparison, he describes aesthetically and thereby fundamentally identifies his subjects. There are those who are almost white—fair to look upon and well-proportioned; there are those who are in between—almost white like mulattoes; and there are those who are as black as Ethiopians, whose existence is deformed. Their existence suggests bodies come from the farthest reaches of hell itself.[14] Zurara invokes, in this passage, a scale of existence, with white at one end and black at the other end and all others placed in between.

This is not the first time the words *white* and *black* indicate something like identity. Their anthropological use in the Iberian and North African regions has an episodic history that extends well before Zurara's utterances.[15] Zurara, however, exhibits an aesthetic that is growing in power and reach as the Portuguese and Spanish begin to join the world they imagined with the world they encounter through travel and discovery. In the fourteenth-century geographical novel *The Book of Knowledge of All Kingdoms* (also known as *The Book of Knowledge*), these two worlds, the imaginary and the real, are joined.[16] It is fundamentally a Christian text, beginning with its invocation of the triune identity of God in proper orthodox form. At the beginning of the book the author situates his own history within multiple accounts of time—Jewish, Christian, pagan, Muslim— in a way that could, with appropriate qualifications, be seen as quite culturally generous, if not downright pluralist. This work, known to Prince Henry and Zurara, does not offer a straightforwardly derogatory view of black flesh.[17] Rather its comparison is subtle. Black is the result of environmental harm. Such harmed flesh, burnt flesh is not present among whites.

The author, in recounting his travels to different places, notes several times that the people are black, or black as pitch. They are Christian, yet they are black. As the author draws near the land of Prester John, the priest-king believed to govern a holy realm and a great army of African warriors, he again notes the people's particulars: "But they are as black as pitch and they burn themselves with fire on their foreheads with the sign of the cross in recognition of their baptism. And although these people are black, they are men of good understanding and good mind."[18] Christian and black are juxtaposed—the one overcoming the other. The land is hot but Christian, so the people are black yet in a condition of grace. This graced but harmed condition of black bodies stands in stark contrast to the bodies of those from the land the author describes as India. That land is equally hot as the land of the blacks, but the towns are close to the sea, and the moist air tempers the heat. The result is a different body: "And in this way they derived beautiful bodies and elegant forms and fine hair, and the heat does nothing else to them except make them brown in color."[19] Few of Zurara's or Prince Henry's contemporaries seemed to question the veracity of the author's accounts of people, places, and routes. Prince Henry in fact considers *The Book of Knowledge* one of his indispensable guides as he envisions further conquest of Africa. These accounts faltered as Iberian travelers pressed the real world against this imaginary one. Yet land and body are connected at the intersection of European imagination and expansion. The imagined geography diminished in strength as a more authentic and accurate geography emerged. The scale of existence, however, with white (unharmed) flesh at one end and black (harmed) flesh at the other, grew in power precisely in the space created by Portuguese expansion into new lands.

The often-used term *European expansion* fails to capture the spatial disruption taking place at this moment, a moment beautifully captured by Zurara. This Portuguese chronicler is watching and participating in the reconfiguration of space and bodies, land and identity. This is the newness present in Zurara's simple observation. Again, land and body are connected at the intersection of European imagination and expansion, but what must be underscored is the point of connection—the Portuguese and the Spanish, that is, the European. He is the point of connection. He stands now between bodies and land, and he adjudicates, identifies, determines. The position of the agent is equal in importance to the actions. Zurara is capturing the twin operations of discovery and consumption. With those twin operations, four things are happening at the same time: first, people are being seized (stolen); second, land is being seized (stolen); third, people are being stripped from their space, their place; and fourth, Europeans are describing themselves and these Africans at the same time. There is a density of effects at work here far beyond a notion of expansion.

In this chapter I register that density of effects, especially as it relates to the formation of human identity in modernity.[20] Centrally, I register the effects of the reconfiguration of bodies and space as a theological operation. That theological operation, heretical in nature, binds spatial displacement to the formation of an abiding scale of existence.

DISPLACING CHRISTIAN VISION

The ordering of existence from white to black signifies much more than the beginnings of racial formation on a global scale: it is an architecture that signals displacement. Herein lies the deepest theological problem. Zurara brings into view the crossing of a threshold into a distorting vision of creation. This distorting vision of creation will lodge itself deeply in Christian thought, damaging doctrinal trajectories. My use of the word *distortion* does not imply a prior coherent, healthy, and happy vision of creation that will be lost in the age of discovery. The newness of the world was unanticipated by all. That newness coupled with European power, greed-filled ambition, and discursive priority drew distorting form out of Christian theology.

The royal chronicler's account of the slave auction, intended to immortalize the exploits of the Navigator, collapses into the crucifixion narrative in which the Son is subjected to evil powers. In Zurara's narrative, these evil powers find their parallel in Prince Henry, who, of course, would never have understood himself as such.[21] Instead, the Infante understood himself and Zurara described him as the good son sent for the sake of the nation. In his *Chronicle of the Capture of Ceuta* Zurara masterfully ascribes to the prince the trappings of anointed sonship. His mother, Queen Philippa, is described in *theotokos*-like ways. Her deathbed imperial oration to her sons, especially to Henry, prophesies and commands him to lead the elite of the nation to the glory that is their due. This holy beginning of his reign is further established by the appearance of the Virgin Mary next to Philippa as she lay dying. On her deathbed Philippa contemplates the divine, transfigured in the Holy Virgin's presence.[22] The religious reality of Prince Henry approximates that of the chronicle. A very pious and theologically astute man, he was known to quote Scripture to strengthen his arguments and had even considered taking religious vows. In his latter years, he established a chair of theology at Lisbon University and had at hand when he died a copy of Peter Lombard's *Libri sententiarum quatuor*.

Henry thus dually represents Christ and Christ's executioners. This contradiction is made possible by a Christianity contorting through travel and discovery. Zurara's aesthetic judgments move with the Iberian and other colonial empires, refine through contact with other peoples, and merge into what will come to be believed as obvious. Slowly, out of these actions, whiteness emerges, not simply as a marker of the European but as the rarely spoken but always understood organizing conceptual frame. And blackness appears as the fundamental tool of that organizing conceptuality. Black bodies are the ever-visible counterweight of a usually *invisible* white identity. My use of the term *scale* should not be conflated with what will later develop as racial hierarchy, intellectual, cultural, or religious, although there are present at this time profoundly hierarchical elements. The explanatory power of the notion of racial hierarchy does not capture the density of the operation of this scale. Scale here refers to the possibility realized from the legacy of Prince Henry onward of seeing and touching multiple peoples and their lands at once and *thinking them* together. This process will be theological.

The process is theological because it is ecclesial. This kind of comparative thinking was not simply the child of burgeoning colonial nation-states. Church and state, popes and kings and queens enfold each other in bringing forth new ways of interfacing with their world. This is truly an inter-course. However, in this joining the church establishes the framework within which the nations will interpret not only their statecraft but also the peoples they encounter through exploration and conquest. In his bull *Romanus Pontifex* of January 8, 1455, Pope Nicholas V displays the power of ecclesial dictum by summarily awarding regions of the known world to Portugal. This papal power over space, which will be exercised repeatedly, rested on an abiding christological and ecclesiological principle — that the church exists for the sake of the world. It is the fount of salvation, and the pope, servant of the servants of God, for the sake of Christ and through Christ, lays claim to the entire world. *Romanus Pontifex* rehearses this central power of Christ's successor:

> The Roman pontiff, successor of the key-bearer of the heavenly kingdom and vicar of Jesus Christ, contemplating with a father's mind all the several climes of the world and the characteristics of all the nations dwelling in them and seeking and desiring the salvation of all, wholesomely ordains and disposes upon careful deliberation those things which he sees will be agreeable to the Divine Majesty and by which he may bring the sheep entrusted to him by God into the single divine fold, and may acquire for them the reward of eternal felicity, and obtain pardon for their souls. This we believe will more certainly come to pass, through the aid of the Lord, if we bestow suitable favors and special graces on those Catholic kings and princes, who like athletes and intrepid champions of the Christian faith . . . not only restrain the savage excesses of the Saracens and of other infidels, enemies of the Christian name, but also for the defense and increase of the faith vanquish them and their kingdoms and habitations.[23]

The contemplation of the Vicar of Jesus Christ is a beautifully sublime and incredibly powerful action described here. It captures the central soteriological action of the church; seeking and desiring the salvation of all peoples. The position of the church in relation to the nations echoes the original constituting relation, that between Israel and the world. Here Israel has been superseded and the framework reconstituted through the Vicar of Christ so that the whole world is viewed through boundless desire. This presents the deepest theological problem and the greatest theological possibility. This boundary-less desire is to "bring the

sheep entrusted to him by God into the single divine fold," presenting a totalizing vision that activates a thoroughgoing antiessentialist rendering of peoples.
Through this rendering all peoples become simply sheep bound under paternal-
ecclesial care.

This salvific concern is at the heart of the Christian gospel, its radicalism
breathtaking, but, placed by the pope in the hands of those whom the pope
called the "athletes and intrepid champions of the Christian faith," it becomes
a different kind of radicalism. This radical concern becomes, through the pope's
own official narration, embodied in the energy, efforts, and exploits of Prince
Henry:

> And so it came to pass that when a number of ships of this kind [caravels] had
> explored and taken possession of very many harbors, islands, and seas, they at
> length came to the province of Guinea, and having taken possession of some
> islands and harbors and the sea adjacent to that province, sailing farther they
> came to the mouth of a certain great river commonly supposed to be the Nile,
> and war was waged for some years against the people of those parts in the name
> of the said King Alfonso and of the infante; and in it very many islands in
> that neighborhood were subdued and peacefully possessed, as they are still
> possessed together with the adjacent sea. Thence also many Guineamen and
> other negroes, taken by force, and some by barter of unprohibited articles, or
> by other lawful contracts of purchase, have been sent to the said kingdoms.
> A large number of these have been converted to the Catholic faith, and it is
> hoped by the help of divine mercy, that if such progress be continued with
> them, either those peoples will be converted to the faith or at least the souls of
> many of them will be gained for Christ.[24]

It would be a mistake to conclude that Prince Henry's commercial interests are
hidden inside the pope's theological interests. Both concerns are joined and in
the open. Indeed, it is precisely the joining of these concerns, commercial and
theological, that enables the translation of soteriological radicalism into a racial
radicalism. As the pope narrates Henry's holy exploits, including the taking of
"many Guineamen and other negroes," a large number of whom, he notes, have
been converted to the Catholic faith, he inscribes a new reality for black flesh.
He never mentions their tribal, linguistic, or geographic specifics; these aspects
of their identities are rendered irrelevant.[25]

Nicholas V's description is a superficial reading of human communities that
ignores their intimately particular characteristics, a descriptive practice that will
be used by many explorers and priests. Yet one should not simply excuse this
description as naïve anthropology or harmless generalization. Nicholas V offers

insight into the power of a theological account of peoples that draws life from the doctrine of *creatio ex nihilo,* the creation by the Creator of all things out of nothing.

Envisioning the world as created out of nothing yields two bedrock hermeneutical principles. First, there is a fundamental instability to all things. Nothing is sure in itself. All things are contingent and held together by God. Rather than rendered through a godlike stability, the world *ex nihilo* means that all things carry inherent possibilities of continuity or discontinuity. Indeed, the fragility of human existence marks humans' inherent instability.

When viewed through this hermeneutical horizon, peoples exist without a necessary permanence either of place or of identity. This kind of antiessentialist vision facilitates a different way of viewing human communities. The essential characteristic of people is their need—for pardon and life, that is, for salvation from God. Nicholas V notes in hope that people may "acquire . . . the reward of eternal felicity, and obtain pardon for their souls."[26]

The second hermeneutical principle is the identity of the Creator. Christ is the creator of all things. Locating the Creator in space and time establishes the most important aspect of the incarnation. God has come and fully entered the reality of the creation. In space and time, into the instability of the world came a new point of stability and life. Equally important is the *arche, the beginning.* Jesus Christ is the beginning of all things. All things belong to him as text to author. The doctrine of divine enfleshment yields both the idea of divine ownership and that of salvation embodied in the here and now. This special sense of embodiment undergirds Nicholas V's sense of geographic authority over all peoples and all lands. God in Christ allows humans to participate in his life, and within that participation there exists a transferability of his authority to humans. As the central point of transferability, the representative of Christ, Nicholas V, may delegate Prince Henry and his cohort to act on his behalf. It is precisely this point of delegation that establishes a trajectory reaching from Henry through the pope back to the incarnation itself—a trajectory of ownership and salvation. Nicholas V states that the Infante from his youth geared his entire life to "cause the most glorious name of the . . . Creator to be published, extolled, and revered throughout the whole world, even in the most remote and undiscovered places."[27]

I have not entered fully into the intricacies of a Christian doctrine of creation or the doctrine of the incarnation. However, the use of those doctrinal logics can be seen working to frame the concepts that will enable the thinking of peoples together with regard to race. These doctrinal logics help one understand the oft-quoted and equally theologically underinterpreted papal permission given to King Alfonso and Prince Henry:

To invade, search out, capture, vanquish, and subdue all Saracens and pagans whatsoever, and other enemies of Christ wheresoever placed, and the king-doms, dukedoms, principalities, dominions, possessions, and all movable and immovable goods whatsoever held and possessed by them and to reduce their persons to perpetual slavery, and to apply and appropriate to himself and his successors the kingdoms, dukedoms, counties, principalities, dominions, pos-sessions, and goods, and to convert them to his and their use and profit . . . the said King Alfonso or by his authority, the aforesaid infante, justly and lawfully has acquired and possessed, and doth possess, these islands, lands, harbors, seas, and they do of right belong and pertain to the said King Alfonso and his successors.[28]

Repeating in part the permissions given in *Dum diversas*, his bull of June 18, 1452, Nicholas V granted this request of King Alfonso in light of the ongoing mili-tary struggle against Islam.[29] But there is more at work here than the vicissitudes of church-statecraft. The pope granted Portuguese royalty the right to reshape the discovered landscapes, their peoples and their places, as they wished. These actions inscribe the contingency of creation itself within the will and desire of church and the colonial powers. The inherent instability of creation means that all things may be altered in order to bring them to proper order toward saved exis-tence. Church and realm, represented in this moment by Nicholas V and Prince Henry (and King Alfonso), stand between peoples and lands and determine a new relationship between them, dislodging particular identities from particular places. Through a soteriological vision, church and realm discern all peoples to exist on the horizon of theological identities.

Displacement is the central operation at work here. The subtleties of its opera-tion move in two directions, both of which one must see in order to understand the depth of this theological mistake. One direction is detectable from the early moments of New World discoveries. Consider the words of Christopher Colum-bus from the account of his third voyage to the New World. He has dropped anchor at the southeastern tip of Venezuela, near Trinidad, a place he named Punta del Arenal: "The next day there came from the east a large canoe with 24 men in it, all of them young and bearing many weapons. . . . As I said, they were all young and fine looking and not negroes but rather the whitest of all those that I had seen in the Indies, and they were graceful and had fine bodies and long, smooth hair cut in the Castilian manner."[30] This is simply a description intended to help Ferdinand and Isabella grasp the details of Spain's New World, especially the lucrative new find of a continent. But it is also a down payment on things to come. The logic of Columbus's description is obvious—the comparison begins with the known, the self. Thus the whiteness he names is reflective, even reflexive of their European bodies—graceful, fine, with long, smooth hair, even cut like theirs. Rotem Kowner writes that for European explorers at this time "the color white, did not carry explicit racial connotations but signified culture, refinement, and a 'just like us' designation."[31] However, its origins or originators are not what make this point of comparison critical for us.

The power of Columbus's description lies in its comparative range. It connects the bodies of the new land (Africa) to the bodies of the other new land (the Americas), through the exercise of an aesthetic with breathtaking geographic flexibility. The aesthetic is of the land but not of the land, of the people but not of the people. It is of the land and the people in the sense that Columbus, like his intellectual predecessors, speculates that specific environs cause the specific characteristics of people. It is not of land and people because these specific characteristics become a racial transcendental, present among completely different peoples with supposedly similar climates. Again, as Columbus reflected on his discovery of a new continent and offered his famous observation that the earth is pear-shaped or like a "woman's nipple on a round ball," he substantiates his hemispheric theory by drawing on this aesthetic: "I find myself 20 degrees north of the equinoctial line, right of Arguin and those lands, where the men are black and the land very burnt. And when I went to the Cape Verde Islands I discovered that the people there are much darker, and the farther south one goes the more extreme their color becomes so that, at the same latitude on which I was, namely, that of Sierra Leone, where the North Star at nightfall was five degrees above the horizon, the negroes are the blackest."[32] Columbus, however, believes that, given the true shape of the earth, conditions at the island of Trinidad and the land of Gracia (his name for modern-day Venezuela) create a different result in people: "I found the mildest temperatures and lands and trees as green and beautiful as the orchards of Valencia in April, and the people there have beautiful bodies and are whiter than the others I was able to see in the Indies and have very long and smooth hair; they have greater ingenuity, show more intelligence, and are not cowardly."[33] Columbus with great precision exhibits the power of the racial scale. One sees that power in its mobility and its flexibility. It is of the world but not of any specific world. It is tied to specific flesh, but it also joins all flesh. Such identity markers do not establish racial essences as their first work. They quietly, beneath the surface, join human beings and in effect uncouple their identities from specific places. Yet the first point of uncoupling is the European himself. Consider the famous statement of Garcia de Escalante Alvarado (1548), the Spaniard who provided the first actual account of Japan and the Japanese: "It is a very cold country. . . . The inhabitants of these islands are good-looking, white, and bearded, with shaved heads. . . . They read and write in the same manner as do the Chinese; their language is similar to German. . . . The superior classes are dressed in silk, brocade, satin, and taffeta; the women have mostly very white complexions and are very beautiful; they are dressed in the same manner as the women of Castile."[34] His vision of the Japanese draws them into a reality that is physical yet without spatial boundary, a reality signaled by whiteness. Escalante and his compatriots are by no means singular in this operation. As all the European empires draw on the flexibility of the racial scale, they pull themselves into this boundary-less reality. This is nothing less than a theological operation. Like the designations of sinner and saint, convert and heretic, believer and unbeliever, faithful and apostate, this linguistic deployment alters reality, blowing by and through the specifics of identity bound to land, space, and place and narrating a new world that binds bodies to unrelenting aesthetic judgments. The European himself is the key to this theological act of displacement. It is not incidental that Columbus, like so many who follow in his footsteps, envisions a soteriological motive for his exploration and colonialism: "The Holy Trinity inspired Your Highnesses to undertake this enterprise of the Indies and through His infinite goodness made me His envoy on account of which I came with this plan into your royal presence, you being the most noble Christian princes toiling for the faith and its propagation."[35] The gospel is always embodied in the acts of faithful Christians, and yet the gospel is without constrictors of space. It is quintessentially movable, elastically stable over vastly different locations. The age of discovery entails that the European body will take on these exact characteristics. But not simply the European body but also, equally important, the African body will take on similar characteristics. These body differences will be articulated through white and black in such a powerful way that their similitude will extend to all peoples. These bodies, black and white, become almost spectral, more precisely, conceptually able to be superimposed over all other bodies. These bodies become visible and invisible in different ways with different purposes. That performed visibility and invisibility shows itself in the constant turnings and evolutions of comparative thinking.

The brilliant Jesuit Alessandro Valignano (1539–1606) shows this incredible ability to capture all flesh within the logic of white and black existence. Born of an elite Neapolitan family and quickly moved through the Jesuit ordination process and ranks, he arrived as vicar-general and visitor to Japan in 1579. In his famous *Sumario* of 1580 he offers his studied reflections on the Japanese and the viability of the mission to Japan: "These people are all white, courteous and highly civilized, so much so that they surpass all the other known races of the world. They are naturally very intelligent, although they have no knowledge of sciences, because they are the most warlike and bellicose race yet discovered on the earth."[36] Later on in the *Sumario* one of his points of comparison appears: here he reflects on the superiority of Japanese conversion based on their supposed racial difference:

> There is this difference between the Indian and Japanese Christians, which in itself proves that there is really no room for comparison between them, for each one of the former was converted from some individual ulterior motive, and since they are blacks, and of small sense, they are subsequently very difficult to improve and turn into good Christians; whereas the Japanese usually become converted, not on some whimsical individual ulterior move (since it is their suzerains who expect to benefit thereby and not they themselves) but only in obedience to their lord's command; and since they are white and of good understanding and behavior, and greatly given to outward show, they readily frequent the churches and sermons, and when they are instructed they become very good Christians.[37]

Valignano's use of *black* in this derogatory fashion was not unusual. As the historian C. R. Boxer noted, it was not at all strange to hear the Indians, Chinese, or even Japanese referred to as "niggers." Francisco Cabral, the Portuguese superior of the mission to Japan (1570–81) who resisted developing an indigenous clergy, stated that "the Japanese are Niggers and their customs barbarous."[38] In order to understand the elastic power of the term *black* in its derogatory form one must remember the nature of the comparative thinking that is in operation.

Because Valignano's concern as vicar-general and visitor was to evaluate the possibilities of an authentic Christian existence and identity in the new lands—Africa, India, China, and Japan—his comparative analysis was driven by a deeply ecclesial concern. The concern was whether the performance of Christian practices was rooted in a saving effect in the individual or was merely a façade covering disingenuous behavior or impenetrable ignorance. The questions at stake were not only who could become a true Christian, but also who might ascend the heights of Christian identity and become a lay leader, priest, or even possibly a Jesuit brother. Valignano understood himself to be engaged in nothing less than an act of spiritual discernment.

What informed Valignano's powerful spiritual discernment of the salvific possibilities of alien flesh was the presence of the most decisive and central theological distortion that exists in the church, a distortion that was growing in power and extension with each new generation. That distortion was the replacement of Israel, or, in its proper theological term, supersessionism. Crudely put, in supersessionist thinking the church replaces Israel in the mind and heart of God. It will take my entire treatment, each chapter adding layers to my account of this decisive distortion, to describe the awesome effects of this way of thinking on the imagination of Christians. At this point one can begin to glimpse the supersessionist effect in Valignano's comparative thinking. This effect begins with positioning Christian identity fully within European (white) identity and fully outside the identities of Jews and Muslims. The space between these identities, Christian on the one side and Jews and Muslims on the other, became the space within which one could discern authentic conversion. This discernment constituted an ecclesial logic applicable to the evaluation of all peoples.

The comparative work built from this ecclesial logic and its most important precedent. In the medieval Iberian world two groups of Christians were already seen as deeply suspect in regard to the veracity of their Christian identity: *moriscos* (converted Muslims or Christian Moors) and *conversos* (converted Jews or New Christians), sometimes referred to with the derogatory term *marranos* (meaning swine in Spanish). It did not matter whether the conversion of Jew or Muslim was forced or chosen; their Christian identity was troubled. It was a dangerous Christian identity owing to the possibility of their return to Judaism or Islam. There was also the frightening possibility that they might be secretly practicing Jews or Muslims, lodged deep in the Christian body. This fear and suspicion had an Augustinian-like multigenerational effect so that anyone with Jewish or Moorish "blood" must be ferreted out and barred from leadership in the church.[39]

Such suspicion and fear, though common in Christian Spain and Portugal as well as in other parts of medieval Europe, indicated a profound theological distortion. Here was a process of discerning Christian identity that, because it had jettisoned Israel from its calculus of the formation of Christian life, created a conceptual vacuum that was filled by the European. But not simply qua European; rather the very process of becoming Christian took on new ontic markers. Those markers of being were aesthetic and racial. This was not a straightforward matter of replacement (European for Jew) but, as I have suggested, of displacement and now theological reconfiguration. European Christians reconfigured the vision of God's attention and love for Israel, that is, they reconfigured a vision of Israel's election. If Israel had been the visibly elect of God, then that visibility in the European imagination migrated without return to a new home shaped now by new visual markers. If Israel's election had been the compass around which Christian identity gained its bearings and found its trajectory, now with this reconfiguration the body of the European would be the compass marking divine election. More importantly, that new elected body, the white body, would be a discerning body, able to detect holy effects and saving grace. Valignano performs this new reconfigured vision of election precisely in the discernment of racial being.

The mobility and flexibility of the racial scale carried with it a doubtfulness of being, a strong suspicion of instability precisely at the point of embodied Christian commitment. Without Israel as the point of elected stability, the idea of an elected people became an idea without its authentic compass and thereby subject to strange new human discernment. Valignano discerns in two ways—those capable of salvation and those capable of the ministry, priesthood, and ecclesial leadership. At the bottom, chained to the deepest suspicion of incapability, are the *conversos* (or *marranos*) and *moriscos*. Valignano locates Africans with these New Christians and Christian Moors as those he strongly doubts capable of gospel life: "They are a very untalented race . . . incapable of grasping our holy religion or practicing it; because of their naturally low intelligence they cannot rise above the level of the senses . . .; they lack any culture and are given to savage ways and vices, and as a consequence they live like brute beasts. . . . In fine, they are a race born to serve, with no natural aptitude for governing. . . . But through a just though hidden judgment of God, they are left in that state of impotence and regarded as a sterile reprobate land which gives no hope of yielding fruit for a long time to come."[40] This astounding statement, reflecting on the people of Monomotapa in Mozambique, shows Valignano drawing the logical conclusion of black incapacity—reprobation. Reprobation is not simply the state of existence opposite election; it is also a judgment upon the trajectory of a life, gauging its destiny from what can be known in the moment. Reprobation joins the black body to the Moor body and both to the Jewish body. All are in the sphere of Christian rejection and therefore of divine rejection. At the other end of capability are the Japanese (and possibly the Chinese). As is apparent in the quotation given above, Valignano believed that as a white race the Japanese showed potential to enter the depths of Christian formation. The Indians, as also noted above, fell short of the Japanese and Chinese. A sense of reprobation lies with them as well: "A trait common to all these people (I am not speaking now of the so-called white races of China or Japan) is a lack of distinction and talent. As Aristotle would say, they are born to serve rather than to command. They are miserable and poor beyond measure and are given to low and mean tasks. . . . Most of them are very poor, but even the rich tradesmen have to hide their wealth from their tyrannical rulers. They go half-naked and live unpretentiously. More, they are all of a very low standard of intelligence."[41]

A Japanese convert, in Valignano's view, could become as good a Christian as a purebred European or an even better one. Their intelligence and cultural superiority made Japan a fertile, attractive ground for Christian growth. Valignano knew that the work in China and especially in Japan was the most sought-after assignment for Jesuits because of they could identify with intelligent and affable "white" Asians. Thus only the very best workers were allowed on that ground.[42] His comparative analysis also informed his classification of the people appropriate for ecclesial service. Most appropriate were purebred Portuguese (that is, Europeans). Second in terms of appropriateness but regarded with significant reservations were those of pure European parentage but who had been born in India or elsewhere "outside." After these groups, the so-called half-born were quite dubious: *mestiços* (or Mestizos), also called Eurasian, those born of Portuguese fathers and native mothers; and *castiços* (or Castizos), those born of European fathers or mothers and Eurasian or *mestiço* mothers or fathers. Clearly beyond the veil of possibility for service were those whom Valignano termed the "dusky races, [as they are] stupid and vicious," and those of Jewish blood. Valignano's analysis proved decisive, as Rome agreed with all his recommendations for recruitment and the formation of priests in and for mission lands, especially Jesuits.[43]

It would, however, be a mistake to summarize this comparative performance as simply a particular historical characteristic of the Jesuit. Alessandro Valignano was not an innovator in either the theological or historical sense. His orthodoxy was without question, his spirituality and political ability of the first order. He spoke with the mind of the church and with the church in mind. What makes his comparative work so crucial is that in him one sees Christian formation being reconfigured around white bodies. A schematic of this reconfiguration might begin with the constellation shown in figure 1.

As may be seen from the arrows of the schematic, black and white add precision and definition in discerning peoples' salvific possibilities. Technically, doctrines of election first refer to peoples, not individuals. However, individuals may be configured within the overall assessment of a people's salvific viability. Black indicates doubt, uncertainty, and opacity of saving effects. Salvation in black bodies is doubtful, as it was in (Christian) Jews and Moors. White indicates high salvific probability, rooted in the signs of movement toward God (for example, cleanliness, intelligence, obedience, social hierarchy, and advancement in civilization). Europeans reconfigured Christian social space around white and black bodies. If existence between Christian and non-Christian, saved and lost, elect and reprobate was a fluid reality that could be grasped only by detecting the spiritual and material marks, then the racial scale aided this complex optical operation. For example, Valignano notes that Africans, like other reprobates, show the following characteristics: they go around half naked, they have dirty food, practice polygamy, show avarice, and display "marked stupidity."[44] The sta-

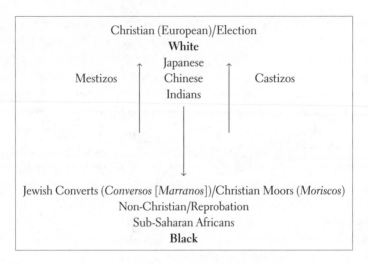

Figure 1. A Trajectory of Salvific Possibilities

bility within this fluid reality is white and black. The racial scale signifies not only a point of exchange—white European election for Jewish election—but also a process of becoming.

Valignano inherited his supersessionist thinking. His use of that thinking, however, brilliantly exhibits its development at this pivotal moment. Through a racial calculus, comparative analysis becomes the new inner logic of how one deploys supersessionist thinking. Supersessionist thinking depends on acts of discernment, that is, of reading the observable for its actualization. Valignano actualizes not simply a way of reading native bodies but a way of inscribing native bodies in the drama of redemption's journey, a journey marked by easy paths (white bodies) and rough terrain (black bodies).

I examine this new inner logic of supersessionist thinking in the next chapter as I consider the thought of José de Acosta. But one important implication of this development stands out: in the age of discovery and conquest supersessionist thinking burrowed deeply inside the logic of evangelism and emerged joined to whiteness in a new, more sophisticated, concealed form. Indeed, supersessionist thinking is the womb in which whiteness will mature. Any attempt to address supersessionism must carefully attend to the formation of the racial scale and the advent of a new vision of Christian social space. Valignano's inherited derogatory vision of black flesh was also present among Muslims.[45] Indeed, one would be hard-pressed to find a positive view of the sub-Saharan African in this time, especially given the attractiveness of the black slave trade. Muslim slave traders drew aesthetic distinctions between white European slaves and black sub-Saharan African slaves, not only because white slaves could potentially bring more money in their sale to Christians, but also because black slaves were considered inferior in body and mind to whites.[46] The fifteenth-century Islamic historian Ibn Khaldun noted that "[Negroes] have little that is (essentially) human and possess attributes that are quite similar to those of dumb animals."[47] Like Christianity, Islam held a comparative sensibility that distinguished, in the words of the tenth-century Persian Islamic historian Tabari, all blacks from the Arabs and Persians, who have "beautiful faces and beautiful hair."[48] However, my concern is not simply with the operation of a derogatory view of black bodies, but also with how Europeans reconfigured Christian social space and in turn entered into their own act of displacement.

Displacement operates within the expansion of worlds. In time the Iberian world will extend from South America to Africa to India to China to Japan to Australia.[49] These nations will not be alone in reach or remain preeminent in power. But the reach of the Iberian nations or any other nation existed within the wider vision of the church. As I have shown, the world of the church was coextensive with that of these young colonialist powers and worked in and through them as well, providing a theological framework that extended their identities onto a spiritual plane and enabled them to articulate their forms of life in their encounters with other peoples. This extending of worlds deeply affected the African as well. In fact, mercantile and theological interests conversed and converged on the African at this moment, not only vivifying the idea of perpetual slavery, but also drawing African bodies onto a plane of existence that involved constant spiritual and material comparison with white bodies.

The subtleties of this displacement moved simultaneously in two directions. The first was conceptual, exhibited in a comparative habit of mind that was facilitated by the racial scale and that was organized within a theological matrix. The second was material, activated by the joining of European and African bodies within an economic arrangement that indicated a fundamental transforming of space. Europeans were willingly leaving their homes. Newly discovered natives were unwillingly being taken from their lands. Historically, this is so obvious as to seem trite, but the parallelism at work here, while almost imperceptible, was earth shattering. With this leaving, this exiting, one approaches the depths of this theological mistake. It will not be easy to articulate the material reality of displacement because it is the articulation of a loss from within the loss itself. To fully tell it requires the very thing that is lacking, indigenous voices telling their own stories of transformation through current concepts of space, identity, and land. Equally difficult is the attempt to peer into a theological mistake so wide, so comprehensive that it has disappeared, having expanded to cover the horizon of modernity itself.

THE ARCHITECTURE OF LOSS

I must now engage in an act of fragment thinking in hopes of seeing the new order that emerged during the age of discovery and conquest. In "gather[ing] up the fragments that remain that nothing may be lost" (John 6:12), I want first to examine another episode in the life of Alessandro Valignano that will help uncover the reality of loss inside the movement of displacement.

Approaching Holy Week in March of 1581, two years after his arrival in Japan, Valignano and his retinue set out on horseback to the city of Miyako (now Kyoto) to visit the Azuchi castle, home of the most powerful leader in Japan, the ruler of Tenka, Oda Nobunaga. Valignano, as was customary, was bringing gifts for the dignitaries: sets of vestments, small oil paintings, musical instruments, books, rosaries, and other things. However, the most interesting thing Valignano brought along with him for that eventful visit was his slave, a dark-skinned African. The intricate route to the castle, past Yao, Wakae, Sanga, and Okayama (Kawachi), crossing the river Yodogawa, and on to Takatsuki, took several days, right into Tuesday of Holy Week, and en route, as the historian Josef Franz Schütte relates, the party drew special attention: "All along the way the people gathered in crowds curious to catch a glimpse of the party; the giant figure of the visitor and the dark-skinned Negro who accompanied him as servant were objects of special interest."[50] Arriving in Takatsuki, Valignano performed that most sacred of liturgies, of Holy Week and Easter, celebrating the body of Christ, in suffering, death, and resurrection. He then proceeded to Miyako to prepare his own body for formal presentation and audience with the ruler. The parallel of presentation of bodies here is striking. Valignano was an usually tall man (over six feet), but as he and his black slave stood in the presence of Oda Nobunaga, the ruler's interest turned to the African. Nobunaga was not alone in showing utter fascination with the African. A large, excited crowd had gathered outside the place where Valignano and his attendants were housed, hoping to catch sight of this black body. Some people had come to blows jostling for position. As he stood before Nobunaga, just a few days after Easter, the body of this African came under careful scrutiny. The astonished and puzzled ruler ordered that the upper body of this black man be uncovered, and then he proceeded to have him washed over and over again to see if the blackness would disappear.[51]

Valignano and his black slave standing there together before the ruler are instructive. Two bodies are in presentation with a third body in the background. For Valignano, it is the third body, that of Christ crucified and resurrected, that has brought him to these shores. Yet the crucial body at this moment is not the body of Jesus, but the body of an African enslaved — *Hoc est enim corpus meum* (This is my body). Nobunaga performs another liturgy after Holy Week, an anti-liturgy, as it were, in which the stripping and repeated washing of the dark African confirms his identity as black and slave. This moment of visitation represented the joining of the white body to the black body — together they appear. Valignano stood before the ruler and presented the new world of the "southern barbarians," as they were called by the Japanese. He showed European mastery over lands and peoples by having this black body in servitude. Though he spoke and presented himself and his church in friendship, this was also a moment of closure, as the African was not permitted to speak for himself. Indeed, even if he had spoken his native language he would probably not have been understood. Standing there half-naked, he had been taken from his home and given a new identity calibrated to his body and articulated by his Christian master. There in that new space the slave had no name, unless it was given by Valignano. For Ruler Nobunaga, whoever this African was would issue out of an examination of his black body and the words of the visitor.

Valignano entered this moment of dislocation by choice, the slave by force. In this new space, Japan, Valignano is a white man among "white people," established in the knowledge that being there was not a disruption of his identity, but an expansion of it into a spiritual and quasi-national network. That new space, however, meant utter disruption for the African. Gone was the earth, the ground, spaces, and places that facilitated his identity, and what remained, embodied in his master, was a signified and signifying reality of whiteness, not simply by his master's speech but by the very location of the master's body operating in power next to his.

This episode exemplifies a spatial disruption that the European Christian would enact and to which he would be almost oblivious, but never innocent. The age of discovery and conquest began a process of transformation of land and identity. And while worlds were being transformed, not every world was changed in the same way. Peoples different in geography, in life, in different worlds of European designation — Africa, the Americas, Europe — will lose the earth only to find it again in a strange new way. The deepest theological distortion taking place is that the earth, the ground, spaces, and places are being removed as living organizers of identity and as facilitators of identity.

What if your skin was inextricably bound to "the skin of the world," to borrow that marvelous phrase from Calvin Luther Martin's text *The Way of the Human*

Being.[52] What if it seemed strange, odd, and even impossible for you to conceive of your identity apart from a specific order of space—specific land, specific animals, trees, mountains, waters, and arrangements of days and nights? Martin, a historian and quasi-theologian who spent years among the Yup'ik Eskimos on the Alaskan tundra and significant time in the Navajo nation, suggests an order of things present among the indigenous peoples of the New World that a mind detached from deep participation with the earth cannot easily appreciate. In contrast Martin points to a different identity form: "People who can define themselves as cardinal points, primary colors, segments of the day, the seasons, even the journey of life itself—people such as this are clearly engaging a reality different from the usual western points of reference."[53]

It is a truism to say that humans are all bound to the earth. However, that articulated connection to the earth comes under profound and devastating alteration with the age of discovery and colonialism.[54] A central overlooked implication of that sense of connection is the articulation of place-bound identity, a form of existence before or "below" race, within place itself. In Martin's account, "Native Americans universally maintain that human and animals were made to occupy the same skin—the skin of shared personhood. Here at creation's origin, there was nothing really to distinguish humans from animals: one lived in human shape and yet was still groundhog, rabbit, tortoise, or what have you. In the native world, men and women existed more broadly as plenipotential people, people who 'are themselves—a Clam, a Dog, a Birch Person—yet they take human shape as well. Each form contains the other. In some ways, they are seen as being both at once.'"[55] Before reading this as a form of ethnographic essentializing (Martin, remember, is a historian, not an anthropologist), one should see the important claim Martin makes, a claim that joins many peoples who remember that they are tribes or peoples. Identity here requires spatial realities endowed with irreducible, even irreplaceable points of reference. What Martin invokes is difficult to capture because it must be read in light of the complex history of the social construction of Indianness and the very real politics of Indian identity in America.[56] Like the African, the Indian is a necessary fiction, a pothole-filled pathway made through discursive practice that allows one to move toward understanding what is at stake in the loss of ways of life and the troubled yet admirable attempts to gather the fragments that remain.[57] In this regard, one should not stumble at the usage of *Indian* or *African* or of invoking what I understand as an aspect of tribal reality for fear of falling into mind-numbing essentialism.

The greater trap is the failure to see the specifics of the loss for indigenes that includes but is not completely captured by European discursive hegemony. As Philip Deloria points out, identity construction must be understood in the context of land appropriation: "The indeterminacy of American identities stems, in part, from the nation's inability to deal with Indian people. Americans wanted to feel a natural affinity with the continent, and it was Indians who could teach them such aboriginal closeness. Yet, in order to *control the landscape* they had to destroy the original inhabitants."[58] Deloria correctly notes a history of Indian-use which, like African-use, bolsters a sense of freedom and independence from the trappings of the old European world, connection to land *as private property*, and the possibilities of being self-made in America. The sense of connection Martin seizes upon is bound neither to nobility myths nor to European Indian invention. It is not "imperialist nostalgia."[59] Martin echoes the words of native peoples, creatively using language to capture that which is beyond the sight of many. He tells the story of an Eskimo from a tiny village by the Bering Sea, Charlie Kilangak, whose Yup'ik name means Puffin. He explained to Martin exactly what it means to be Puffin:

> I am a puffin.
> I live on the cliffs or on the steep hillsides.
> I know and choose to live where my family will be safe.
> I love to fish, and know which fish to ingest for my children.
> I could both fly in the skies or under sea and master the winds and the
>   currents.
> I know where to go by looking at the world around me.
> I am a puffin . . . from . . . my ancestral tree, and in blood.
> I choose to dress in black and white so my children will know who they are
>   too.
> I have this wonderful colorful beak. It helps me identify my own kind, so
>   others would know who I am.
> I am a puffin, and I am what my creator has made me to be.
> I am a puffin, and my son is too.[60]

Martin tells another story of a young Iroquois man who had an argument with his Iroquois uncle about Indian identity. The uncle asked the young man, who had just graduated from college, who he (the young man) was?

> When the nephew matter-of-factly replied that he was who his name said he was, the older man was not impressed. "Yeah, that's who you are, I guess." Pause. "Is that all?" Sensing he was being set up for something, the young man expertly traced his parentage on both sides and then ran back through his clan. [Seeing that he was not giving the answer the uncle wanted, he conceded, angrily asking the uncle,] "Well, who the hell am I then?" The older man calmly replied, "I think you know but I will tell you. If you sit here, and look out right

over there; look at that. The rocks: the way they are. The trees and the hills all around you. Right where you're on, it's water. . . . You're just like that rock. . . . You're the same as the water, this water. . . . You are the ridge, this ridge. You were here in the beginning. You're as strong as they are. As long as you believe in that . . . that's who you are. That's your mother, and that's you. Don't forget."[61]

Martin is not romanticizing Native Americans, claiming for them some essentialized ecological genius, but instead is simply noting the remnants of a sensibility concerning identity. We are the very things we may invoke spatially.[62] His recounting of part of a Navajo hymn illustrates this:

The mountains, I become part of it . . .
The herbs, the fir tree, I become part of it.
The morning mists, the clouds, the gathering waters.
I become part of it.
The wilderness, the dew drops, the pollen . . .
I become part of it.[63]

This Native American insight draws one into a self-description built within a vision of creation bound to specific locations. This union with the world through "unbounded kinship," as Martin calls it, turns on geographic specificity[64] and on a kinship with plants, places, and animals.[65] Martin isn't noting a recalcitrant "primitivism" heroically standing against the tides of modernity. Rather, he has come upon ancient ways of articulating existence. That articulation was rooted in an ongoing conversation with the world in a "reciprocal aesthetic that announces kinship."[66]

Martin suggests, unsympathetically, that those first Christians who came to the new worlds "were at the furthest limit of their conception of the real and though utterly unaware of it were fingering the 'skin of the world.'" Those Christians went unknowingly beyond geography into identity.[67] They entered what for them was a frontier of strangeness. Already fearful and angled toward isolationist practices, they enacted a spatial vertigo, renaming places, peoples, and animals and reconfiguring life.[68]

Christian faith and theology carry within them the possibilities of knowing and renarrating identity with geography. The Greek Orthodox theologian S. A. Mousalimas tells the story of an Orthodox Yup'ik hunter whose way of life articulates his Christian identity through his familial oneness with animals and land.[69] But these were possibilities of self-articulation never to be fully realized, never to be truly explored.

Instead, the new worlds were transformed into land—raw, untamed land. And the European vision saw these new lands as a system of potentialities, a mass of undeveloped, underdeveloped, unused, underutilized, misunderstood, not fully understood potentialities. Everything—from peoples and their bodies to plants and animals, from the ground and the sky—was subject to change, subjects for change, subjected to change. The significance of this transformation cannot be overstated. The earth itself was barred from being a constant signifier of identity. Europeans defined Africans and all others apart from the earth even as they separated them from their lands.

The central effect of the loss of the earth as an identity signifier was that native identities, tribal, communal, familial, and spatial, were constricted to simply their bodies, leaving behind the very ground that enables and facilitates the articulation of identity. The profound commodification of bodies that was New World slavery signifies an effect humankind has yet to reckon with fully—a distorted vision of creation.

This is the troubled existence humans have entered upon without realizing their loss. This occurrence cannot be easily discerned because it is deeply embedded in the loss of knowledge itself. Martin, without inscribing a cultural pathology, invokes this overarching sense of loss for Native peoples in Alaska and other places:

> The prison is overflowing with Yup'ik men, mostly, who are lovely and sweet people who got drunk and blacked out and did something awful. They are sad, orphaned from their old world, and what they have now is a hybrid that doesn't work. They are a people who've lost the story. Or had it drowned in bootlegged vodka or watched it perish from diphtheria or influenza or tuberculosis—or put a bullet in it. Starting with the Russian fur merchants in the eighteenth century and continuing with the missionaries a hundred years later, then the teachers and government bureaucrats, all the while battered by appalling epidemics, a tidal wave of alcohol, and now the din of television sets switched on all the time, plus snowmobiles and powerboats and rifles and videos—with all this, the moose don't dream themselves into people any more. At least, not many people. Nor do salmon, caribou, or bears or seals or walrus. I doubt the blueberries and cranberries and salmonberries give their spirit to many Yupiit, either.[70]

This is not the scene of the corroding effects of modernity on "primitive peoples" but an example that builds directly from the imposition of racial agency into indigenous worlds. Consider another vignette from Martin about Robert, whom he met during a visit to a prison:

[Robert] wished sometimes he could just disappear into "someone nothing."
Annihilation. His grandfather told him long ago that he could learn the white
man's ways and language, but could never become a white man. The Eskimos,
warned the old man, would eventually become a "spot," a dot, to the whites.
Irrelevant. Robert reached for a paper napkin to wipe his eyes. He walked away
to the chain-link fence, beneath the sign that says the guards can shoot anyone
standing that close to the fence—to weep in private. Alcohol put him here.
He drank and lost consciousness . . . and did something frightening. I asked if
he's an artist. "Oh yes, somewhat." He told me how he once carved an Eskimo
hunting a seal out of *pure ivory.* . . . . Robert put his right hand up over his head
and assumed the hunter's waiting posture . . . the patient hunter poised above
the breathing-hole. Robert, I realized, had carved himself.[71]

Martin delineates a sense of perception that enfolded native peoples in a reality
immensely beyond the idea of an isolated body.[72] He also begins to outline the
loss that accompanies the slow destruction of that sense of perception. This loss
is the loss of land—dispossession and resettlement—and, even more crucially,
the imposition of a new calculus of signification built around white bodies. The
grandfather's warning voiced not simply a concern about overwhelming numbers
of white people, but also about the reduction of indigenes' visibility. This invisibility is not only diminished Indian populations, but an invisibility that shrinks
their presence from the land and animals, water and sky. It is white perception
that is at play here: "The Eskimos . . . would eventually become a 'spot,' a dot, to
the whites. Irrelevant."

Irrelevancy here points to the draining of significance of particular people in
particular places. The invisibility of indigenes' ways of life ironically is carried
inside white perception of those ways of life. Martin points to the emergence of a
form of perception of bodies in space that makes invisible the spatial dimensions
of the identities of those bodies.

Elizabeth Marshall Thomas, in *The Old Way: A Story of the First People*
(2006), also captures this sense of perception and loss and in an equally instructive way.[73] She is a member of the famous Marshall family, who during the 1950s
lived among the so-called San people, the Bushmen of the Kalahari (their world
surrounded by Namibia, Botswana, Zambia, and Angola), more properly designated the Ju/wasi and /Gwi peoples. Although neither she nor any of her family
members were at the time anthropologists or ethnographers, together they produced some of the most important work on the Ju/wasi and /Gwi and are cred-
ited with introducing their world to the "modern West" and in turn giving witness
to the ongoing effects of the colonial and postcolonial worlds on the Ju/wasi.[74]

The Ju/wasi were considered one of the last hunter-gatherer societies in Africa and in the world. Marshall Thomas's text builds from her equally important book of 1958, *The Harmless People*, in which she offered her initial account of life among the Ju/wasi.[75] The second book, *The Old Way*, places her experiences with these people of the Nyae Nyae in an evolutionary framework, one understandable, even admirable, yet deeply problematic: "We found people who called themselves Ju/wasi and were living the lifestyle of our ancestors, a lifestyle of the African savannah that began before we were human beings, changing in form but not in essence as time passed and the climate fluctuated and lasting until the last third of the twentieth century. That any of us are here at all is due entirely to the long-term culture that these hunter-gatherers, with their courage, skill, and knowledge, continued to uphold. To me, the experience of visiting this place and these people was profoundly important, *as if I had voyaged into the deep past through a time machine.* I feel that I saw the Old Way, the way of life that shaped us, a way of life that now is gone."[76] What brought the teenager Elizabeth Marshall to the Kalahari with her family was her father, the founder and former president of Raytheon, and his desire to explore a world still relatively untouched, the wilderness world of the Bushman. Her initial sense of temporal and spatial displacement continues to shape Marshall Thomas's anthropological and literary account of the Ju/wasi people and their slow, painful demise. Unlike her earlier treatment of the Ju/wasi in *The Harmless People*, this text, *The Old Way*, leans heavily on a particular construal of time, what Johannes Fabian describes as radically dehistoricized "evolutionary" time.[77]

Fabian's critique of flawed uses of time in constructing an anthropological object helps one see how Marshall Thomas's vision of the Ju/wasi both sheds light on the problem of displacement and reflects the problem. Fabian, in his seminal text *Time and the Other*, suggested that the hermeneutic through which anthropologists and other Western intellectuals interpret native peoples has been through the spatialization of time. Spatialized time becomes naturalized time. Fabian lodges the origins of this way of configuring time in the Christian tradition. Enlightenment traditions found a resource in the Christian vision of the history of salvation in space and time and refashioned that vision into an immanent, observable reality of progress. This is not a new insight, yet Fabian captures an important effect of this refashioning, that is, the ability to discern "temporal relations" between geographic locations and peoples of the world.

Fabian argues that Western intellectuals, especially anthropologists, are the inheritors of an evolutionist epistemology that "imperceptibly replaces real ecological space with classificatory, tabular space."[78] Not denying the idea of development, he is trying to capture the epistemological conditions under which anthropologists and other interpreters of culture do their work. Those conditions produce such notions as primitive peoples, which is "essentially a temporal concept and a category, not an object, of Western thought."[79] He notes three uses of time in anthropological discourse: physical time, mundane time, and typological time. None of these brings clarity to anthropological description as much as they indicate the muddled thinking that has been present in the interaction of Western and colonialized peoples. Physical time is nonculturally conditioned time. It is time which, whether calibrated in evolutionary, prehistorical reconstruction or demographic or ecological terms, is objective, neutral, and natural. Mundane and typological times are improvisations on physical time. Mundane is, as the word suggests, nonprecise or "loose," everyday attributions of periodization. And typological time denotes types of time, that is, "intervals between events," that may be comparable: for example, feudal versus industrial, agrarian versus urban. This designation of time indicates "quality of states" and creates in effect the possibility of designating real people without history. Here "time may almost totally be divested of its vectorial, physical connotations."[80]

Fabian believes these uses of time are a kind of coping mechanism. Naturalized and spatialized time "gives meaning(s) to the distribution of humanity in space."[81] This is a strong reversal of the idea that the vast distance of human cultures in space self-generates temporal relations through the discovery of ages. Spatialized time allows the "distancing of those who are observed from the time of the observer." In this way, spatialized time is a means to an end, that is, to show that "natural laws or law like regulations operate in the development of a human society and culture."[82] In contradistinction, Fabian notes another kind of time, intersubjective time. Intersubjective time is time shared, shared by object and observer, shared by the referent and the speaking subject. The term he uses for this shared reality is *coeval*: "In fact, further conclusions can be drawn from this basic postulate to the point of realizing that for human communication to occur, coevalness has to be created. Communication is, ultimately, about creating shared Time."[83]

Fabian's is a powerful, even deeply theological idea, one that I shall return to later. However, at this point, one can begin to see what Fabian is moving toward. He notes that even where people recognize shared time there will be "devices of temporal distancing."[84] The unrelenting production of such devices results from a habit of mind Fabian calls the denial of coevalness. It is "a persistent and systematic tendency to place the referent(s) of anthropology in a Time other than the present of the producer of anthropological discourse."[85] For Fabian, this problem yields a choice: "Either [the ethnographer or anthropologist] submits to the condition of coevalness and produces ethnographic knowledge or he deludes himself into temporal distance and misses the object of his search."[86] Fabian is careful to note that even the best intentions and highest morals of the cultural observer have not guaranteed overcoming of the denial of coevalness. The denial in part is inherent in the bequeathed trajectory of Enlightenment cultural chauvinism that would never treat colonialized societies on their own terms. But the denial is also due to the reconfiguration of space and time in relation to bodies. The denial is equally of shared time and of shared space. This latter denial emerges out of a simultaneous recognition of bodies different and racialized and terrain alien to the observer. Marshall Thomas, not so much an exemplar of the denial as someone who I believe achieves Fabian's condition of coevalness, constantly deploys devices of temporal distancing. She shows that space has the same cultural density as time. In so doing, she performs a spatial distancing that is decisive in her interpretation of the Ju/wasi. In Marshall Thomas one can see, in addition to what Fabian noted as the replacement of "ecological space with classificatory, tabular space," the effects of alienated space enacted on bodies.

The "old way" for Marshall Thomas is the way of life the Ju/wasi lived. It is the way of life that reaches back to Paleolithic times. In that reaching back humans figuratively hold hands with their mothers reaching back millions of evolutionary years when they were the animals that roamed the rain forests. The Ju/wasi, for Marshall Thomas, thus are their own unique reality, but also, more decisively, they re-present humankind (as once they lived) on the land, attuned to its subtle ecologies and sophisticated economies of food, water, and sharing. This account of the Ju/wasi is first and foremost an evolutionary tale that suggests more about humanity than about the Ju/wasi. It is a kind of swan song to a life now gone that attempts to draw implications for moderns from the Ju/wasi way of life. Such use of a people requires pause, to see both the beauty of the Ju/wasi and their tragedy. Yet tragedy exists here in two senses: the tragedy of their demise and the tragedy of their use in the narrative. They are made to signify humanity in ways that turn their lives into transparencies. Looking through them, one sees the Paleolithic.

I am not accusing Marshall Thomas of intentionally casting a derogatory gaze on the Ju/wasi. Marshall Thomas's account draws on colonialist ways of viewing black flesh in which black bodies signify the constructs of Western minds. From the detection of the demonic to the myth of the noble savage to the interpretation of embodied cultural artifacts, the history of this vision is to conjure intelligibility from (primitive) blackness itself. Not every aspect of this troubled way of seeing is present in Marshall Thomas's treatment, yet her unrelenting rhetorical strategy to see, that is, to imagine, in the Ju/wasi the ancient patterns of humanity's becoming draws its logic from this derogatory optic. Be that as it may, Marshall Thomas does expose something very important, namely, the reality of the interwovenness of the Ju/wasi and the land.

The cultural logics of the Ju/wasi are inseparable from the ways of the animals of the southwest African savannah. Not only the animals, but Ju/wasi everyday practices are completely unintelligible without discerning the contours of the Nyae Nyae landscape: "On the savannah, the seasons begin and end with rain."[87] Marshall Thomas holds up this reality of space as the way the Ju/wasi count time. Water and its scarcity are keys for understanding Ju/wasi movement. Settlement and travel are shaped around the places of water. The location of waterholes is fundamental knowledge that they carry from generation to generation. In an amazing catalog of practices, she details the joining of land and the life of a people. Yet she also reveals the distance of her family from the land even as they inhabit it along with the Ju/wasi. This can be seen in something as simple as the supplies they (as opposed to the Ju/wasi) need for survival on the land: "We had tents, cots, sleeping bags, folding chairs, and tables, a compass, cameras, film, recording equipment, reference books, notebooks, pens, ink, pencils, disinfec- tants, antivenin kits for snakebites, brandy, cases of canned foods, boxes of dry foods, dishes, cooking pots, frying pans, knives, forks, spoons, cigarettes, matches, spare tires, auto parts, inner tubes, tire patches, jacks, toolboxes, winches, motor oil, drums of gasoline, drums of water, bars of yellow soap, towels, washcloths, toothpaste, toothbrushes, coats, sweaters, pants, boots, sneakers, shirts, under- wear, socks, reading glasses, safety pins, scissors, a sewing kit, binoculars, bullets, a rifle. The Ju/wasi had sticks, skins, eggshells, and grass."[88]

The land was *in* the Ju/wasi in an extraordinary way. Families, or, more pre- cisely, the women of a family, were the *kxai k' xausi*, the "owners who possess" the land or the *n!ore*.[89] This concept of ownership was far more organic than that of property ownership:

> What is a territory or a *n!ore* to a group like that? Not what it would be to us, a carefully delineated piece of property that can be bought and sold, with marked-off boundaries. A Ju/wa territory belonged to those who were born there, whose rights were acquired through a parent who was born there, on back through time. The ownership could not be transferred, and the land had no formal boundaries but faded off into no-man's-land on the far sides of which other, different groups might hold equally extensive territories. Thus the impor- tance of *n!ore* derived less from its conditions as a tract of land and more from the plants and animals that lived on it, the firewood that could be found there, and, most important of all, the water. . . . Thus the *n!ore* was not property, it was life, and the concept of *n!ore* was deep in the soul.[90]

The Ju/wasi moved around various areas of the Nyae Nyae as land, animals, and plants were available, their settlements forming semicircles or circles with grass shelters facing in every direction to guard against animal attack. As they sat, their group configurations always matched the contours of the trees' shade from the sun. They sat close to each other for protection and comfort. They calibrated their hunting and gathering around periods when the heat of the savannah was bearable. If the land was in them, the animals were always with them, body and soul. Hunting determined almost every transition in Ju/wasi life, especially male life. Hunting produced a staple of their diet, meat, and marked a young man's capability to enter marriage, confirming the health and well-being of a community. It also showed the complexities of the knowledge of land and animals that the Ju/wasi carried across generations: "The tracking ability of the Bushmen is legendary, and rightly so. I happened to be traveling with three Ju/wa men who had occasion to track a hyena across a wide slab of bare rock. How they did it I have no idea. . . . The feat seemed effortless. The trackers thought nothing of it and, being at the time unfamiliar with the general ignorance of white people regarding the natural world, they were mildly startled by my amazement. To us, however, the ability of the Ju/wasi to track a wounded antelope if the antelope is with a herd seems equally amazing."[91] Moments like this in the narrative illumine Marshall Thomas's awareness of her difference, a difference she marks racially. Another moment of marked awareness was when she went to gather edible plants with the Ju/wasi women. These plants (roots, nuts, berries, melons, spinach-like leaves, and fruits) were the main staple of the Ju/wasi diet. Gathering was as educational and humbling for her as being with the hunters. Again she was amazed by the ability of the Ju/wasi to identify edible buried plants by only "a bit of grass-like stubble about an inch long."[92] The Ju/wasi could remember the precise locations of various melons, fruits, and other plants that had been spotted the previous season and were now ripe. This land memory stretched over vast areas that all looked exactly the same to her, but not to the Ju/wasi.

In careful detail Marshall Thomas depicts how a sense of identity can flow directly from the land. For example, elders are highly respected and valued because they are the bearers of knowledge of how to live in the world of plants, animals, earth, and sky. Elders represent not only the epistemological limits of life-knowledge but also the epistemic structure of practices for the Ju/wasi. The standard explanation for ignorance about anything was "their old people hadn't told them," and thus they did not know how to proceed.[93] She also marks the shared social sensibilities of Ju/wasi with lions, elephants, and other animals. In one beautiful passage she describes how lions of the Nyae Nyae rarely attack the Ju/wasi because the elders of both lions and Ju/wasi taught their young not to hunt each other.[94] The Ju/wasi distinguished other peoples from themselves through categories of outsider shaped by their horrifying encounters with Europeans farmers and Bantu pastoralists who usurped their land and in many cases enslaved them. As Marshall Thomas writes, "They lumped them together with the predators, calling all of them, very simply, *!xohmi*, the word that they would use for lions and hyenas, meaning interestingly enough, that like the lions and hyenas, the newcomers had no hooves."[95]

Marshall Thomas's narrative sheds light on ways of life that are patterned not after but actually *with* space, with land, trees, water, animals. However, there is also in her account an embodied sense of alienated space. She actually does not need the land as the Ju/wasi people need it. She has water, food, and escape. She is at all times completely clear that she is a white woman different from them. She respects them, cherishes them, loves them, but she is white and they are black Africans. Here spatial distancing is embodied racially. Marshall Thomas recognized she was different from the Ju/wasi and respected that difference. Although the Ju/wasi renamed her Di!ai, drew her into their everyday practices, shared their stories, introduced her to their cultural logics, and in turn drew from her knowledge, both in terms of her history and cultural sensibilities, she did not see herself as inhabiting the same space as the Ju/wasi.[96] This is not primarily an issue of language. She learned their language. She and her family as well committed themselves to helping the Ju/wasi.

What is at play here is the overturning of space and the disruption of identity facilitated by its carriers. Marshall Thomas tells of an incident in 1998 that occurred during a showing of her brother's famous documentary on the plight of the Ju/wasi, *A Kalahari Family*. She lashed out at someone in the audience who suggested that the Marshall family had initiated the spoiling of the Ju/wasi way of life by bringing the Western world to their doorstep. Her spirited reply to the accusation claimed the change was inevitable. However, on further reflection, she realized the accusation had merit: "I didn't hear what he [the audience member] said because I was still fuming, but in fact, we were partly responsible for starting the change, and not just our truck tracks. Our presence certainly alerted the Ju/wasi (those who had never been slaves on farms) to the life beyond the Kalahari, and our presence in the Nyae Nyae certainly reminded the white settlers and the Bantu pastoralists of the great, untouched grasslands that lay beyond the farms."[97] The accusation had merit because the Marshall family's presence marked the land in a new way. It marked the land as a separate reality from the reality of the people. Their presence effected a conceptual separation that became a material one. They separated the people from the land. This judgment may seem counterintuitive. Their existence on the land, even for a brief time, enacted an optic that has existed from the very beginnings of Iberian expansion and conquest. That way of seeing land drew indigenes unrelentingly, unforgivingly away from land and encapsulated their identities in typological and racial space. That is, it drew them inescapably into the same space as white identity. This way of seeing turns the earth into land *in potentia*: "[My father] . . . had known what the Bushmen could not have known, that their future was uncertain, that they were already wanted as laborers, and that other people wanted their land and were only too ready to take it from them, because in the eyes of the white farmers and Bantu pastoralists, the Bushmen 'did nothing' with it. They 'didn't use it,' and the whites and pastoralists would. My father also knew something about the governments of the countries that shared the Kalahari and understood how ready they were to assist their constituents in land acquisition. Perhaps no one could have predicted the year that the Old Way would end, but obviously it wasn't going to last forever."[98] The irony here seems to escape Marshall Thomas. She is describing precisely the logic of the colonialist. Her father saw clearly the matrix of utility that would be placed on the Ju/wasi and their space. Both would be interpreted through two forms of use-value, one for people and the other for land. What neither she nor her father could see was their participation in that colonialist logic through their own encapsulation in a space different from the Ju/wasi. Again, Fabian is helpful in pointing to the implications of this encapsulation procedure. In commenting on Parsonian functionalism, he notes that its effect was to encapsulate time within a given social system, thereby enabling the study of time within cultures. This process "virtually exorcised time from the study of relations between cultures." "'Theories of Time' held by various cultures could now be studied with 'timeless' theory and method."[99] Fabian's point here is that a bracketing comes into effect that pushes out the possibility of seeing time as a "dimension of intercultural study."[100]

Translated to the reality of space, this encapsulation meant the Ju/wasi were placed in, conceptually speaking, a cultural-spatial bubble in which their land logic could be seen and evaluated. The Marshalls evaluated it positively, even romantically, but the white farmers and Bantu pastoralists evaluated it negatively. Both saw it in fundamentally the same way, as the unreal, the symbolic of a configuration of bodies in space that was functionally dissonant (figure 2).

How the Marshalls aided in the separation of Ju/wasi from their land was by enacting through their presence a new relationship to the land at the very moment they "touched" the Ju/wasi. They had reached beyond geography into identity, and in so doing they showed that continuities of identity did not require specific land or specific relationships to land. In the modernity the Marshall family embodied, identities are encapsulated by language and race, along with the important tropes culture and (ethno-)rituals. That is, as the Marshalls were in the land (in respect, in honor, even in ecological care) but not of the land, so too

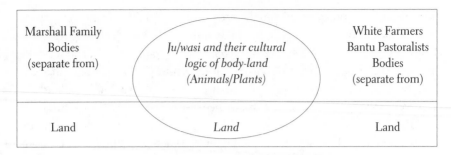

Marshall Family	*Ju/wasi and their cultural*	White Farmers
Bodies	*logic of body-land*	Bantu Pastoralists
(separate from)	*(Animals/Plants)*	Bodies
		(separate from)
Land	*Land*	Land

Figure 2. Symbolic Configuration of Bodies in Space

could the Ju/wasi be: "Our presence certainly alerted the Ju/wasi (those who had never been slaves on farms) to the life beyond the Kalahari, and our presence in Nyae Nyae certainly reminded the white settlers and the Bantu pastoralists of the great, untouched grassland that lay beyond the farms."[101] The Ju/wasi were therefore construed as people bound to the land, but not necessarily so; their binding was a matter of choice, much like the presence of the Marshalls. The Ju/wasi could now be interpreted both in their location and their being as transitional.

In less than twenty-five years, the South African government and private interests utterly inverted the Ju/wasi relation to land. It was a process rooted in centuries-long colonialist practices that had transformed the New Worlds. Beginning in 1959 with the establishment of a government outpost in Tsumkwe that would oversee Bushmen affairs from the ground to the disastrous proposal in 1960 that European-style farming be practiced through the introduction of goats, corn, and millet, the Ju/wasi were pulled into ecological holocaust. The goats, corn, and millet compromised the ecological integrity of the area. In 1970, the South African government established a Bushmen homeland (for Ju/wasi, Herero, Tswana, Kavango, and Ambo), with various groups assigned land tracts, and then prohibited all Bushmen from hunting traditional game. However, game was hunted vigorously by whites. By 1975, with limited options for finding sufficient food to eat, most Ju/wasi concentrated in Tsumkwe. By the 1980s, the Ju/wasi were forced by the South African government to live in government housing in "a location" in Tsumkwe. Marshall Thomas's description captures the reality of life in a South African township: "The sedentary, unsanitary, overcrowded conditions of course brought disease, and the people began to get all manner of sicknesses to which they had no immunities, including TB, malaria, bilharzias, venereal diseases, and later, of course, AIDS."[102] The recruitment of Ju/wasi to military service, fighting guerrilla warfare against the South West Africa People's Organization, and the introduction of alcohol were the final blows to the Ju/wasi way of life. Military service was one of the only means of securing income for many, and alcohol overconsumption unleashed the demons of violence and death. The people turned on each other out of frustration over limited options for thriving and the loss of their land. Indeed, some Ju/wasi committed suicide with the poison arrows they had once used for hunting life-giving game. Her quotation of a song composed by N!ai, the daughter of the woman with whom Marshall Thomas shared her Ju/wasi name, captures this horror: "Now people mock me and I cry. / My people abuse me. / The white people scorn me. / Death dances with me."[103] A few Ju/wasi continued to struggle as farmers, but the reality of the vast majority was the death of a way of life, if not of a people: "Only a small area squeezed between the nineteenth and twentieth parallels [of assigned land] remain to the Ju/wasi we knew. Of the fourteen waterholes of the former Nyae Nyae, only five are within the area, which is now known as the Nyae Nyae Conservancy. But, thanks largely to my brother [John Marshall], the Ju/wa residents of the conservancy are the only group of Bushmen in Namibia who have any land at all. The rest live on *white people's farms as farm workers* or on the outskirts of pastoralist villages without rights of tenure. In Namibia, as in all southern African countries, the Bushmen are the poorest ethnic group by far, with the greatest unemployment."[104] The transformation is complete — the Ju/wasi have been turned into an ethnic group captured in poverty. As her brother so powerfully argued, it would be impossible for the Ju/wasi to return to the Old Way or anything approximating it. But sentimentalizing this impossibility of return as the loss of the premodern world that has come upon us all dehistoricizes this reality of transformation by isolating the Ju/wasi as simply a "tragic people" who were out of step with the Enlightenment processes of cultural evolution. They cannot return because white presence first interrupted the connection of land to identity and then very quickly reconfigured both.[105]

Elizabeth Marshall Thomas is correct that the arrival of the Marshalls was only a harbinger of the global change that was moving toward the Ju/wasi. However, her text does not recognize the crucial loss of a reality of connectivity. This reality meant not only a form of life bound to specific space but also a form of identity that reached beyond the typological and the racial, a form that was an invitation to all humankind. In its place, she proposes, she imagines the typological, the universal, by reaching back into time to an *arche*, a beginning that joins "us" (as the distant offspring of ancient humans) to the Ju/wasi. This is a powerful form of temporal distancing. In this way Marshall Thomas can evoke only an evolutionary connection because the other forms of connection are no longer available to her or to anyone. Their significance now is only in terms of human evolutionary beginnings. The Ju/wasi exist without contemporary significance. Now they are nothing more than poor black people, and the world has many poor black people.[106]

Marshall Thomas's *The Old Way* attests to the seriousness of the loss of space. There is yet another dimension of loss, a dimension where memory, language, and history intertwine with space to give the moral content of identity. She hints at this other dimension when she describes the destruction of *xaro*, the practice of sharing and gift giving. This practice required all Ju/wasi to give gifts of things formed from the land, whether gathered, hunted, or made, to people of their communities or related ones. Jealousy's and envy's corrosive effects on the community were thereby averted, especially in times of water or food scarcity. The loss of land can in effect disrupt moral vision. In order to understand this one must imagine moral sensibilities as being space-textured. Keith H. Basso, in his text *Wisdom Sits in Places: Landscape and Language among the Western Apache*, shows powerfully how landscape functions to cultivate wisdom and moral authority in a community. His work among the *ndee*, commonly known as Western Apache, in the village of Cibecue in Arizona on the Fort Apache Reservation (north of Tucson and east of Phoenix and situated at an elevation of forty-nine hundred feet) exposes the connections between landscape and how native peoples remember, learn, and perpetuate moral vision.[107]

Basso identifies Western Apaches for whom, in ways that reflect the Yup'ik sensibility described by Martin, specific spatial reality is the hermeneutical horizon on which they see themselves and the world. The Apache practice of naming places carries with it a constellation of identity markers. Fundamentally, place-names are the means through which Apache tell their history. As Basso states, "What matters most to Apaches is *where* events occurred, not when, and what they serve to reveal about the development and character of Apache social life."[108] The "where" is key because it indicates "the path or trail (*'intin*)" the founding ancestors traversed both in their actual movements and in their moral and social actions. How do the Apache access that path when it becomes no longer visible, "beyond the memories of living persons"? The path must be imagined in a disciplined way from the tracks, that is, the stories, songs, relics, and, most important, place-names. When the name of a place such as *Goshtł'ish Tú Bił Sikąné* (Water Lies with Mud in an Open Container) is spoken, it repeats the very words of the ancestors and invokes their presence and their actions on behalf of themselves and their progeny. In this case, they arrived at and then decided on the precise location where the Apache would begin to create their future. The names enable Apache to remember what was done in a particular place. As Basso says, they answer the question, "What happened here?"[109] Authentic historical accounting for Apache requires these spatial realities. It also requires a narrator or storyteller of Apache history, whom Basso called the "place-maker."[110] Anyone may function as a place-maker narrating "place-worlds," the world of the Apache ancestors and their world as well.

The place-maker becomes the indispensable guide, revealing the bond of place to bodies through the narrative: "The place-maker's main objective is to speak the past into being, to summon it with words and give it dramatic form, to *produce* experience by forging ancestral worlds in which others can participate and readily lose themselves. . . . The place-maker often speaks as witness on the scene, describing ancestral events 'as they are occurring' and creating in the process a vivid sense that what happened long ago—*right here, on this very spot*—could be happening *now*."[111] Basso understands that this way of telling history stands at odds with Anglo-American versions of native history, which seem to Apache to be "distant and unfamiliar."[112] History as place making is a performance that cultivates an aesthetic. Through that aesthetic, Apache tell their stories to make the past present in dramatic form, linking it to place. Such linking aims at "instilling empathy and admiration for the ancestors themselves."[113] This aesthetic looks at Anglo-American (Western) historiographic practice, especially regarding Apache history, as "geographically adrift" because it is detached from local landscape with "few spatial anchors," with places often not identified, obsessed both with dating historical events and placing them in "tightly ordered sequences" organized through some totalizing theory.[114] Equally important, Western historiographic practice regarding the Apache loses sight of the central purpose of telling history—to cultivate Apache people and their moral and social sensibilities, that is, to build community.

A sense of particular places anchors community building. By holding on to place-names, Apache not only understand their ancestors' world but how their own world has changed. Changes in landscape teach them lessons about their own behavior, whether they have been faithful or not to the ways of their peoples' past. The loss of a body of water or the absence of animals once very familiar to an area of land may mark past or present acts of disrespect. Basso recites the story of the place named *Tłiish Bi Tú'é* (Snake's Water), an inactive spring west of Cibecue. At that site the activity of the people who long ago came to this place for water was framed for him through the narration of a place-world. They found snakes lying on the rock by the spring. They surmised that the snakes owned and protected the spring. A lone Apache man separated from the group who were headed for the water and approached and spoke to the snakes respectfully and correctly. The snakes left and the group approached and retrieved some water.

The water was good, and the people were grateful. The story having brought the past into the present, the Apache narrator concludes that something disrespectful probably happened for the water to now be gone.[115]

In Apache cultural ecology, place-names preceded and helped to constitute clan names. Their local moral universe then came into place as they lived on the land and formed "commemorative names."[116] Commemorative names were place-names tied to ancestral actions of deep moral consequences. Apache express commemorative names through a form of narration called 'ágodzaahi, or historical tale. These brief, quickly told historical tales take center stage in the process of moral formation: "Historical tales are intended to edify, but their main purpose is to criticize social delinquents (or, as the Apaches say, to 'shoot' them), thereby impressing these individuals with the undesirability of improper behavior and alerting them to the punitive consequences of further misconduct. . . . Nowhere do place-names serve more important communicative function than in the context of historical tales."[117] 'ágodzaahi stories capture people and place them between "historical events and geographical locations," between Apache ethics and a person's current behavior in order to reveal to him or her what it means to be Apache.[118] The place-name *Chąą Bi Dałt'ohe* (Shades of Shit) is a powerful example. The people who lived at this place had a great harvest and had much corn, while their relatives who lived nearby had a poor harvest and had little corn. They asked the relatives with much corn to share, but they would not. In anger, they forced their corn-abundant relatives to stay home, not letting them leave even to defecate. Unable to get to the spot of land that functioned as a toilet, they were forced to defecate at their home in their shaded areas. Their camp filled with the smell of bodily waste, and they got very sick. The relatives said, "You have brought this on yourselves. Now you live in shades of shit!" The story concludes, "Finally, they agreed to share their corn. It happened at Shades of Shit."[119]

When stories such as these are told, the actors in the story join with the one to whom the story is addressed in a form of moral analogical predication. They intend to suggest that the similarities of behavior between persons past and the person addressed by the story may yield similarly damaging consequences now. This is certainly not a unique feature of a culture, yet for Apache both the stories and the land itself are active agents, stalking or hunting people, reminding them that their actions are not without consequences. The land speaks and bears witness not only to the ancestors but to the acts that are immoral and death dealing:

> This is what we know about our stories. They go to work on your mind and make you think about your life. Maybe you've not been acting right. Maybe

you've been stingy. Maybe you've been chasing after women. Maybe you've been trying to act like a whiteman. People don't *like* it! So someone goes hunting for you—maybe your grandmother, your grandfather, your uncle. It doesn't matter. Anyone can do it. . . . Many things jump up at you and block your way. But you won't forget that story. You're going to see the place where it happened, maybe every day if it's nearby and close to Cibecue. If you don't see it, you're going to hear its name and see it in your mind. It doesn't matter if you get old—that place will keep on stalking you like the one who shot you with the story. Maybe that person will die. Even so, that place will keep on stalking you. It's like that person is still alive.[120]

This extraordinary account from Nick Thompson, one of the most crucial of Basso's Apache interpreters, elucidates what Basso terms "the moral significance of geographical locations."[121] This sense of places as moral agents means that specific lands carry a power to, as one Apache woman said, "make people live right. . . . The land looks after us." To lose the land is a very serious matter and may be seen as forgetfulness of the story or of the land itself.[122] The testimony of Wilson Lavender in 1975 is a profound illustration of the consequence of land-forgetfulness: "One time I went to L.A. training for mechanic. It was no good, sure no good. I start drinking, hang around bars all the time. I start getting into trouble with my wife, fight sometimes with her. It was bad. I forget about this country here around Cibecue. I forget all the names and stories. I don't hear them in my mind anymore. I forget how to live right, forget how to be strong."[123]

Land and storied memory together work to vivify the moral imagination for Western Apache. This is true of many native clans and tribes for whom places and their names, whether mountains, rocks, or vacant fields, "endow the land with multiple forms of significance," which actively give shape to a vision of the good and their embodiment of wisdom.[124] Basso shows the close connection of language and landscape in creating a world. Together, language and landscape offer up the unfamiliar of a people never before encountered:

The shapes and colors and contours of the land together with the shifting sounds and cadences of native discourse thrust themselves upon the new-comer with a force so vivid and direct as to be virtually inescapable. Yet for all their sensory immediacy (and there are occasions, as any ethnographer will attest, when the sheer constancy of it grows to formidable proportions) land-scape and discourse seem resolutely out of reach. Although close at hand and tangible in the extreme, each in its own way appears remote and inaccessible, anonymous and indistinct, and somehow, implausibly, a shade less than fully believable. And neither landscape nor discourse, as if determined to accentuate these conflicting impressions, may seem the least bit interested in having them resolved.[125]

It is precisely this "strangeness" of land coupled to language that faced the emerging colonialist powers as they entered the New Worlds. It is also precisely this foreignness that they overcame by splitting open the connection of people to land and to language. Here one can begin to capture the other dimension of the loss of connectivity of peoples to land, to specific spaces: disruption, even mutilation of the paths to the wisdom necessary to live in the world.[126] The loss indicates the destruction of the fine webs that held together memory, language, and place to moral action and ethical judgment.[127] It is a loss almost imperceptible except to the bodies of those for whom specific geography and animals continue to gesture to them deep links of identity. The loss is the overturning of space that *is* modernity. However, one must invoke the notion of modernity here very carefully because it may cause one to lose sight of the specifics of agency and agency recreation at work in the historic reality of displacement.

Europeans established a new organizing reality for identities, themselves. Yet to say Europeans created otherness, as Tzvetan Todorov notes in his classic text *The Conquest of America*, is quite imprecise and theologically beside the point.[128] Europeans enacted racial agency as a theologically articulated way of understanding their bodies in relation to new spaces and new peoples and to their new power over those spaces and peoples. Before this agency would yield the "idea of race," "the scientific concept of race," the "social principle of race," or even a fully formed "racial optic" on the world, it was a theological form—an inverted, distorted vision of creation that reduced theological anthropology to commodified bodies. In this inversion, whiteness replaced the earth as the signifier of identities. It would be a mistake to see this replacement as a discursive practice fully controlled by Europeans. It *is* a discursive practice, but one that presented itself as the only real option given the aggressive desacralization of the world. When you disrupt and destroy the delicate and contingent connection of peoples' identities bound to specific lands you leave no alternative but racial agency. As Zurara exhibited, a scale was being formed—white, almost white, mixed, and black—a scale that captured even Europeans.

However, lack of full control of this discursive practice does not mean Europeans were passive. Whiteness was being held up as an aspect of creation with embedded facilitating powers. Whiteness from the moment of discovery and consumption was a social and theological way of imagining, an imaginary that evolved into a method of understanding the world. It was a social imaginary in that it posited the existence of difference and collectivity for those in the Old World faced with the not easily explainable peoples and phenomena of the New World. It was a theological imaginary because whiteness suggested that one may enter a true moment of creation gestalt. Whiteness transcended all peoples because it was a means of seeing all peoples at the very moment it realized itself. Whiteness was a global vision of Europeans and Africans but, more than that, a way of organizing bodies by proximity to and approximation of white bodies.

With the emergence of whiteness, identity was calibrated through possession of, not possession by, specific land. All peoples do make claims on their land. But the point here is that racial agency and especially whiteness rendered unintelligible and unpersuasive any narratives of the collective self that bound identity to geography, to earth, to water, trees, and animals. People would henceforth (and forever) carry their identities on their bodies, without remainder. From the beginning of the colonialist moment, being white placed one at the center of the symbolic and real reordering of space. In a real sense, whiteness comes into being as a form of landscape with all its facilitating realities.

I want to begin to outline some of the central ramifications for Christian theology and for a racial theory created by this reality of displacement. In chapter 2 I will explore further these ramifications as I consider the transformation of theology itself into a discourse of displacement. Here, however, I want to show how the conceptual and material processes of displacement worked together to enable a new ground for imagining identity. It is this new ground that enabled the formation of the racial self. The issue of identity now invokes a universe of modern conceptualities, some of which are respected in academic circles as new healthy convergences of multiple scholarly fields and interests, others of which are denounced as faddism, that is, creating undisciplined anachronisms running roughshod over historical periods and peoples.

In theology and other fields, the idea of identity, like the idea of culture, is prone to conceptual slippage and political signaling that is difficult to contain. This chapter is concerned less with defining identity than with showing that a form of identity coupled with processes of identity formation emerges from the colonialist moment, the effects of which scholars have not begun to conceptualize. I have also been hesitant to invoke the modern notion of self for fear of signalizing that my focus is on the emergence of a self, racial or otherwise. It is not. My concern is the arrival of new ground that replaces the land and specific places as primary signifiers of identity. On this new ground, a self grows, extends into the world, and becomes or, more precisely, enters the freedom of multiple processes of becoming.

RACIAL BECOMING

European Christians, from the Iberians through the British, saw themselves as agents of positive, if not divine, change, as it were, the markers of creaturely contingency. They saw themselves as those ordained to enact a providential transition. In so doing they positioned themselves as those first conditioning their world rather than being conditioned by it. They performed a deeply theological act that mirrored the identity and action of God in creating. The theologian Karl Barth, in §28 of his *Church Dogmatics*, II/1, speaks of God as the One revealed in his act. God is the One whose *being* is revealed in divine action.[129] Such a recognition not only banishes our abstractions regarding the identity of God, but also renders a God who is unconditioned by us. For Barth, the concrete reality in which this unconditioned God is found is Jesus of Nazareth. The unconditioned nature of God does not mean aloofness. It points to the history of a God in Israel and in Jesus, who loves us unconditionally, faithfully, and in freedom, not out of necessity. This is the way of the Creator with the creation. The freedom of the Creator to love us engenders our freedom. Barth's positive ontology of divine being, of a God revealed in divine act, a being in becoming, casts light on the distorted ontology of being that is found in the colonialist moment.[130]

The relation between the colonizers and the colonized does show mutual conditioning, but that mutual conditioning was mitigated by God-like action in which the relation became as those conditioning to those conditioned, European to native. What is decisive here is that a creative authority, a creative regime, gets channeled through white presence. That creative regime activates simply by the performance of whiteness. All peoples touched by the machinations of colonialist operations get caught up in that creative regime. In order to grasp the subtlety at work in this act, consider its positive opposite articulated in Barth's account of divine freedom and creaturely dependence:

> No created beings are in fact so independent of each other that in spite of this relative mutual independence they have not also to some extent a certain mutual interdependence, in the sense that ultimately none of them would have its being and nature apart from its interlocking with the being and nature of all the others. But God confronts all that is in supreme and utter independence, i.e., He would be no less and no different even if they all did not exist or existed differently. God stands at an infinite distance from everything else, not in the finite degree of difference with which created things stand towards each other. *If they all have their being and a specific nature, God in His freedom has conferred it upon them; not because He was obliged to do so, or because His*

purpose was influenced by their being and nature, but because their being and nature is conditioned by His being and nature.[131]

Barth's weighty and theologically intricate statement about divine conditioning of the created beings must be turned on its head to understand the operation of racial ontology. Racial being is an act of continual conference in which mutual interdependence is not suspended, but placed on a trajectory toward an endless becoming organized around white bodies. European colonialists in acts of breathtaking hubris imagined the interlocking nature of all people and things within their own independence of those very people and things. This is an independence that facilitates the constant turnings of existence.

The scope of that independence is crucial—not simply of indigenes but also of landscape. Vine Deloria Jr., in his important essay "The Coming of the People," argues that the specific realities of the land—rivers, valleys, mountains, and so forth—and the animals together with the people constitute an interconnected community. All are relatives (family members), and all must be listened to in order to live rightly. This is to be distinguished from the world wrought by European settlers:

> The white man, where viewed in this context, appears as a perennial adolescent. He is continually moving about, and his restless nature cannot seem to find peace. Yet *he does not listen to the land* and so cannot find a place for himself. He has few relatives and seems to believe that the domestic animals that have always relied upon him constitute his only link with the other peoples of the universe. Yet he does not treat these animals as friends but only as objects to be exploited. While he has destroyed many holy places of the Indians, he does not seem to be able to content himself with his own holy places . . . for his most holy places are cemeteries where his forefathers lie under granite slabs, row upon row upon row, strangers lying with strangers.[132]

Deloria's comments capture two joined actions, disconnection and destruction, but added to Barth's thoughts one sees those actions within the act of conference. The conference of "a *being* and a specific nature," to quote Barth again, is precisely the operation of racial attribution, of white and black with everyone in between. Yet one must see this attribution within the refashioning of the landscape. Races becomes as the land becomes—something new. This entails a reciprocal determination, both temporal and spatial. In the minds of the European settlers, the instability of both land and people called for the stability of transition. The natives, black, red, and everyone not white, must be brought from chaos to faith. The land, wetlands, fields, and forests must be cleared, organized, and brought into productive civilization. The stability is in the transition, held together by racial attribution.

Once the stability of transition is in place, then the ideas and rhetoric of mutual interdependence, mutual conditioning may be superimposed, as if one were placing layers of frosting on a cooling cake. But this is a fabricated mutual interdependence, one built upon a new ordering of things and people. Reciprocity of racial being was in play in the formation of the New World racial order, but that reciprocity must never be construed as creative equality. Toni Morrison, in her epic text *Playing in the Dark: Whiteness and the Literary Imagination*, captures this sense of reciprocity as she notes the uses of an Africanist persona in American literature and the Euro-American imagination: "For the settlers and for American writers generally, this Africanist other became the means of thinking about body, mind, chaos, kindness, and love; provided the occasion for exercises in the absence of restraint, the presence of restraint, the contemplation of freedom and of aggression; permitted opportunities for the exploration of ethics and morality, for meeting obligations of the social contract, for bearing the cross of religion and following out the ramifications of power."[133] Morrison pictures a God-like freedom similar to that described by Barth regarding God's own being. Of course, she is referring to fiction and the work of the writer, but she is also capturing racial reciprocal being. The creativity at play here is enabled and reinforced by the power to change native worlds, to reconfigure space, uproot peoples and replant them. It is nothing less than a *creatio continua*, a continuous creation, and a continuous recreation. Whiteness is co-creator with God. Morrison states further, "If we follow through on the self-reflexive nature of these encounters with Africanism, it falls clear: images of blackness can be evil *and* protective, rebellious *and* forgiving, fearful *and* desirable — all of the self-contradictory features of the self. Whiteness, alone, is mute, meaningless, unfathomable, pointless, frozen, veiled, curtained, dreaded, senseless, implacable. Or so our writers seem to say."[134] The analogy I draw between God as Creator and whiteness as Creator is not a tight one. It falls apart at the point of ascribing immutability to white being. Immutability is not the point. Indeed Europeans are inside this racial becoming. The point here is conference bound to creativity. Conference and creativity are the dual realities within which racial being is in its becoming. That becoming is not simply assimilation, but more decisively a becoming facilitated by whiteness, an agency born inside the racial imagination. Morrison's description of whiteness turns more toward a replacement — whiteness for landscape, whiteness as landscape. That is, landscape not only as Deloria envisions it, alive, speaking, instructing, but also landscape as the ground ready to be built upon, ready to have fashioned upon it racial existence.

One cannot understand what is at stake in the formation of whiteness until one understands this new order of things unleashed by colonialism. The refashioning of bodies in space to form racial existence makes little sense without seeing simultaneously the refashioning of space.[135]

The point here is not simply the loss of indigenous stability. I am not positing an immutability of native existence. The loss here is of a life-giving collaboration of identity between place and bodies, people and animals. The loss here is also of the possibility of new identities bound up with entering new spaces. Absent these possibilities peoples are invited into an ever-tightening insularity of collective identity and collective narration.

People today continue to live in a dual trajectory of constantly shifting geographic spaces made more mutable by the dictates of capitalistic logic and racial identities that are free-floating and changeable, yet constantly stabilized through the reciprocity of racial being. As I shall explicate in more detail later, without land functioning as identity signifier, racial designations historically understood and politically activated continue to be compelling sensible ground on which to envision collective agency. Until one begins to reflect on the interconnected turnings of space and the formation of racial being as mirrored processes, every attempt to destabilize racial identity, argue for a common humanity, and claim race as fiction, social construction, or essentialized nonsense will be superficial at best.

Theorists and theories of race will not touch the ground until they reckon deeply with the foundations of racial imaginings in the deployment of an altered theological vision of creation. We must narrate not simply the alteration of bodies but of space itself. The narration must be of both. There is an aspect of delusion in racial theory and theology that suggests possibilities of resistance to racial identity, or seeks to discern powers of racial improvisation, or advocates renouncing white privilege all without seeing how these identities are reflexively calibrated to the turnings of spatial habitations. Racial identities have taken on landscape and geographic characteristics and cannot simply be overcome by thought, any more than a mountain may be moved by turning one's face away from it.

This means that strategies that "renounce race" often are unwittingly socially and culturally counterproductive and may lead to economically imperialist practices regarding land and claims on land because the freedom they claim by resisting discursive practices, or cultural logics, or processes of structuration flows directly out of the spatial dislocation of bodies.[136] Thus the freedom to renounce race is a direct descendent of the theological power to deny and undermine geographically sustained identities. No easy answers follow. It should be clear at this point that I am not an advocate of race. Nor am I resolved to a race-by-default position. Neither do I envision a return to life before race. At this point my concern is to illumine an intensely tangled mistake that cannot be improved by race-antinomian intellectual forays. Antiessential, antirace positions tend to move toward odd configurations of individualism that are spiritually vapid.[137] The way forward, if there is a way forward, will involve several more conceptual steps before a future of communion might be envisioned.

The equally pressing concerns, however, are ones of Christian theology. This reality of displacement means deep internal shifts in theology. Theology will be formed from the colonial moment forward without what Heidegger called "the way of dwelling," that is, the way of being mortal that requires specific spaces formed into places of organizing centers of identity.[138] Without place as the articulator of identity, human skin was asked to fly solo and speak for itself. Heidegger himself would not share a notion of a "landscape that hunts for us." His sense of signification works in only one direction, from us to the land (and certainly not the land signifying us or other creatures doing the same). Yet for Christian theology the effects of a world displaced and racialized would be devastating. Western Christian theology continues to misunderstand the theological power of white and black identities. Christian theologians and all other intellectuals continue to theologize and theorize those identities very poorly. Indeed, we continue to ignore Zurara's tears.

ACOSTA'S LAUGH

On April 27, 1572, an eager young Jesuit named José de Acosta Porres disembarked from a Spanish ship onto the soil of Lima, Peru. He had most recently spent several months in Santa Domingo, having traveled from Spain three months earlier. By everyone's account this young man was exactly what the new emerging order, the Compañía de Jesús, the Society of Jesus, hoped for—a supremely trained, profoundly devout agent of ecclesial renewal who would help foster in those he taught a learned piety. José de Acosta Porres seemed bound before birth to be a Jesuit. Born in 1540, the year Ignatius of Loyola's dream of an order received papal approval in the bull *Regimini militantis ecclesiae*, José de Acosta enjoyed a family life that reflected the doctrine of providence.[1] His father, Don Antonio de Acosta, was a wealthy merchant in Medina del Campo, the commercial center of Castile, and he, along with José's mother, Doña Ana de Porres, was deeply committed—body, soul, and money—to the Society of Jesus.

Jose's parents did not want their marriage or the children to deflect attention from their fervent religious devotion or from their desire to become coadjutors. Don Antonio de Acosta not only wanted to join the Society of Jesus, he generously provided land and financial resources to support its flourishing. Doña Ana de Porres desperately wanted the order to promise her that upon her death she would be buried next to her sons in a Jesuit cemetery. The other Acosta children felt the shaping power of their parents' religious devotion. Of their six sons, five became Jesuits, and of their three daughters, two joined religious orders. José de Acosta, as would be appropriate for a child born to prosperous parents in Medina, would be provided the best possible education. Having inherited his parents' zeal, however, his educational journey would be determined primarily by his own religious fervor.

Acosta ran away from home at the tender age of twelve, journeyed fifty miles from Medina, and entered the Society of Jesus in Salamanca before being sent back to Medina to begin his education in the order. His zeal, clear to everyone, was matched by his intellectual prowess. Acosta's abilities perfectly matched the developing character of this powerful young order. The Jesuit order, the first Roman Catholic order intentionally self-defined as a teaching order, would take up as one of its major ministries the provision of formal education for all who wanted it.[2] By the time Acosta began his formal education, the Jesuit order was already a significant presence in the church and the academy, and by the time he arrived in Peru, the order was a dominant force in the educational communities of Europe. The founding figures of the order, principally Ignatius of Loyola, and with him Francis Xavier, Juan Alfonso de Polanco, Jerónimo Nadal, Peter Canisius, Diego Lainez, Alfonso Salmerón, and Francisco de Borja, envisioned an order that would draw deeply from the intellectual well of Scholastic theology without imbibing its preponderant speculative and abstract character. This order would carry forward a humanistic agenda beginning with a commitment to education as fundamental to moral formation and continuing with a strong appreciation for classic rhetoric and the study of classic languages—Latin, Greek, and Hebrew. This agenda would be pursued without uncritically accepting everything propagated by Renaissance humanism. The Jesuit order would embody a mystical theology that bound learning to aggressive piety and inward examination and service without being misidentified as *alumbrados*, medieval spirituals who sought spiritual perfection through internal illumination and whose commitment to orthodoxy seemed dubious.[3] By making clear its steadfast commitment to go anywhere to serve the church in obedience to the pope, the order would also not be equated in any way, shape, or form with Luther's Protestants.[4]

José de Acosta lived in the intellectual house these early Jesuits were building, and in him the Jesuits' *modus procedendi* created one of the most impressive examples of work done well. This good work showed through the Renaissance humanist education he received first in Medina and then at the University of Alcalá de Henares and the Jesuit College connected to the university. His years in Medina introduced him to a version of the *modus parisiensis*, a pedagogical and curricular schema made famous at the University of Paris and encouraged by Ignatius, which emphasized an ordered progression toward more complex subject matter. Acosta's four-year program—(year 1) *infirma*, (year 2) *media*, (year 3) *suprema*, and (year 4) rhetoric or Latin compositions and poetry writing—immersed him in the study of Latin, Greek, and their classical literatures. The student so formed would exhibit the ability to speak and write with great eloquence and power. This was the goal of humanist education: articulate intellectual performance that bespoke of a life ready to be lived in virtue and public service. This was similar to the kind of *Bildung* (formation) that Hegel would envision two centuries later; yet with Hegel it would be without the deep Aristotelian and Thomist, that is, theological, underpinnings.[5]

This curricular goal, for the Jesuits, existed within the wider idea of the interpenetration of devotion and knowledge that was the hallmark of the formation desired by the order. The crucial foundational documents of the order, Ignatius's *Spiritual Exercises*, the *Formula*, the *Constitutions*, and *Autobiography*, all drew the Jesuit reader to desire both intellectual excellence and inward purity of soul established in obedience to Christ and his church. Acosta understood not only the inseparability of Christ-centered spirituality and higher learning but also the need for this synthesis to be embodied in Christian life and performed through service. His academic performance garnered attention at the Jesuit school in Medina, and Acosta quickly gained a reputation as a brilliant Latinist, orator, and playwright.[6] His education at the University of Alcalá strengthened this synthesis and increased his reputation. Studies at the university followed an ordered structure similar to that at Medina. At Alcalá, a Thomist vision shaped not only each year of study but the overall pedagogical logic of the curriculum. The instruction of the first four years was philosophical in nature and theological in intent—(year 1) *súmulas*, a year dedicated to the study of Peter Spain's *Súmulas logicales*; (year 2) *logic*, the study of Porphyry's *Predicables* and Aristotle's *Predicaments*; (year 3) study of Aristotle's *Natural Philosophy*; and (year 4) Aristotle's *Metaphysics*.

Four years of philosophy study were followed by four years of theology taught to him by some of the finest theologians of Spain. Students were instructed through the practices of formal lectures, disputation and debate, and preaching. Acosta learned Thomist theology, moral philosophy, and Sacred Scripture and was further required to take private courses at the Jesuit College, which gave him even more significant exposure to Thomist as well as Scotist and Nominalist thought. At the Jesuit College, Acosta was instructed in positive theology, a kind of practical theology that emphasized instruction in the teaching and preaching of Scripture, along with the other sources of theology in the church fathers and the councils, for the edification of the faithful.[7] His education at Alcalá reflected a form of Scholasticism deeply influenced by the theological luminaries of the First School of Salamanca: Melchior Cano, Mancio de Corpus Christi,

Domingo de Soto, and the great Francisco de Vitoria. That form of Scholasticism was sensitive to the humanistic critiques of Scholasticism's arid speculations and very interested in the classic practices of rhetoric and reading of original sources.[8] Acosta listened well to his teachers and carried forward their sensibilities.

His deepest theological sensibility was that of a Thomist, with a clear, precise doctrinal understanding and articulation joined to a conceptually clear vision of how the world is and ought to be ordered. As a Thomist, Acosta understood what the joining of Augustinian and Aristotelian logics meant for the rational articulation of Christian faith. His teachers understood that in Acosta they had one of the very best, very brightest students who could easily assume their place as a professor of theology. He was a talented intellectual, preaching and teaching with great skill and furthermore had administrative gifts that were put to good use in carrying out regular official correspondence between the order in Alcalá and the Jesuit superior general in Rome. However, Acosta's zeal, now cultivated through intense theological formation, turned toward the mission enterprise. Acosta wanted to serve in the field. A portion of his letter to Vicar-General Francisco de Borja displays his earnest desire: "I do not have any inclination to go to any particular part, except that it might be a help for me to be amongst people that are not too brutish and have some capacity, although there might be things that weigh against that. Of course, the way to the West Indies from Spain having begun to open, it has occurred to me that I might be able to play my part somewhere there if I were to be sent to do what I do here, that is, to read theology or some other sort of ministry."[9] Acosta got his wish. He stepped onto the shores of Lima a theologian of the first rank ready to do ministry. Not simply a Catholic theologian in the New World, he was one of the most important, if not the most important, bearer of the theological tradition of Christianity to set foot in the New World in his time and arguably for at least one hundred years after his arrival. Indeed Acosta was the embodiment of theological tradition. He was a traditioned Christian intellectual of the highest order who precisely, powerfully, and unrelentingly performed that tradition in the New World.

A TRADITION SHAPED ACOSTA

In several seminal texts Alasdair MacIntyre has argued that traditioned intellectual inquiry constitutes the forms of rationality of the medieval epoch, José de Acosta's epoch. MacIntyre's equally important claim is that traditioned intellectual inquiry constitutes the conceptual plateau from which one should engage, evaluate, and construct moral vision. MacIntyre's work focuses on an intellectual holism, the inseparability of rational forms and moral formation. Drawing from the thought of Thomas Aquinas, MacIntyre grasps the pedagogical depth and interconnectedness of moral formation and intellectual judgments:

> It is only individuals . . . educated into the making of certain kinds of discrimination that enable them to order the expression of the passions in the light of an ordering of goods—something which in the first instance they will have had to learn from their teachers. . . . For someone who lacked altogether the kind of training and development which Aquinas—and Aristotle—takes to be required would develop the expression of their desires in a piecemeal, uncoordinated way so that they would come to have in adult life desires which appeared essentially heterogeneous, aimed at goods independent of one another and without any overall ordering. From the standpoint of such a person the unity of the goods aimed at in the moral life, as described by Aquinas, could only appear as a symptom of some kind of monomania.[10]

The kind of education MacIntyre described here and in many other important texts is precisely the kind of education and the kind of moral formation Acosta received.[11] MacIntyre's advocacy of tradition for the right ordering of philosophical and ethical reflection resonates with a wide range of modern theologians who see in his work a crucial point regarding tradition.[12] Theological reflection is quintessentially a traditioned enterprise. Beyond that recognition, many theologians realize that MacIntyre is signifying the spiritual reality of tradition; a life ordered toward the good is a life graced by God and endowed with the Holy Spirit. Most important, lived Christian traditions are inseparable from Christian communities that teach the virtues whereby people may see and understand their sin and learn how to live faithful lives before the triune God. In this way Christian tradition is a living reality bound to the people of God. Christian tradition houses their attempts to live faithfully in the world.

A tradition is embodied both in a community and in its individual members. In Acosta one can see this embodiment. The embodiment is not a matter of perfection, but of faithfulness and a consistency to working out the questions that face a tradition from within the *telos* of that tradition itself. Again MacIntyre captures the sense of animation at work in a living tradition:

> We are now in a position to contrast three stages in the initial development of a tradition: a first in which the relevant beliefs, texts, and authorities have not yet been put in question; a second in which inadequacies of various types have been identified, but not yet remedied; and a third in which response to those inadequacies has resulted in a set of reformulations, reevaluations, and new formulations and evaluations, designed to remedy inadequacies and overcome limitations. Where a person or a text is assigned an authority which derives

from what is taken to be their relationship to the divine, that sacred authority will be thereby in the course of this process exempt from repudiation, although its utterances may certainly be subject to reinterpretation.[13]

José de Acosta was the beneficiary of conceptual reformulations not only with the formation of the Aristotelian–Thomist tradition but also of the church, both by his membership in a renewal movement, the Society of Jesus, and by his humanist education that improved on customary Scholastic training. MacIntyre is important here at the beginning of this exploration of José de Acosta, his world, and his thought, because of his key insights into the nature of a tradition and because of his crucial understanding of what a traditioned individual or community, or a tradition itself may face—an epistemological crisis. That is, MacIntyre captures the specific characteristics of a tradition facing a threat to its conceptual integrity. Such threats arise as a tradition develops, gauging its own standards of progress and finding in its articulations the exposure of new problems based on the inner logic, that is, the internal trajectory of its beliefs:

> Central to a tradition-constituted enquiry at each state in its development will be its current problematic, that agenda of unsolved problems and unresolved issues by reference to which its success or lack of it in making rational progress toward some further state of development will be evaluated. At any point it may happen to any tradition-constituted enquiry that by its own standards of progress it ceases to make progress. Its hitherto trusted methods of enquiry have become sterile. Conflicts over rival answers to key questions can no longer be settled rationally. Moreover, it may indeed happen that the use of the methods of enquiry and of the forms of argument, by means of which rational progress had been achieved so far, begins to have the effect of increasingly disclosing new inadequacies, hitherto unrecognized incoherences, and new problems for the solution of which there seem to be insufficient or no resources within the established fabric of belief. This kind of dissolution of historically founded certitudes is the mark of an epistemological crisis.[14]

José de Acosta marks an epistemological crisis in the history of Christian theology. He himself did not perceive his life to be in the midst of any crisis of thought, nor did he articulate any crisis of Christian tradition. Nor have historical theologians, systematic theologians, or church historians discerned any crisis of theology in the person or work of José de Acosta. The crisis I will elaborate in this chapter does not quite match MacIntyre's description because in effect it is a crisis that is yet to be fully recognized by Western theologians, but it is a crisis nonetheless. It is a crisis that expresses a form of modernity in its denial of certain kinds of authority and in its connection to a refashioning of worlds.

In this regard, one could fault MacIntyre but more importantly those theologians who have followed his thinking on tradition for not seeing the effects on the Christian tradition triggered by the modernist elements at the beginning of the age of Iberian conquest. In a very telling comment in *Which Justice, Which Rationality?* MacIntyre registers the phenomenon of the colonialist gaze but to little effect in his elaboration of tradition: "When those educated in the cultures of the societies of imperialist modernity reported that they had discovered certain so-called primitive societies or cultures without change, within which repetition rules rather than transformation, they were deceived in part by their understanding of the claims sometimes made by members of such societies that they are obedient to the dictates of immemorial custom and in part by their own too simple and anachronistic conception of what social and cultural change is."[15] MacIntyre invokes a history of reflection on "native" existence that demands a new kind of calibration of his retrieval or reinvention of tradition. That calibration requires that one carefully watch how traditioned Christian existence, first that of the Iberians and then that of all Europeans, fundamentally changed as they ascended to hegemony in the New Worlds. It is indeed traditioned imperialist modernity.

And José de Acosta marks the theological beginning of imperialist modernity. This form of modernity was articulated within and is born of an Aristotelian–Thomist tradition. Modernity is not the sole child of Christian tradition or theology. Nor is Acosta its sole progenitor. I am not suggesting either, with philosophers such as Jeffrey Stout, that MacIntyre and some traditionalist theologians ignore how deeply embedded they are in modernity. Stout's modernity, like MacIntyre's and some traditionalist theologians' visions of tradition, has yet to reckon with the machinations of imperialist modernity.[16] They all have yet to face José de Acosta and what he means for Christian (and modern democratic) traditions embodied and articulated.

The difficulty I shall face throughout this chapter is reckoning with the fact that this crisis of theological tradition was not discerned by Acosta, and for the most part has still not been discerned, as a crisis of Christian tradition. From the moment Acosta (and all those like him) placed his feet on the ground in Lima, the Christian tradition and its theologians conjured a form of practical rationality that locked theology in discourses of displacement from which it has never escaped. The metaphor of "feet touching the ground" is an important one here. Acosta stepped into a world, the Indias Occidentales, that was being radically altered and that in turn would alter the way he perceived the world.[17] More specifically, it would not alter the creedal substance of his doctrine of creation but the way in which its logic would be performed. The ground on which Acosta was to stand was disappearing and reappearing in a new way. His theological vision was formed in the midst of that transformation.

THE *PACHACUTI* (UPHEAVAL) OF THE WORLD AND CHRISTIAN THEOLOGY

Whose world did José de Acosta enter as he disembarked onto Peruvian soil? He stepped into the Inca and Andean world only in a qualified sense. Primarily, Acosta brought his world with him, his world of spiritual powers, intellectual excellence, holy disciplines and exercises, and ecclesiastical authority disseminated through a strict chain of pious beings. That old world, Acosta's world, joined its mirroring image in the New World. This mirroring world began in Peru with the work of the conquistador Francisco Pizarro, who captured the city of Cajamarca in 1532 and executed the Inca supreme ruler, Atahualpa, in 1533 and in the process obtained incredible riches. The process of regicide begun by Pizarro reached a conclusion forty years later in the year of Acosta's arrival. In that year, the rebel and last Inca leader, Túpac Amaru, was executed by civil agents of the Spanish viceroy Toledo, thereby announcing the utter subjugation of Andean peoples.[18]

Pizarro's world brought unimaginable death to the peoples of the Andes. Pizarro, even as quintessential conquistador, was arguably simply another, albeit radically foreign, agent of conquest among agents that included the Incas themselves. There is no doubt that the Incario, the Incan state, was in the process of solidifying power through the forced migration of peoples in order to secure the state from attacks by insurgents. Nor is it in doubt that many peoples were very willing to aid in the overthrow of the Incas. The Iberian societies that entered the New World in conquest were shaped by war and hardened by battle, and, like Iberian societies, the world of the Incas and that of its neighbors were violent cultures. Yet neither the ongoing culture of war nor the brutality of the cultures serves well as a hermeneutic lens through which to understand the colliding of worlds. Neither will they help one grasp the transformation of theological speech that will find expression in theologians like Acosta. The strongest, most helpful term at my disposal is the Andean term *pachacuti*, meaning "world turned around" or "world turned upside down." As the historian Sabine Mac-Cormack writes, "Andeans used the concept of *pachacuti* when confronted with the Spanish invasion, for the invasion marked the end of an epoch more radically than any preceding upheaval had done."[19] The drama and flexibility of the term *pachacuti* mark its appropriateness. It may refer to epochs or individuals who facilitate the transformation of the world or "the turning about of time." Strictly speaking, only Incan royalty were connected in a positive sense of *pachacuti*, that is, only those associated with the power of the divine could transform the world for the better.[20] However, I suggest that it could be applied negatively to particular agents of Spanish rule.

Pizzaro initiated *pachacuti*, and Acosta operated within it, extended it through the march of his world into Andean space and time. In the forty years between Pizzaro's victory and Acosta's arrival, much had happened to the Andeans. Even before Pizzaro's arrival, Spanish presence was being increasingly felt in the New World through the spread of Old World pathogens. Smallpox, influenza, tuberculosis, measles, and other diseases established "virgin soil epidemics," which blew through New World populations with no immunological familiarity with these disease organisms and therefore no defense against them.[21] By the time of Pizzaro's military campaign, Old World diseases were in full assault on the Andeans.[22] By the time of Acosta's arrival, millions had died, and many were dying daily. The initial feuding between Pizzaro, his brothers, family, and supporters and Diego de Almagro, a fellow conquistador who felt cheated by Pizzaro, and his men over control of this new slice of the prosperous New World slowly gave way to a more stable situation with the *encomiendas*, areas of land (including the Andean people who lived in them) granted by the king to Spanish settlers. True Spanish stability, however, came with the arrival of Viceroy Francisco de Toledo y Figueroa.

Of the three viceroyalties that made up the Spanish colonies in the sixteenth-century New World—New Spain (Mexico), New Granada (Panama, Colombia, Ecuador, and Venezuela), and Peru—the Viceroyalty of Peru was, at the beginning of Viceroy Toledo's tenure, about to take center stage in the political interests and financial fortunes of the Castilian kingdom.[23] Peru's ascendency depended upon the wealth that would be generated by the silver and mercury mines in Potosi (1545) and Huancavelica (1563), respectively, that were beginning to be fully exploited. As the representative of the king in the New World, the viceroy was the Spanish ruler on the ground representing the interests of the crown. In Viceroy Toledo, King Philip II had a sure surrogate. Toledo, a battle-hardened, deeply religious soldier-monk and member of the military Order of Alcantra, arrived in Peru in September 1569, with orders from Philip to bring Peru into full compliance with royal wishes.

Toledo was the fifth in a line of what had been fairly unsuccessful viceroys. His predecessors' failures were in large measure due to their inability to enlist the *encomenderos*, those who owned encomiendas, in the goal of maximizing the profitability of the new lands for the empire as well as establishing complete political and military control of the New World. That kind of viceroyalty ended with Toledo. Immediately upon his arrival, Toledo began a five-year inspection tour of the colony with sixty inspectors. From 1570 to 1575, Toledo examined every aspect of the colony, especially the state of the encomiendas and the threat posed by rebellious elements, including the reigning Inca leader, Túpac Amaru, whom Toledo had killed. MacCormack describes the execution scene and registers part of an eyewitness account in which Túpac Amaru is coerced into self-denunciation and Christian confession:

> On the appointed day, over one hundred thousand Indians with their curacas [native chiefs], along with the Spanish inhabitants of Cuzco, were gathered in Haucaypata to witness the death. The Inca rode into Haucaypata on a donkey draped in black and from the scaffold turned to address the assembled multitude.... *Raising both hands, with his face turned to where most of the curacas were standing, the Inca Topa Amaru made the sign that Indians are accustomed to make toward their lords and in his mother tongue said with a loud voice....* My lords ... hear now that I am a Christian and they have baptized me, and I wish to die in the law of God, and I must die. Everything that so far I and the Incas my ancestors have told you, that you should adore the Sun, Punchao, and the huacas, idols, rocks, rivers, mountains, and vilcas, is false and a lie. (italics indicate the words of the eyewitness account)[24]

Viceroy Toledo also had plans for the encomiendas. He reorganized the Indian populations, relocating them into concentrated villages called *reducciones*. The reducciones, like the encomiendas before them, were created to control and exploit the indigenes and their labor potential. A new kind of bureaucrat was created to manage the reducciones, the *corregidores de indios*, or *corregidores*. Like encomenderos, corregidores eventually controlled their own lands, or *corregimientos*. The advantage Toledo gained through this shift was to bring total control of native labor under the state. Now Indian labor could be more smoothly distributed among the mines, the encomiendas, the newly emerging farming estates called haciendas, and even the textile workshops, the *obrajes*. Toledo and those before him organized native, exploited labor through a system called the *mita*, originally used by the Chimor and Inca regimes. It demanded of the Andeans that a portion of the men, those between the ages of eighteen and fifty, work in the mines; no one escaped the back-breaking, mind-numbing labor. The mines were simply horrific. Descending hundreds of feet into hot, poorly lit and poorly ventilated, toxic, and extremely dangerous mines, Indian adults and children would work mercilessly for hours on end. As they ascended from the pits on unstable ladders, their backs were laden with ore. When they reached the top their only reward was to be greeted as they emerged from the mine by frigid Andean winds. Thousands died in the mines or from the lung diseases contracted through this torturous work. Unrelenting servitude, like death, shadowed the Indians in the mines, in the reducciones, in the encomiendas, on the haciendas, and in the obrajes.

I do not wish to deny Andean agency in the formation of this new system. The encomenderos and corregidores utilized another point of cultural stability in native societies, the curacas, or *caciques*. These were the nobles who were in power when the Spanish arrived, and they maintained it under Spanish hegemony. They were the go-betweens, translating Spanish economic and cultural interests into native modalities and interpreting native realities to their Spanish overseers. But they also quickly adapted Spanish practices, both cultural and especially economic, while remaining in contact with indigenous cultural networks. In this way, they lived in both the *república de españoles* and the so-called *república de indios*.[25] However, the social space of the caciques, no matter their political dexterity, was not a zone that was safe from Spanish control and manipulation. Viceroy Toledo is crucial because José de Acosta arrived to do theological work at the beginning of his reign. In fact, Acosta joined Toledo for part of the viceroy's *visita*. I am not pressing a church–state distinction too much with Acosta and Toledo. While it is true that Toledo executed royal desire through his administration, he bore a steadfast ecclesial mind in his work. Tensions developed later between Toledo and Acosta, but they were not over state control and church independence. They were, rather, over the proper deployment of ecclesial and spiritual power to bring order to the New World. In such matters, Toledo understood himself to be more clearsighted than any one church official or theologian, or even an entire order. Acosta disagreed, not with the imperial strategy but with local tactics.[26]

In Peru, Acosta entered a Spanish world in the making and a native world in collapse, two worlds so intertwined that both are transformed in this colonialist moment. The transformation is visible in the reformation of Indian life that took place through the reconfiguration of habitat. The encomienda and the reducción began the Spanish disruption of Andean space and interruption of Andean identities. In this regard, the reconfiguration of living space is the first reflex of modernity in the New World, that is, the denial of the authority of sacred land. The Spanish rejected an authority constituted spatially, in this case, a divinely established native authority over space itself.[27]

The encomienda came to Peru through Pizzaro, who gave land and the *ayllus*, the groups of indigenous families and peoples living on that land, to his conquistadors. Although these peoples remained in large measure on their land, their lives on that land were irreversibly altered. Their native leaders became managers of encomenderos' holdings, and they all became servants of particular encomenderos. Bartolomé de Las Casas, whose thoughts on Peru preceded Acosta's arrival and whose work marked the theological landscape, gives an apt description of the effects of the encomienda system on the Indians:

> All the towns of the region stood amid fertile lands of their own. Each of the settlers took up residence in the town allotted to him (or *encommended* to him as the legal phrase has it), put the inhabitants to work for him, stole their already scarce foodstuffs for himself and took over the lands owned and worked by the natives and on which they traditionally grew their own produce. The settler would treat the whole of the native population—dignitaries, old men, women, children—as members of his household and, as such, make them labour night and day in his own interests, without any rest whatever; even the small children, as soon as they could stand, were made to do as much as they could and more. Thus have the settlers exterminated the few indigenous people who have survived, stripping them of their houses and all their possessions and leaving them nothing for themselves. . . . They have oppressed the many people of the province, worn them to a shadow and hastened their demise.[28]

Pizzaro introduced the unimaginable to the Andeans, a world in which the bodies of countless thousands and vast reaches of landscape would be reconfigured around the bodies and lives of a few encomenderos. Like many other peoples, these natives interpreted their lives through the land; their ancestors walked the land, signified their existence through trees, mountains, rivers, rocks, animals, earth, and sky. MacCormack notes a vital difference between the Andeans and the Spanish: "Andeans perceived the land differently than Spaniards. It was not merely that the majestic heights of the Andes and the far-flung plains of the lowlands sustained the presence of the living as much as that of the dead. It was also that these heights and plains, and the springs and lakes that demarcated them, were so many pointers to humankind's remote origin from and identity with that august environment."[29] The gods, the land, and their identities were bound together. But encomienda meant the interruption of everything.[30] For when the Spanish arrived, they did not arrive alone. They brought pathogens, plants, and animals: wheat, barley, fruit trees, grapevines, flowers, and especially weeds; horses, pigs, chickens, goats, cattle, attack dogs, rats, and especially sheep. The world changed—the landscape became alien, profoundly disrupted. Daily patterns that depended not only on sustaining particular uses of certain animals and plants, but also on specific patterns of movement, migration, and social practices in certain places met violent disruption or eradication.

This environmental imperialism was shaped around what environmentalists call ungulate irruptions. Ungulates, "herbivores with hard horny hooves," when introduced to lands with an overabundance of food, reacted to this wealth of food as the Spanish themselves reacted to the wealth of gold and silver: "They increase[d] exponentially until they [overshot] the capacity of the plant communities to sustain them."[31] They ate everything in sight, decimating existing crops, destroying cycles of food growth and harvest, changing the biological regime of the New World, and altering the spatial arrangements of native life. Lands that once sustained particular ways of life disappeared as these new animals ate away the plants that supported that life. As Elinor Melville notes, this was especially the case with sheep:

> By the end of the sixteenth century, only eight decades after the Spaniards arrived, the picture had changed. The Indian populations were decimated and their fields reduced. The once fertile flatlands were covered in a dense growth of mesquite-dominated desert scrub, the high, steep-sided hills were treeless, and the piedmont was eroded and gullied. Sheep grazing, not agriculture, took precedence in regional production. . . . Sheep did not simply replace men . . . although that was the final outcome; rather, they displaced them—ate them, as the saying goes. The processes by which sheep grazing displaced agriculture, and sheep displaced humans, resulted in the formation of a new and far less hospitable landscape within which the indigenous populations were marginalized and alienated, their traditional resources degraded or lost, and their access to the means of production restricted.[32]

The conquerors as pastoralists established a new system of relating to the land and a new point of evaluation for indigenous agriculturalist practices: themselves. This meant that the skills and abilities of native peoples to work the land were rendered null and void even as the Andean peoples tried to continue their own pastoral practices. It also meant that they were forced to place their "products" into new economic networks alongside new alien crops and produce. The reputation created by this transformation meant that the native peoples' agricultural practices were perceived as backward at best or of poor stewardship of the natural resources at worst.[33] Spanish pastoralist practices were truly a plague on the land because ungulates were allowed to roam unhindered, oblivious to Indian land rights and particular land traditions and customs. Everywhere they roamed they transformed land, eating the plants to the ground, destroying ecological balance, making it suitable for new kinds of cultivation, even before encomenderos sought to claim it as their own.

The Andean peoples resisted and adapted as best they could. They resisted by remembering the stories of their gods and their connection to the land, even land that was transforming in front of their eyes, reinterpreting their connections to the land in and through new spaces. They also learned Spanish pastoralist practices and adapted to the new animals in their midst. However, one must place these acts of resistance and adaptation within the new economic and social network created by the encomiendas. This system placed Andean bodies in a new order of space and time. Indian life was lived between the economic stations of the encomenderos.[34] Their places of residence in the towns, their farming areas, their mines, their entry ports for goods, their market outlets, even the haciendas and the obrajes all formed a living circuit that shaped the daily routine of indigenous subjects.

The absolute power of the encomiendas in Peru and other places was curtailed formally first by the *Laws of Burgos of 1512–1513* and later by the *New Laws of 1542*, laws vigorously resisted by the Spanish landowners. What actually challenged the encomendero power was the swelling of the Spanish population, which made it increasingly difficult for such power and wealth to remain in the hands of only a few people. The encomiendas were collapsing under the weight of so much power. In Peru, Toledo inflicted the final blow on the absolute power of the encomenderos with his sweeping changes. His changes, however, did not destroy the encomienda system; they exaggerated one fundamental element: the control and the manipulation of Andean peoples. His reducciones, labor villages, placed Andean peoples of highly diverse groups together on one baseline of identity: labor. Inca, Ayarmaca, Maras, Anahuarque, Canas, Canchis, Lupaqa—whatever customs and rituals helped to form their various identities were now compromised by the overarching, unrelenting activity of work.[35]

In addition to the new alien environment created by the Spanish came the introduction of new people. The Spanish from the very beginning brought their slaves, the Africans. With the black slaves, the Spanish continued a history of Iberian self-perception that by Toledo's and Acosta's time was well over one hundred years old. Black slaves in Peru performed displacement. They were peoples stripped of land and identity, joined at the hip to the Spanish, and charged with the articulation of Spanish desire. They were new people not only in the sense of being geographically new to these lands, but also in the sense of being recently constructed as black and African and, most important, slave. They were fashioned to instruct the Indians in their destiny—service to empire. Yet this instruction was not simply education for service to empire but also instruction into new identity, racial identity. More precisely, black slaves were not the instructors, as the Spanish were always the instructors of racial being; but the indispensable racial illustrations. As the negative anchor at the bottom of the racial aesthetic, as "blackness," they illumined the awesome majesty of the top, Iberian "whiteness."[36]

At this point, however, the Andean peoples were being introduced to the Iberian obsession with *limpieza de sangre*, purity of blood. The theological power of blood purity, historically rooted in hatred of Jews, energized the racial optic that would now view the Andean peoples, replacing in the minds of the Spanish the cultural and religious identifiers and landscape signifiers that informed Andean self-articulation.[37] Native identities were now enclosed in this new racial reality. C. R. Boxer notes the effect of this "pigmentocracy": "Persons of mixed blood were usually regarded with suspicion, dislike, and disdain, due to the erroneous belief that the colored blood [*sic*] contaminated the white, as the history of *mesticos* in the Portuguese empire and of *mestizos* in the Spanish empire shows. There were exceptions in all times and in all places. But both Iberian empires remained essentially a 'pigmentocracy' . . . based on the conviction of white racial, moral, and intellectual superiority—just as did their Dutch, English, and French successors."[38] One must, however, keep in mind the act that very often stood behind the appearance of so-called mixed blood people, namely, the rape of Indian women and, before it and with it, the rape of African women.[39] Michele de Cuneo, who accompanied Columbus on his second voyage, left an account indicative of the sexual violence of conquest. Columbus had given a captured woman to him as a gift: "I captured a very beautiful Carib woman, whom the aforesaid Lord Admiral gave to me, and with whom, having brought her into my cabin, and she being naked as is their custom, I conceived the desire to take my pleasure. I wanted to put my desire to execution, but she was unwilling for me to do so, and treated me with her nails in such wise that I would have preferred never to have begun. But seeing this (in order to tell you the whole even to the end), I took a rope-end and thrashed her well, following which she produced such screaming and wailing as would cause you not to believe your ears. Finally we reached an agreement such that, I can tell you, she seemed to have been raised in a veritable school of harlots."[40] This tale of "sexual triumphant" invokes the interpersonal order that will characterize the New World.[41] The slow but sure migration of Iberian women to the New World and the continuation and cultivation of Old World marital and familial practices in the new space of places such as Peru did not abate. However, those Old World practices lived within New World sexual subjugation with its racial calculations. Both mestizo and mulatto and all designations in between were new racial signifiers that reigned over Andean self-designations.[42] As may be seen from the following lists of race-mixture nomenclature, that calculus not only reflected the tortured logic of pure-blood obsession but also introduced a racial gaze into the everyday practices of Andean peoples.

Embedded in this nomenclature is a racial consciousness that pivots on the possibility of being identified as white, of becoming white.[43] The Spanish placed

Table 1. Comparison of Nomenclatures

Sixteenth-century (Spanish) Peruvian Nomenclature	Eighteenth-century (Spanish) Peruvian Nomenclature
1. española + negra = mulato	1. Spaniard and Indian woman beget mestizo
2. mulato + española = testerón or tercerón	2. Spaniard and mestizo woman beget cuarterón de mestizo
3. testerón + española = quarterón	3. Spaniard and cuarterona de mestizo beget quinterón
4. quarterón + española = quinterón	4. Spaniard and quinterona de mestizo beget Spaniard or requinterón de mestizo
5. quinterón + española = blanco or española común	5. Spaniard and Negress beget mulatto
6. negro + mulata = sambo	6. Spaniard and mulatto woman beget quarterón de mulato
7. sambo + mulata = sambohigo	7. Spaniard and cuarterona de mulato beget quinterón
8. sambohigo + mulata = tente en el aire	8. Spaniard and quinterona de mulato beget requinterón
9. tente en el aire + mulata = salta atrás	9. Spaniard and requinterona de mulato beget white people
10. española + india = mestizo real	10. Mestizo and Indian woman beget cholo
11. mestizo + india = cholo	11. Mulatto and Indian woman beget chino
12. cholo + india = tente en el aire	12. Spaniard and china beget cuarterón de chino
13. tente en el aire + india = salta atrás	13. Negro and Indian woman beget sambo de Indio
14. india + negra = chino	14. Negro and mulatto woman beget zambo[b]
15. chino + negra = rechino or criollo	
16. criollo + negra = torna atrás[a]	

Notes

a. David Cahill, "Colour by Numbers: Racial and Ethnic Categories in the Viceroyalty of Peru, 1532–1824," *Journal of Latin American Studies* 26:2 (May 1994): 325–46; 339.

b. Cited in Mörner, *Race Mixture in the History of Latin America*, 58–59.

this possibility, this becoming of white identity, in the midst of the complex multiplicity of Andean identities and attempted to gauge Indian flesh by its many miscegenational permutations. There were "ethnic" distinctions or evaluations present in Incan and pre-Incan societies prior to the conquest by the Spanish. But the power of the new racial calculus caused these racial permeations to dismiss any ethnic distinctions among the Indians. With the Spanish, the new had arrived: an Inca, Ayarmaca, or Maras, for example (and the many variables within these categories of identity), may be mestizo, or mate with a Spaniard and produce a mestizo, or mate with a black and conceive a *sambo*, or produce a "pure blood" by mating within her race.[44]

I rehearse this history in order to capture the theological operation already at work as Acosta gained his bearings in the New World. What I have outlined is a matter of creation and recreation, an act of power as awesome as any rite of Christian baptism. In fact, one should envision this as an act of Christian initiation. It would be a mistake to see the church and its ecclesiastics as entering the secular workings of the state in the New World, or to posit ecclesial presence as a second stage in the temporal ordering of the New World. No, the church entered with the conquistadors, establishing camp in and with the conquering camps of the Spanish. The reordering of Indian worlds was born of Christian formation itself. Though the church may not have been in control, it was also not marginal. The church in Peru, as everywhere in the New World, was partner with the state, each maintaining its own administrative structures. Yet the church and its priests of every order established their presence, their parishes, inside the reality of the encomienda system.[45]

Holy space stood within reconfigured physical space, and in this new space the priests who educated the indigenous peoples within the parish, *doctrineros*, functioned as theological teachers. James Lockhart and Stuart Schwartz capture the new situation of the native inhabitants: "Given the fact of conquest, the sedentary peoples by and large took conversion for granted. The question was one of learning just what a converted person should do and how much of the old could be retained. Thus the emphasis was on instruction rather than conversion, on teaching Christian duties, beliefs, and sacraments."[46] The doctrineros taught Iberian custom along with Christian theology and cultural practices, imposing among other things a new sexual division of labor that mirrored Castilian practices.[47] What is crucial here is the new groundlessness within which Christian theology was presented to the indigenes. Detached from the land, oblivious to the ongoing decimation of native ecologies, deeply suspicious of native religious practices, and, most important, enclosed within Iberian whiteness, the performance of Christian theology would produce a new, deformed, and deforming intellectual circuit.

CHRISTIAN THEOLOGY AS A
DISCOURSE OF DISPLACEMENT

The young theologian who came to Peru in 1572 was not the healthiest of men. José de Acosta was often incapacitated by a bleeding chest sore that was usually accompanied by a fever. It could be that his physical challenges forced him to focus his mind. But whatever the case, his poor health stood in stark contrast to his brilliance. Like all Jesuits with his level of training, he was assigned in his early ministerial work in Spain as a teacher of theology, first at the Jesuit school in Ocaña and then in Plasencia, in schools that were much like modern-day private secondary schools. Acosta's professorate work coincided with the explosion of Jesuit schools and the rise of the Jesuit order as the preeminent religious educators of Europe. During these years, excellent teachers were in great demand, and few were more desired than the young Acosta.[48] Although he had expressed to Vicar-General Francisco de Borja, the leader of the Jesuit order, his desire to go to Spain's new territories, Borja had envisioned something different for Acosta — replacing Francisco de Toledo, the celebrated theologian at the Collegio Romano. Toledo had taught at the University of Salamanca before joining the Jesuit order and carrying out his teaching and writing ministry from one of the highest profile ecclesiastical sites of the order. He became one of the most important Jesuit theologians of their early period, so for the leader of the order to choose Acosta as Toledo's replacement was no small matter. However, it finally seemed clear to Borja that to stabilize the Jesuits in the New World what was needed in Peru was a theologian of the highest caliber. Acosta got his wish. He would arrive as the first Jesuit theologian in residence in Peru.

José de Acosta was arguably the most thoroughly trained, intellectually accomplished, and doctrinally prepared theologian to enter the New World in the sixteenth century. From his privileged beginnings through his elite education to his associations with the most powerful figures of the Jesuit order, Acosta was paradigmatic of a theologian in the New World. He also displayed the character of theological expression in this new realm of European empires. It is crucial not to imagine a bifurcation between formal theology, the theology of classically trained university theologians, and the organic or practical theology of the parish priest. Such a distinction makes no sense in the case of Acosta or the Jesuit order, as Acosta was indeed a theologian on the ground in Peru, as much as that was possible. He arrived in the New World and made his base of operations in the college at Lima, where he taught a range of subjects, especially theology proper. And from there he carried out other ministerial duties such as preaching as well as visitations to other cities of the Spanish territories. He also taught at the University of San Marcos, Viceroy Toledo's special interest. Acosta's intellectual gifts soon garnered for him the significant leadership in Peru of the rector of the college in Lima, and he was appointed provincial of Peru by the Jesuit visitor, Father Juan de la Plaza.

These roles gave Acosta extraordinary power in overseeing and guiding the work of the order in Peru. His position also put him in direct contact and often in conflict with Viceroy Toledo over jurisdiction and judgment concerning where Jesuit efforts should be deployed. What was not at issue in their relationship was the rightness of conquest, the providential reality of Spanish imperial presence, and the viceroy's refashioning of the Andean world. Unlike his Jesuit brothers who were not enthused about being pressured by the viceroy to take on the work of *doctrinas*, Acosta strongly endorsed the recommendation as a tremendous opportunity for the theological instruction of indigenes. Acosta also appreciated the potential of the reducciones for facilitating Christian formation, and he was excited by the Jesuit work of overseeing the reducción at Juli. Acosta thus fashioned a theological vision for the New World that drew its life from Christian orthodoxy and its power from conquest.

It would be a mistake to see his intellectual work as simply a reflex of colonial power. It is a manifestation of colonial power, but it also reveals in a very stark way the future of theology in the New World, that is, a strongly traditioned Christian intellectual posture made to function wholly within a colonialist logic. The colonial moment changed the trajectory of the teleological framework of Christianity. This new trajectory established a strange kind of insularity and circularity for Christian traditions of inquiry. The telos of Christian faith and life was yet in place, but faith's intellectual way of proceeding was now unclear and troubled in relation to the earth, the ground, new spaces, and landscapes.

By *faith* here, I am referring not to the content of faith, the *fides quae creditur*, but to the faith of the intellectual at work, the *fides qua creditur*. This is not to say the content of faith remained safe and secure, hermetically sealed from colonialism's effects. It did not remain safe. As we will see, the content of faith takes on strange new purposes and with it new characteristics in its explication. The faith that believes and the faith that is believed are tightly bound together, and the ambiguity of the new situation rests first in the believing subject but soon enters the content of faith. The inner coherence of traditioned Christian inquiry was grafted onto the inner coherence of colonialism. The colonialist economic circuits running from the Old World to the New and back again joined with what

Michel de Certeau calls the intellectual circularity of production, "the production of the Other and the production of the text," and both took hold of theological reflection, directing it to turn in on itself.[49] The journey of faith's articulation
was now quite unclear.

NARRATING THE NEW WORLD

Francisco López de Gómara made an infamous dedication statement to King
Charles V in his book *Historia general de las Indias* (1552): "The greatest thing
after the creation of the world, omitting the incarnation and death of him who
created it, is the discovery of the Indies; and so they call them the New World."[50]
Gómara's comments at once seem exaggerated, but in another instance they
place the supposed discovery of the Indies on its proper horizon for the Old
World. That discovery stands with the creation of the world in its sheer epistemological immensity. Gómara equates the realization of the world created by God
with the stunning surprise of vast parts of that creation theretofore unknown.
He conceptually brackets the importance of the life of Jesus Christ in birth and
death, probably out of respect, so as not to weaken the pivotal reality of salvific
history by making it of lesser significance in relation to the discovery of the New
World. Yet it is also the case that for many intellectuals of the sixteenth century,
theologians or not, it was not clear how that salvific history related to creation
and discovery.

It is precisely this conceptual struggle of grasping the creation in the newness of discovery and then relating it to salvific history that characterizes the Old
(theological) World as it meets the New World.[51] Textual authorities, theological
and philosophical, were now unknowingly being altered by New World experiences.[52] The most fundamental alteration was a split between geography, philosophy, and theology. In effect, theology and philosophy could no longer lay
claim on a sure grasp of the creation. Acosta was one of the first theologians in
the New World to sense this necessary alteration:

> I shall tell what happened to me when I went to the Indies. As I had read the ex-
> aggerations of the philosophers and poets, I was convinced that when I reached
> the equator I would not be able to bear the dreadful heat; but the reality was
> so different that at the very time I was crossing it I felt such cold that at times I
> went out into the sun to keep warm, and it was the time of year when the sun
> is directly overhead, which is in the sign of Aries, in March. I will confess here
> that I laughed and jeered at Aristotle's meteorological theories and his philoso-
> phy, seeing that in the very place where, according to his rules, everything must
> be burning and on fire, I and all my companions were cold. For the truth is that

[in] no place in the world is there a calmer and more moderate region than that under the equator.[53]

Acosta laughs, and with his laugh he shows he was an articulate observer of the New World. His laugh signifies the stark difference between the conceptualities he had learned so well in the Old World and the physical realities of the New World surrounding his flesh. Yet there is more than the ironic at play in his laugh. It also points to the potential destruction of philosophical and theological textual authority regarding the real world. But his experiences, like those of so many others, did not challenge Old World textual authorities; it extracted from them geographic authority and laid that supposed authority to the side. But what is the effect of a geographic extraction from the performance of ancient textual authorities, Christian and non-Christian? How does that removal of true speech, true sight regarding the materiality of the world affect a doctrine of creation? A Christian doctrine of creation is not dependent on geographic precision; however, it is not wholly independent of geographic accuracy. Belief in creation has to refer to current real-world places or it refers to nothing. Acosta understood this and made adjustments to Old World theories, both philosophical and theological. It is with exactly these conceptual adjustments that Acosta opened up a new performance of the doctrine of creation and paved the way for the enfolding of theology inside racialized existence, inside whiteness.

José de Acosta is crucial here for the theological texts he conceived or wrote (or both) while in the New World, most notably *Historia Natural y Moral de las Indias* and *De Procuranda Indorum Salute*.[54] His *Natural and Moral History of the Indies* (hereafter *Historia*) was translated into multiple European languages, reprinted for centuries, and served as a crucial resource in the development of Enlightenment science. *The Procurement of Indian Salvation* (hereafter *De Procuranda*) was the first book written by a Jesuit in the Americas, and it was arguably the most theologically sophisticated text written in the New World in the sixteenth century. *De Procuranda*, written while Acosta was in Peru, built from his lectures at the college in Lima and at the University of San Marcos. Acosta sent the manuscript to Rome in 1577, and it was published in 1588 in Seville. Acosta began writing *Historia* in Latin in Peru (chapters 1 and 2), but it was not until he returned to Spain that he translated it into Spanish, finished the other chapters, and published it in 1590. He dedicated the Spanish translation to Infanta Doña Isabel Clara Eugenia de Austria in hopes she would read it and recommend it to her father, Emperor Phillip II.[55] A comprehensive analysis of the two texts, *Historia* and *De Procuranda*, is beyond the scope of this chapter, and it is not my concern here to draw out the implications of these two texts for the historical development of Christian doctrine. The texts are crucial because they reveal the adjustments Christian theology will make in the New World, adjustments that will undermine theology's deepest materiality, its humanity, and its intimacy.

Decades later the *Historia* earned Acosta the title the Pliny of the New World from the Benedictine monk Benito Jerónimo y Montenegro. This work of Acosta's mature years was one of the most comprehensive and elegant descriptions of the Americas for its time.[56] It presents the kind of traditioned rationalist response suggested by MacIntyre's description of one who is able to discern the truth of a particular position: "Those who have reached a certain stage in [the] development [of a tradition] are then able to look back and to identify their own previous intellectual inadequacy or the intellectual inadequacy of their predecessors by comparing what they now judge the world, or at least part of it, to be with what it was then judged to be. To claim truth for one's present mindset and the judgments which are its expression is to claim that this kind of inadequacy, this kind of discrepancy, will never appear in any possible future situation, no matter how searching the enquiry, no matter how much evidence is provided, no matter what developments in rational enquiry may occur."[57] As an Aristotelian-Thomist, Acosta understood himself to be doing exactly this, evaluating truth-claims about the world, separating through his experience in the New World the actual case of material specifics from Old World speculations. Acosta did not reach, in his own estimations, what MacIntyre refers to as an epistemological crisis—that conceptual space in which Acosta might acknowledge new inadequacies, incoherencies, and new problems for which "there seem to be insufficient or no resources within the established fabric of belief."[58] In fact, however, Acosta reached if not an epistemological crisis, then certainly an epistemic rupture, one he had to slice from the body of the tradition, its textual authority and geographic discernments, as one slices away dead material from a plant so that it might continue to live. Once this operation was underway, Acosta had to replace ancient philosophical and theological geographic authority with another geographic authority, himself.

If Acosta established a new geographic authority based on his experiences in the New World, then the goal of that new authority had to be to reestablish ecclesial and ancient Christian authority regarding spaces. This new authority, however, would remain textual. The *Historia* was to serve as the conceptual architecture for the way in which many people in the Old World would interpret the new, serving as what Walter Mignolo calls an "encyclopedia of the exotic."[59] Mignolo notes that the *Historia* in general follows the outline of Pliny's *Natural History* in treating the cosmos, the earth, and its specifics, all the way down to animals and plant life. Actually, the *Historia* has a feel more like Aquinas's *Summa*

Theologiae, not in its Scholastic manifestation but in the way Acosta begins with concerns about the Christian tradition's teachings regarding the creation and specific locations (books I, II), then turns his attention to the specifics of the New World (books III, IV).He concludes with an anthropological treatment of the Indians (books V–VII). In effect, Acosta is explicating a doctrine of creation through the geographic specifics of the New World. This is a groundbreaking and stunning intellectual move. In the face of geographic upheaval in Old World theology and philosophy, Acosta attempts to reframe the world inside of a theological vision. Although he entered the New World, his central epistemological gesture was bringing the New World inside his theological vision, rendering it intelligible inside Christian theology.

Acosta's would be a totalizing epistemological gesture that was a harbinger of the kind of Western conceptual hegemony that has come upon the world since the sixteenth century. Mignolo is surely correct when he notes the Christian signature on that conceptual hegemony: "Confronted with previously unknown groups of people, the colonizing Christians in the Indias Occidentales (or simply the Indias) began determining individuals on the basis of their relation to theological principles of knowledge, which were taken as superior to any other system around the world."[60] If, as Mignolo says, "theology provided the authority of the locus of observation and cartography [of] the truth of the world being observed," then in Acosta one can see how that authority is enunciated in light of theology's epistemic rupture.[61] Theology will indeed become the trigger for the classificatory subjugation of all nonwhite, non-Western peoples. But that classificatory subjugation began simply as the reassertion of a doctrinal logic—that God created the world. Here, with Acosta, the theoretically sublime Christian doctrine will create space and then conceal in his own time and in the centuries to come the morally hideous.

Acosta's goal was quite honorable: render ancient textual patristic witness steady and sure while acknowledging its theretofore unknown limitations. He writes,

> No one should be offended, or think less of the doctors of the Church, if on some point of philosophy and the natural sciences they hold opinions different from what is chiefly received and approved by sound philosophy; for their whole study was to know and serve and preach the Creator, and this they performed excellently. And because they were wholly employed in this, which is the important thing, it is of small concern that they were not always wholly correct in the study and knowledge of creaturely things. Certainly the wise men of our day, and vain philosophers, are more to be blamed, for, although they know and grasp the nature and order of these creatures and the course

and movement of the heavens, these unfortunates have not come to know the Creator and Maker of all this. And while all of them were occupied in these excellent deeds and writings they did not rise with their thought to discover their sovereign Author, as divine wisdom teaches; or even when they acknowledged the Creator and Lord of all, they did not serve and glorify him as they should have done, being vain in their thoughts, for which the Apostle justly blames and accuses them. (*Historia*, I:1)

From the very beginning of *Historia*, Acosta asserts theology as the queen of the sciences. Yet now its royal reign seems more localized. In Acosta, theology has returned from speculations regarding the earth to its semantic-specific *theologia*, words about God in knowledge, service, and proclamation. As any theologian would, he renarrates Christian tradition, but more specifically he adjusts the pedagogical trajectory of the teachers of the church, offering his readers a more precise locus for the church's intellectual reflections. This is already a retreat, a surrender made necessary by the New World. Acosta is aware of this. He wants to minimize not merely ecclesial error, but the error of the teachers of the church who grasp the Creator clearly, if not the creation. But what does it mean to say they may not grasp the creation correctly, especially in the face of creation's newness? Acosta himself was a case in point. Even as he wrote the *Historia*, he remained a geocentric Ptolemist. Although Copernicus had published his *De revolutionibus orbium caelestium* in 1543, it was yet to have an effect on theologians such as Acosta. The effect of the New World on his thinking was to separate theology from the earth for the sake of theology's coherence.

Acosta's formal training had established marked distinctions between theology, philosophy, and what would later be called natural science. Now philosophy was coming into critical view not for its failure to understand the world (in ways that theology's faulty knowledge was declared to be exempt from), but because its knowledge had not risen to theology, that is, to knowledge of the Creator. Acosta would, however, find and note at length various faults in ancient philosophers' speculations about the earth, but his point at the beginning of the *Historia* is to register a spiritual failure: as Paul notes in Romans 1, the pagan philosophers knew but did not serve or glorify the Creator. Acosta's criticisms did not amount to a wholesale rejection of his own philosophical formation. He remained a thoroughly Aristotelian Thomist. His commitment to an Aristotelian anthropology was unwavering even in light of his withering rebuttal of Aristotle's meteorological speculations. The moment of innovation here is Acosta's bracketing of theology by means of an intellectual sleight of hand. Theological critique masks theological limitation. This adjustment will be rehearsed countless times as Acosta's modernity gives way to the Enlightenment's modernity. With Acosta, however, theology launched itself into the unknown world doing self-protective commentary.

Theology in the New World was not under attack, having to defend itself against nascent secular discourses. In the New World it surely remained queen of the sciences. However, it was now a queen over a realm too vast to control. Acosta exhibits the stretching of theological speech in an attempt to make intelligible its vision of the world to the faithful of the Old World. This is a matter of coverage, of coherence, and of holding the entire world within theocentric sight. Acosta's efforts imitated the economic circuit that was quickly enfolding the expanding known world in cycles of production and consumption. The economic circuit's coherence was beautiful and constantly self-correcting. The economic circuit showed how merchants were able to adapt to newness, overcoming geographic barriers, transforming the inhospitable into livable habitation, and exacting goods and services from all it touched. The economic circuit was taking the New World and channeling it through the Old World and taking the Old World and performing it through the New World.

Could theology do or be anything less than equally beautiful, coherent, and self-correcting? Acosta's act of retrieval of ancient Christian thought is a delicate operation of subtle redeployment. For example, in his gentle "correction" of Augustine's claim that the antipodes did not exist because people in the antipodes would have to "move about upside down," Acosta is much more subtle than Las Casas about Augustine's errors.[62] Acosta finds that Augustine, like Gregory of Nazianzus, simply had no knowledge of how people could traverse the great expanse of the ocean and therefore had reached the limits of his knowledge and imagination:

> Surely [Augustine's] motive in denying the existence of antipodes was taken from the innermost parts of sacred theology, through which Holy Writ teaches us that all mankind descends from the first man, who was Adam. Therefore, to say that men were able to pass over to the New World by crossing that infinite expanse of the Ocean Sea seemed an incredible thing and completely nonsensical. And indeed, if palpable events and the experience of what we have seen in our own time had not opened our eyes, this reasoning would have been considered irrefutable to the present day. And now that we know that the reasoning I speak of is neither conclusive nor true, yet we will be at some pains to give an answer: I mean to declare how and by what means the lineage of men could arrive here and how and whence they came to people these Indies. (*Historia*, I:8)

Augustine's basic vision of the world as elaborated in the *City of God* remains correct, according to Acosta: the truth of a created world as revealed through Scripture. But now the specifics of that creation exposed by the New World raise difficult questions: how did people get there if in fact they descended from Adam by way of Noah's sons? Acosta's famous answer that they crossed over some theretofore undiscovered land mass was a brilliant deduction that tried to remain faithful to Scripture (*Historia*, I:20). Acosta was one of the first Western intellectuals to venture this thesis, yet what is crucial here is his powerful suturing of Scripture and tradition to this new space in order to bring doctrinal logics to bear on the New World.[63]

Acosta's redeployment of Scripture and tradition yields another, equally important conceptual maneuver. He articulates a vision of providence with an incredible new elasticity. He discerns the guiding hand of God in the way the Spanish arrived and remained in the New World, while discerning no such divine involvement in the lives of native peoples. Divine providence, however, could be seen in everything, from the technological advances that made travel to the Indies possible to the alleged discovery of the silver and mercury mines: "Since Heaven decreed that the nations of the Indies be discovered after lying hidden for so long, and that this route had to be made familiar so that many souls would come to know Jesus Christ and attain his eternal salvation, Heaven also provided a sure guide for those who follow this path, which was the guide of the compass and the virtue of the lodestone" (*Historia*, I:17). To tie providence to the happy use of the compass (although it was not invented by Iberians) was exquisite theological improvisation, and the idea was to be repeated by countless theologians and Christian intellectuals in the centuries that followed.[64] It indicated how a doctrine of providence was to become a powerful tool not only in situating European presence in their mysterious and inexplicable new surroundings, but also in calming fears of being in the midst of the unknown, both physically and conceptually. However, Acosta understood that the central mystery of the New World was the natives themselves, their origin, nature, and ways of life.

Acosta dismisses the idea of finding the source of Indian origin in the Scripture itself. The first dismissal in this regard is of natives' connection to any people in Scripture, and the second dismissal is of any genealogical connection between the indigenes and the Jews: "Ignorant folk commonly believe that the Indians proceed from the race of Jews because they are cowardly and weak and much given to ceremony, and cunning, and lying. In addition to this they say that their dress appears to be the same as that of the Jews. . . . But all these are very idle conjectures and have much more evidence against them than for them" (*Historia*, I:23). Acosta must distance Indians from Jews in order to safeguard the salvific possibility of the natives. The idea of Indians being Jewish descendents would complicate Acosta's theological narration of the New World beyond his ability to render it intelligible. His refutations, however, expose a weakness. Acosta has reached the epistemological limits of his theological vision. As he states, "It is easier to refute what is false about the Indians' origin than to discover the truth, for among them there are neither writings nor any certain memories of their first founders" (*Historia*, I:24). Ironically, Acosta's dismissals of Old World theories stand alongside his dismissal of native knowledge regarding their own origins.

Native knowledge exists beyond the limits of Acosta's imagination. It exhausts his theology. So he concludes that "it is not very important to know what the Indians themselves are wont to tell of their beginnings and origin, for what they relate resembles dreams rather than history" (*Historia* I:25). He cannot imagine a theological appropriation of native knowledge as an act of theological reflection itself. Such an act is prohibited by his deep commitment to a Western episteme that is emerging at the precise moment of colonialism's emergence.[65] To say Acosta's theological conceptuality has reached exhaustion does not mean it ends his discursive project. He describes without hesitation native objects and the native as object, both formed in native silence with Acosta beginning a discursive procedure that will mark Western reflection on nonwhite flesh for the next several hundred years—he speaks for them.[66]

This epistemic imaginary was launched from within a vision of divine providence. As Acosta describes Spain's new environment in its new territories, he weaves together descriptions of land, animals, and plants, noting the work of the hand of God. He masterfully articulates providence in this literary performance of Castilian ownership. Acosta's literary elegance, however, does not conceal the thorny theological problems he must address, such as the wide variety of animal species as well as their origins. As one can see from the precision of his thought, he surmises a complex migration of animals from Noah's ark:

> We must then say that, even though all the animals came out of the Ark, by natural instinct and the providence of Heaven, different kinds went to different regions and in some of those regions were so contented that they did not want to leave them; or that if they did leave they were not preserved, or in the course of time became extinct, as happens with many things. And if we look at the matter carefully it is not only the case of the Indies but the general case of many other regions and provinces of Asia, Europe, and Africa. . . . We must also consider whether these animals differ specifically and essentially from all others or whether their difference is accidental; this could be caused by various accidents, as in the lineages of men some are white and others black, some giants and other dwarfs.[67]

Acosta's careful Aristotelian sensibilities allow him to envision the working out of the divinely placed telos in all the multiple varieties of plants and animals. While his theorization had implications far beyond theology, it never left the hermeneutic of providence—God had prepared the Spanish and this New World for their intercourse. One of Acosta's most famous analogies of providence is his *hija fea*, or "ugly daughter," analogy. It appears in the *Historia* and is suggested in *De Procuranda*:

> But it is a circumstance worthy of much consideration that the wisdom of our Eternal Lord has enriched the most remote parts of the world, inhabited by the most uncivilized people, and has placed there the greatest number of mines that ever existed, in order to invite men to seek out and possess those lands and coincidentally to communicate their religion and the worship of the true God to men who do not know it. Thus the prophecy of Isaiah has been fulfilled that the Church shall pass on to the right hand and to the left, which is, as Saint Augustine declares, the way the Gospel must be propagated, not only by those who preach it sincerely and with charity but also by those who proclaim it through temporal and human aims and means. Hence we see that the lands in the Indies that are richest in mines and wealth have been those most advanced in the Christian religion in our time; and thus the Lord takes advantage of our desires to serve his sovereign ends. In this regard a wise man once said that what a man does to marry off an ugly daughter is give her a large dowry; this is what God has done with that rugged land, endowing it with great wealth in mines so that whoever wished could find it by this means. (*Historia*, IV:2)

Here Acosta places his historic moment between Scripture (Isaiah) and tradition (Augustine). In this moment, Spain is beginning to reap unprecedented financial return from the rapidly increasing mining production. Acosta binds the economic circuit to Christian teleology through what he claims to be the work of the Eternal Lord, who enriched the land with mines as a preparation for the gospel, a *praeparatio evangelica*, to create the possibility of colonial desire. Here a doctrine of providence yields the grotesque: God is responsible for colonial desire. The people are not the point of desire; the land itself is the sensual focus. As Acosta states, "Hence there is great abundance of mines in the Indies, mines of every metal: copper, iron, lead, tin, quicksilver, silver, and gold" (*Historia*, IV:2).

The poignancy of Acosta's ugly daughter analogy comes into view when one considers the two modes by which, according to Acosta, the gospel may be propagated. On the one hand, the gospel may be presented through preaching in sincerity and charity, and on the other hand it may be proclaimed "through temporal and human aims and means." Acosta is not drawing a sharp distinction here. His point is divine sovereignty, God's "sovereign ends." As God has always used worldly powers to fulfill the divine will, so now God works inside the temporal relation between Spain and the New World, guiding its misdirected *eros*, an *eros* not for the daughter but for the dowry. The subtleties of Aristotelian–Thomist divine causality are in play here, so one cannot simply say that divine agency works singularly; rather, the actions of the Spanish are truly their own actions. Yet God enables in multiple ways. The literary effect of the analogy is far-reaching. Acosta's analogy not only renders the lives of native peoples unappealing in their supposed barbarity, but also voids their lives as any essential place of *communio* for the Spanish. Acosta outlines the presentation of salvation without the desire for communion. The analogy witnesses a strained ecclesiology and a troubled church in the New World.

The hermeneutic of providence in the hands of this Jesuit enables an insularly economic reading of the New World. As Acosta writes regarding the precious metals and the mines, he notes the increased revenue the church receives from this industry: "Today his Catholic Majesty receives, year after year, a million pesos simply from the royal fifths of silver that come from the mountain of Potosí, not counting further wealth from quicksilver and other prerogatives of the Royal Treasury" (*Historia*, IV:7). He calculates the dramatic increase in wealth to Spain and the church as irrefutable signs of the workings of God through them not just for the propagation of the gospel but also for the financing of wars against the enemies of Christianity. The fact that Acosta entered Peru during Spain's most lucrative years of conquest shadowed his theological reflection and enabled a way of seeing the specifics of the New World while not seeing its specific suffering. Acosta seemed oblivious to the suffering of the people who did the mining, the Indians and Africans. He describes the work of mining in great detail, except one thing is missing, the humanity of the miners:

> They work there in perpetual darkness, with no idea of when it is day or night; and as these are places never visited by the sun, not only is there perpetual darkness but it is also extremely cold, with a very heavy atmosphere unfit for man's nature; and so it happens that those who enter the mine for the first time feel weak and dizzy, as happened to me, experiencing nausea and cramps in the stomach. . . . They carry the ore on their backs up ladders made of three strands of leather plaited into thick ropes, with sticks placed between one strand and another as steps, so that one man can be descending while another is climbing. . . . Each man has a fifty-pound load in a blanket tied over his breast, with the ore it contains at his back; three men make the climb at one time. The first

carries a candle tied to his thumb so that they can see. . . . They climb by catching hold with both hands, and in this way ascend the great distance . . . often more than 150 *estados*, a horrible thing about which it is frightening even to think. Such is the power of money, for the sake of which men do and suffer so much. (*Historia*, IV:8)

Acosta failed to acknowledge the miners' humanity because his theological vision was now overdetermined, drawn into a circular logic energized on the one side by concern for addressing the problems raised by the New World for inherited biblical and theological accounts of the creation and population of the world, and on the other side by the need to assert the hand of the Christian Creator—God at work in the New World and in control of the process of discovery.[68] As Acosta theologically narrated the New World, he was also renarrating the old with the new inside it. The newness of the Indias Occidentales was slowly but surely being domesticated by means of Christian vision. In Acosta's hands, Christian discernment took on a painful superficiality. In an astonishing statement in the *Historia*, Acosta, contra Las Casas, speculates that the reason for the rapid depopulation of many areas and the massive deaths of natives is their own fault: "In our time the population of these coasts or plains is so much diminished and impaired that twenty-nine out of thirty of its inhabitants have disappeared; and many believe that the remaining Indians will disappear before long. People attribute this to various causes, some to the fact that the Indians have been overworked, others to the changes of food and drink that they adopted after becoming accustomed to Spanish habits, and others to the excessive vice that they display in drink and other abuses. As for me, I believe that this latter disorder is the chief cause of their reduced numbers" (*Historia*, III:19). Acosta makes this statement after witnessing the reorganization of native bodies into new units for labor, labor that was taxed by unrelenting demand. He also witnessed the tightening of land control and mining production by Viceroy Toledo and the continued abuse of native women and children. He could not have known about the spread of lethal pathogens. But he did understand the devastating effects of the introduction of new animals on the land and on indigenous crops. Knowing this, he yet concluded that it was the immorality of the Indians that was leading to their demise. The insularity of his theological vision draws him away from the obvious. While Acosta did recognize the abuse of the natives, that recognition was complicated by his profound commitment to colonial rule. In another strange analogy he compares the refining process for silver to the holy refining process of humanity, quoting Mal 3:3 in the Vulgate, "He shall purify them, and refine them as silver" (*Historia*, IV:12). It is strange not as a spiritual analogy, but in light of the countless deaths being caused precisely by the extracting and refining processes themselves.

The most serious problems of discernment appear in Acosta's treatment of Andean religions. One must use *religion* here in a nuanced way because what in fact Acosta perceives to be a religious performance is fundamental to the problem. One must also keep in mind the anachronism that attends to a modern use of the concept of religion at the birth of the colonial moment. As Anthony Pagden noted in his seminal text *The Fall of Natural Man*, Acosta's innovation was his "attempt to distinguish between the various Indian cultures in the New World."[69] It is inside this innovative procedure that Acosta theorizes religions and the religious consciousness of not only the Indian but all "discovered" peoples.

Acosta's experience in Peru was not the only source of his knowledge of native religious practices. He also learned a great deal from the work of Licentiate Juan Polo de Ondegardo, who had written on Inca religion and was advisor to Viceroy Toledo. In fact, Ondegardo's work served as an indispensable guide in helping Acosta understand what he was seeing in fragments. Acosta was seeing religious fragments because by the time he arrived in Peru, "Inca religion," as MacCormack notes, "was a memory only," and other religious rituals and practices existed in splintered form inside a burgeoning Christian cultural hegemony.[70] However, Andean religions were still perceived as a very real threat to colonialist Christian society by people such as Acosta and Toledo. Regardless of the actual strength of Andean religions, Acosta offered, on the basis of Ondegardo's work as well as that of Fray Diego Durán, what he considered to be a definitive theological treatment of them for his readers in Spain. It was not definitive in the sense of showing a comprehensive, sympathetic understanding of native religious practices. It was definitive in fully lodging those practices within a Christian narrative that evacuated them of any substantially sui generis reality and meaning. In Acosta's conceptuality, Andean religious practices reflected two realities, innate inferiority and demonic agency.

For Acosta and the vast majority of his religious brothers of all orders theological interpretation stood at a great distance from Andean religious self-perception.[71] Although this gap between perception and interpretation is a matter of historical record, moderns have yet to reckon with the deeper implications of Acosta's misperception. MacCormack, in her insightful essay "Demons, Imagination, and the Incas," notes crucial signs of the problem:

> Throughout the Andes, people thought their ancestors had sprung from the land itself, from mountain or rock, lake or spring. A place of origin, often described as *pacarina* (from *pacari*, "dawn"), was a fixed point, always present,

immovable. To be buried in the open country thus meant in some general sense to return to one's origin. . . . The relationships Andeans perceived between life and death, and between humankind and the natural environment, were thus *profoundly different from Spanish and Christian equivalents.* The land surrounding one told the story of one's first ancestors as much as it told one's own story and the story of those yet to come. It was right that the familiar dead were seen walking through the fields they had once cultivated, thus sharing them with both the living and with the original ancestors who had raised the first crops in the very same fields.[72]

I am neither suggesting that Andean religions were monolithic nor simplifying a complex history of contestation and transformation of religious communities and practices, which at the time of Spanish invasion were in tremendous flux owing to Incario domination. MacCormack's observations do, however, capture a basic relation that attends Andean religious performance, and these observations begin to situate Acosta's misperception. He cannot discern the spatial logics of Andean life, in which "the plains and mountains, the sky and the waters were both the theater and the *dramatis personae* of divine action."[73] This inability will have tragic effects on how Acosta interprets Andean sacred objects, the *huacas,* and the complex calculus of sacred presence they represent. Equally important, Acosta will match the way in which the colonialists physically tore Andean life from geographically specific locations with his own conceptual ripping and will thereby solidify Christian theology's insularity and circularity in its literary performances and enunciative practices.

In the second half of the *Historia,* Acosta seeks to examine Indian moral history, which is the customs and deeds of the Indians. However, the fundamental agency that shapes his narrative of Indian moral history is *del demonio ("the devil"):* "The devil's pride is so great and so obstinate that he always longs and strives to be accepted and honored as God and to steal and appropriate to himself in every way he can what is owed only to the Most High God. He never ceases to do this in the blind nations of the world, those that the light and splendor of the Holy Gospel has not yet illuminated" (*Historia,* V:1). The central work of the devil in "blind nations" is to embed in them idolatrous practice. Acosta is not an innovator in this critique; he is simply elaborating an ancient Christian posture in relation to non-Christian peoples. However, it would be a mistake to quickly conclude that this accusation of idolatry is simply a reflex of ethnic chauvinism or a failure to appreciate cultural difference. Seeing a world in which idolatry is not only a possibility but a probability requires a thoroughgoing theological vision. To denounce idolatrous declaration out of hand is to inevitably reason from within secular space. Such was not an option for Acosta. This is not to say that Acosta's vision of idolatry is exempt from critique because it is a sign of his times. Rather, in order to grasp the tragedy at work here one needs a deeper analysis than to see idolatry simply as ethnic chauvinism or as a movement within cultural and epistemic hegemony. Both are true, yet both are incomplete.

The central question that attends Acosta's narration of Indian moral history is this: how does a hermeneutic of providence modulate into a hermeneutic of idolatry? The answer may be sought in the theological performance of *De Procuranda* (see below). However, the *Historia* exposes the essential steps in this modulation because it gives the conceptual mapping that enabled Acosta's reading of native practice. Acosta deploys a scriptural logic—the worship of the true God excludes and then discerns the worship of the idol (facilitated by the devil). Here Acosta stands solidly and precisely within the Christian tradition. Unfortunately, like the tradition he has inherited, he reads this scriptural logic backward: church has replaced Israel as the bearer of the vision of the true God, and all those outside the church are pagan.

Acosta perpetuates the supersessionist mistake, but now in the New World the full power of that mistake is visible. Acosta reads the Indian as though he (Acosta) represented the Old Testament people of God bound in covenant faithfulness and taught to discern true worship from false. Acosta reads the religious practices of indigenes from the position of the ones to whom the revelation of the one true God was given, Israel. Christian theology contains at its core a trajectory of reading "as Israel," as the new Israel joined to the body of Jesus through faith. Yet by the time Acosta performs his reading, this christological mediation has mutated into the replacement of Israel as the people that make the idea of idolatry intelligible as a primarily Christian insight.[74] From this position of holding an idea of idolatry resourced solely by a supersessionist Christian vision, Acosta speculates as to the possibilities of whether Indians as pagans under the control of the devil may be led to the light. Within this backward scriptural logic, Acosta then reads various texts (for example, Wis 14 and Rom 1), with Israel evacuated and replaced. Consider the application of his exegetical vision applied to Acts 17:23: "First, although the gross darkness of unbelief has obscured the minds of those nations, in many ways the light of truth and reason works in them to some small degree; and so most of them acknowledge and confess a supreme Lord and Maker of all, whom the Peruvians called Viracocha. . . . They worshiped him, and he was the chief god that they venerated, gazing heavenward. And the same belief exists, after their fashion, in the Mexicans and the Chinese today and in other heathen peoples. This is very similar to what is told in the Book of Acts of the Apostles, when Saint Paul was in Athens and saw an altar with the inscrip-

tion 'Ignoto Deo,' to the unknown God" (*Historia*, V:3). Acosta replaces Paul as
the exegete of pagan ritual. In relation to the Indians, Acosta notes in astonishment that they have no word to name God: "For if we try to find in the Indian
languages any word corresponding to this one, *God*, as it is *Deus* in Latin and
Theos in Greek, and *El* in Hebrew and in Arabic *Allah*, it cannot be found in the
language of Cuzco, nor in the Mexican tongue" (ibid.). His reading suggests he
would not position himself with the Indians within a history of Gentile (that is,
non-Jewish) existence.

Acosta is cut off from a simple Gentile remembrance that would enable a
far more richly imagined possibility of movement toward faith from within the
cultural logics and spatial realities of Andean life. That is to say, he is cut off from
active remembering that he and his people were also "like the Indians." Such
remembering does not exclude discerning "the demonic," yet it surely opens up
analogies, analogies of both synchronic (that is, relating native worship practices to the formation of *new* Christian possibilities) and diachronic (relating
possible transformations in *Christian* worship practices in the New World to historic transformations of Christian worship that took place in societies of the Old
World). This is not to say that Acosta failed to claim all peoples as having a pagan
past prior to Christianity. I am not saying either that Acosta did not recognize the
mission strategy of building Christian ritual practices on top of native ritual as
much as possible.

What I suggest would have entailed a different imaginative modality, one that
was possible for Acosta, given his stunning ability to think in new ways yet remain within his intellectual and theological tradition. For Acosta this would have
meant embodying a generosity of spirit that was sorely lacking in his assessments
of native practices. Instead, Acosta imagines intricate networks of demonic activity. And he imagines the demonic work to be far more extensive, expressive,
and operative than the work of God could ever have been had the Spanish not
been in the new world. What triggers this demonic imagination and conceals
redemptive cultural analogies is Acosta's vision of native intellectual and cultural
inferiority. The symbolic Christian imaginary within which Acosta functioned
believed Indians lacked intelligence because they lacked European languages
and especially their signifiers for God. This lack, coupled with Acosta's supersessionist vision, meant that the demonic becomes a compelling heuristic through
which to interpret Andean societies.

Acosta looked at the religious life of the Andeans and imagined a reversal of
Christian logic and practices, a demonic *imitatio Christianitas*. Following early
church theological sensibilities, and again reflecting on Wis 12–14, he organized idolatry into two forms, each in two modalities: first, the worship of natu-

ral things, which included celestial bodies and what Acosta understood as the huacas—rivers, springs, trees, mountains, and so forth—and, second, the worship of things "imagined or fabricated by human ingenuity," which included idols made of wood, metals, and stone as well as the ancestors and their possessions (*Historia*, V:2–6).[75] What directed idol production was the cunning of the devil, who mimics the divine in all things. By means of this imitation the evil one holds the Indians in utter subjection:

> The devil in his arrogance, and in competition with God, has taken over the things that God in his wisdom has ordained for his cult and honor, and for man's good and his salvation; these the devil strives to imitate and pervert so as to make himself honored and man more deeply damned. And so we see that, just as the Supreme God has sacrifices and priests, and sacraments, and religious persons, and prophets, and people dedicated to his divine cult and sacred ceremonies, so, too, does the devil have his sacrifices and priests, and his kind of sacraments, and people living in seclusion and feigned holiness, and a thousand kinds of false prophets. . . . So he tries to usurp the glory of God for himself, and to counterfeit light with his darkness. (*Historia*, V:11)

Andean religious practices understood as Christian counterfeiting runs all the way to churches, theological schools, monasteries, and even the mystery of the Holy Trinity (*Historia*, V:28). Ultimately, Acosta will lodge Andean immorality and find its generative source in its idolatry. Acosta finds space to praise Incan forms of government and the forms of trade that flow from the ordering of that society. He even acknowledges their innate intelligence in this regard and believes this signals their teachability. This praise, however, is not transferable to their religious practices, which are in constant need of extirpation.[76]

Acosta's hermeneutic of idolatry vivified in the New World was an outgrowth of his Aristotelian–Thomist training, which understood that the true nature of an object was discernable only through correct intellection.[77] In regard to the religious realities of the New World this meant Acosta saw himself as constantly cutting through the deceptions of the senses that held the natives blind by Satan's hand to theological truth. Just as Acosta was able to discern the hand of God at work in the creation of the New World and thereby establish providence at work, so he could pierce through their religious practices to detect the clandestine operations of evil. Using this Aristotelian–Thomist sensibility, Acosta establishes a transparency that will be fundamental to the colonialist gaze. This transparency will be an ability to always see through the natives—their words, their logics, their practices, their beliefs—and discern the underlying logic, in this case a religious logic, that attends their actions. Unfortunately, for Acosta that underlying logic comes from the devil. Acosta, while not alone in this hermeneutic of idolatry, represents the dominant modality in reading native religious practice during his time. However, Acosta's derogatory vision of Andean religious life was not a historical necessity.

When Las Casas considered Indian religious practices, he came to conclusions that were different from Acosta's. I do not intend to examine Las Casas's perspective on native religious practice. I simply wish to highlight his theological generosity, especially in light of Acosta's vision. In his famed *In Defense of the Indians*, in argument against the Aristotelian scholar and theologian Juan Ginés de Sepúlveda, Las Casas takes up among other things an argument for the defense of the Indians from the standpoint of what many considered their most heinous practice, human sacrifice. It is precisely the accusation of human sacrifice (concomitant with cannibalism) that, according to Sepúlveda, justified going to war and enslaving the natives.[78] This should be done, he suggests, in order to protect the innocent. Las Casas argues in chapters 34–38 of his *Defense* that the native peoples cannot be persuaded to end their current religious practices simply by being told by the Spanish that they are morally wrong, because the horrific behavior of the Spanish living among the natives is the first deterrent to any Indians taking seriously Spanish ethical admonishments.[79] Even more important for his argument, Las Casas argues that native human sacrifice is consistent with their theological visions. This in a fundamental way is a groundbreaking position.

Las Casas on Christian theological grounds argues for the coherence and integrity of non-Christian religious practice. His four reasons for recognizing the theological coherence of native practices are that (1) all peoples operate out of some knowledge of God, even if little or confused; (2) all people are led to worship God by their capacities and cultural ways; (3) the highest way to worship God is through sacrifice; and (4) sacrifice, no matter under what custom, is always offered to the true God as that god is understood by the native peoples. All Las Casas's points flow out of the logic of natural law theorization. Yet each makes space for a sui generis religious reality. He suggests that native peoples are worshiping God "as they understand god." This understanding is through the natural light of reason and not through grace or doctrine. MacCormack suggests that Las Casas overcame what I am calling a hermeneutics of idolatry by moving the examination of native religious practices away from its two points of comparison, ancient (false) religions of classical antiquity and Christianity, and toward study of "the origin and nature of human perceptions of God."[80] She writes that Las Casas laid the groundwork for considering "American religions as, *inter alia*, cultural phenomena capable of being studied independently of Christian theological conviction."[81] Tzvetan Todorov believes Las Casas introduced "perspectivism into the heart of religion":[82]

> But to acknowledge that their god is true for them—is that not to take a first step toward another acknowledgment, i.e., that our God is true for us—and only for us? What then remains common and universal is no longer the God of the Christian religion, to whom all should accede, but the very idea of divinity, of what is above us; the religious rather than religion. . . . Las Casas is led to modify his position and to illustrate thereby a new variant of the love for one's neighbor, for the Other—a love that is no longer assimilationist but, so to speak, distributive: each has his own values; the comparison can be made only among certain relations—of each human being to *his* god—and no longer among substances: there are only formal universals. Even as he asserts the existence of one God, Las Casas does not a priori privilege the Christian path to that God. Equality is no longer bought at the price of identity.[83]

Todorov has overreached Las Casas here. He makes Las Casas conjure secular space in which theological vision is private, individual, and shaped in alterity. In finding in Las Casas the suggestion that "religious feeling is not defined by a universal and absolute content but by its orientation, and is measured by its intensity,"[84] Todorov has made Las Casas sound too similar to the German Romantic theologian Friedrich Schleiermacher in his famed *Über die Religion*.[85] Todorov thus renders a too-modern Las Casas, one who has left theology and entered religious studies and who reduces all theological statements to the cultural musings of religious subjects. Such a reduction is actually closer to Acosta, albeit without his derogatory trajectory.[86] Las Casas is able to grant conceptual space for native religious practices precisely on the ground of a Christian vision of creation in which such visions have their own integrity. Such a Christian vision does not, as MacIntyre reminds us, evacuate its theological claims of their substance, turning them into simply emotive-cultural religious form.

Las Casas's theological generosity does not solve the problems either of Western epistemological hegemony, or of what Daniel Castro calls Las Casas's ecclesiastical imperialism, or of his inability to reckon with black flesh and African suffering in any theologically substantial way.[87] Las Casas, like Acosta, carries forward a supersessionist reading of Scripture that established the invaders as the imperial readers and extirpators of idolatry. However, in Las Casas's treatment of native religious practices one can catch glimpses of a Gentile remembrance in the ways he situates pagan worship as a part of Christian history, albeit sinful history, and not simply the history of classic antiquity. Most important, his treatment of native religious practices sharpens the distinct contours of Acosta's vision. Acosta was well aware of the controversial advocacy of native rights in the thought of Las Casas and his followers, the debates at Valladolid between Las Casas and Sepúlveda, and even the earlier seminal work of Francisco de Vitoria, who established in his *De Indis et De Ivre Belli Relectiones* (1539) the possibilities of Indian obedience to God. Acosta, however, in his reflections on native religious practices, kept his distance from Las Casas.

Acosta was, in effect, moving toward a more modern vision, more modern even than Las Casas's. In Acosta, the hermeneutics of idolatry was modulating into something new—an ethnographic, anthropological vision of cultures arranged hierarchically. This is not a movement away from a theological vision but a modulation within it.[88] The implications of this modulation will be seen in the pedagogical vision within which Acosta sees the future of theology unfolding. In Acosta, as in many of the articulators of the Christian tradition in the new worlds, the native students will always remain the barbarians.

THE MAKING OF COLONIALIST THEOLOGICAL SUBJECTIVITY

At the beginning of *De Procuranda*, Acosta considers the vast diversity of peoples of the New World and then categorizes them into three distinct classes of barbarians (table 2).[89] The first group, the highest in civilization and development,[90] are those barbarians who are in effect civil beings who have stable cities, established governments and bureaucracies, regular commerce, and, most important, the knowledge of letters.[91] The Chinese, Japanese, and peoples of eastern India fit in this group. They, much like the ancient Greeks and Romans, should not be converted by force of arms but by the force of reason. Once the gospel is presented to them, God will, by divine grace, work through their reason to establish its truth in them.

Barbarians of the second group lack a developed system of writing, philosophy, and civil wisdom, but they have a system of government marked by defined leaders, custom, law, and social order. The Mexicans and Peruvians fill this category. These barbarians have innate abilities that simply need to be cultivated. Their elementary writing and accounting systems show ingenuity and promise, but their collective life lacks proper organization in that it is inundated with customs, rites, and rituals. However, when they are brought under the power of "Christian princes and Magistrates," they should be able to grow in the gospel.[92]

The third class of barbarian are those peoples who live like wild animals, hunting and gathering in packs and having no governmental sensibility or system of writing. They "hardly have human feelings—without law, without agreements, without government, without nationhood, who move from place to place."[93] There are quite a few of this class of barbarian in the new worlds, according to

Table 2. Barbarian Typologies

	Language; Writing System	Government	Examples	Means of Conversion
Barbarian (a)	advanced communication networks; intelligible systems of writing	monarchy; the rule of law; commerce; bureaucracies; urban societies	Chinese; Japanese; Eastern Indians; Ancient analogies: Greeks and Romans	through reason and the presentation of advanced technologies
Barbarian (b)	elementary writing and accounting systems; elementary communication systems	ruled by councils; free associations; settlement and kinship life	Mexicans; Peruvians; Incans	through appropriation and translation of existing rituals and religious symbols under the tutelage of Christian princes and magistrates
Barbarian (c)	live like wild animals; barely have human feelings; no writing system	nomadic—no fixed dwelling; no rule of law; rudimentary forms of government	Caribs, Chuncos, Chiriguanes, Moxos, Yscayingos, Brazilians; Floridians	by force; imposition of pedagogy facilitated by the Christian state

Acosta offers one of the earliest theological ethnographic visions of the new worlds. He draws crucial distinctions between barbarian types by means of the white theological gaze. That is, by looking through their rituals, idolatries, behaviors, language, and practices, he is able to categorize barbarian identity. Native being presents a fundamental transparency through which he can discern their level of civilization and human maturity. Most important for him, he is able to look all the way through the native body to discern the degree to which the demonic is at work in a given population.

White Gaze → Native Ritual, Practice → Barbarian Identity → Demonic Influence
            Idolatry, Behavior,   Native Being
            Language

Acosta. This third type, which may be dominated by force, is characterized by docility. They have some elementary or rudimentary forms of government, but "their laws and customs are childish and laughable."[94] Since they are docile they may be "attracted through flattery," and if that fails, then they must be constrained by force "to enter the Kingdom of Heaven."[95]

De Procuranda was written during Acosta's early years in Peru, before the *Historia* and before his return to Spain. Yet one can see in these finely drawn distinctions between barbarian types the architecture for the important distinctions he will later articulate regarding idolatry and the three forms of government which closely follow the three types of barbarians. The intellectual posture from which he will interpret the New World shows through the work. Here, too, is the merger of two circuits, the theological defined by the Jesuit emergence and the colonialist-economic defined by the program of subjugation and transformation established by Spanish presence.

At its inception the Jesuit order was an order of educators. What Jesuits brought to all the lands they inhabited was a theologically shaped process of evaluation, a form of what Pierre Bourdieu termed a *habitus*, "systems of durable, transposable dispositions, structured structures predisposed to function as structuring structures."[96] This theologically shaped pedagogical habitus was deeply Christian in its desire to form Christian character mediated through the humanist vision of *Bildung* in anyone willing to be so shaped. Yet when Acosta looked out onto the New World, the Christian habitus in which he had been shaped became the expression of a colonialist logic. The central reason for this transposition has to do with forms of evaluation that were not simply alien to the New World but overpoweringly alien:[97]

> Now it is worth noting that the Cross, being unique, brings to us as ministers of the Gospel different difficulties, in fact ones that are quite the opposite to those experienced by the Apostles, in order that we might admire the counsels of God. *For in our case it is the stupidity and the ignorance of the Barbarians* that militates against us, whereas in the case of the Apostles, it was the opposite—the inflated and lofty wisdom of the Jews, the Greeks and above all that of the Romans, making the Apostles seem ridiculous when they presented themselves as uneducated people before the synagogue, the academy and the senate. . . . [The Apostles] were pursued by the powers that be of that time, when the lictors threatened them. Yet we have no fear here of the magistrates who are Barbarians; here the rod of authority lies with the Christians. . . . The Apostles had to struggle against wily, proud and inflexible people, for their manner of life continually rejected the simplicity of the Faith in those times. We, on the other hand, suffer the inconsistency and *the natural stupidity of the*

Indians, obliging us to sow the divine seed in shifting, sandy soil and not on the solid rock like them. Labor without respite, poverty, ignominy, storm and daily dangers of death, wore out the Apostles. We, in turn, are fatigued by boredom, the lack of debate, the lowliness of the inhabitants, the loneliness, depression, and frustration. (*De Procuranda*, I:4, emphasis added)

Acosta invites his readers to gain strength and set their bearings by the holy efforts of the apostles. Acosta translates ancient, non-Christian resistance to the gospel into Indian (that is, barbarian) stupidity, ignorance, and intellectual weakness. It also translates ancient apostolic suffering into contemporary suffering from the lack of intellectual community, the kind which had formed him in the Jesuit order. Acosta is displaying here far more than problems of adjustment to the New World. He draws theology and theological tradition into an evaluative form from which it cannot escape. What comes into effect is a new form of ecclesial habitus in which the performance of theology—in teaching, preaching, writing, and other ministry—becomes the articulation of processes of colonialist evaluation. These processes of evaluation carry within them what Acosta perceives as the soteriological and social distance between himself and his student-barbarians.

Unlike the apostles, whose efforts at converting pagans by sowing gospel seed were productive, Acosta and his brothers will sow gospel seed in what looks to be unproductive sand.[98] The apostles and their challenging world mirror the world of Acosta and his fellow priests, and in this way Acosta and his contemporaries abide with the disciples of Jesus in the same Christian tradition. In Acosta's time and among his barbarians, will the gospel truly take hold in them? Acosta moves theology into this question and then performs the evaluative form unrelentingly in relation to the indigenes. This profound conceptual move must not be interpreted as hatred or disdain for the natives. Acosta understood his actions to be in concert with loving Christian service.[99] Theology would stand over native flesh, calling the natives to a higher form of life. Theology existed in constant evaluative mode, exposing native deficiency: "Doctrine promises rewards that we cannot see, and commands that we scorn and cast aside the goods that we see, and so doctrine transports human feeling to that which is beyond human feeling, and demands that men live a life of angels" (*De Procuranda*, I:3). Regardless of its Neoplatonic overtones, Acosta believed theology draws the student into a new reality, a godly reality. While this is an ancient Christian sensibility, it is also tragic in its form of transposition. Acosta stands conceptually in one place and demands that "the barbarians" move toward him. Acosta's formation in piety, Scholasticism, and Renaissance humanism established in him typical "master patterns of behavioral style" that captured both his theological and spiritual vision as well as his pedagogical performance.[100] At another level, however, something unusually and profoundly distorting is happening here. Acosta transposed his pedagogical dispositions into a new key in the New World. He expanded those dispositions to capture theology itself, theology inside a humanistic pedagogical sensibility.

Christianity is a teaching faith. It carries in its heart the making of disciples through teaching.[101] Yet its pedagogical vision is inside its christological horizon and embodiment, inside its *participatio Christi* and its *imitatio Christi*. The colonialist moment indicates the loss of that horizon and embodiment through its enclosure in exaggerated judgment, hyperevaluation tied to a racial optic. Pedagogical evaluation in the New World set the context within which the theological imagination functioned. Theology was inverted with pedagogy. Teaching was not envisioned inside discipleship, but discipleship was envisioned inside teaching. Pedagogical evaluation was normatively exaggerated, expanded evaluation. The inversion of theology with pedagogy meant that evaluation became the constant operation of what Michel Foucault called the modality of knowledge/power.[102] Through that modality, the native subject was formed into a deficient barbarian in need of continuous external and internal self-examination and evaluation. How well or how poorly the evaluations are done stands inside this human subject–generating discursive formation, and thus those evaluations (good or bad, strong or weak) are simply permutations on a hegemonic pedagogy.[103]

Acosta's evaluative modality is the glue that holds *De Procuranda* together. The six chapters—"Hope That the Indians May Be Saved"; "On the Justice and Injustice of War"; "The Obligations of the Civil Administration"; "The Spiritual Ministers"; "The Catechism and the Method of Catechizing"; and "The Administration of the Sacraments to the Indians"—elaborate the pedagogical challenges facing the formation of Christian subjectivity in the Indians as indeed the white (Spanish) man's burden. Acosta narrates a new vision of Christian suffering, one in which Christians suffer in the New World not with the native inhabitants but with their weaknesses—moral, spiritual, intellectual, and environmental. These native weaknesses engender weaknesses in the Spanish in terms of the deficient Christian workers who are drawn to the New World as well as the corruption of their moral strength. Such a vision of suffering will be repeated countless times as colonialist Christianity grows in the new worlds.

One must not, however, lose sight of the alteration at work in this moment of loss. Colonialism is not the beginning of the loss but is its most exquisitely painful manifestation. If theology becomes the kernel inside a humanist evaluative shell, gauging the possibilities of indigenous Bildung, then what becomes of Christian tradition(s) and what MacIntyre envisions as traditioned inquiry, that is, the ability of a tradition to question itself and generate principle-referential arguments that expose its own internal incoherence? The internal becomes a new kind of internal. Christian traditioned inquiry is not only internal to the practical rationality enabled by its first principles, but now it is also internal to an evaluative modality reborn in awesome power in the New World as colonialist evaluation. However, according to MacIntyre, tradition, in this case Christian tradition(s), carries within itself the apparatus of judgment. This allows Christian tradition(s) to cultivate the ability to make judgments in regard to the excellence of its practices, its practitioners, and even its conceptual tools for making judgments. But the colonialist moment encases this Christian apparatus of judgment in new worldly power.

Christian scholastic and Renaissance humanist intellectual forms join together and harden into an evaluative form that in a real sense stands outside the reach of Christian tradition. Embodied and active in intellectuals such as Acosta and constantly vivified in the presence of subordinate natives, this evaluative form becomes the means through which Christian tradition must be articulated in the New World. This necessity is born of colonial power constituted through the economic circuit and its manufacturing mechanisms. The operation of forming productive workers for the mines, encomiendas, haciendas, the obrajes, and the reducciones merged with the operation of forming theological subjects.

Following Foucault's suggestive ways of reading power, one can see how processes of Christian cultivation not only join easily to those of production, but also signal a comprehensive oversight of the body, especially the native body. The kind of power witnessed in Acosta is an example of what Foucault calls "pastoral power."[104] Pastoral power is a form of power not localized in one position, here the parish priest; rather this power disperses through a network of relations that include the priest, his actions—communicative and symbolic—his response to native actions, and his activity in relation to the actions of others upon native bodies. The central reality in this form of power is that it extends from the communal to the individual, from governmental processes—governmental in the sense of oversight—to mental or internal processes, that is, from heaven to earth, and back again. According to Foucault,

1. It is a form of power whose ultimate aim is to assure individual salvation in the next world.
2. Pastoral power is not merely a form of power that commands; it must also be prepared to sacrifice itself for the life and salvation of the flock. Therefore, it is different from royal power, which demands a sacrifice from its subjects to save the throne.

3. It is a form of power that looks after not just the whole community but each individual in particular, during his entire life.
4. Finally, this form of power cannot be exercised without knowing the inside of people's minds, without exploring their souls, without making them reveal their innermost secrets. It implies a knowledge of the conscience and an ability to direct it.[105]

Foucault understood that pastoral power had, since the eighteenth century, moved beyond its ecclesiastical trappings into a life of its own in the state "as a modern matrix of individualization."[106] Indeed, Foucault's central interests revolve around the modern formation of subjects and the relations of power that constitute reflexive subjectivity. However, his finely grained accounting of power and subject formation helps one recognize the kind of power that flowed through Acosta's evaluative form. More than the creation of subjects, Acosta's pedagogical inversion means that Christian theology has in front of it a false optic, an optical illusion. Acosta reads the New World pedagogically and not theologically, though he imagines he is reading it theologically. Foucault suggests that there is no knowledge and truth outside of power relations and that there are no power relations without the articulations of knowledge and truth. If one takes this suggestion to heart, then Acosta may be seen as articulating not primarily a new form of theology, but theology in a pedagogical form that constantly reimagines the world and especially native subjects by gauging their intelligence and intellectual capacities.

The obsession to understand the New World joins with the assessment of whether native peoples understand what they are being taught, each reinforcing the energy of the other. In Acosta, the Augustinian–Anselmic dictum *faith seeking understanding* mutates into *faith judging intelligence*. The former is not merely a theological slogan of faith; it is a way of perceiving proper Christian intellectual activity as rooted in a faithful response to the revelation of God. That response defines Christian identity not as a quest to verify divine existence or activity in the world, but as an endeavor to understand the world and humankind from the standpoint of belief in God. Faith generates the seeking and enables through grace the understanding.[107] Yet the mutation at work in the New World sets up a condition right in the middle of the faith seeking understanding. That condition refers to the possibility of understanding given the intellectual immaturity and inferiority of New World peoples. Acosta, the Jesuit pedagogue and Aristotelian–Thomist, recognizes that faith is in a fundamental sense a matter of formation, of habit, of training. Acosta believes that natives can be trained in the faith, but only with much struggle, much effort, and with their world shaped in disciplinary realities.

Put bluntly, these disciplinary realities for Acosta transform the New World into one large, ever-expanding classroom with no beginning or ending period, an unrelenting pedagogical eternity. This is the optical illusion, but its effects on native bodies are very real. This is the ground upon which the ideologies of white supremacy will grow: a theologically inverted pedagogical habitus that engenders a colonialist evaluative form that is disseminated through a network of relationships, which together reveal the deep sinews of knowledge and power. In *De Procuranda*, Acosta wishes to juxtapose two disciplinary realities: the holy minister, who embodies and performs doctrine, and a holy community that echoes back that performance, but now made native. Discipline in this sense is not punishment (though punishment is included); rather, following Foucault, discipline is the formation of docile bodies: "Thus discipline produces subjected and practiced bodies, 'docile' bodies. Discipline increases the forces of the body (in economic terms of utility) and diminishes these same forces (in political terms of obedience). In short, it dissociates power from the body; on the one hand, it turns it into an 'aptitude,' a 'capacity,' which it seeks to increase; on the other hand, it reverses the course of the energy, the power that might result from it, and turns it into a relation of strict subjection. If economic exploitation separates the force and the product of labour, let us say that disciplinary coercion establishes in the body the constricting link between an increased aptitude and an increased domination."[108]

It is precisely the kind of discipline Foucault outlines here that Acosta is at pains to try to enlist from the ministers in the New World. Acosta's struggles with the failures of clergy in the New World center on their inability to perform a disciplined life in front of the Indians, one that would foster native imitation. For Acosta, the fact that the clergy's immorality is a massive stumbling block to Indian conversion only intensifies the need to establish coherence between the effectiveness of the gospel in the Old World and life in the New. Throughout *De Procuranda* Acosta desperately reiterates the essential elements he believes will enable the *párrocos* to exhibit a learned piety, purity of life, knowledge of doctrine which will be cultivated by an ongoing reading of the church fathers and knowledge of the Indians' languages and customs (*De Procuranda*, IV:10).

These rabid recommendations mirror not only his Jesuit sensibilities but his life, a life whose intellectual confidence faces the eroding effects of the New World. Acosta blames the lewdness and avarice of the priests on the barbarian women, who are in his opinion "no different from female animals" in their sexuality (IV:14).[109] Native women are like a fire, and Acosta asks, "Who will come out of such a fire unscathed?" He answers, "Only the person that is protected by divine grace, and through daily mortification of the flesh builds a strong wall around himself" (IV:14, also cf. IV:15). This temptation is yet another reason for Acosta's advocacy of the reducciones, which would enable a greater level of control over the native population through the marshaling of priests together for mutual protection against this temptation. Yet Acosta, astonishingly, recognizes the power of the priests and others as itself a temptation: "There is another grave temptation that cannot be overcome without great fortitude of soul. It is the exercise of despotic power over the Indians, who are so used to it and take it for granted, being also slow to oppose it. They give wing to the commands of those who direct them, and carry out at once all that is commanded of them. So, there are many who abuse the submission of their subjects, commanding them harshly, and ordering them about senselessly whenever the mood takes them, for better or worse. . . . Such people are so fond of ordering people about, that they cannot tolerate help from others, even if they might be people of integrity and sound doctrine and experience in the work of the Lord."[110]

Although Acosta does not make the connection between this clear appearance of power and the sexual order of things that his compatriots are enacting in the New World, his acknowledging of this power is no less amazing. To name power in this regard as a temptation is to name not simply an activity of the colonialist but also the very reality within which New World colonialist society will rise from the ground and create the future. Acosta names poor deployment of power as the problem, not the power itself. There is no renunciation of power at work in his critique. Indeed, the deepest offense in this display of the poor use of power is the resistance of priests and others to receive counsel on how properly to handle the natives from theologians like Acosta, people of "integrity and sound doctrine and experience in the work of the Lord" (*De Procuranda*, IV:14). Acosta's comments here expose an erosion of pedagogical possibilities in relation to the Indians. The exercise of such power in this manner precludes a holy *imitatio* between priest and Indian.

Regardless of evidence that erodes confidence in the ministry of the gospel, Acosta remained convinced in *De Procuranda* that theology is crucial to establishing the faith in the New World. Given the newness and tenderness of Christianity in the New World, Acosta believed that "theology [was] of vital importance to root out hereditary errors and defend the newly planted religion" (*De Procuranda*, IV:11). Yet theological governance of the New World depended on pedagogical acumen, and unfortunately, as Acosta concluded, those priests charged with the teaching ministry were quite deficient. They rarely knew the languages of the Indians, brought no energy or creativity to their teaching, and did not know how to build on the pedagogical traditions that formed priests, like the Jesuits in the Old World:

> What *doctrinero*, for example, has ever asked the Indians to explain to him what he was talking about? Who has ever used dialogue as a method of teaching from the known to the unknown? Whenever has an Indian heard these sorts of words from a priest: "Look, remember what I have said. Now I will give you this task to learn in the next three days about who this Christ is that we, the Christians, worship and that you see there, represented in that image. He is God, who reigns in the sky throughout all eternity, and who became man, and came down to earth, to give us the Kingdom of heaven. Now if you answer well, you will get a reward and praise, and if you fail to, you will be punished and humiliated in public." When has that sort of thing ever been done? (*De Procuranda*, IV:3)

As in the Old World, Acosta places the calculus of rewards and punishment within the teaching of theology and the formation of Christian habits. As will be the case throughout his tenure in Peru, Acosta is especially concerned to extirpate idol worship, which thoroughly thwarts the inculcation of theological virtues. He is convinced that effective teaching is the key to rooting out idolatrous habits. In a telling comment, Acosta notes the stubbornness of the natives' commitment to their religion, especially as it relates to their perspectives on nature: "Now, it ought not to be sufficient for the diligent catechist to reject the vanity of idol worship in a general way, but he must also make a specific refutation of gods, *guacas* and superstitions that are common-place in his community. . . . The Indian gazes at the rising sun and greets it; he placates the river that he is going to swim across, asking for benevolence; he observes the squawks or the songs of nocturnal birds and animals; he casts lots about what he plans to do; he offers the first fruits or seeds to the earth; he consecrates his firstborn to the stars; he dedicates marriages with certain songs" (*De Procuranda*, V:10).

Acosta and his theological compatriots slowly but steadily work in this "horrid situation of uncultured barbarity," stripping away Indian idolatry until Christ be formed in the Indian (*De Procuranda*, I:8). Acosta will not allow ignorance, no matter how grotesque, to hinder the work:

> So then we need to teach the Indians, and all other unfaithful people, about the mystery of Christ. To exclude any human lineage from this general principle is a grave error, not to say open heresy. . . . But then you well may ask— What about a person who is incapable, ignorant, stupid, old and decrepit, or some Ethiopian black, thick as two short planks, a bison that is hardly different

from the wild beast? Are you going to oblige them and others like them to learn about the mystery of the Trinity, which is difficult even for the greatest and sharpest of minds? Are you going to require something that goes beyond the capacity of human reason from a person of such stolidity? Well, I say that I am not obliging people to understand the mystery of Christ . . . but I am obliging them all to believe it, which is something that everybody can do, for nobody is incapable of thinking about God and man. It is possible to teach them that God was made man, and that He is Christ. (*De Procuranda*, V:4)

Acosta's quest to teach and thereby create orthodoxy even in those he designates the most ignorant flesh, black Africans, produced a reductive theological vision in which the world's people become perpetual students, even where and when faith is formed. What will grow out of this horrid colonial arrangement is a form of imperialism far more flexible, subtle, and virulent than could be explained by appeals to cultural difference or ethnic chauvinism. This imperialist form drew life from Christianity's lifeblood, from its missionary mandate and its mission reflexes. It was therefore poised to follow its currents all along its geographic length and its nationalist breadth, profoundly marking its body.

ACOSTA AND THE ORIGINS OF PEDAGOGICAL IMPERIALISM

Acosta wrote *De Procuranda* on his way to writing *Historia Natural y Moral de las Indias*. By the time he arrived at the completion of the *Historia*, he was a different man. He left Peru somewhat demoralized: the effectiveness of his tenure as provincial was questioned, and his physical condition was made worse by significant weight gain. Although he left the New World physically weaker, he attained greater power upon his return to Europe, becoming an advisor to both the king and the pope and at last becoming a serious ecclesiastical powerbroker. Acosta had fulfilled the promise of his youth.

Acosta's work is an outstanding example of the intellectual journey Christian theological traditions will take in the New World. Tradition here is understood as an intellectual process guided by constant consultation with ancient Christian texts, a practical rationality whereby judgments that reflect the inner logic of Christian identity and story are made, and a way of envisioning the world scripturally. This tradition, in the hands of Acosta and many like him, became docetic. If Docetism is the denial of Christ's materiality, of his becoming fully human, then this form of Docetism is Christian tradition faltering in the face of a new materiality. In one sense, the form of denial here is incarnational, in that divine presence was denied while demonic presence was claimed in the places and peoples of the new worlds. Rendering the material demonic is certainly intrinsic to this Docetism, yet what is at heart docetic in traditioned theological reasoning in the new worlds is its failure to discern its new spatial situation.

Christian intellectual life draws back in the face of this newness. Traditioned intellection fails to enter into the spatial and landscape logics of these new peoples. The first denial is not of incarnational presence but of incarnational practice. It's not that Christian intellectuals entering the new worlds of Africa and the Americas were capable of claiming or should have claimed divine presence in those worlds beyond the possibilities inherent in natural law theorization.[111] Given the hermeneutics of providence and idolatry, such a modern theological claim of divine presence would have been a very far reach for Acosta and theologians like him. And as I shall consider in subsequent chapters, claiming divine presence after the advent of the colonialist moment has been fraught with thorny problems. With those problems comes the danger of claiming divine presence without its appropriate christological mediation. The point here is the continuation of the logic of the incarnation. Incarnational logic here is not analogical but participatory; it is the logic of discipleship and mission, the going forth in the triune name. The denial of incarnational practice is precisely the failure to go forward as the Son came forward and wishes to go forward in intimate joining. An intimate joining, conceptual and nonviolent, would have been challenging though possible simply because these worlds, old and new, while different shared some basic sensibilities.[112]

Unfortunately, with the seizure of land and the destruction of the connections between native spatial logics and identities, the possibilities of cultural intimacy configured around landscape were never to be realized. Christian intellectual tradition in the New World denies its most fundamental starting point, that of the divine Word entering flesh in time and space to become Jewish flesh. Such denial was certainly not inevitable. Not only were the cultural logics of the Iberian world close enough to those of the native peoples of Africa and the Americas that deeper forms of imaginative connection and conceptual merger were possible, but Christian intellectuals such as Acosta had in front of them one of Christian history's most powerful moments of conceptual, intimate joining, that is, the use of Aristotle.

Acosta learned from his teachers why and how the thought of the philosopher Aristotle and his culture's way of imagining life might be used to clarify Christian vision. Acosta entered a Christian tradition in the West that had found a profound way to step inside the inner logics of Aristotelian thought. The appropriation, however, of Aristotelian thought could only have been a partial example because that appropriation lacked the spatial dimensions present in the

New World situation. To enter a new land was to enter a newness that required careful listening to the rhythms of creation played by the indigenous peoples so that the sounds of Christian witness might be joined in harmony (with its proper dissonances) with those rhythms. Moreover, to enter a new land was to touch the skin of a people, joining skin to skin, with the inevitability of being changed, of being transformed, not simply by the people but by creation itself.

Where spatial coevalness was denied, however, the temporal dimensions of Christian intellectual tradition and the desire for orthodoxy became overdetermined and rendered a pedagogical nightmare. The native peoples of the world received a Christianity exaggerated in evaluative habit and poised to merge brutality with intellectual formation. It would create a deeply troubled theological subjectivity. Yet native peoples became Christian. Native peoples remain Christian in large numbers. However, the question becomes, what kind of Christianity, given these realities of displacement, have they received? What kind of Christianity has been possible given the advent of the racialized structures of human existence? And most important, what kind of vision of Christian intellectual life could be formed in the shadow of this pedagogical imperialism? A more nuanced reading of Christianity and orthodoxy here might prefer to speak of Christianities and various visions of orthodoxy. Indeed, as Protestants enter the colonialist picture one sees different configurations of Christianity and different valances of orthodoxy. One could also discern differences in approach to native subjects by the different religious orders, different personalities in those orders, and different popes. However, my argument does not presuppose a monolithic vision of Christianity or orthodoxy. It does presuppose a consistent commitment by various Christian communities to form theological subjectivity along the lines witnessed in Acosta.

It could be argued that colonialism does show cultural intimacy and joining, but this is surely the kind of joining that is assimilationist and that created what Walter Mignolo, following the insights of Frantz Fanon, termed the "colonial wound":

> Coloniality names the experiences and views of the world and history of those whom Fanon called *les damnés de la terre* ("the wretched of the earth," those who have been, and continue to be, subjected to the standards of modernity). The wretched are defined by the *colonial wound*, and the colonial wound, physical and/or psychological, is a consequence of *racism*, the hegemonic discourse that questions the humanity of all those who do not belong to the locus of enunciation (and the geo-politics of knowledge) of those who assign the standards of classification and assign to themselves the right to classify. The

blindness toward histories and experiences lying outside the local history of Western Christianity, as shown by secular Europeans, grounded in the Greek and Latin languages, and unfolded in the six vernacular imperial languages (Italian, Spanish, Portuguese, French, German, and English), has been and continues to be a trademark of intellectual history and its ethical, political, and economic consequences.[113]

The colonial wound is real and remains largely untheorized within Western Christian theology, with one major exception. Three hundred and seventy-seven years after Acosta returned to Spain from Peru, a young Peruvian priest named Gustavo Gutiérrez, who began his formal education at the university founded by Viceroy Toledo and where Acosta had taught for a brief time, the University of San Marcos, wrote what would become one of the seminal texts in liberation theology, A *Theology of Liberation*, printed in Lima.[114] One cannot appreciate the historical significance of Gutiérrez's work or of that of the other forms of liberationist thought without understanding the legacy of José de Acosta. Neither can one really make sense of Christian theology or Christian intellectual life since colonialism without reckoning with theologians such as Acosta. Yet one would be hard-pressed to find even a small treatment of Acosta in standard systematic or historical theological texts offered up in theological educational institutions and programs in religious studies.

Acosta is missing from standard theological texts not because of simple intellectual oversight, but because he exposes the imperialist matrix within which orthodox Christian tradition continues to exist. The work of Acosta and of many theologians like him remains relegated to missionary texts, or mission or intercultural studies texts, or even early ethnography or anthropological texts, not, as it should be, to standard texts on the performance of theology in the New World. Such a performance demands far more analysis and reflection. Theologians must strongly reject the current pedagogical schemas that separate missionary texts from theological texts, missiology from theology, both historical and systematic. The current practice of teaching systematic theology (and all its varieties—dogmatic, pastoral, and so forth—and all its historical epochs) and then of teaching missions (historically conceived) or intercultural studies or both as separate realities only slightly related may in some instances be pedagogically defensible, but ultimately it is immoral in the current situation.

The immorality here lies in the loss of historical consciousness: the world of theology and the theological world of Christianity changed with the moment of discovery of the new worlds. The global situation that is thrust on theology from 1444, when Prince Henry surveyed his first cargo of slaves, forward has rarely made its way into how theologians, historical or systematic, have told the story of theology as it entered the modern world and changed in the Enlightenment. It has therefore not made its way into how theological education and the formation of Christian intellectual life continue to function in the Western world. There remains in many of the pedagogies of Western theological education a deep form of alienation that reaches back to the conceptual arrangements of Acosta. Theologians are still at a loss to grasp the deeper connections between theology on the ground in the New World and theology in the Old World. Theology was sealed off from the theology on the ground of the priests and the merchants. Freed from being asked to make sense of the New World and the world's new flesh, theologians turned their attention to safeguarding or refashioning Christian intellectual life as that life entered the deep waters of modernity. Yet before the advent of the Enlightenment and all it would signify, a Jesuit theologian stood on a ship in deep water bound for Lima, and there on that ship he laughed. Moderns have yet to reckon with his laugh.

Part II

TRANSLATION

3

COLENSO'S HEART

John William Colenso set foot on the shores of Durban at Port Natal, in what is now South Africa, on Monday, January 30, 1854. This newly minted bishop of the Anglican Church was about to begin one of the most important odysseys of a missionary bishop in the history of the Christian church. The world of Bishop Colenso was far removed from that of José de Acosta. Colenso was an Anglican bishop of the nineteenth century, shaped by a Protestant church and an England still feeling the effects of the French Revolution, immersed in the industrial revolution and in the intellectual revolution that was the Enlightenment. Acosta was a Jesuit of the late fifteenth century, shaped by a Roman Catholic Church and a Spain being transformed by the discoveries of new worlds and troubled by the overturning of ecclesial life brought about under the Protestant Reformation. Yet both were missionaries at the emergence of two nation-states, successive global world powers, and both entered new worlds as those worlds were being radically transformed.

COLENSO'S FIRE: THE CRUCIBLE OF A TRANSLATOR

The forty-year-old man who came to Natal as its first Anglican bishop in 1854 had not had an easy life. The untimely death of his mother and the financial collapse of his father's business meant that young John had been largely responsible for raising his younger siblings. His early life was defined by unrelenting hard work, but also by an innate intelligence and abiding academic ambition. At St. John's College, Cambridge, he distinguished himself as a brilliant student, particularly in mathematics, and as an extremely overworked student owing to his chronic financial situation. Yet John was from the beginning a very serious Christian, and his commitment to his faith and the church deepened as he progressed through his education.[1]

Colenso's intellectual vision was shaped by the theological romanticism of Samuel Taylor Coleridge and Frederick Denison Maurice. These two thinkers, introduced to him by the young woman who would become his lifelong companion, Sarah Frances Colenso (née Bunyon), drew his vision out from the Protestant evangelicalism of his early years into a wider theological imagination characterized by Enlightenment sensibilities.

Coleridge introduced him to the idea of a universal religious consciousness that only needs to be accessed inwardly to establish its validity. In this regard, Coleridge's views had much in common with the thought of the great German Romantic theologian Friedrich Schleiermacher. The Christian God articulated by Coleridge was not dependent on proofs, evidence, or demonstrations. As Coleridge says in his famous text *Aids to Reflection*, "All the (so called) demonstrations of a God either prove too little, as that from the order and apparent purpose in Nature; or too much, namely, that the World is itself God."[2] Coleridge offered Colenso an intuitive faith that gently but firmly drew space between itself and the Scriptures, releasing the Bible from service as the basis of Christian faith itself.[3]

In a telling passage that presages much of Colenso's intellectual journey, Coleridge comments on the meaning of the well-known text "There is no other name under heaven by which a man can be saved, but the name of Jesus" and offers a view of the moral Bible, a Bible freed from literalist interpretation and drawn into a wider pedagogical vision:

> It is true and obligatory for every Christian community and for every individual believer, wherever the opportunity is afforded of spreading the *Light* of the Gospel, and making known the name of the only Saviour and Redeemer. For even though the uninformed Heathens should *not* perish, the *guilt* of their perishing will attach to those who not only had no certainty of their safety, but who are commanded to *act* on the supposition of the contrary. But if, on the other hand, a theological dogmatist should attempt to persuade me, that this text was intended to give us an historical knowledge of God's future actions and dealings—and for the gratification of our curiosity to inform us, that Socrates and Phocion, together with all the savages in the woods and wilds of Africa and America, will be sent to keep company with the Devil and his angels in everlasting torments—I should remind him, that the purpose of Scripture was to teach us our duty, not to enable us to sit in judgment on the souls of our fellow creatures.[4]

Coleridge inserts the peoples of Africa and America as tropes for those at the farthest edge of soteriological possibility. They are the "uninformed Heathens" who, along with Socrates and Phocion, had been relegated in the dominant theological systems of his day to damnation and tormenting hell. Coleridge had little patience for such an inadequate idea of the reality of the divine. His compelling intellectual vision grew out of his deep and abiding involvement with the thought of Immanuel Kant and the German Idealist tradition articulated in the works of Johann Gottlieb Fichte, Friedrich Schelling, and Schleiermacher. Kant's profound reformulation of what constituted adequate theological speech found exciting articulation in Coleridge, who channeled the sensibilities of German Romanticism into English. Most notably, Coleridge not only enabled religious consciousness and Enlightenment reason to happily coexist but also suggested that reason properly understood manifests religious consciousness. Unlike pre-Kantian visions of religious truth based on objective metaphysical truth, Coleridge echoed Kant's critique of such thinking and invited people to turn inward in order to locate the source of the truth of religion. Colenso will carry forward this Coleridgean critique of the older (pre-Kantian) theological vision as well as the deployment of Africans as tropes of damnation to indicate a kind of theological vulgarity.

Maurice offered Colenso a breathtaking vision of a loving Father-God, one whose power flows through indefatigable love. For Maurice, the divine presence in the world was already a saving presence: "The truth is that every man is in Christ; the condemnation of every man is, that he will not own the truth; he will not act as if this were true, he will not believe that which is the truth, that, except he were joined to Christ, he could not think, breath, live a single hour."[5] From Maurice, Colenso inherited this christological universalism, which greatly shaped his powerful humanitarian sensibilities. He also gained from Maurice, himself a disciple of Coleridge, a vision of theology and Christian doctrines driven by an overarching moralist hermeneutic. All theological statements and doctrinal axioms, if they are rooted in universal truth, issue really only in lessons for the moral life.[6] The goal of theological statements is to deepen one's understanding of the moral structure of human existence. In this way, doctrinal statements in the powerful construal of Maurice drew attention to humans' life together and the formation of their character. Much in line with German Romanticism, Maurice envisioned religion and religious language's central purpose to more clearly express the authentic human person in his or her individuality and universality. Thus Christian doctrine functioned inside a kind of circularity. That is, theology and doctrine, as the articulations of universal moral truth, only completed what was already possible to know, even if in embryonic form, through nature. Colenso seized on this moralist hermeneutic and explicated a vision of God that did not require doctrine with any metaphysical density for the formation of Christian identity.

Colenso, however, arrived in Natal not simply a budding theologian; he was also a translator come to Africa to convert and educate. He came to the colony of Natal, nestled on the eastern seaboard of southern Africa between the majestic Drakensberg Mountains to the west and the Indian Ocean to the east and between the Thukela River to the north and the Mzimkhulu River to the south. It was home to many peoples, including the Zulu people. In the face of the ubiquitous presence of Europeans, the many peoples that traditionally inhabited that region had seen and were seeing their ancient worlds collapse and reemerge fundamentally changed.

The peoples of this region were being squeezed on all sides by Europeans. The Portuguese presence to the northeast and especially at Delagoa Bay had for decades before Colenso's arrival disrupted life by drawing native peoples into detrimental trading practices involving ivory, hides, maize, and slaves. The Portuguese inserted their hunting and trading practices into an already fragile ecological system that saw, in the years prior to Colenso's arrival, environmental strain through drought and famine. Portuguese hunting and trading also affected sociopolitical systems easily manipulated through trade. These capitalist operations resulted in stimulation of tribal conflict and reconfiguration and ultimately in the disruption and displacement of peoples.[7] The British presence in the southeast and the Boer/Voortrekker presence in the south-southwest created an unrelenting appetite for land and laborers that drove ever-increasing patterns of deception, subterfuge, manipulation, injustice, and violence. Armed with weapons given to them by the British and Dutch, and often in collusion with them, the Griqua, Kora peoples and other armed horsemen based on the southwest middle Orange and lower Vaal rivers descended upon unsuspecting peoples, raiding and killing and taking prisoners who would become laborers for the British and Boer colonialists.[8] Chiefs, tribes, and individuals were also being placed in a moral universe controlled by white opinion displayed in print media. The morality or immorality of every African was determined by how much he supported white interests, accepted European culture, and yielded land, labor, and life to European control.[9]

Furthermore, by the time of Colenso's arrival, settler and merchant interests were beginning to narrate their presence as salvific, bringing order to chaos and cultivation to empty, uninhabited lands. They attributed the chaos to the legacy of a Zulu chief, Shaka Senzangakhona, and his terrorist behavior. What would soon come to be designated as the *Mfecane*, "the crushing, the destroying," in which Shaka and the Zulus were interpreted as the central cause of disruption, disorder, displacement, and death in the region, had its beginning in European discursive control of the multiple narratives Africans themselves told of intertribal conflict and war. Shaka was only one of many excuses used by the white settlers for aggressively seizing lands and pulling peoples from the hands of "despotic chiefs" and into labor systems.[10] African agency was intact; there were intertribal conflicts, war, violence, and death as chiefs constantly sought to consolidate power, establish stability, and ensure the peace and prosperity of their peoples. However, African agency was always articulated ultimately by settlers and settler-merchants, who made sure that the grand narrative performed in England and in other communication centers of the Old World juxtaposed African despotism to white benevolence.

The colony of Natal was saturated with two interrelated forms of desire: the merchant and the missionary. Settler existence began in 1824 with the entrepreneurial interests of traders from the Cape colony to the southwest. Francis Farewell and Henry Francis Fynn, along with other merchants, came in search of trade agreements with Shaka, the Zulu king. The Boer gained control of the colony and the surrounding area after a bloody conflict with the Zulu and the defeat of the Zulu king, Dingane kaSenzangakhona, son of Shaka. They had named the spoils of their war the Republic of Natalia. But the Boer victory was short-lived. The colony became property of the British crown in 1842 after the British pushed out the Boer/Voortrekker. British involvement in this area was at first less than enthusiastic because Natal was not considered an area brimming with lucrative possibilities. But the British believed that Boer expansion was a threat that merited their military intervention. Natal, however, struggled to fully integrate itself into the imperial economy.[11]

Caught in the middle of all this were the many native peoples. The attempt to reestablish and refashion themselves became a permanent characteristic of their existence. On the one hand people were trying to maintain precolonial African institutions with chiefs, *indunas*, headmen or chiefly councilors, and *ibutho*, age-grouped men or women who served the chief by carrying out various duties. Indigenes, who functioned without that kind of institution, wished to remain free of chiefs while maintaining common traditions and practices. On the other hand, the white settler presence had brought the entire region into a capitalist system such that no native agricultural practice or tradition involving the land would go untouched or unaltered. All the land and animals, especially the cattle, came steadily under settler influence or control.

The settlers exploited Natal as a significant entrepôt. Because of the linkages between farming efforts and trade, native inhabitants' lives were steadily woven into ever-expanding commercial networks. White settlers' aggressive desire to make life profitable in Natal was matched only by their impatience with indigenous landowners as their direct competition in trade and farming. Moreover, white settlers' need for laborers was feverish, and Africans outside of their control were a source of deep frustration. These Africans, for their part, were increasingly displaced even on their own ancestral lands. Pursued by land speculation companies such as the London-based Natal and Colonization Company, which allegedly owned hundreds of thousands of acres, many displaced peoples found themselves living the lives of squatters and tenants. Many contracted as labor tenants for white farmers, or they rented land and were subject to arbitrary rules, laws, and evictions.[12]

The land and native life were also steadily woven into missionary networks. Between 1835 and 1880, there were at least seventy-five mission stations covering the Natal, Zululand, and Mpondoland, missions representing a host of denominations, including Methodist, Scottish Presbyterian, Roman Catholic, Lutheran, Church of England, Congregational, and American Presbyterian. German, Swedish, Portuguese, English, Dutch, and American missionaries spread across the Natal landscape building churches and schools and proselytizing Africans.[13] Some societies worked closely with colonization and land companies such as the Joseph Byrne Emigration and Colonization Company, establishing enterprising settlers and planting missionaries in one single operation. This is the world that John Colenso, bishop and translator, entered.

It would be impossible to understand the life and actions of Bishop Colenso in his new world without considering the one man who had the single greatest effect on his life and that world, Theophilus Shepstone. There were others who were important in Colenso's life—his fiercely intelligent wife, Frances Colenso; the presiding bishop of Cape Town, Robert Gray, with whom Colenso was to wage the theological struggle that was to define his public image in England; and William Ngidi, with whom he studied the Zulu language and who was to become a crucial figure in Colenso's theological program. All were crucial, yet in truth, Shepstone is the necessary hermeneutical horizon upon which to grasp the theological vision Colenso enacted in the new world of Africa. Indeed it would be quite appropriate to characterize the young bishop's early years in Natal as the Colenso–Shepstone years. Upon Colenso's arrival in Natal, the two men quickly became close and began what looked to be a deep and abiding friendship.

Shepstone was in many ways the ideal companion for a missionary translator come to a strange new world. He was the son of a Wesleyan missionary, John William Shepstone, who shared the same first and middle names as his newfound friend. Theophilus grew up in Methodist itinerancy in the Cape colony. This meant that home for him and his siblings had been in Bathurst, Theopolis, Grahamstown, Wesleyville, Morley, and a host of other places on the Cape. It also meant that Theophilus's gift of language acquisition was to become quite useful as he mastered the Nguni languages, that family of languages spoken by the many groups that inhabit what is now southern Africa. By the age of fourteen, Theophilus was already aiding missionaries in translation work.[14] He was also to serve with distinction as an interpreter for colonial officials and the military. A deeply devout Christian man, Shepstone understood missionary life and what was necessary for it to thrive. Moreover, he had gained intimate knowledge of native practices, cultural logics, and belief systems that he used to great effect. So when Colenso found Shepstone in Pietermaritzburg at the beginning of his first visit to Natal in 1854, he thought he had discovered a gift set in place for him by God.

One must understand Colenso and Shepstone as two translators. Although it would be several years before Colenso gained mastery of the Zulu language and Nguni language systems, the work of translation was mirrored in the lives of these two men, with one significant difference: Shepstone translated much more than Christianity into native worlds. He stood at the center of the translation of native worlds into European hegemony. Shepstone was in charge in Natal. Colenso's early years in Natal were just the opposite of the period of very strained relationship between the theologian Acosta and the Christian colonial ruling agent Viceroy Toledo. Colenso and Shepstone were two sides of the same coin, joined in the same process, translation. Colenso brought Christianity into vernacular languages, and Shepstone used vernacular languages to bring the natives into colonial existence. Colenso had willingly and with great joy stepped into the Shepstone system.

In 1846, at the age of twenty-eight, Theophilus Shepstone (whose first name means "lover of God" in Greek) became the diplomatic agent to the native tribes of Natal. Later named secretary for native affairs, Shepstone ruled the colony for thirty years. His Nguni name, Somtsewu, means "Father of Whiteness."[15] And as the great white power, Shepstone put in place a system of control, masterful in its use of native logics. The historian Jeff Guy suggests that the reason Colenso and Shepstone became fast friends was not only because they were close in age and personality, but also because they shared a vision of how to move African society forward:

> Shepstone and Colenso held that the proper answers to the challenges created in a rapidly changing social situation should be found in the utilisation

of older social forms. Shepstone argued that it was necessary to retain and develop those aspects of African life which did not conflict with civilised standards and that care had to be taken not to provoke the African into resistance
by violently changing his way of life. From Maurice, Colenso had learnt that
the good worked by the presence of God could be discovered in all men, and
that the missionary had to identify this and build upon it—not destroy everything in an attempt to rout that which was abominable.[16]

Guy surmises that Colenso and Shepstone shared a native anthropology:
"Colenso had rejected the idea of hopelessly fallen man, Shepstone the totally
barbarous one. It was upon this that their friendship was founded."[17] While this
sunny summation of their comparable conceptual dispositions may be true, it
also points toward the deeper strategies of paternalistic manipulation that will
characterize the Shepstone system and mark South African life right up to and
through the apartheid years.

Shepstone bore a reputation as an expert on the native mind, a reputation he
endlessly cultivated through his administrative machinations. One sees in Shepstone the outcome of linking language mastery to whiteness. In one way, his mastery of native dialects joined the work of the missionary and that of the colonial
agent in the colonization of language. Yet in another way, his language mastery
shows the growth of colonialist operations from missionary roots. It would certainly be unfair to paint these missionaries as nothing more than colonialists.
However, one must not miss the point of the unintended consequences of language acquisition and the cultivation of intimate relations. Personal (missionary)
knowledge is put to colonialist use. As he transitioned from a missionary translator and helper to colonial interpreter to colonial agent to the central power
running the colony, Shepstone was poised to build the colonialist system on top
of existing native networks. This was the heart of his system.

Shepstone's deepest impulse was to gain full control of the African. His initial
plan, which was rejected by the colonial office for its cost, was to place all Africans on reservations under the strict control of white magistrates.[18] What Shepstone ultimately managed to do was place a canopy of British administrative and
judicial structure on top of precolonial African institutions.[19] What this meant
was that Shepstone himself would become the (operational) chief of chiefs, with
everyone under him—resident magistrates, administrators of native law, chiefs,
indunas, and headmen. On the surface this system appeared to respect context, indigenous life and custom. In truth it was a system of profound control.
Africans would be governed by native law administered by indunas, under the
guidance of chiefs. Above the chiefs, overseeing the administration of native law,

were the white magistrates and administrators, and over them all was Shepstone, the lieutenant-governor (the supreme chief), and the Legislative Council. Shepstone ensured loyalty throughout the system by returning a portion of the fees, fines, and in-kind penalties (for example, cattle) to chiefs and indunas as payment for administering justice. But the demonic genius of the system lay in its taxation schema.

Many white settlers and farmers, especially those from inland farms and villages, despised Shepstone and his system of distributing land to Africans. They believed he favored the Africans by granting land rights, allowing them to live on tribal lands as well as on land owned by land companies, and by allowing them to participate in the emerging market economy. All of which meant that Shepstone's policies created a small, stagnant pool of black labor. On the surface, his policies did give the appearance of leaving the Africans' ways of life intact, but in truth Shepstone had chained African ways of life tightly to capitalism. He taxed almost everything associated with the everyday practices of indigenous life. Chiefs had to pay a hut tax calibrated to the number of huts in their villages; an increase in the number of huts through population growth meant increased taxes. There were fees for marriage and divorce, and fines for violations of policies and laws. But the greatest revenue scheme involved the custom duties on imported goods. Through the Legislative Council, Shepstone was able to place charges on goods that were used exclusively by Africans, while goods used by white settlers carried slight charges or were duty free. Goods bound for inland Africans also were priced higher.

On the one hand, Africans earned money by supplying food to the markets through backbreaking labor on their land, by trading within a trading system unfair to them, and by working for white employers under conditions that matched and exceeded the harshness of life in England during the emergence of industrial capitalism. Furthermore, they were taxed far more than the white settlers. As the historian Norman Etherington notes, "Whenever more revenue was needed, new charges were levied on African consumer goods."[20] Indeed, the government was paid for on the backs of Africans.[21]

The powerful coastal farmers and merchants, overseas businessmen, and colonial companies in England all appreciated Shepstone and his policies. They understood he had achieved a remarkable level of social stability and financial solvency through his operations. Indeed, Shepstone ambitiously promoted his system as a model transferable to other parts of Africa.

It is not clear whether Bishop Colenso could see at the beginning of his life in Natal the devil in the details of the Shepstone system. What is clear is that Colenso agreed in principle with Shepstone's policies because he was at heart, like Shepstone, a British citizen deeply committed to the colonialist civilizing project in Africa, and he was shaped to read African societies through white paternalism. Yet from the very beginning of his time in Natal, Colenso demonstrated that he was not perfectly aligned with the Shepstone way of treating the native peoples. During his first ten-week journey in Natal, Bishop Colenso recounted the events of February 10. On that day he went with Shepstone and his aide to survey the land a few miles outside of Pietermaritzburg where he would build his episcopal residence, Bishopstowe. Upon his return to the city, he learned that a native worker had been crushed by a stone. Bishop Colenso was moved as he observed the grief of the dead man's brother and found the bond between himself and the Africans growing closer. It was after this event that Ngoza, one of Shepstone's native headmen, wanted to pay his respects to Colenso. The event of their meeting typifies the colonial operation as well as Colenso's ambiguous relationship to it. Colenso had been advised to "keep the Kafir waiting." After he dressed, he stepped into the courtyard where Ngoza was waiting:

> In due time, I stepped out to him, and there stood Ngoza, dressed neatly enough as an European, with his attendant Kafir waiting beside him. I said nothing (as I was advised) until he spoke, and, in answer to a question from Mr. Green, said that he was come to salute the inKos'. "Sakubona," I said; and with all my heart would have grasped the great black hand, and given it a good brotherly shake: but my dignity would have been essentially compromised in his own eyes by any such proceeding. I confess it went very much against the grain; but the advice of all true Philo-Kafirs, Mr. Shepstone among the rest, was to the same effect—viz. that too ready familiarity, and especially shaking hands with them upon slight acquaintance . . . did great mischief in making them pert and presuming. Accordingly, I looked aside with a grand indifference as long as I could, (which was not very long,) and talked to Mr. G., instead of paying attention to the Kafir's presence.[22]

Colenso entered the courtyard in the colonialist persona. Ngoza in European dress stood in front of Colenso, while Colenso, by instruction, minimized his presence by ignoring him. Silence, indifference, and indirect speech all performed the colonialist relation, and the bishop enacted it perfectly, except that the actions did not quite fit him. He wanted to shake Ngoza's hand, he could not sustain the look of indifference for long, and in the end he spoke directly to him, in benediction, as he left, "*hamba kahle*—walk pleasantly," to which Ngoza replied, "*tsala kahle*—sit pleasantly."[23]

After his initial reconnaissance tour of Natal, Colenso returned to England to gather his mission party. In May of 1855, Bishop John William Colenso returned to his new home. He made his way to Pietermaritzburg and then to Bishopstowe, where his historic tenure officially began. The colony held about six thousand whites and over one hundred thousand Africans. Given that the colony had two major cities, the port city of Durban and, fifty miles away, Pietermaritzburg, the seat of the government, and comprised thousands of square miles, the bishop had his work cut out for him. At Bishopstowe, Colenso began his ambitious project to establish the mission station, Ekukhanyeni (meaning the Place or Home of Light or Enlightenment). He envisioned that Ekukhanyeni would impart the best of European civilization. It would offer training in agriculture and mechanics, which would form farmers and artisans with skills vital to the colony. It would teach reading and writing and cultivate intellectual excellence.[24]

It was no accident that Bishopstowe stood in the shadow of the magnificent Table Mountain. John and Frances Colenso fell deeply in love with the area, the view of the mountain, the slopes and hills of the land, the sounds of the land, and the breathtaking beauty of its sunrises and sunsets. The beauty and power of Bishopstowe and the view of the mountain, which Frances called "that majestic altar," centered Colenso's dreams and work.[25] Also central to the bishop's dreams and work was the translation of the Bible into the language of the people. To this he turned considerable energy. One of the first structures erected at Bishopstowe was a hexagonal summer house, which was lined inside with bookshelves. There Colenso would sit with his native informants, that is, his language teachers, and do the difficult, painstaking work of learning the language and translating. The bishop carried on a full slate of pastoral duties: teaching, preaching every Sunday, visiting, church administration, missionary fundraising, and looking for and cultivating priests. But he understood the center of his mission to be translation.

Colenso strongly believed that the gospel must be preached and presented to the natives in their own language. This was the hallmark of the Protestant Reformation and the central energy behind the translation endeavor of every Protestant mission. Ministry must be in the vernacular of the common people. Everything revolved around understanding native words and presenting a Christian world in those words. Colenso's insight was far deeper than he realized. Indeed, his intuition was going to place him in unimaginable difficulty and unanticipated suffering. Yet his work of translation exposed an unbroken thread that tied his life together, from his early days as the principal caretaker of his younger siblings, through his years of struggle at Cambridge, to the summer house: unrelenting hard work.[26]

Showing frustration with those who did not understand the hard work, necessary patience, and great urgency of translating, Colenso wrote, "I have no special gift for languages, but what is shared by most educated men of fair ability.

What I have done, I have done by hard work—by sitting with my natives day after day . . .—conversing with them as well as I could, and listening to them conversing,—writing down what I could of their talk from their own lips. . . . [P]icture to yourself what it is to have the whole Diocese waiting for books in the Native Language, which I must personally not only make and write, but make as *correct* as possible in the minutest detail, and be as careful to the *printing* as I must to the *writing*, (to say nothing of the cares of a household of some 70 souls)."[27] Colenso gained through struggle what Shepstone had through birth, namely, access to the everyday speech of the native peoples. Colenso also gained access to a space in which his nascent theological vision would encounter the thoughts and hopes, the pain and suffering of Africans. This was a place where the possibilities of "resistance and new consciousness may emerge."[28] It was also a place where the subterranean cracks in his synthesis of the British colonial project, his theological vision, his ecclesial identity and commitments, and his commitment to the implementation of Shepstone's colonial system began to show.

As he began his work of translation, Colenso was still greatly enamored of Shepstone's vision of managing African flesh. He was wholly convinced that Shepstone's pipe dream of setting up an African colony in Zululand with himself as chief and Colenso as spiritual director was an urgently needed plan of action to address the "overcrowding" of Natal with native refugees. This "black kingdom" would be a model city displaying the civilizing and Christianizing effects of careful planning and engineering of native lives.[29] If the massive contradictions in the Shepstone system were concealed to Colenso when he began his translation work, it is because his mind was preoccupied with the theological revolution that was forming in his thinking. As he shared space with black bodies, space born in speaking and listening, the theological seeds planted by Coleridge and Maurice began to grow and take new shape. Fully a man of his time, he was also in many ways ahead of his time.

Colenso's time was not a great one for Christian missions in southern Africa. Most missionaries in the colony were moving inextricably toward supporting full-blown British imperialism and the stark segregation of the races. Such movement was due to the fact that few denominations were having overwhelming success in converting large numbers of natives. Most mission stations were modest affairs, and the people who usually came to and inhabited mission stations were the outcasts of African societies—homeless, displaced natives and those seeking refuge from chiefs or clans. Mission stations stood between worlds—Christian and non-Christian, European and African—and created tensions between those worlds. Those Africans who became *ikholwa* or *kholw*, Christian converts, were caught between two worlds.

These Christians converts were estranged from and resisted by both worlds, but especially by the white settler world, which saw them as one of their greatest threats. They represented the success of strategies of Western domesticity. Increasingly educated, economically able and savvy, socially and politically ambitious, the kholwa represented the possibility of full inclusion, biracial community, and equality. For the many chiefs within the Shepstone system, the kholwa presented subversive elements, people who resisted the old ways, especially the authority of chiefs to guide their lives. By whites, they were denied full citizenship in the colony, especially the right to vote and freedom from the jurisdiction and demands of chiefdoms. By blacks, they were shunned, ostracized, and held in suspicion.[30] The kholwa consequently failed to prosper in the colonial world of Natal, their lives witnessing a system set to deny the very thing it claimed to promote: Christian civilization. If the kholwa exposed the deepest contradiction of the colonialist Christian vision, it was not a contradiction that factored into the missional or pedagogical vision of Bishop Colenso.

For Colenso, Ekukhanyeni was a place of vision. He approached his Zulu students as people who were to be prepared to lead their nation and participate in a universal human society. Drawn to this school were John and William Ngidi and Magema Magwaza Fuze. John and William Ngidi had been converted by an American missionary who employed them as assistants. When that missionary died, John and William looked for new employment and came to Colenso and Ekukhanyeni. William Ngidi and Magema Fuze became Bishop Colenso's primary assistants, but the term *assistant* does not capture the impact of their lives on Colenso. He enlisted them as conversation partners who not only were learning how to read and write in both English and isiZulu but who were also publishing their own work.

Bishop Colenso began the education of Africans on a footing that was unprecedented. On a trip to visit the Zulu king, Mpande, Colenso encouraged the students who were accompanying him—Magema Fuze, Ndiane Ngubane, and now assistant teacher William Ngidi—to keep journals of the visitation. Those journals, published in 1860 as *Three Native Accounts of the Visit of the Bishop of Natal in September and October, 1859, to Umpande, King of the Zulus*, were among the first English/isiZulu texts written by natives.[31] Another important text published at Ekukhanyeni was Magema Fuze's *Abantu Abamnyama, Lapa Bavela Ngakona (The Black People and Whence They Came)*, considered the first book written by a Zulu in his native dialect.[32] These fruits of mission labor are crucial because they indicate that the trajectory Colenso's Africans students were on was toward self-articulation.

Colenso granted the students access to a workbench in the building of European discursive operations, to the literary weapons of warfare and defense, to the tools for engaging in emancipatory politics, and to the building blocks of nationalist existence. Indeed, Colenso could be appropriately construed as the spiritual father of a particular moment and region of African literary consciousness. However, all his efforts were under the canopy of preparing proper colonial subjects. The central plan shaping the educational mission of Ekukhanyeni was Shepstonian in nature. Shepstone convinced him that success at the mission required a top-down approach, which meant that Colenso would seek to educate the first sons (and a few daughters) of chiefs. The philosophy was straightforward: where the British-educated head goes, the native bodies will follow. British education, in the hands of Colenso and Shepstone in these early years, never lost sight of this hegemonic overlay.

Colenso's missionary vision, however, led him into the ecclesial tensions and theological conflicts that ultimately defined his life. The historic struggles among Bishop Colenso, Metropolitan Robert Gray (bishop of Cape Town), and the Anglican Church, which led to charges of heresy against Colenso and his excommunication, have been well documented, and their complex details need not be recited here.[33] However, of crucial import is the theological vision that surfaced through Colenso's work and his historic struggle for his ecclesial-professional life. For it is precisely that theological vision, along with the full development of the white supremacist state, that destroyed the spectacular trajectory of the Bishopstowe mission station. That theological vision also exposes much of the conceptual architecture of modern-day white, Western theological engagements with non-Western Christians. Equally important, Colenso's reflections show the ambiguous inner logic of strategies of contextuality. With Colenso one gains a vision strongly rooted in the European Enlightenment, in frustrations with industrial capitalism, and in the exhaustion of an orthodox imagination. Together they created in Colenso a flight to the universal, a flight that illumines both the great riches and tragic dimensions of his theology. Yet most centrally, Bishop Colenso's thought reveals the deeply contorted ground on which translation of the Christian world had been forced to proceed.

COLENSO AND THE FLIGHT TO THE UNIVERSAL

It would be difficult to find a more productive Christian intellectual in the mission field than John William Colenso. His translation output was simply breathtaking. Less than three months after his mission party's arrival, he produced a massive Zulu dictionary, a Zulu grammar, and a revised Zulu version of the Gospel of St. Matthew. By the end of his first seven years in Natal, he

would add the entire New Testament, Genesis, Exodus, and Samuel, all translated into isiZulu. He would also publish a Zulu liturgy, a treatise on the Decalogue, and Zulu readers in astronomy, geography, geology, and history.[34] This list
does not include the other publications Colenso oversaw through the operation
of the station's printing press. By his side, along with other assistants, was William
Ngidi, constantly asking questions, probing Colenso's theological responses, and
suggesting alternative readings and interpretations. In this context one can see
both the maturation and alteration of his theology since his arrival in Natal and
entry into the everyday practices of translation and mission work. At the heart
of that thinking was his commentary on Romans, entitled *St. Paul's Epistle to
the Romans: Newly Translated, and Explained from a Missionary Point of View*,
published at Bishopstowe in June of 1861 and republished in 1863.[35]

The commentary on Romans, not his more famous and more widely disseminated work *The Pentateuch and the Book of Joshua: Critically Examined*, led to
the charges of heresy brought against Colenso.[36] In fact, the text on the Pentateuch only enacts a portion of the theological agenda outlined in the Romans
commentary. In writing a Romans commentary, Colenso stands in a historical
line of theologians that extends before him to Luther and after him to Karl Barth.
Like them, Colenso was compelled to return to the text that elaborates the foundations of the Christian life in order to reestablish Christian existence in this new
world, not only the British world but the world of Natal. As Andrew Walls notes,
the book of Romans, especially Rom 1 and 2, has played a crucial role in the
theological imaginations of missionaries. The Romans epistle was their strongest
ally as they sought to articulate a theological vision of their efforts. Missionaries
saw in Romans 1 a corrective to Christian arrogance.[37]

If, as Colenso believed, "the great work of the Christian Teacher of to-day is
to translate the language of the devout men of former ages into that of our own,"
then he understood his commentary work to read the fundamental aspects of
faith from the standpoint of the missionary situation and thereby articulate more
precisely the very nature of Christianity.[38] Colenso's commentary comes in the
midst of two historic developments. First, he writes within the continuation of
the comparativist hermeneutic that we have seen modeled in Acosta. That hermeneutic drew historical and immediate comparison between Christianity and
other religions. In contrast to that of the Renaissance Catholic Acosta, Colenso's
work stands in the midst of the modern Protestant recapitulation of that theological operation. That is, Colenso's thinking reflects the new conceptual arrangement of being able to compare the religious practices of different indigenes
from multiple colonialist sites by analyzing side by side the different native religious subjects and their different religious systems. However, in Colenso's time

comparative procedures were being decoupled from their theological moorings and were in effect reinventing the religions of the world through racial and cultural taxonomies.[39] This meant that by Colenso's time native religions were increasingly read outside of such Christian theological frameworks as, for example, manifestations of the demonic. Rather, native religions were read as affirmations of racial character and indicators of civilization and human development.

The modern invention of religion again is, first, a reinvention of the trajectory taken by the Portuguese and the Spanish, who, as we have seen, first drew up the possibilities of (theological) anthropological reflection through descriptions of body differences (for example, skin color, hair texture, manner of dress, and so forth). The need to explain unforeseen, exotic peoples invoked through descriptive practices new ways of creating knowledge. The same questions regarding the status of a religious consciousness among the natives who were present with Acosta and his colleagues were also at work in Colenso's epoch. That is, these questions grew out of descriptive procedures that bound assessment of religious consciousness to the assessment of the body. It had been argued in Colenso's time that the tribes of southern Africa lacked religion because they were developmentally deficient. As David Chidester notes in *Savage Systems: Colonialism and Comparative Religion in Southern Africa*, the comparativist strategy was calibrated to the desire for land accumulation: "Such total denial [of African religions] was a comparative strategy particularly suited for the conditions of a contested frontier. On the battlefield, the enemy had no religion. At the front lines of a contest of religions, Christian missionaries adopted this strategy of denial. However, denial was also a strategy that suited the interests of European settlers who during the 1820s and 1830s had increasingly established their presence, and their claims on land, in the Eastern Cape. In addition to missionary accounts, therefore, the frontier also produced settler theories of religion."[40]

Such logic is not new. From the beginning of the age of discovery, Europeans perceived Africans as having the most bestial, debased forms of religious practice. Colenso's time also saw the continuation of another aspect of the vision of deficient black religion: that lack of religion was bound to a lack of any inherent claim on the land. The designation of native religious practices as superstition rather than religion became an important discursive practice within this stratagem of denial. But the stratagem fell out of direct use in Natal at the time of the Shepstone system. With the land safely in the hands of the colonialists, "the Zulu lost political autonomy but gained the recognition by Europeans commentators that they had an indigenous religious system."[41] Such recognition resulted from the growing awareness that earlier assessments of the religious status of the Zulu were fundamentally incorrect as well as from the fact that such an acknowledgment had no effect on the seizing and transformation of the land. Thus, religion became a signifier within the loss of land control. Religion as a signifier for African identity grew in direct proportion to African alienation from their land, so that by the beginning of the twentieth century African life in Natal reflected a long history of geographic displacement and loss.[42]

These spatial dimensions are subtextual in Colenso's commentaries and an important, albeit unrealized, aspect of his critique of the arrogance of the settlers and missionaries. Colenso will draw Zulu religious practice into a positive theological vision. This in and of itself is a powerful and revolutionary act given the prevailing missionary and theological sentiments of his day. Yet he will operate within the emerging ideological use of religion and African religious consciousness displaced from specific claims on space and place. Equally important, Colenso's theological vision will form yet another strategy of land displacement. This is not to say that Colenso and his European colleagues failed to see Africans' connection to the land. They simply dismissed that connection as nonessential except in the most basic form of use-value.

The other historic development that intersects with Colenso's commentary work is the advent of what Jonathan Sheehan has termed the Enlightenment Bible.[43] By this Sheehan refers to the transformation of the Bible in modernity through "a complex set of practices whose most sophisticated instruments were *scholarship*—philological, literary, and historical—and *translation*."[44] Sheehan's insightful reading of this history accurately lodges its beginning in the Protestant Reformation (as well as the Renaissance and scientific revolution). Protestantism was from its beginning a movement shaped by the desire for a vernacular Bible in the hands of the people, the Reformation motto of *sola scriptura* capturing Protestants' hopes to restore the Bible to its central place in understanding divine authority. As Sheehan notes, however, "If Protestant vernacular translation bridged the gap, once again, between heaven and earth, it *also* revealed the very human side of the biblical text that the doctrine of *sola scriptura* could never admit."[45] Protestants encountered the real dilemma of articulating the divine authority of Scripture without the benefit of a magisterium or a canonical process vivified by ecclesial oversight or the proliferation of vernacular translation checked by any overarching priestly authority. The reformers, Sheehan argues, established "a new vernacular biblical canon" as a way to stabilize the authoritative texts and lodge Christian tradition into a single text, the Bible itself, but this process also gave birth to the "tools of biblical decanonization."[46] Thus the "sixteenth-century vernacular Bible represented . . . both a successful break with tradition *and* a successful consolidation of a new tradition."[47]

That new tradition as it was articulated especially in Germany and England would give rise on the one hand to an explosion of textual scholarship and on the other hand to "the vernacular translation project."[48] As Sheehan notes, both of these endeavors would move the Bible beyond theology. Biblical scholars and translators (often one and the same) perceived theology (here understood as doctrinally disciplined and traditioned reflection on Scripture) as nonessential commentary on the Bible. Sheehan is not suggesting that this development is antitheological in its inception; rather, it established a steady and fundamental distancing from theology.[49] Sheehan's account of the complex, rich history of Reformation and post-Reformation biblical development is sparse but effective. His central point is crucial: "If the Bible had always functioned in Christian Europe as an essentially unified text—indeed, its theological importance depended on this unity—the post-theological Enlightenment Bible would build its authority across a diverse set of domains and disciplines. Its authority had no essential center, but instead coalesced around four fundamental nuclei. Philology, pedagogy, poetry, and history: each offered its own answer to the question of biblical authority, answers that were given literary form in the guise of new translations."[50]

The Enlightenment Bible comprised four emanations. The textual emanation, the Bible understood as a set of documents, allowed philological investigation to circumvent theological questions and controversies by cultivating textual criticism. Textual criticism inserted and consequently hid (theological) commentary inside the criticism itself, within the marginalia of textual display, apparatus, and translation. The pedagogical emanation presented the Bible as a distillation of moral truths. The pedagogical Bible instilled a timeless moral vision for all humanity. It was this vision of a morally compelling thrust at the hermeneutic center of the Bible (as well as of other crucial texts) that fueled nineteenth-century romanticism. The poetic emanation viewed the Bible through the lens of the historical and timeless reality of poetic expression that is present among every people. The poetic Bible exhibited the literary heritage of humanity and revealed the Bible's complete translatability, which makes possible its utter rebirth into diverse national literatures.[51] The historical emanation drove the Bible deeply within the historiographic imagination, and it issued as a historical archive. As archive, the Bible became "an infinitely variegated library of human customs and origins. And in this historical Bible, the ideal of a familiar text was abandoned for one perpetually in [historical] translation."[52] The historical Bible was a powerful emanation of Enlightenment mentality in its ability to police theology by enfolding theological reflection with the Bible itself into a broader search for common human imaginings and knowledge.

These Enlightenment emanations converge and coalesce around what Sheehan calls the cultural Bible. In Germany and England, the cultural Bible becomes the sacred text of a nation and a people. The cultural Bible is fruitful for the cultivation of society and the formation of civilization; the Bible becomes, especially in Germany, the Ur-text of civilization. Central to the creation of a cultural Bible was the dismissal of Judaism and Jewish people from any claim, not only to the Bible, but to any cultural heritage which might undermine the articulation of the Bible as Christian literature. The presence of Jewish people was hermeneutically sealed off from the vision of the Bible as a national treasure, as the cultural expression of the national spirit, and, in the case of Germany, the German soul.

There was great fear in England over the transformation of the Bible into the Enlightenment Bible. As Sheehan puts it, "English theologians and critics abandoned the thorny paths of historical criticism for the smooth highways of orthodoxy."[53] Yet the transformation was happening with the increasing intellectual concourse between Germany and England. The publication in 1860 of *Essays and Reviews* (one year before Colenso published his Romans commentary), a collection of seven essays, six of which were written by Anglican churchmen, acknowledged the demand for a new Enlightenment vision of the Bible.[54] That demand also presented the Bible as foundational to civilization; that is to say, the Bible emerged in England, as in Germany, as culture-constituting. The idea of culture evolved as an abstraction and as an absolute.[55] As Raymond Williams notes in his powerful account of the development of the idea in England in the nineteenth century, the idea of culture was turned against the dehumanizing effects of the Industrial Revolution.[56] This is not the idea of culture as it will be articulated within the social sciences and modern anthropology and ethnography, that is, as a descriptor of particular ways of life, rooted in language, rituals, and everyday practices. Rather, this is a vision of culture which captures the humanizing, spiritual essence of a people; here "culture represented that 'heritage of an accumulated ineluctable racial memory' that undergirded the essential qualities of 'western civilization.'"[57]

The Bible thus emerged in England in Colenso's time as the epicenter of two points of crisis and conflict. On the one hand, the Bible stood between the forces of Enlightenment change and a recalcitrant and fearful orthodoxy. On the other hand, the Bible stood between unrelenting forces of societal change bound to the Industrial Revolution and capitalism and the romanticist voices pressing for cultivation of the cultural and national spirit of a people in order to assert or reestablish as an imaginative act its moral center. The Industrial Revolution was reducing human beings to elements in the mechanization and routinization of processes of production. The romantic impulse responded to these reductive processes by proclaiming the infinite worth of the human spirit and the need to attend to exaltation through education. A third point of crisis and conflict, though lacking the Bible as its epicenter, informs Colenso's life and work: the conflict between low church and high church, between a Protestantism pushing further away from its Roman Catholic past and a Protestantism that was retrieving a catholic identity rooted in Christian antiquity and turned toward the formation of a national church. Colenso for his part thought near the epicenter of these points of crisis and conflict. He was an evangelical Pietist who became a centrist Anglican bishop influenced by intellectual figures deeply implicated in his country's Enlightenment movement. He was in many ways an expression of the Enlightenment Bible; yet Colenso was unable to grasp the dangers of thinking near this epicenter.

Sheehan's account does not map cleanly onto Colenso because Colenso carries forward a genuinely theological agenda, though that theology exists under strained conditions articulated through the Enlightenment Bible. One must, however, hold together the Enlightenment markings of Colenso's scholarship and his normalization of the spatial disruptions of Africans in his thought. The transformation of the Bible and the transformation of space play against each other in his thought. Neither becomes an articulated theme, yet each enables the other. Together they display the modern abandonment of place-centered identity, an abandonment rooted in a particular theological vision. Colenso offers a highly refined vision of the whiteness hermeneutic, the interpretative practice of dislodging particular identities from particular places by means of a soteriological vision that discerns all people on the horizon of theological identities. This discernment in and of itself is not the problem. The problem is the racialization of that soteriological vision such that racial existence is enfolded inside the displacement operation and emerges as a parasite on theological identity. But here that hermeneutic is in service, he believes, to the greater good of the African and the integrity of the mission church.

Colenso's commentary opens quite tellingly with heartfelt dedicatory thanks to Shepstone. Colenso conversed with Shepstone about the very ideas he works out in the commentary. In fact, Colenso hoped a commentary on Romans written from the perspective of "some questions, which daily arise in Missionary labours among the heathen" would serve as the theological foundation for the great work Shepstone planned in Zululand.[58] The Zululand project, as noted, was Shepstone's plan to move tens of thousands of so-called surplus Africans from Natal to another place, where he would reside as their chief. Colenso's commentary on Romans would serve as a kind of theological charter for the governmental operations in this new site. Even as he wrote his commentary, he was still convinced of the symmetry between his work and Shepstone's efforts at "advancing the civilisation of [native] tribes" of the colony.[59] He would match his theological reflections to Shepstone's God-given ability "for influencing the native mind."[60] He envisioned that they would together create a humane, Christianized domesticity for the Africans. In this way, Colenso joins theological work to the advancement of civilization. He was, however, unaware that the theological vision outlined in his commentary would be at great odds with both that civilizing vision and the Shepstone system.

Colenso's Romans commentary is in some ways a conventional nineteenth-century work. He situates the text in its historical setting, and, as a New Testament scholar would, he posits the identity of the audience for the epistle and then displays his evidence for his contention. Colenso understood the letter to be written to Jewish believers. But unlike conventional New Testament scholars, Colenso has a more pivotal concern in mind than establishing Paul's audience when he posits Jewish believers as the central addressees in Romans. The Jews in the text stand in for arrogant English Christian settlers in the new world of Africa. The Zulu, by contrast, do not simply stand in for the Gentile/heathen; they are *in fact* the Gentile/heathen. In schematic form his analogy would look like this:

English Christian Settlers   ⟵——————————⟶   Zulu People
Jewish Converts   *Gentile/Heathen*

Colenso is not engaged in straightforward anti-Semitism in his commentary, although he does have a very denigrating vision of Jewish identity.[61] What he puts forward is much more complex than a simple derogatory deployment of biblical Jewish identity. Colenso is reading salvation history inside settler-Zulu relations and attempting to render the particularities of identity inconsequential to Christian existence. In order to do this, Colenso must racialize those identities to then transcend them. Key to this interpretive move is the slow construction of the divine character based on his reading of Romans in such a way as to make Jewish particularity of no importance to God. Indeed, God will quickly appear in Colenso's commentary as being fundamentally opposed to Jewish priority and election. God is ultimately opposed to that priority because God takes no stock in particular (racial) Jewish identity. In this regard, Colenso suggests Nicodemus as a Jewish archetype:

> Nicodemus also had no doubt as to his own right, not merely as a true believer in God, but as a true born Jew, a child of Abraham, to have a share in it. What he wanted to know was . . . how he might best attain a worthy place in that kingdom. . . . Our Lord throws him back at once in His reply to the only true

ground of hope. It is as if He had said, . . . "You are come to me very confident of your concern in this Kingdom. You are sure, you think, of a place in it. But why are you sure? What ground have you for thinking that you have any place at all in it? Do you imagine that, because you are born of Abraham, your claim will be allowed? But I tell you this will avail you for nothing. Your mere natural descent is no ground at all for any such expectation. . . . This, then, was an instance of a devout Jew, fully prepossessed with the infatuation of his people, and requiring to have this false ground of hope struck away from under his feet at the very outset, if he would heartily embrace the faith of Jesus.[62]

Colenso imagines the conversation between Nicodemus and Jesus as a deconstructive one. Jesus removes from Nicodemus any presumption of divine privilege, any connection of divine life with particular human flesh. This statement as an implicit critique of English settler mentality would be a powerful word against that form of Christian hegemony. But it already exposes the problematic equation of white (English) Christian with Jew. That equation demands a deep commitment to a moment of transition, a supersessionism that enables the analogy itself. The transition for Colenso allows one to move from an ethnocentrism to a theocentrism, from imperfect Christian doctrine yet trapped in "Jewish sentiments" to the true spirit of the gospel. That spirit is a universal spirit. Colenso's first major hermeneutic move is to place all peoples under the fundamental problem, ethnocentrism. The Jews of Paul's day, like the Romans and Greeks before them, like the settlers and the Zulu, all read the world as being composed of one people with the rest of the world as "foreigners, men of the nations" (for example, Jews and Gentiles, Greeks and barbarians).[63]

It is precisely this assumed racial supremacy of a people that is "a worm lying at the root of all [the] Christian profession" of so many pious believers in Rome.[64] For Colenso, Israel reveals this original mistake. One finds three primary errors in Jewish believers in Rome: birth, messianic expectation, and law. He writes,

1. The Jew said, "I am a favoured creature—a child of Abraham, and *therefore* a child of God, and an heir of His kingdom, whatever my life may be. What have *I* to do with a message of salvation? Perhaps, for the heathen it may be needed. But the Kingdom of God is mine, by virtue of the promise made to my great forefather. I have a *right* to enter it. I *claim* it as mine." This error St. Paul must correct by showing that he had no such right, that he, the Jew, needed the free gift of *Righteousness*, as well as all others of the human race—that he too was "concluded under sin" like others, and had no claim whatever, because of God's promises to Abraham. . . .[65]

2. But the Jew might say, "Suppose that I admit this, yet, at all events, the Mes-

siah is to come specially for us. He is to be the carrying out and realization of those promises to our forefathers, which made us the favoured people above others. You do not surely mean to say that we, Jews, the children of Abraham, the chosen family of God, are to be put on an *equality* with the common Gentile in this respect?" "Yes!" St. Paul would say, "you are to be put on a perfect equality with the meanest Gentile. You will stand no better than they in this respect—not a whit more *safe* from God's wrath—not a whit more *sure* of entering the Kingdom. . . .

3. Still, however, the Jew might persevere and say: "But surely our *Law* is not to be done way with. At all events, the Gentiles, if they are to partake of the Gospel, and even to be admitted to share on equal terms with us, must conform to our religion, and practise those observances, which have come down to us through fifteen hundred years on the authority of Moses, with the Divine Seal upon them. . . ." "No!" says the Apostle again, "Faith, simple faith, a true, living, childlike faith and trust, that worketh by love, this is all that God seeks of all—no circumcision—no Jewish practices or peculiarities. . . . These are all now done away in Christ Jesus.

These theological points not only reflect nineteenth-century Protestant theology but also in essence reflect some of the strongest interpretive tendencies in Christian accounts of Israel's identity in relation to Christian identity. Colenso's Paul negates any soteriological character to Jewish identity. This also means that messianic expectations geared to the concrete salvation of their people are also meaningless. Israel loses any historic trajectory of liberation, any political hope born in the past that should shape the present. In addition, the negation of the law means that their salvific future requires them to abandon the very practices that have defined them. Colenso thus offered up through his reading of the early chapters of Romans a Jewish people that has nothing of saving importance to offer the world of the Gentiles. They are quite literally the foil to faith, the carrier pigeon of the gospel. Moreover, any attempt to offer anything of particular communal or "racial" substance to the Gentiles that would be in any way binding on the Gentiles would be an exercise in sinful futility. This, according to Colenso, is the heart of Paul's critique of his Jewish family.

The analogy with the settlers breaks down rather quickly at this point. Unlike Colenso's Roman Jews, English settlers did indeed believe they had something of saving importance to offer the heathen, even if Colenso's exegetical reflections denied that belief. Indeed Colenso's own vision of civilization grants to Britannia what he refuses Israel, namely, the refashioning of a people's way of life for theological reasons.

The entire commentary builds from this logic and this massive blind spot, but the heart of Colenso's Romans commentary, the central image he powerfully develops, is that of God the loving and merciful father. In his use of this brilliant image lie both the riches and the poverty of Colenso's theological vision. If Israel serves any purpose, it is to expose to humankind the God who loves them. Colenso's twist on the "righteousness of God" exemplifies how a specific history within which righteousness becomes intelligible disappears and becomes a universal sense of divine righteousness: "This 'righteousness of God,'—this righteousness which comes from God—which is the free gift of God—which . . . God has given to the whole human race, before and after the coming of Christ,—is being 'revealed,' he says, that is, unveiled, in the Gospel. It is there already, in the mind of our Faithful Creator, in the heart of our Loving Father. The whole human race was redeemed from the curse of the Fall, in the counsels of Almighty Wisdom, from all eternity—the Lamb was slain 'from before the foundations of the world.' . . . [T]he whole family of man, in the ages gone by . . . were yet 'justified,' *made* just or righteous, dealt with as children, before any clear revelation was made of the way in which that righteousness was given to them."[66] Colenso here draws on an extremely powerful theological position that will be performed in countless ways by a variety of theologians in the nineteenth and twentieth centuries. It discerns the saving work of God as a completed act that must govern the ways one thinks about the material enactments of that accomplished work. Colenso came to this radical position from seeing its opposite in the missionary field. Colenso was painfully familiar with the theological position propounded by many missionaries that placed those who had died without Christian faith under damnation in hell and eternally punished. Colenso, in his book describing his first visit to the Natal colony, *Ten Weeks in Natal*, tells the story of sitting by the Tongaat River having lunch and reading in the *Missionary Intelligencer* something that greatly disturbed him. He had a section from the paper that an American missionary had used to wrap Colenso's lunch. He read stories in which natives were told that everyone who dies without the gospel is burning in hell from the moment of death: "I quote these passages, not for a moment wishing it to be supposed, that the good American Missionaries of Natal hold and preach, as a body, these fearful doctrines—God forbid!—but to enter my own solemn protest against them, as utterly contrary to the whole spirit of the Gospel,—as obscuring the Grace of God, and perverting His message of Love and 'Goodwill to man,' and operating, with most injurious and deadening effect, both on those who teach, and on those who are taught."[67]

A few years after the publication of his Romans commentary, in a speech before the Anthropological Society of London, Bishop Colenso recalled with revulsion a prayer he had seen published by a missionary institution associated with his church. The prayer included the words, "O Eternal God, Creator of all things, *mercifully remember* that the souls of unbelievers are the work of Thy hands, and that they are created in Thy resemblance. Behold, O Lord, *how hell is filled with them*, to the dishonor of Thy Holy Name."[68] Colenso rightly discerned a presumption lodged deeply in this position: the ideas of sin, damnation, and punishment are collapsed into divine enactment.

According to this skewed logic, to believe in these tenets is to also believe that they are now temporally in effect. Moreover, the strength of that belief is bound to the surety of one's ability to discern its realities in humanity, especially in and among the Africans. While the roots of this flawed theological vision were ancient by Colenso's day, they carry an intensely imperialist character. Essentially, it inserts humanity, and in this case Europeans, in a God-position vis-à-vis decisions of eternal significance. It draws colonialist hubris deeply inside a constellation of theological ideas. It is that hubris that triggers what would become in the late nineteenth century and twentieth a formulaic way of articulating the relation between sin, damnation, and eternal punishment. What is concealed in that formulaic articulation is the centered white subject who discerns moral deficiency, salvific absence, and the eternal state after death. Colonialism is not the cause of this theological problem but, bound to Enlightenment reconfigurations of theological knowledge, surely is its refinement.

Colenso presses against this constricted vision of salvation that says, once *I see* that you believe in Jesus you are saved, but if *I discern* disbelief or the absence of belief in you, then upon your death you will be eternally punished in hell. However, he cannot escape its imperialist presumptions. Colenso will offer up its mirror image, an image that will carry an inverted constriction:

> Already, side by side with this revelation of God's wrath for willful sin in the heart of man, there is a revelation of His Mercy—a secret sense that there is forgiveness with our Father in Heaven, in some way or other, possible or actual. The Jews, before the coming of Christ, had their system of sacrifices given them, to remind and assure them of this. The heathen had their various modes of quieting their hearts, with what served to them as a pledge of Divine forgiveness. But all men, everywhere, have had all along, and still have, a belief in such Divine Forgiveness, as well as in such Divine Wrath upon willful sin; they have a feeling that it must exist, it must somehow be provided for them. Nay, coupled with the very sense of sin, there is a dim sense of a righteousness which they already possess.[69]

Colenso folds all humanity into righteousness, not damnation. Central to this universal affirmation is the leveling of all peoples through their particular religious experiences. Divine righteousness enables religious ethnography, an ability to discern a theological sameness in all people. As Jonathan Draper notes, for Colenso, "God has simply provided a righteousness to the whole human race in Christ, whether they knew it and accepted it by an act of faith on their part or not. . . . All of us, Christians, Jews, heathen, were dealt with by Creator God as righteous creatures, not only now, but 'from all eternity'. This was the reason for the universality of human religious experience, which impels people to live moral lives."[70] One can discern the German Idealist tradition in this method of articulating the relation of revelation to salvation. This way of grasping the religious subject enables a benign, even generous posture toward different peoples. Colenso puts the Enlightenment romanticist ideas to powerful use.

Colenso's way of describing the religious subject, especially the Zulu, is elegant. All people operate in the moral and spiritual light they have been given. Punishment is calibrated by their moral failure or integrity in operating in their inherent sense of sin or righteousness. Christian faith is the revelation of this very fact—that is, of inherent righteousness—and the Zulus are a perfect example. As he says, "We know that they exhibit certain virtues, and are capable of brave and kind and just and generous actions. But we know also that they practise habitually, without any restraint, a certain gross form of vice, that they kill for trivial causes, sometimes, apparently, for none at all."[71] Colenso goes on to say that sin is the disregard for the light they do have. In this way Colenso, like many nineteenth-century theological figures, naturalizes Christianity, domesticating it by making Christianity the architecture of religious experience. What is also crucial is the way he does this in the colonialist mission theater.

Colenso rewrites salvation history as the history of religious consciousness. In this way he is able to name Christian arrogance and misbehavior as a great impediment to the flourishing of that religious consciousness and its possible, but not necessary, movement toward Christianity. In a passage astonishing for its level of insight, given the virulent forms of anti-Semitism of his era, Colenso recognizes that Jewish resistance to Christian faith in his day was due not to a Jewish "reprobate mind" but to Christian behavior: "It is far more likely that the acts of abominable cruelty, injustice, and contemptuous bigotry, with which, in Christian lands and by Christian people—too often, alas! by Christian ministers—they have been so frequently, and are even now, treated, have gone far to fix them in holy and righteous horror of a religion, which taught that such outrages were right. All, surely, that an humble-minded Christian can allow himself to say of the present state of the Jews generally, is that they are not actually incurring great moral *guilt*—(he cannot judge of that,)—but suffering great moral and spiritual loss from the acts of their forefathers."[72] Colenso makes religious consciousness the given reality within which God is already working out a drama of salvation and conversion. Romans, Jews, and other Gentiles each follow their inherent moral light and will be judged accordingly. So, too, for Zulu and settler alike God has graciously forgiven them and wants them to hear "by means of any one of Earth's ten thousand voices" the Father's declaration of righteousness.[73] In Colenso's hands, the message of the gospel becomes one of acceptance and awareness: acceptance of the gracious gift of God's righteousness and awareness of God's fatherly love, ultimately revealed in Jesus. Colenso's theology draws a straight line from biblical Jews and Gentiles/heathen to Christian settlers and Zulu/heathen. What holds them all together in his vision is the fatherly love of the Creator God who has shed light "into their very hearts."[74] Their moral duty—white settler, Zulu, Gentile, Jew—is to move toward the inward light that is also reflected in the Son: "The Apostle does not say that *God is reconciled to us* by the Death of His Son, but that *we are reconciled to God.* The difference in the meaning of these two expressions is infinite. It is our unwillingness, fear, distrust, that is taken away by the revelation of God's Love to us in His Son. There is nothing now to prevent our going, with the prodigal of old, and throwing ourselves at His Feet, and saying, 'Father, I have sinned; but Thou art Love.'"[75]

The bishop drew on the biblical story to fill in his description of God the Father and thereby render at times an exquisite picture of divine love. But at the same time, Colenso's vision evacuated Christian identity of any real substance. All theological identity is essentially the same, Jewish, Christian, or Zulu—an internalized struggle of the religious consciousness to hear the word of love and acceptance from God the Creator-Father and his son, Jesus, and to follow the dictates of the moral universal inherent in all people. What looks like a radical antiracist, antiethnocentric vision of Christian faith is in fact profoundly imperialist. Colenso's universalism undermines all forms of identity except that of the colonialist.

This reading of Colenso's theological position in his Romans commentary may seem counterintuitive. It was Colenso who, among others, reversed the idea that the Zulu had no religion and no knowledge of God. He pressed the position that among the Zulus God was known and had been called *uNkulunkulu,* the Great-Great One, or *umVelinqangi,* the Supreme Creator. Indeed, Colenso's deep commitment to recognizing Zulu religious consciousness helped fuel Zulu cultural nationalism. Moreover, Colenso, like Shepstone, believed in building Christian civilization on top of existing native logics, such practices as cattle or property exchange as part of arranged marriages and polygamous family life. Yet in Colenso's hands, the (religious) cultural particular says nothing productive. In fact, he already knows what is the telos of all religious consciousness. Jeff Guy summarizes Colenso's geographic teleology:

> Colenso's role as a missionary bishop in Natal was to promote commodity production and capital accumulation through the propagation of the standards and expectations of the Christian way of life — the Christian way of life as perceived by the Victorian middle class, of course. The purpose of his mission was to produce the scrubbed, well-dressed, properly trained African family, living in a square house, separated from other households, faithful to the precepts of individualism, hard work and the Bible, the husband selling his labour, spending his income wisely, and thereby advancing the economic progress of the colony and his own social status, his wife in the home, his daughters in service, and his sons in training and preparing to marry monogamously, to reinforce and repeat the process.[76]

Colenso's flight to the universal carried forward colonialism's reconfiguration of the earth. It was precisely this deep connection that Colenso could not see. As Guy correctly captures, Bishop Colenso wanted the Christian way of life described above without its consequences: "that men and women be driven off the land and into wage labour, the dispossession of families and the dismantling of the polygamous household, together with the laws, customs and beliefs associated with it."[77] The moral resonance of Colenso's theological vision was incompatible not only with the Shepstone system of exploitation, but also with the telos of his mission, the complete transformation of Zulu life into mid-Victorian domesticity. However, much more is at play here than a missionary who brought his cultural baggage along with the gospel he preached. Such common culture and gospel analyses are tragically superficial and miss the wider problematic.

First, Colenso's universalism was the other side of his colonialism. His ability to conceptualize a God who is not only beyond but in some sense opposed to the strictures of Jewish identity draws life from colonialist abilities to universalize the earth, that is, to free it from the strictures of particular ways of life. Of course, missionary life is by its proper nature boundary crossing, but his universalist vision reduces the power and presence of the very things it claims to grasp, the particularities of African peoples. He resolves those particularities into signposts for potential development. Crucially his universalism made Christianity the landscape of religious consciousness while all identities are drawn toward sublime futility. For instance, while Colenso beautifully captures the humanity of Jesus as the ground for redemption, that humanity is merely symbolic: "And at last He sent His own dear Son, to make more plain than ever the beauty of Holiness, and the excellence of the Law, with the full message also of His Fatherly Love to all the world, that as sin had reigned and revelled, as it were, through the death which it had brought on all the race, so now might grace reign through the righteousness, which it would give to all the race, unto Life Eternal, through Jesus Christ our Lord."[78] True to his Enlightenment sensibilities, Colenso would quickly affirm the historical realities of Jesus, just as he affirmed the historical limitations of all biblical figures. Jesus as a speaking Jew does not matter soteriologically. Although Colenso's universalism did not deny cultural particularity, it denied that it mattered theologically. Particular identities had no prescriptive authority, only descriptive utility.

Taken together, his universalizing of the earth and his denial of cultural particularities' prescriptive authority, all inside the canopy of a loving Father Creator-God, meant that Christian theology in the bishop's hands could offer no compelling vision of a genuinely new way of life for anybody. As noted earlier, Colenso lived in the midst of a depleted orthodoxy. In nineteenth-century England, theological orthodoxy was desperately looking to establish its identity in the face of the cataclysmic shifts in society, namely, the creation of industrial capitalism, which was rabidly bringing the New World into global capital processes. That orthodoxy was also unsure of its identity vis-à-vis Catholicism and a burgeoning nationalism and so was engaged in an obsessive theological retrieval of the theological and liturgical sensibilities of the early church. That orthodoxy was also under pressure to articulate itself in the face of a growing number of intellectually agile voices expansive enough to incorporate orthodox ideas within wider streams of thought that were in effect corrosive to orthodoxy itself. The orthodoxy of his day left Colenso with few options in envisioning the mission situation.

Colenso is in fact a theologian-in-colonialism, and he is also a theologian with a spent orthodox imagination. His account of the kind of missionary he needed in Natal to support his mission operation is exemplary: "Men with large hearts, cultivated minds, and generous views, fit to be entrusted with such work. Of course, if the object aimed at is chiefly to multiply the professors of Church doctrine,—if men are wanted merely to cram the native mind with creeds and catechisms, and raise a number of human parrots, repeating dogmatic phrases and formularies,—it might not be so difficult to find suitable instruments; more especially as the income and position of a missionary are far superior to what such teachers would probably be likely ever to attain at home."[79] Given the overturning, securing, and accumulating of space within imperialist economies, orthodoxy and piety in the mission situation were performing a single theological option. But in order to see this, one must keep in view the long dilemma of nineteenth-century orthodoxy. That dilemma had its roots in the transformation of the world wrought by colonialism itself, the expansion of the world beyond the ability of theology to grasp that world and the destruction of a vision of creation with the advent of discovery. The consequences of Colenso's theological vision follow the route taken by Acosta. Colenso offers a theology that lacks indigenous cultural prescription.[80] No vision of cultural engagement or joining is forthcoming, and certainly no possible vision of missional cultural submission.[81]

The act of translating is the unrelenting submission to another people's voices for the sake of speaking with them. Yet it is precisely this submission that is denied in the overarching colonialist process of translation. There was, however, a form of submission. The submission that was initially concealed from Colenso's theological reflections was in fact submission to white settlers' ways of life and spatial reconfigurations. It is exactly this form of forced Christian submission that would beget a tortured Christian cultural nationalism among nonwhite peoples and would also reduce theology to a level of uselessness that theologians have yet to comprehend.

Colenso's universalist thought brought him into deep conflict with his church. In 1863, his nemesis Bishop Robert Gray, lord bishop of Cape Town and metropolitan, brought charges of heresy against Bishop Colenso for "false, strange and erroneous doctrine and teaching."[82] As a sign of protest against Bishop Gray's right to remove him on account of his scholarly positions, Colenso never attended the trial, which began on November 16, 1863. The details of the trial are beyond my concern here; however, the charges brought against Colenso are important because they capture the level of engagement his church had with his thought:

1. That he denied that our Lord died in man's stead, or to bear the punishment or penalty for our sins, and that God is reconciled to us by the death of his Son.
2. That he taught that justification is a *consciousness* of being counted righteous, and that all men, even without such a consciousness, are treated by God as righteous, and that all men are already dead unto sin and risen again unto righteousness.
3. That he taught that all men are born into righteousness when born into the world; that all men are at all times partaking of the body and blood of Christ; denying that the holy sacraments are generally necessary to salvation, and that they convey any special grace, and that faith is the means whereby the body and blood of Christ are received.
4. That he denied the endlessness of future punishments.
5. That he maintained that the Bible contained but was not the word of God.

6. That he treated the Scriptures as a merely human book, only inspired as any other book might be inspired.

7. That he denied the authenticity, genuineness and truth of certain books of the Bible.

8. That, by imputing errors in knowledge to our Lord, he denied He is God and Man in one person.

9. That he brought parts of the Book of Common Prayer into disrepute (e.g. the Athanasian Creed and the vow at the ordination of deacons which spoke of "unfeigned belief" in the Scriptures).[83]

Absent from every official engagement and assessment of Colenso's thought by his initial accusers was any consideration of why he came to his theological positions. In his Romans commentary he describes the situation of having to answer complex theological questions for which he had not worked out his own thinking, questions that facilitated the refashioning of his theology: "Such questions as these have been brought again and again before my mind in the intimate converse which I have had, as a Missionary, with Christian converts and Heathens. To teach the truths of our holy religion to intelligent adult natives, who have the simplicity of children, but withal the earnestness and thoughtfulness of men,— to whom these things are new and startling, whose minds are not prepared by long familiarity to acquiesce in, if not receive them,—is a sifting process for the opinions of any teacher, who feels the deep moral obligation of answering truly, and faithfully, and unreservedly, his fellow-man, looking up to him for light and guidance, and asking, 'Are you sure of this?' 'Do you know this to be true?' 'Do you really believe that?'"[84]

Colenso was in fact an overwhelmed theological teacher caught in the middle of the intensely challenging situation of a translator.[85] Not only was he trying to translate Christian Scripture into another language and thereby bring that native world into a Christian discursive universe, but he was also trying to respond to the questions raised by indigenes. Those questions focused light on precisely the fit of that Christian discursive world with native logics. In so doing, those questions pressed Colenso into grasping both the inner logics of Christian theology and inner native logics. This was beyond his ability.

The questioning itself, by revealing the exhaustion of his orthodoxy, exposed the poverty of his theology. Colenso was not an unimaginative thinker, as some have suggested, not at heart still just a mathematician working out of his depth.[86] His scholarship shows great familiarity with the theological currents, ideas, and challenges of his day, and his literary output shows his ability to understand the theological tradition that had been given him, albeit a tradition that in his mind was in need of strong renovation. Rather, Colenso, like many of his contemporaries, was unable to perceive what was being asked of him as a theological teacher in the new world of Africa. Grasping the inner logics of both worlds required a depth of intimacy with both that Colenso lacked. His theology dismissed the Jewish realities of Christian existence, and his colonialist sensibilities joined with the reformation of African geography made his Shepstone-influenced account of the African mind little more than a white construction. That is to say, the very patterns of indigenous life Colenso was observing were being drastically altered not only as he watched but because he and other settlers were watching. They altered African worlds even as they observed them. They transformed those worlds as they sought to understand and control them.

Colenso's theology in effect retreated from intimacy and advanced toward a kind of didactic use of the native.[87] The (non-Western) world comes to have a central educative function for the West. We saw in Acosta how the Indian came to signify an educational opportunity for the Spaniards to learn about themselves through the native. By the nineteenth century, as John Willinsky observes, travel and living abroad not only carried this educative weight but became the path to greater self-knowledge.[88] Colenso turned native questions into occasions for theological self-absorption. It was as though he heard their questions, turned away from them, turned toward England, and began to theologize.

RENDERING THE AFRICAN

Fundamentally misdirected, Colenso turns away from the African in order to gather what for him is a more compelling concern, theology's renovation. In fact, his accompanying habit is equally decisive—he draws the African into his own theological struggle, positioning the African's voice as a tool in that struggle. Colenso did not invent this colonialist habit of mind, but in him one sees a particular kind of refinement. His work, especially his accounts of how "native questioning" drove him toward theological reassessment, represents a trajectory that continues today. That is, Colenso exhibits a pattern of turning away from indigenous theological questions, shunning the necessary intimacy needed for serious grappling with those questions, and drawing indigenous voices into forms of utility not only in Western theological struggles over orthodoxy or heterodoxy, both also in the project of nation building.

In March of 1865, at the height of the controversy that surrounded him, he was asked to give a lecture at the Anthropological Society of London, a response to W. Winwood Reade's racist lecture "Efforts of Missionaries among the Savages," in which Reade contended that missionary efforts among Africans were futile.

According to Reade, Africans had no aptitude for Christianity and lacked any sustainable Christian moral conscience.[89] Colenso's response to Reade was a limpidly contextual one.

Colenso suggested that Reade's visit to West Africa was probably too brief for him to capture a full picture of the situation. Furthermore, Colenso reminded his listeners that West Africa had been deeply shaped by the slave trade. To him this meant that if in fact Reade's description of African behavior was accurate, it was due in large measure to the bad example of white settlers. With this less than thunderous response to Reade's derogatory comments as the preface to his thoughts, Colenso goes on to recount the arguments he made in his Romans commentary regarding hell, punishment, missionary preaching, theology, and so on. His goal was to situate missionary work on surer footing. Colenso offered a candid assessment of the failures and efforts of missionary enterprises but pressed the continued importance of the endeavor, using his own work at Bishopstowe as the example. Toward the end of the lecture Colenso offered proof of his positive missional effect by quoting from a letter written by William Ngidi, his native informant. As the bishop stood before the learned gentlemen of the society, he translated the letter from Zulu. The letter affirmed the ministry of Bishop Colenso and confirmed some of his theological positions:

> But sir, there is a thing which I was wishing to tell you clearly, to wit, that in fact as to the doing of the people, I don't wish to worry myself to no purpose, with the plentiful talk which comes from the people, white and black, of ours. "Sobantu has gone astray; he is condemned; he has no truth." About these matters, sir, they make my heart sink. . . . But in all that I am looking for your return, because truly I put all my trust in all your teaching of me. It was that which gave me strength to know thoroughly our Father Unkulunkulu, who is over all. Sir, I supplicate blessing for you from our Father above; may He confirm you in that truth in which you confirm (others). And I too myself still hold fast that truth which I received from you, to wit, we are Unkulunkulu's, — He knows us. All that I received from you, that is what I stand by — I mean to know Him, — I mean to trust in Him, — everything of that kind.[90]

Colenso used these comments to suggest to Reade that here was some good evidence of positive results from missionary efforts.[91] After years of learning Zulu, translating the Christian world into Nguni languages, and building his mission station, Colenso is able to offer up an African speaking his mind. What is central is that this is an act of translation. That is, Colenso conjures the translated African, symbolizing the building of a Christian people. It is precisely this question of whether Colenso's work is in fact aiding in the building of a Christian people that fuels the controversy surrounding his commentary on the Pentateuch and draws the figure of William Ngidi deeply inside English ecclesial/nationalist concerns.

The lecture was not the only time Ngidi appears in England in discursive presence. He is the African who troubles Colenso's Pentateuch commentary. He is, in Colenso's rendering, the "native mind," reflecting childlike simplicity but with thoughtfulness and intelligence. It was Ngidi who asked the bishop many of the haunting questions regarding the flood, creation, and so forth. It was not only concern over the historical facticity of biblical narratives that drew Ngidi's unyielding questions, but the moral implications of those narratives. Ngidi's re-action to Colenso's quotation of Exod 21:20–21 captures this challenge for the bishop:

> If a man smite his servant, or his maid, with a rod, and he die under his hand, he shall be surely punished. *Notwithstanding*, if he continue a day or two, he shall not be punished, for *he is his money.* (Exod 21: 20–21)
>
> I shall never forget the revulsion of feeling, with which a very intelligent Christian native, with whose help I was translating these words into the Zulu tongue, first heard them as words said to be uttered by the same great and gra-cious Being, whom I was teaching him to trust in and adore. His whole soul re-volted against the notion, that the Great and Blessed God, the Merciful Father of all mankind, would speak of a servant or maid as mere "money," and allow a horrible crime to go unpunished, because the victim of the brutal usage had survived a few hours. My own heart and conscience at the time fully sympa-thised with his.[92]

Ngidi takes the role of the intellectual provocateur in Colenso's theological project. It is noteworthy that the African becomes an intellectual dialogue part-ner, someone whose thoughts, even if expressed only as questions, make real his humanity. Unfortunately, it was William Ngidi who received unflattering implicit acknowledgment in Matthew Arnold's devastating critique of Bishop Colenso's Pentateuch commentary.[93] Jeff Guy is right to discern in Arnold's critique of Colenso a manipulation of the assumptions of white supremacy that would re-volt against the idea that "an Englishman and a bishop could find, in a Zulu's questions, an intelligent critique of contemporary religious belief."[94] Arnold's biting sarcasm echoes the famous derogatory poem published in Natal regarding the bishop and William Ngidi:

A Bishop there was of Natal,
Who had a Zulu for a Pal,

Said the native "Look here,
"Ain't the Pentateuch queer?"
Which converted my Lord of Natal.[95]

In his essay "The Bishop and the Philosopher" Arnold used the occasion of reviewing Colenso's Pentateuch commentary to establish literary criticism as the
appropriate judge of the twofold utility of theological works: they must either
"edify the uninstructed" (that is, the masses) or "inform the instructed" (that is,
the educated elite).[96] The bishop's work, according to Arnold, fails at both tasks.
Arnold's crucial intervention in the Colenso controversy not only highlights theology's utility in nation building, but also reveals the problematic nature of invoking African presence as somehow helpful in this task.

Ironically, Bishop Colenso would agree with Arnold's vision of Christian theology's role in enlightened England, namely, to promote the cultivation of a cultured self. And Arnold for his part shared Colenso's critical sensibilities regarding
the Bible and theology. Arnold's problem with Colenso's work is that he believed
it would have the reverse effect, that it would upset the dangerous masses that
were already primed for revolution and anarchy. For Arnold, Colenso's work falls
short of a proper demythologization of the Scriptures, one that would translate
Scripture and doctrine into poetic form for the formation of a nationalistic, politically and socially conservative culture. As Terry Eagleton notes, Arnold believed "the scriptures must be stripped to a suggestive poetic structure for shor-
ing up a conservative social morality."[97] According to Eagleton, Colenso was, in
Arnold's view, "unpoetical and so politically dangerous."

Arnold's important essay points to the forest of intellectual issues Colenso
wandered into with his scholarship. It also points to the role his African inter-
locutors would be forced to play in relation to these issues. If Colenso's body was
in Natal during his early years, his mind was in England. He would bring into his
mind's world people such as William Ngidi, whose words would be called on to
do battle on Colenso's theological and ideological side. However, the battle itself
would reduce African presence to a single task, to show the markings of civilization taking hold. That task would also reduce the theological voice of the African
and theology itself in tragic ways.

Colenso, however well intentioned and considerate of the African, rendered
that African through his translation before the Anthropological Society of London a theological novice, one whose thinking will only bring him to the same
conclusions reached by white theologians. Surely, he could not have rendered
him otherwise. Africans were, for the missionaries and the emerging anthropologists, at the beginning—of civilization, of knowledge, of maturity. Yet the mar-

riage of Darwinian evolutionary thought and white supremacy meant that the
African would remain, through representation, theologically infantile. Colenso
believed that the African would, like the Englishman, evolve to a civilized state,
but the point here is one of representation, of spectacle.[98] Colenso's translation
constricts the use-value of the black voice. The African's theological commodification is complete. That native voice now speaks only to substantiate—an argument, a criticism, a concept, a plan of action, a belief of—white presence. What
is lost in translation is the possibility of a theological conversation partner who
would significantly affect the outcomes of modes of life. The translated Zulu
arrives in England, by means of his letter and in the midst of a lecture and in the
midst of a theo-political struggle, a solitary witness to Colenso's truth.

A common though shortsighted way of interpreting the Colenso–Ngidi collaboration has been as misguided questions that begat misguided answers.[99] It
betrays the complexity this collaboration signifies to suggest that African Christianity has not been occupied with Ngidi's kinds of questions or Colenso's types
of answers. There is indeed a distorted joining of worlds taking place in the translators' relationship. However, that joining cannot be captured through the now-
standard dualistic perspective on such collaborations. On the one side is the phenomenon of westernized Christian Africans who exhibit a westernized (false)
consciousness, and on the other side are Christianized Africans who carry out a
different set of questions and concerns reflecting an African consciousness.

Translation not only leads to textual representation; equally important, it is
an invitation to a process of concurrency, not simply linguistic, social, or cultural, but also theological. This process of concurrency describes the possibilities
of cultural inner logics being joined together, to the possibility of freedom in
the transgression of boundaries. However, the Colenso–Ngidi collaboration displayed a lack of the initial bedrock of concurrency, the Gentile joined to Israel
through the body of Jesus. The tragic effect of its absence is a Christian theology
that is unable to enter fruitfully into the cultural inner logics of peoples. Thus, in
Colenso, Christian theology is not only provincial, locked inside a false universal,
but also lacks patterns of communion.

The result was to constitute Christian theology as a matter of nationalistic
utility, as a resource for the reiteration of cultural identities. Whether one understands Christian theology as historically situated discursive practices or as ways of
life shaped within disparate liturgical, social, and cultural worldviews or simply
as doctrines carried forward through the articulation of the practical rationalities
of traditions, the result is the same: theology as the catalyst for cultural recapitulation. Theology invites peoples to look culturally inward in search of a theological reiteration of the collective self.[100]

Colenso's work illuminates the question of the essential purpose of Christian translation: What is the translation of a Christian world supposed to create? Centrally, translation should beget Christian agency. Even this example of colonial self-absorption does not negate the important developments of African agency and African Christian agency particularly. However, what is at stake here is precisely the character and shape of agency, given the work of translation that is deeply bound up inside colonialist operations. In the previous chapter we saw Christian theology bound up in an evaluative insularity, a pedagogical imperialism. Now I add to that portrait another layer: Christian theology producing through translation isolating and reductive forms of Christian agency. This latter claim puts in a different light the possible positive historical benefits of Christian translation. The positive historical benefits of Christian translation must be seen inside this wider tragedy.

THE TRANSLATION OF A TRAGEDY

Two of the most powerful accounts of the positive historical benefit of Christian translation come from two eminent historians of Christian missions, Lamin Sanneh and Andrew Walls. A brief consideration of the central theme in each of their visions of translation will show the implications of the colonialist trajectory undertaken by Bishop Colenso. Sanneh, in several groundbreaking texts, has attempted to articulate the unintended consequences of vernacular translation. Indeed, he interprets Christianity itself as a vernacular translation movement.[101] He reads colonial history through the unintended consequence of the formation of black agency and cultural being. He in no way denies the mechanisms of colonial control or the history of horror produced by the age of discovery and conquest. However, Sanneh wants to read the history of the colonial moment, especially in Africa, within an ecclesial history. That is to say, he draws the colonial history inside a longer, wider history of missionary activity. He understands vernacular translation as the hermeneutic horizon through which one must see and interpret the actions not only of missionaries but of Christianity itself.[102] Sanneh's reading of translation begins not with colonialism but with Israel.[103] Like Colenso, Sanneh theorizes a historical Christianizing process through the idea of a universal humanity that transcended Jewish particularity. Paul is key to this process in that his writings are the embodiment of that process: "Paul's ambiguous and often very critical relationship to Judaism cannot be isolated from his participation in the Gentile mission, and with good reason. As missionaries of the modern era were to find, encountering the reality of God beyond the inherited terms of one's culture reduces reliance on that culture as a universal normative pattern. . . . Contrary to much of the prevailing wisdom in this field of study, mission implies not so much a judgment on the cultural heritage of the convert (although in time the gospel will bring that judgment) as on that of the missionary. . . . The center of Christianity, Paul perceived, was in the heart and life of the believer without the presumption of conformity to one cultural ideal."[104]

The Apostle Paul, for Sanneh, establishes the logic of an internal cultural critique that happens whenever the gospel is presented to another culture. The gospel casts light on the cultural moorings of the carrier culture. The reality of God exposes those connections between a particular culture and the gospel itself, showing the difference between what is indeed simply one cultural vision and another, different cultural vision. Israel, in Sanneh's reading of Paul, exposes the universal movement of divine activity, which in no way belongs to Israel itself: "That remorseless [divine] consistency drives a sword through the heart of our cultural complacency, and by its thrust we are healed."[105] This providential historical process yields two options for reading the history of Christian missional faithfulness or infidelity.

Missionary culture may make itself "the inseparable carrier of the message."[106] Mission as translation is something very different. It "make[s] the recipient culture the true and final locus of the proclamation."[107] Mission as translation means that cultural rejection is not inherent in Christianity and, most important, "it carries with it a deep theological vocation, which arises as an inevitable stage in the process of reception and adaptation."[108] Sanneh imagines these options woven together in the messiness of Christian history, always showing the possibilities of translation.

In this way the act of translating creates a theological relativism. That relativism means that concepts bound to one language system give way to alteration or eradication when drawn toward another language. For Sanneh, these discursive practices are culturally specific. Equally important, translation necessitates a form of alienation from the original: "The original is assumed to be inadequate, or defective, or inappropriate, but at any rate ineffective for the task at hand. Thus a peripheral role comes to be assigned to the original mode. In addition, translation forces a distinction between the essence of the message, and its cultural presuppositions, with the assumption that such a separation enables us to affirm the primacy of the message over its cultural underpinnings. Thus translation involves some degree of cultural alienation on the part of the translator, though the recipient culture may eventually compensate him or her with the consolation of an adopted member."[109] Sanneh wants to balance the idea of the culturally particular with the universalistic reign of God. He says, "God needs to be close and specific enough to be recognizably real to us, and yet be untrammeled enough by our cultural presuppositions to be searchingly true to the divine self."[110] Sanneh is reading Israel through his analysis of the historical process itself. And he has discerned in his historiographic imagination an animated theological essence that moves through time from one cultural situation to another. Sanneh discerns God at work in history.

Sanneh believes that the practice of translation engaged in by the missionaries opened to them the possibility of repudiating cultural imperialism.[111] If the practice of translation disrupted colonialist hegemony, it did so by making room for something else, cultural nationalism: "Mission furnished nationalism with the resources necessary to its rise and success, whereas colonialism came upon it as a conspiracy. At the heart of the nationalist awakening was the cultural pride that missionary translations and the attendant linguistic research stimulated. We might say with justice that mission begot cultural nationalism."[112] Modernity and one of its signature realities, cultural nationalism, and their relation to theology, demand a slower, more studied reflection than Sanneh allows with his vernacular thesis. To become a modernizing agent is a very complex and thorny acknowledgment, one that demands a more ironic historical rendering. Sanneh acknowledges that the notion of mission as "unwarranted interference in other cultures" merits careful consideration, but he wants to attend more earnestly to the possibilities of cultural exchange and change.[113] He also holds to a developmental logic that wants to acknowledge the good of modernity with its technological and material advantages. However, Sanneh does not attend carefully to the other form of translation operative in and with vernacular translation, that is, the translating of native worlds into the old worlds of Europe, that is, into colonialist worlds.[114]

Sanneh relegates the colonial effects to a general understanding of the historic phenomena of colonialism, which for him are less important than what he calls the "theological enfranchisement of mother tongues, and the modern missionary application of it."[115] Sanneh discerns within the cultural imperialism of missions a place for African agency that is a "space for indigenous self-understanding and the basis for resistance."[116] While this is certainly a historical point, it is a far more precise theological point. Sanneh is rehearsing the embodiment of divine freedom in flesh. He is improvising on a christological insight. He discerns a reality of freedom within bondage, victory within defeat and suffering.[117]

Sanneh's reflections in this case, however, engender a significant lack of theological specificity. Sanneh envisions a God quickly clothed in multiple discourses and thereby clothed in multiple conceptualities throughout the historical process. His historicism in effect nationalizes theological formation. For Sanneh, vernacular translations, with their concomitant local theologies, indicate an appropriate relativism of all cultures as mediums of the gospel. This cultural relativism, he believes, challenges ethnocentrism, theological and otherwise.

Walls, like Sanneh, draws crucial lessons from the historical reality of vernacular translation. Yet for Walls, translation is an even more decisive theological category: "Incarnation is translation. When God in Christ became man, Divinity was translated into humanity, as though humanity were a receptor language. Here was a clear statement of what would otherwise be veiled in obscurity or uncertainty, the statement 'This is what God is like.'" . . . Bible translation as a process is thus both a reflection of the central act on which the Christian faith depends and a concretization of the commission which Christ gave his disciples. Perhaps no other specific activity more clearly represents the mission of the Church."[118] Translation becomes, in Walls's vision, the way in which Christianity, when performed correctly, enacts a tentative posture toward one's culture, people, and nation. Christians are those people who live between the home, or indigenizing principle, and the pilgrim principle. The pilgrim principle tells Christians that they have no abiding city and that they wait for their true home to appear. The home, or indigenizing principle, tells Christians that Christ comes to their home and joins himself to them.[119] The Christian life in this vision is always a matter of translation. This Christology of translation in which the Son is always being translated "in terms of every culture where he finds acceptance among its people" establishes the true form of Christian existence.[120]

Like Sanneh, Walls posits Israel and the Jew–Gentile relation as paradigmatic. The movement out of Israel is the movement toward the universal. The Jewish Christians of the first century reveal the beginnings of what will be the constant overturning of linguistic containment. Gentile believers altered the faith proclaimed by the disciples of Jesus, and this reveals the trajectory for the continuous transformations of Christian faith:

> Those Christian Jews in Antioch who realized that Jesus had something to say to their pagan friends took an immense risk. They were prepared to drop the time-honoured word Messiah, knowing that it would mean little to their neighbors, and perhaps mislead them—what concern was the redeemer of Israel, should they grasp the concept, to them? They were prepared to see the title of their national saviour, the fulfillment of the dearest hopes of their people, become attached to the name of Jesus as though it was a sort of surname. They took up the ambiguous and easily misunderstood word "Lord" . . . . They could not possibly have foreseen where their action would lead; and it would be surprising if someone did not warn them about the disturbing possibilities of con-

fusion and syncretism. But their cross-cultural communication saved Christian faith for the world.[121]

Walls's eloquent account of this movement out of Israel focuses on language as the medium of transformation. The entrance into new language, that is, "cross-cultural communication" as he calls it, is entrance into a new world. Such cross-cultural communication places Christian faith into the world. Christian faith then enters the world under the conditions that constitute all knowledge, subject to the limitations of worldview and epistemic situation. For Walls this limitation of perspective is "a necessary feature of our hearing the Gospel at all."[122] Like Sanneh, Walls draws a tight circle around language and culture and nation with the effect that the incarnational reality of God in Christ embodied in translation resolves itself in nation. Christ enters the DNA of a nation by means of its language.[123]

Walls and Sanneh render translation and, centrally, vernacular translation of the Christian Scriptures the pivotal concept for the promulgation of Christianity. Walls offers a vision of Christianity's central claim—the incarnation of God—as "a massive act of translation" and proceeds to elaborate the historical mission process as the struggle of translation.[124] Sanneh also strongly pulls in this direction, but invites one to see the historical advantages of this development for cultural diversity within Christian unity. However, both Sanneh and Walls (in different ways, to be sure) bypass the deeper concern that shapes the colonialist moment and Christian theology in that moment. That deeper concern has to do with the translation of multiple worlds simultaneously.

While Sanneh and Walls are very familiar with the history of colonialism and do not ignore it, they read the world of translation too narrowly, that is, from within the confines of the modernist problematic established within the colonialist modality itself.[125] Historically, they cannot capture the simultaneity that constitutes the Christian world in the new worlds. The multiple levels of translation, that is, of transference, transformation, transliteration of land, animals, space, language, and bodies, mean that worlds overlap and in that overlap they are altered irrevocably, hybridized, and cross-pollinated. Equally important, new forms of racialized Being are coming into play and driving the performance of oral and written systems in new directions and in the service of new purposes. This means that the formation of colonialist and native agency must be seen in terms of their greater tragedies of frustration and confusion as well as of their possibilities for self-emancipation.

Theologically, Sanneh and Walls have imbibed a subtle form of supersessionism that is now lodged deeply inside their historiographic imaginations. To ques-

tion the matter bluntly: when did we leave Israel's world? Language creates a
kind of mystification in Sanneh's and Walls's work in which translation points
to the world-constituting realities of language. Yet language is inside the world
it constitutes. The worlds of Christian language are inside Israel's house. Israel's
house is a space where people are joined in worship and where ways of life come
into the communion of the common, of eating, sleeping, and living together.
And through language Israel's house indeed covers the entire world. Through
Christian faith, new languages and the people who speak them are drawn into
that house, as the prophet Isaiah reminds us:

> [2] In days to come the mountain of the LORD's house shall be established as
> the highest of the mountains, and shall be raised above the hills; all the nations
> shall stream to it. [3] Many peoples shall come and say, "Come, let us go up to
> the mountain of the LORD, to the house of the God of Jacob; that he may
> teach us his ways and that we may walk in his paths." For out of Zion shall go
> forth instruction, and the word of the LORD from Jerusalem. [4] He shall judge
> between the nations, and shall arbitrate for many peoples; they shall beat their
> swords into plowshares, and their spears into pruning hooks; nation shall not
> lift up sword against nation, neither shall they learn war any more. (Isa 2:2–4
> NRSV)

It is precisely this house that is forgotten and denied in the Christian theological
formation processes of the West. Unfortunately, Sanneh and Walls execute their
intellectual programs inside the denial. By drawing the incarnation so tightly inside translation they eclipse a deeper historical movement with its concomitant
theological scandal. Christians are, through Jesus the Christ, brought into the
story of Israel, which is indeed God's story. What is at stake is not simply particularity and certainly not the dialectic between the particular and the universal,
but rather the scandal of particularity.

The historical process elaborated through the phenomenon of translation as
articulated by these two historians presents particularity as examples of a continuous modality of divine–human interaction. In this way translation disarms
Christian particularity of its central scandal, the election of Israel and through
Israel the election of Jesus. Sanneh and Walls are correct to see that through
Jesus, Israel's particularity does not mean linguistic containment, but neither
does it mean linguistic supersessionism.[126] Israel's particularity bound up in Jesus
means that his scandalous particularity is the means through which Christian
faith acquires its social and political materiality. That social and political materiality draws our imaginations not first to the translation of the gospel message but
to the joining of peoples in the struggle to learn each other's languages in the

process of lives joined, lives lived together in new spaces, and constituting a new history for a new people.

The particularity Sanneh and Walls inscribe underwrites cultural national-isms wedded to theological formation. Unfortunately, they don't offer a sufficient account of the tragic theological history that lay behind the rise of nationalism. Neither do they see the abiding connection between cultural nationalism and ethnocentrism. Sanneh believes his vision of particularities embraced through the occurrences of vernacular translation actually undermines ethnocentrism by showing the possibility of multiple languages serving as revelatory mediums. Indeed, both authors are less concerned with nationalism than with showing how the gospel may protect and celebrate the cultural integrity of peoples while calling them beyond the mere celebration of their own culture. However, as Colenso shows, the formation of cultural nationalisms is a far thornier problem for Christian identity than either Sanneh or Walls suggests. Equally important, it is precisely at this point of their work that these historians seem strangely ahis-torical. As we have seen in this chapter, the rise of cultural nationalism carries unique racial, social, political, and economic signatures that cannot be divorced from ecclesial embodiments or the violence of nation-states.

In one sense, Colenso's early years in southern Africa divulge a theologian yielding to the temptation to control, a translator reframing native worlds within colonialism. But in another sense, in his later years in southern Africa Colenso gives witness to the destabilization of his world and its colonizing project. In-deed, the full testimony of the life of Colenso in South Africa outstrips his colo-nizing theological project, outstrips his stratagems for native domestication, and outstrips his fabricated goals of translation and brings him powerfully and pain-fully to the authentic goal of translation, joining.

BISHOP COLENSO AND THE END OF TRANSLATION

If translation is necessary to Christian theology, it is also dangerous. Colenso began his missionary career in the colony of Natal a deeply committed trans-lator of the gospel message to a people previously unknown to him. In those early years, he was joined at the proverbial hip to another translator of worlds, Theophilus Shepstone. The bishop envisioned his work as being inseparable from the work of this colonial administrator and yet, the more he translated Christian words into the isiZulu language the more his ears became attuned to the con-cerns of native voices. Little did he know that the very act of translation would place him on a path that would end one of his most important friendships in southern Africa. His break with Shepstone was occasioned by Chief Langaliba-

lele, the son of Chief Mtimkhulu of the Hlubi. Seeking asylum from Zulu domination, Langalibalele, his people (the Hlubi within the Zulu kingdom), and the
Ngwe people arrived in Natal in 1848.[127] Shepstone exercised absolute power
over Langalibalele and his peoples, placing these seven thousand displaced souls
on land at the foot of the Drakensberg Mountains with the understanding that
they would help guard white farm settlements from renegade marauders. By the
1870s, Langalibalele and his peoples, to the searing consternation of white English settlers, were thriving on the land. The settlers saw Langalibalele and the
Hlubi and Ngwe peoples both as unwanted competition in the marketplace because of the crops they produced and as much-wanted servile labor untapped
because of their flaunted independence. They also saw these natives as a military
threat owing to their increased access to guns received in exchange for their work
in the diamond fields. Yet it was not their prowess as excellent farmers, or their
influence on market prices through their goods and services, or even the presence of weapons among them that led to their tribulations, but the disrespect
that Shepstone perceived Langalibalele showed him personally. The Hlubi chief
failed to show proper, continuous deference to the great white chief.

It was the idea of Africans with guns that provided the pretext for the powerful
display of the Shepstone system. The Natal government demanded that all Africans register their firearms, an order exceedingly difficult to carry out given the
wide dispersion of weapons in the colony and the region. In fact, Chief Langalibalele did try to comply but without success. Shepstone ordered the chief to
appear before him to explain his actions. Out of fear for his life, the chief refused,
preparing the ground for Shepstone to pursue military action. A final envoy was
sent in pseudosupplication to the chief, an envoy who, it was claimed, Langalibalele's men threatened and humiliated. Insulted by this action, Shepstone ordered
the people to be captured and "broken up"—land was taken, cattle seized and
sold, men were marched from the mountain in chains, the elderly were abandoned destitute, and women and children were turned into "servants" for the
settlers.[128] In the end, the settlers got exactly what they wanted. Everything.

Langalibalele was captured and paraded in chains through the streets of
Pietermaritzburg, surrounded by a hostile white crowd. The chief's trial was a
spectacular example of colonialist injustice. The verdict was never in doubt, and
on February 9, 1872, he was found guilty and banished from Natal for life and
eventually exiled for a time to Robben Island. Colenso watched these events with
great interest and concern for the inconsistencies he saw in the entire affair. He
was also greatly troubled by the behavior of his dear friend Shepstone. The truth
came to Colenso through Magema Fuze, a former student and the man who ran
Colenso's printer, himself a Hlub, as well as through other Hlubi living on land

at Bishopstowe. They revealed to Colenso that the key witness of Langalibalele's alleged insurrection was lying and that the whole affair was steeped in deception. Colenso confronted Shepstone with this truth, and it was clear Shepstone was not interested in the facts. It also became clear that Shepstone was deeply involved in perpetrating this injustice. At this point, Colenso was faced with a decision the consequences of which would forever change his life in Africa. Guy powerfully captures the unfolding tragedy:

> If he did act further in support of Langalibalele it would make his position as Bishop in the colony virtually untenable. First he would alienate the colonists, and although his own income was secure he did not have sufficient funds to maintain his clergy without the support of their congregations. Already ecclesiastically isolated, he would cut himself off from his last body of adherents if he took up Langalibalele's cause. Furthermore it was already clear that Shepstone had not, as he had previously thought, been dragged into the affair unwillingly, but was deeply implicated. And Shepstone was not only his closest friend, he was also his most influential lay supporter. Their families had grown up together, the Shepstones had helped the Colensos in many ways over the years, and the Bishop had always spoken for Shepstone to those with power and influence in England.[129]

Colenso chose to listen to his cotranslators: not Shepstone, but Fuze and Ngidi. This choice painfully ended his friendship with Shepstone and turned him from colonialist collaborator to colonialist enemy. Thus began the transformation of Bishop Colenso. From the Langalibalele affair forward all the intellectual, political, social, and ecclesial tools he had honed in defining and defending his theological positions were placed in the service of the black body. His unrelenting advocacy for the chief and his people opened up the world he thought he knew into the world he would now understand. The change was evident upon his return to England to advocate for justice for the chief. Colenso turned down an opportunity to preach at Westminster Abbey to press his theological positions out of concern that it would detract from the Langalibalele situation. Again, Colenso chose the African.

His actions were certainly consistent with his theology. Given what he believed, he saw his advocacy for the Zulus and others as the only option. As is always the case, however, theological beliefs are always more than one imagines. Whether those beliefs are weak or strong, they leave open a door, and through that door came collectors on those beliefs, demanding a life consistent with that confession. For Colenso, the voices he had heard carefully year after year in translating were now speaking to him in a new way, and now that he had chosen the African he had new ears to hear: "As the months, and then years passed, more and more Africans from further and further afield confided in Colenso or turned to him for advice and assistance. And as they did so the Bishop's understanding of how Natal's rulers were perceived by those they ruled increased, his antagonism towards the authorities intensified, and his sympathy for the colonised deepened."[130] Colenso the translator, the one who had paid careful attention to the syntactical structures and semantic configurations of native languages, was now seeing practices concealed to most settlers: "The unthinking cruelty of the official announcement, the unconscious distortion in the formal report, and the unperceived injustice in the impartial legal judgement."[131] These were the operations of colonialist administration that settlers had chosen not to see, yet the bishop and his family could now see clearly. Bishop Colenso and his family were to see not only the injustice done to Langalibalele but also the horror of the war brought on the Zulus and their majestic chief, Cetshwayo kaMpande. Shepstone's old obsession with creating his own black kingdom in Zululand was a central driving force in his manipulation of colonial officials, officials already disposed toward destroying the fantasized Zulu military threat. Colenso watched and learned from the Zulus of Shepstone's imbecilic and humiliating attempted coronation of Cetshwayo after he ascended to the Zulu throne. Shepstone did this to claim his right and power as the "chief of chiefs" and to continue his efforts to obtain the land for his black kingdom. Colenso watched and learned from the Zulus of Shepstone's betrayal at the meeting near Blood (Ncome) River. Shepstone reversed his position and sided with the Transvaal in a dispute with the Zulus for Zulu-owned land. Colenso watched as the Shepstone clan drew the English inexorably toward war with the Zulus.

Bishop Colenso and his family did not simply receive information. They acted. The mission station at Bishopstowe, which had once so idealistically carried out its work of conversion, was now a place of political resistance to colonialist rule. The printers that had churned out translated texts — Scripture, theological commentaries, readers, and grammars — now printed the information Colenso and his family had gathered that documented colonialist judicial and administrative indiscretion, violence, and crimes against the Zulu nation. Magema Fuze and William Ngidi, who had joined Colenso in his missionary work, now supported the work of Zulu liberation. With the initial military setback of the British against the Zulu at Isandhlwana, Colenso refused to side with settler rage at the African. Instead, he pressed forward his translation not of Scripture but of Christianity: "Colenso knew the consequences of exposing white injustice to an already bigoted audience which had just suffered such terrible personal losses at the hands of a black enemy, and whose racial prejudices were now fed by terror."[132]

Resistance was a family affair, including not only Bishop Colenso but Sarah Frances and their children: their eldest daughter, Harriette Colenso, who most directly carried on her father's work, and Frances Ellen and Agnes Mary, along with two sons, Francis Ernest and Robert John, both of whom lived principally in England during their adult years but supported their father as best they could. The bishop made his choice in full knowledge of its consequences, and it became their choice as well. In the end, where his church would not follow and where his nation was surely not to go, his family faithfully and willingly went.

After only a few years, the mission ended. Once the theological controversy began, nothing else seemed to matter. There were very few, if any, truly new converts to Christianity, and in the end Colenso was rejected and despised by the very settlers he was sent to shepherd. Colenso's love of England and its civilizing mission turned sour: "This English rule, barely distinguishable in Colenso's eyes from God's rule, had initiated a 'Saturnalia of wrong-doing' and 'an apotheosis of force' in Zululand. For twenty-five years Colenso had based his actions on the assumption that he represented a system which 'can hardly be looked at apart from the Divine Government.' Now, as the result of the British invasion of Zululand, 'the name of Englishman' had become 'in the Native mind the synonym for duplicity, treachery, and violence' and with reason."[133]

Guy suggests that the Zulu "war, in destroying twelve thousand [Zulu] lives . . . also destroyed the meaning of Colenso's life."[134] Colenso became the translator against colonial translation. He became a translator bound to the flesh and bound to the plight of the African, and in so doing he interrupted a life of translation bound to the remaking of native worlds. This was a place his theology could not take him, but precisely where the Africans drew him. The practice of translation, the daily acts of sitting with black flesh seeking to say what the Scriptures say, opened Colenso to a path different from his own articulation of his work. His translated theology and his translated life were of different worlds. His translated theology was of a world already formed prepared to instruct, guide, and mangle. His translated life was of a world forming, moving inextricably toward binding, toward communion. His life and his work were of one piece.

The theological implications of Christian translation were often concealed to the colonialist translator. The story of Israel connected to Jesus can crack open a life so that others, strangers, even colonized strangers begin to seep inside and create cultural alienation for the translator and, even more, deep desire for those who speak native words. These implications are far greater than emancipatory possibilities for indigenes rooted in vernacular Christian agency or budding cultural nationalisms, but in joining—loving, caring, intimate joining. That joining is a sharing in the pain, plight, and life of one another. Just as Ngidi felt pathos for the plight of his Sobantu (Colenso), standing against those who called and treated him as a heretic, so Colenso came to feel pathos for the Africans who were called and treated as nonhuman. This, finally, is Christian translation. And such translation cost Bishop Colenso everything.

One should recall what was at stake in Colenso's mistakes. And in order to grasp this theological performance one must think beyond standard critiques of Christian colonialism in which Christianity is construed as allowing Western cultural imposition or simply as being cultural imposition itself. These critiques are beside the crucial point. Christianity in the colonialist moment offers one a gospel that is for everyone of necessity but joins no one of necessity. Thus the incarnation in this order of things comes to signify divine entrance into the world. The specific contours of that entrance lose their social and political character. This docetic problem is matched by another theological heretical habit of mind, adoptionism.

The adoptionist mode of thought found it easy to conceive of a human being whose life announced divine approval, divine presence, and divine election. God claimed this human being as special, unique among the creatures, and made him divine by an act of divine fiat. Jesus becomes the Son of God, which announces a divine fait accompli. His life witnesses this election—this divine presence and the knowledge that is able to rightly name the name of God. Adoptionism in this regard is a way to make sense of divine presence, divine immanence without suggesting a genuine historic entrance of the divine into space, time, and body. Adoptionist thinking in this way does not disrupt the normal patterns of human existence but finds in those patterns possibilities of holiness, transcendence, and divine approval. My skeletal account of a complex theological development is an attempt to capture what I earlier noted as the emergence of a contextual sensibility in Colenso.

For Colenso, God was already present among the Zulus. They had a name for God and knowledge of God rooted in their religious consciousness. At one level Colenso's assumption appears to be an ecumenical breakthrough, a ray of theological sunshine announcing not only religious tolerance for indigenous peoples but possibly even celebration of and respect for their religious sensibilities. Indeed, this has become a way of articulating divine presence serviceable for multiple intellectual projects. Yet at another level, what is apparent in Colenso's conclusions is the formation of a cultural nationalism that fully captures Christian theology. It is theology of and for the nation, for a people, any people, and every people. And in this conceptualization, Israel is historicized as an exhausted theological moment because God is now with everyone else. "Now" is not a temporal designation but a conceptual one. As Colenso noted, God has always been with everyone, they just didn't know it. Once this is expressed, theology must come to exist wholly as a nationalist intellectual exercise.

The point here is easy to miss. The tragedy is not contextual reflection; the tragedy is the way divine entrance is imagined among peoples. God's history is missing—no Israel, no Jesus, no apostles, no material struggle, no divine walking through time and indeed space, real space. Such a walking, such an entrance would be messy, carrying forward Israel's election and carrying forward many peoples, places, voices, ways of life bound to the Jewish Jesus, always announcing that God is with us. Colenso, following a distorted tradition, bypasses the real historical entrance and discerns God as present among all peoples, thereby eradicating theological history. Divine entrance, therefore, requires no relationships with anyone. Just as God is with Christians in Jesus, God is present among all people. But is God present among all peoples, all cultures? Only on this side of the colonialist moment and its antecedent supersessionism does one see this as a legitimate question. It is not. Divine presence revealed in the Jewish Jesus is a disciplining presence, guiding not only what Christians say about God in the world but how they see God at work in the world. That seeing comes with Christian bodies, their participation in the divine work in the world, drawing them toward other peoples, calling them to become one and to love concretely.

The theological imagination that deploys divine presence without concomitant real presence and real relationship may be enacting a form of Gentile hubris that believes we have the right to claim the very reality that was only announced over us by a gracious act of the Holy Spirit in the presence of Jewish believers (Acts 10, 11). Equally important, this adoptionist habit of mind turns peoples toward an isolating theological creativity, imagining the divine among one's own people. Such imagining is not wholly wrong, but it is impoverishing. And Christian theology in modern times has been set in place by this very poverty. So the gospel transmitted means in many imaginations the ways in which different peoples have culturally adopted and adapted Christian faith, ideas, doctrine, and language. And thanks to a supersessionist mistake and a colonialist sensibility, few Christians would discern the tragic history and the ongoing tragedy inside that statement about transmission. Unfortunately, the universal (bound up in docetism) and the contextual (bound up in adoptionism) are currently the dominant options for the contemporary theological imagination. They are two sides of the same coin, the one enabling the other, and neither finding its way to a Christian theology that of necessity creates intimacy.

Christian theology as articulated by intellectuals like Bishop John William Colenso continues to unfold in the world, its translation caught in the dynamics he so powerfully displayed. Like Acosta, Colenso has escaped notice in Western theological textbooks. His eclipse may lie in his heretical thought, his reputation as a protoliberal, or the perception that he was not a very sophisticated thinker. Colenso, however, illumines part of the contemporary theological morass. Indeed, Bishop Colenso marked a path that has been traveled by so many others before and since. One must in the end celebrate that path for showing a courageous Christian bishop who gave his life in missionary service and who in the mature years of his life acted for the good of an oppressed people. One must also grieve over that path for showing Christian theology in translation not only bound to colonialism, but still confining Christians to its options. There is a way forward but to find that way forward requires Christians to truly understand the pathos of this translator.

Yet before leaving his world, it is well to remember the words written by William Ngidi that were later turned into a hymn:

> Yes, indeed, my brothers, the weapons of war should be beaten into ploughs for cultivating the ground, and war-shields be sewed into garments of clothing, and peace be proclaimed, on the north and on the south, and on both sides, through the Father of our Lord Jesus Christ, Unkulunkulu, who ever liveth, and all evil become peace, I mean become goodness. Ah! And soldiers (should) be mustered for tribes which attack those at peace, and be mustered for roads of communication, and all tribes shout and say, "He is the King, He is the King, He is the King, God, Unkulunkulu, who has risen from the dead! By Him, the world, we have overcome it, and all its evil things! All evil is dead, Goodness stands, because the Father of Goodness stands; because the father of evil is dead, evil is dead also! Goodness, and Righteousness, and Holiness, on the north and on the south, and on both sides, stands in Peace! I mean, the Peace which comes from the Holy Spirit.[135]

In the end, William Ngidi and many others like him captured something in the missionary endeavor. Despite its multiple problems, a translation of the original had happened. And even if the original had been mutilated, tortured, and eventually killed in colonialist power, there was a resurrection.

4

EQUIANO'S WORDS

Olaudah Equiano was born in 1745 in a place he called Igbo, an area of Africa that is now southeastern Nigeria and that entered the consciousness of the Western world during the slow and steady ascension of the British nation to military and financial dominance.[1] By the year of his birth, the British had been involved in the slave trade for almost two hundred years, ever since the anti-Catholic sentiment and action of Queen Elizabeth I and the unquenchable greed of the ruthless merchant John Hawkyns. Impatient with Portuguese and Spanish Atlantic domination and angry about arbitrary papal rule that had divided the world up between its two ecclesial servant-nations, the Protestant Queen Elizabeth I sent Hawkyns to Africa with her blessing.

The Hawkyns family of Plymouth was a powerful, well-established merchant clan. Through his father, William Hawkyns, John had learned the ways of the sea and of trade. He also inherited his father's lust for power and his comfort with violence as a means to avaricious ends. Three ships under John Hawkyns's leadership—the *Swallow,* the *Jonas,* and the flagship *Solomon*—arrived on the west coast of Africa in December of 1562. Hawkyns and his men attacked Portuguese traders, coldbloodedly torturing and killing many of them and stealing their cargo, their money, and their human spoils. He stored the human spoils below decks in "rat-infested holds," his only concern being for their survival until such time as they could be sold.[2] The Portuguese claimed Hawkyns stole over nine hundred Africans. Hawkyns's own count claims fewer than that. His third-person account of this brutal beginning of the British slave trade is telling: "From thence he passed to Sierra Leona, upon the coast of Guinea, which place by the people of the country is called Tagrin, where he stayed some good time, and got into his possession, partly by the sword, and partly by other means, to the number of

300 Negroes at the least, besides other merchandises, which that Country yield-eth."[3] The "trade" born in violence took on an international character thanks to English piracy. Hawkyns proceeded from the west Guinea coast to Hispaniola, where he took advantage of the tensions between the settlers and the Spanish crown. These settlers, who felt abandoned by Spain, eagerly bought the goods, both inanimate and human, Hawkyns was selling. Hawkyns returned to England with money in his pocket and money for the queen's eager hands. From these hellish beginnings began the most significant phase of the Atlantic slave trade, the British trade, which far surpassed that of the Portuguese and the Spanish. This slave trade brought Equiano into the modern world in British hands.

The 1560s and two centuries more were years of British expansion. British interests ran from Nova Scotia through the colonies of North America to the Caribbean colonies as well as to its African interests along the Ivory, Gold, and slave coasts. Britain was also pressing its way east toward India and toward the east coast of Africa. Between Equiano's birth and the day of his death in 1797, Britain imported each year millions of pounds of sugar, tobacco, and cotton and millions of gallons of rum. They exported yearly hundreds of thousands of his "sable brethren," as he called them. Equally important, British war and slave ships were growing in size and firepower, becoming superior to every other na-tion's ships. During these years, British military prowess and the British appetite for and consumption of foreign goods, especially sugar, were matched only by its hunger for black bodies to labor in the production gangs of the colonies. From 1707 until 1808, over seven hundred thousand Africans gave their lives to the Atlantic plantation complex, laboring in the British Caribbean colonies. Dur-ing the same period, more than five hundred thousand Africans perished on the march to the slave ships; four hundred thousand died on board the ships; and a quarter million died shortly after the ships docked.[4] Yet during this time Britain was alive, powerfully alive, at sea. This is the world Olaudah Equiano was born within.

According to his own account, Equiano was captured at a young age, separated from his people, forced to march the long journey to the sea, compelled to live aboard British vessels, in the colonies, and in England, and in the midst of all this he became a Christian. What makes his story remarkable is that it became a story, written by himself. An audacious act, the act of writing allowed him to create a self in writing, a human interior. Equiano's powerful self-portrait of a human, an African, and a Christian presents a pivotal moment in the formation of Christian identity in nonwhite flesh, in colonized bodies. Equiano's *Interesting Narrative* is a Christian text, a theological text,[5] a spiritual autobiography.[6] Yet the acknowl-edging of his story as Christian invites one to consider the complexities of that existence for the African in modernity. Chronologically, Equiano comes centuries after Henry the Navigator's chronicler Zurara, and he falls between José de Acosta and John William Colenso. But theologically he comes after them all. We had to see the worlds formed around Zurara and the Jesuit Acosta and that formed around Colenso in order to understand the world Equiano will create through his own words.

THE STORY OF THE SLAVE SHIP

In 1789, Gustavus Vassa, now known by his African name, Olaudah Equiano, published his autobiography. The first volume of the original two-volume work begins with an account of his life in his native country. He posits a simplified yet civilized existence for his people before the invasion of Western civilization. The social order was healthy and logical—there were warriors and militia, musicians, dancers, and poets, chaste wives and responsible husbands and hard-working agriculturalists. Priests and magicians functioned as ministers and physicians. There were slaves, but they labored under the humane conditions of the kinship network.

The bonds of kinship played a tremendous role in Equiano's early life, both as boundaries to stay within and as rules to break. In a poignant episode he talks about his violation of the purity codes of his people during his mother's menstruation. During menstruation, he tells us, it "was forbidden [for a woman] to come into a dwelling-house, or touch any person, or any thing we ate. I was so fond of my mother I could not keep from her, or avoid touching her at some of those periods, in consequence of which I was obliged to be kept out with her, in a little house made for that purpose, till offering was made, and then we were purified" (*Interesting Narrative*, 42). For the sake of intimacy, Equiano risks violation of social codes, even if those codes are religious, ultimately demonstrating the elasticity of kinship bonds. Equiano subversively imagines connection.

These very bonds of connection unraveled for him when he and his sister were stolen from their home by two men and a woman employed by slavers (47). While still a child, Equiano was displaced, taken away from all he knew. Then, before his journey enters its most important life-shaping moments, he is separated from the stolen sister. Without parents, land, a place, or a known future to shape his imagination or to focus his desires, Equiano describes the shock waves produced by the slave ships as they spread the Atlantic slave trade across West Africa.

He was also describing "exchange," a word that now means definitively separating oneself from a product of one's personal labor, but had very different meanings in African political economy. In that context, people did not think in terms of the potential worth of an object in the context of exchange but saw its immediate value in terms of concrete use. Objects made by a person could be loaned, entrusted to the possession of and use by another, but not parted with. It was the indissoluble association of a person with the thing he or she had created, even after that thing might have passed into the hands of another, that produced the bond that always united givers and receivers, a reciprocal connection in personal terms of the association in material terms that arose out of possessing some material extension of another's labor.[7]

Slave traders, however, entered African political economies with a new vision of the relation of material objects to human being and new ways of teasing out the contractual elements of human relations themselves. Africans had viewed human labor as networked and contingent upon longer, more abiding claims to potential service. Given the fragility of life and the tentativeness of human strength and productivity, powerful people sought to solidify their position by acquiring loyalty rather than labor and promise of service rather than immediate payoffs.[8] Leaders and laypeople alike sought stability in long-term obligatory relationships out of which came the logics of exchange and the telos of production.[9]

In a "political economy where human dependence was the most efficacious means of increasing production," the idea of production primarily for exchange rather than communal use was destructively alien.[10] Therefore by manipulating a barter system that was intensely bound to use-value, each agreement, each sale suggested to African peoples engaged in trade the possibility of long-term obligatory relations. However, this communal metaphysic was being slowly eroded by an unbelievably virulent form of contractual individualism underwritten by sheer violence and European technological mastery. Workers were objectified alongside their labor, their products, their land, their animals, their loves, their hates, their hopes, their dreams, and all their everyday practices. This capitalist world of surplus value would introduce vast long-term inflation and the most powerful lever for sustaining uneven exchange ever created: debt. This was not the debt of an individual but of representatives tied to clans and peoples.[11] Guns and alcohol, essential parts of almost every "bundle" of goods, also helped to distort the traditional practices of community building. Joseph Miller powerfully captures these disruptive effects:

> Beyond the obvious coercive potential of muskets and the political prestige of strong drink, the sheer circulation of imports of any sort nurtured social and political stratification in Africa. Goods from the Atlantic accelerated the rates

at which the powerful dislocated the weak and at which people of all sorts were uprooted from their home communities and moved to those of new lords or masters, from villages to kings' courts, from old patrons to new patrons, or from lineage leaders to merchants. . . . [T]he increased velocity with which slaves circulated as the flows of material goods intensified meant that slave dependents moved more frequently and spent greater portions of their lives beginning over and over again as helpless, culturally disabled aliens in a succession of new communities.[12]

Miller notes four exchange strategies growing out of the increased commercialization of black life. The first altered normal patterns of communal consumption by pressing large quantities of foreign goods and services through traditional "domestic circuits of exchange" built on marital alliances, patronage, and tribute. The second strategy encouraged unrelated parties with goods to exchange or "producers with market opportunities among distant populations" to create relationships of alliance, patronage, and tribute, building into kinship networks establishing traditional and semitraditional bonds of obligation and relationship. In this way market opportunities became the underlying reason for the relationship itself. The third strategy involved utilizing trade centers for the "open exchange of material goods between autonomous equals, unbalanced by personal obligation." This strategy stood in constant tension and struggle with traditional patterns of exchange revolving around community building and obligation. The fourth exchange strategy embodied a "modern commercial economy" that rejected the old political economies in favor of "attribut[ing] basic value to useless tokens of exchange rather than to people." Africans committing to this exchange strategy were required to fundamentally alter their way of life.[13]

One can see in these stratagems the slow overturning of native anthropologies of deep human connection that vivify and make intelligible individual actions. The alternative anthropological vision is one that is well known—a vision of individuals freed to draw their own human circle guided by market possibilities. These stratagems served one decisive purpose, namely, to make possible the (hoped-for) eternal enslavement of black flesh. They hoped to make black peoples actors within the global market, peoples of diverse tongues who would now all speak the same language of commerce, knowing its calculation of evaluation. And of course there was one painful difference between actors: Africans could be bought and sold.

The trade entered African dreams and waking consciousness and stayed for centuries, touching every life indirectly and many directly. It slowly drove peoples deeper into alien lands, not only destroying their hopes of returning to ancestral lands in safety, but weaving their designation as aliens into their very being. Miller eloquently summarizes the tragedy of trade's chaos:

The slaving frontier zone thus washed inland in the sixteenth century and surged east like a demographic wave bearing the sea-borne goods of the Europeans on its crest. It tossed people caught in its turbulence about in wildly swirling currents of political and economic change. Like an ocean swell crashing on a beach, it dragged some of its victims out to sea in the undertow of slave exports that flowed from it, but it set most of the people over whom it washed down again in Africa, human flotsam and jetsam exposed to slavers combing the sands of the African mercantile realms left by the receding waters in the west, displaced from their birth places but not distantly so compared to the faraway destinations of the slaves carried off to America. By the middle third of the nineteenth century, the wave had tumbled population all the way to the center of the continent. There it rose to towering heights of chaos as its force combined with a similar demographic surge flooding the area from the Indian Ocean. Behind it, toward the Atlantic to the west, the turbulence subsided into relatively still demographic pools where quiet-flowing currents of reproduction and debt carried off most of the people sent into slaving, and where only eddies of periodic succession struggles and banditry from the distant sweeping tide continued to disturb the calm surface of politics.[14]

None of this would have been possible without the slave ship. What began with the guile of exchange led to violence and violent capture and then to the march of exile. Black bodies were driven out from the higher inland forests, plains, and mountains down to sand, ocean, and hungry vessels. The long, arduous journey prepared them, both physically and psychologically, for the slave ship, slowly carrying them away from home through the trading hands of multiple peoples.[15]

The march was the demonic reversal of a pilgrimage. On holy pilgrimage, those who walk depend on kind, hospitable strangers to offer them food and sometimes shelter. The pilgrimage, step after step, edging exhaustion, reveals the vulnerability of the human creature and humans' longing for God as companion and destiny. The walking pilgrim calls to God her Creator hoping to be received home again, not in heaven but here on earth in communion with the Holy One. For many in the Christian tradition, there was and is no stronger purifier of Christian identity than the aching journey of a pilgrimage. But the march of black flesh in bonds to the sea mocked that journey through reversal. The march of slaves, greedily hurried black bodies, toward death-filled ports demonically mimicked the divine banishment of the first family from the garden. Slavers would not have imagined this brutal march as a theological act, yet it was so in the most sinister way. African peoples walking together, bound together, first in varieties of rope and finally, as they approached the ships, bound in chains, left a way of imagining themselves when they left their lands.

Equiano marched, with his short legs and small feet. This child journeyed toward a destiny not primarily of place or even time but of identity. His walk toward the water brought him briefly to a chance encounter with his stolen sister, when they would be reunited for a single night: "She and I held one another by the hands across [a slaver's] breast all night; and thus for a while we forgot our misfortunes in the joy of being together" (51). The image of a slaver sleeping between these two children, a brother and a sister, was a powerful symbol of the disrupting wave of slavery. Morning meant the return of Equiano's misery as they were separated forever. The morning severed his last connection, reducing him to nothing and returning him to the long journey into nothingness. This is the nothingness out of which he will come to be. Standing in the middle of this nothingness will be the chaos that will order his existence, the slave ship: "The first object which saluted my eyes when I arrived on the coast was the sea, and a slave-ship, which was then riding at anchor, and waiting for its cargo. These filled me with astonishment, which was soon converted into terror, which I am yet at a loss to describe, nor the then feeling of my mind" (55).

If the world was recreated, then the sign of that recreation was the slave ship. Out on the vastness of the ocean, where water and wave superintend sight and sound, the slave ship announced the recreation of the world beyond the eyes and ears of much of the world. The life of Olaudah Equiano shows this. The slave ship floats on the sea, suspended between worlds, announcing the power to displace and translate the young Equiano. The child will be born again, born of a new set of relations he cannot easily grasp. He can only draw on the vision of a world of spirits to capture through his imagination what he cannot understand through their language. The hands that had reached all the way to his village and its intimate spaces now drew him close to its collective white body: "When I was carried on board I was immediately handled, and tossed up, to see if I were sound, by some of the crew; and I was now persuaded that I had gotten into a world of bad spirits, and that they were going to kill me. Their complexions too differing so much from ours, their long hair, and the language they spoke, which was very different from any I had ever heard, united to confirm me in this belief. Indeed, such were the horrors of my views and fears at the moment, that if ten thousand worlds had been my own, I would have freely parted with them all to have exchanged my condition with that of the meanest slave in my own country" (55).

The new ground on which these Africans would fashion the contours of their identities was the ship itself. The wooden world of the ship delivered them into the colonial world, but first it served as a replacement. The ship replaced the land by reformulating ecologies of identity around bodies, as it were, floating in space. Once they arrived at the shore for departure, a process of evaluation that had been gaining strength since their capture disclosed its logic. At the door of the sea, their bodies underwent a new calculation—size, type, age, gender, tribal background, language, beauty, ugliness, strength, compliance, aggressiveness, viability—all geared to determine market potential. This economic calculation was godlike in character. From the unassailable position of the gaze, slavers generated a process of judging black bodies that would take on a life of its own, growing in discursive power with each century. The frightening newness of the ship in the eyes of the Africans foretold a remaking of their lives without their consultation. The child Equiano sensed the newness signified by the chain but thought this newness meant they were now food to be eaten. A child's imagination reached close to the truth: they were now commodities: "When I looked around the ship too, and saw a large furnace of copper boiling, and a multitude of black people of every description chained together, every one of their countenances expressing dejection and sorrow, I no longer doubted of my fate, and, quite overpowered with horror and anguish, I fell motionless on the deck and fainted" (55).

The slave ship presents a particular moment when human beings seize limitless possibilities.[16] The captain stood at the center of slave ship ecology, representing both the European feudal past and its Enlightenment mercantile future. The captain was, as Marcus Rediker notes, "the monarch of his wooden world" and the "representative of the merchant and his capital throughout the voyage.[17] . . . He hired the crew, procured the ship's provisions, oversaw the loading of the original cargo, and conducted all the business of the voyage, from the buying of the slaves in Africa to their sale in the Americas. He saw to the navigation of the vessel, tended the compasses, and gave the working orders. On the smaller ships, he ran one of the two watches. . . . He possessed near-absolute authority, and he used it however he saw fit to maintain social order aboard the ship."[18]

Captains came from the upper classes of the Old World, and on their ships they were the educated, articulate authority figures. Slave ship captains, as the harbingers of the new capitalist order, sought to maintain absolute discipline geared to a central goal—maximum profitability. On the one hand, they embodied the emerging vision of a self-made individualist who manifested a true entrepreneurial spirit with its risk taking and business-making possibilities. On the other hand, they also embodied applied Enlightenment knowledge with their fluency in multiple languages and their abilities to engage in speculation, negotiation, and complex international contractual agreements. They were the eighteenth- and nineteenth-century equivalents of the small and midsize business owner of a twenty-first-century franchise. They also exhibited their unbelievable localized power in ways that would establish much of plantation and New World social logics.

The captain not only carried forward the merchant's sensibilities and interest on the slaving voyage, but also acted out of profound self-interest. A successful slaving voyage would make a captain a very rich man. A captain of a slave ship in eighteenth-century Britain who completed a successful voyage could make the modern-day equivalent of hundreds of thousands of dollars, gaining his own slaves or selling slaves from his own stock. The captain could then invest that money in land, plantation, and farming opportunities. A captain could easily retire after a few voyages to the aristocratic life of a plantation owner or enter a career as a statesman in the New World.

But this was certainly not the case for the sailors. The sailors were in every sense the oppressed proletariat. Few men (and even fewer women) happily or knowingly volunteered for work on a slaving ship. They were driven to the ship by distorted visions of adventure, sheer poverty and financial desperation, or kidnapping or when their debts were manipulatively increased by cunning merchants, landlords, and captains to the point that they had no choice but to sign up for service aboard these dreaded vessels.[19] Crimps, labor agents in the employ of merchants, landlords, or captains, would coerce these unprotected souls into service. A crew of sailors on a slaving ship often represented an international and cosmopolitan group of impoverished laborers with peoples from various corners of Europe and the colonies—Indian, Asian, and, of course, African. African sailors served because other employment options were extremely limited; indeed, the only other option was slavery.

Sailors formed a brotherhood of suffering and violence, serving, as Rediker states, "[as] a third party between two much bigger, heavier dancers: the merchant, his capital, and his class on the one hand and the African captive, her labor power, and her class-in-the-making on the other."[20] This middle position made the sailor both the recipient of and the conduit for the violence of the slave ship. Sailors were beaten, whipped, and tortured in other ways in order to maintain discipline and keep them in strict order on ships far from the judicial structures of land.[21] Sailors in turn took out their anger on black bodies by beating, whipping, and torturing slaves. Thus the possibilities the slave ship may have provided for ethnic confraternity, for freedom, and for the individuals' financial success were engulfed in the one reality of violence. The ship's cosmopolitanism was constructed through violence and on the foundation of the African slave, the one whose body marks the accumulation of profit through time.[22]

The slave ship distorted the power of joining together many different peoples on a common journey and mission.[23] The diverse languages of the crew were subordinated to the voices of the captain and the officers, and the various languages of the slaves were used against them. Slaves of different tongues were often placed together on ships, which both further isolated and individualized them and reduced the possibility of planned rebellion. As one employee of the slave trade stated, "By taking some 'of every Sort on board [the slave ship], there will be no more Likelihood of their succeeding in a Plot, than of finishing the Tower of *Babel.'"[24]

The man, woman, and child drawn in pain from their homeland were greeted by violence, stripped down to a nakedness filled with shame, and reduced from names to numbers.[25] Loved ones connected by flesh and blood who survived the interior march were often separated from one another. Those fortunate enough to remain together entered the horrors of the ship together. On board the ship, men and women were separated and placed below deck, the men most often chained together by twos. When above deck, slaves were separated from the crew by a barricade, sometimes reinforced by musket or loaded blunderbuss and cannon. From the barricade crewmen could fire on slaves in the event of an insurrection.

Those who resisted in any way were beaten or whipped without mercy. Both women and men whose rebellion was thought to be contagious were tortured and killed as examples of the wages of disobedience. The rape of black women was woven into the very fabric of the social order of the slave ship. The captain and the officers selected the women or, most often, the young girls they wanted in their personal stock, and they then controlled sailors' access to the "remainders." That control was without virtue, as sailors shared fully in the brutal rape and torture of women and children.[26]

Death revealed itself aboard the slave ship as a power, as an antilife form pressing its way deep into the ecology of slave ship life. Captains claimed this power and ruled their crews by fear and intimidation. Sailors shared in this power and drew its use to a fine point in the control of the slaves. One must remember, however, that death surrounded captain and sailors as well in the forms of shipwreck, piracy, mutiny, and financial ruin. The west coast of Africa was for half of the sailors who sought its shore their final unhappy resting place, and for the half that did not die on the coast it was still a dreaded place. For all employed in the trade, exposure to the elements, disease, hunger, thirst, easy loss of life or limb were constant companions. All were bound together in this ecology, captain, sailor, and slave by the fragility that is creation.

The fragile creation is subject to death. Slave ships poignantly displayed the character of this vulnerability. They embodied not only the chaos and violence unleashed by human disobedience, but also gave witness to the contingency of human existence out of nothing. Slave ships played in the nothingness—hung African life out in it and dangled black bodies over it, always seeking to join those bodies to the nothingness out of which existence came in hopes of reestablishing African life as called into existence by market desire and the power of whiteness.

The finality of it all on board a ship suggested the final solution: suicide. For some West African peoples suicide in such cases was considered "an admirable act,"[27] a kind of martyrdom, especially for those people who believed that in death they would overcome the nothingness and return home, free and without pain. Yet suicide in this case was more than an option. It was a supreme temptation, a false sign of freedom, and therefore a sign of death's victory. In this temptation the voice of death spoke louder than the sounds of life, muffled as they were by the groans coming from the holds.

Many were prevented from yielding to the temptation of suicide. Instead they were forced to begin life anew on the ships as slaves. For instance, the simple yet profound act of eating became an occasion of torture. Eating on a slave ship did not carry the symbolic weight of affirming community and of offering thanks to God. Africans who refused to eat, choosing instead a slow death at sea rather than a slow death on the plantation were force-fed, often by use of a horrific piece of technology called the *speculum oris,* a contraption that forced the mouth open.

This technological advance in forced feeding stood alongside other disciplinary technologies deployed on slave ships. It was usual to find on a slave ship manacles (for the hands and arms), shackles (for ankles and sometimes wrists), various kinds of chains, neck irons, branding irons, thumbscrews, cat-o'-nine-tails, and other whips.[28] Just as the slave ship destroyed the honor of satisfying labor and its ability to build bonds of respect among different people, so too it turned technological advances malignant.

Bound together by twos and crammed tightly into the ship's holds, these human beings lay side by side in coffinlike spaces fetid with mucus, vomit, blood, and human waste. The heat, paucity of breathable air, and pestilence meant that many died below deck. The fate of those joined to the dying and dead was to have death chained to them until someone removed the dead body. The fate of the dead reinforced the mutilation of community and the disorder of creation: dead bodies were not buried but thrown overboard to the waiting sharks that followed the slave ships. Sharks fed on black flesh as though it was part of their natural food source, and their menacing presence was a stark reminder of death's imperial power reigning on board and of a creation in disarray.

As we noted in chapter 1, the geographic displacement established by the colonialist moment meant the body stood in, as it were, for the land. The slave ship reveals the flexibility and global adaptability of race, an adaptability enabled by the market. Everyone who stepped on a slave ship became racialized, white and black. But it was not only what happened to identity once aboard a ship, but what the arrival of a slave ship signified. As each slave ship docked in the new worlds, it further energized the racialization of human existence already underway through the overturning of peoples from their land. The slave ship for its part was the pivotal identity destabilizer that drew peoples into the performance of racial identities. Rediker writes, "It . . . mattered little what had been the cultural or ethnic background of the sailor, for he would, on the ship and coast of Africa, become 'white,' at least for a time, as the 'vast machine' helped to produce racial categories and identities. It was the common practice for everyone involved in the slave trade, whether African or European, to refer to the ship's crew as the 'white men' or the 'white people,' even when the crew was motley, a portion of it 'colored' and distinctly not white. The sailor's status as a 'white man' guaranteed that he would not be sold in the slave-labor market, and it marked him as someone who could dispense violence and discipline to the enslaved on behalf of the merchant and his capital."[29]

EQUIANO AND FALSE INTIMACY

This world of the slave ship, this remade world, this racial world would now be the world of young Equiano. In this world, he would seek to reestablish that which might make him whole, make him human. He will seek relationships, human bonds that might sustain him. In the third chapter of his narrative, Equiano introduces his readers to his important friendship with the youth Richard Baker, a white youth who befriended him on one of his first voyages after being purchased. A few years older than Equiano and the owner of slaves himself, Dick becomes a true friend. They shared "many sufferings together on shipboard" and laid "in each other's bosoms when [they] were in great distress" (65). The friendship with Richard Baker ended abruptly with his death in 1759. But Equiano draws his loss to an important point: "[His death was] . . . an event which I have never ceased to regret, as I lost at once a kind interpreter, an agreeable companion, and a faithful friend; who, at the age of fifteen, discovered a mind superior to prejudice; and who was not ashamed to notice, to associate with, and to be the friend and instructor of one who was ignorant, a stranger, of a different complexion, and a slave!" (65). With remarkable candor and vulnerability, the writer suggests a white exemplar of friendship even within the hostile wooden world of the slave ship. Equiano is once again grappling with the death that stalks his bonding, his village, his sister, the fragment of his people at the slave market, and now his closest childhood friend, Richard Baker.

These efforts to create intimacy help one grasp the complexity of the master–slave relation as it is played out in Equiano's life. Although he was bought and sold several times on the west coast of Africa, the significant slave masters emerge in the New World. On June 13, 1754, Equiano arrived in Virginia as a "refuse" slave, having been rejected in Barbados by West Indian buyers and having parted there with the few slaves to whom he had some connection.[30] His slave odyssey would be shaped primarily by four men: Mr. Campbell, his first master; Michael Henry Pascal, his most significant master; Captain James Doran, a transitional master; and Robert King, the master who would eventually set him free. Though Campbell was first and introduced young Olaudah to the new world of slave existence in Virginia, it was Pascal who was most determinative of the life he would live and preferred to live. Pascal was a seaman, a lieutenant in the Royal Navy, and in 1754 he purchased the African boy for thirty or forty pounds sterling from Campbell. Most important, as Vincent Carretta notes, Pascal would give him access to surrogates: "He was still a slave, but because of his youth and status as an officer's servant his was a relatively privileged position. He had lost one family but found another, he thought, in his fellow seamen. Most important, he once again appeared to be in a stable relationship with an adult male figure of authority. The orphaned little boy quickly attached himself emotionally to the man who had bought him and who, Equiano assumed, reciprocated that emotional attachment. In Equiano's eyes Pascal filled the role not only of adult, master, and superior officer but, more significantly, of substitute father."[31]

Before Pascal, though, Daniel Queen, the captain's attending sailor, befriended him and taught him some of the rudimentary skills that would be necessary for financial self-sufficiency on and off a ship. Queen taught him how to attend to the captain, how to read and write, and how to buy and sell small items to the crew. Queen also taught him to read the Bible. They would spend countless hours reading and discussing the Bible. As Equiano says, "In short he was like a father to me; and some even used to call me after his name; they also styled me the black Christian. Indeed I almost loved him with the affection of a son" (92). Queen gave the young Olaudah the idea that he could be his merchant apprentice, which greatly fueled his fires of freedom.

Exchange networks became the point of cohesion and in some cases substituted for abiding kinship relationships, just as he was being introduced to Christian ideas. Christianity performed as an exchange network and, understood within categories of capital, would become a severely limited Christianity. It is not clear from the narrative whether Pascal became jealous of the relationship between Queen and Equiano or whether he sensed that the boy (whom he named Gustavus Vassa after the sixteenth-century Swedish king and emancipator) was being led to anticipate freedom. Whatever the case may be, Pascal abruptly and without warning, without allowing him to gather his things, without farewells to the crew, loaded Equiano onto a small boat, took him to another ship, the *Charming Sally*, and sold him to Captain James Doran. Heartbroken by yet more loss and by what he perceived as a deep betrayal, he tried to argue for his freedom with his new master and Pascal: "I told him my master could not sell me to him nor to any one else . . . I have served him . . . many years, and he has taken all my wages and prize-money, for I only got one sixpence during the war; besides this I have been baptized; and by the laws of the land no man has a right to sell me" (93–94).

Captain Doran told Gustavus that he "talked too much English," and if he continued talking he would be tortured in the manner captains inflicted on insubordinate crewmen. The attempt to offer a rational argument against slavery in the face of a captain was ridiculous from the captain's vantage point. What was also unseemly was English in the mouth of a slave, not to mention a slave speaking to white men as though he was their equal. Equiano in this conversation faced the limitations of relationships construed within networks of exchange, even as he tried desperately to deploy those networks to his advantage. We also see the symbol of Christianity's fundamental limitation, the inefficacy of baptism in the presence of a racial calculus. As performed in the slaveholding Christian West, baptism enacted no fundamental change in the material conditions of Christian existence.

Even if at this point Equiano claims he had not fully understood the way of salvation, he attributed a Christian perspective to his younger self in this moment of betrayal: "In a little time my grief, spent with its own violence, began to subside; and after the first confusion of my thoughts was over, I reflected with more calmness on my present condition: I considered that trials and disappointments are sometimes for our good, and I thought God might perhaps have permitted this in order to teach me wisdom and resignation; for he had hitherto shadowed me with the wings of his mercy, and by his invisible but powerful hand brought me the way I knew not. These reflections gave me a little comfort, and I rose at last from the deck with dejection and sorrow in my countenance, yet mixed with some faint hope that the *Lord would appear* for my deliverance" (95–96). This is a beautiful statement of divine providence, a reflection one might attribute to a seasoned Christian whose spirituality reflects a disciplined interpretive practice. Equiano places such reflection in the mind of his younger self. This revealed to his white readers that even if the appropriate social relations promised by Christian faith were thwarted by the exchange networks constituted within slavery, his connection to God would not be so thwarted or compromised. Yet this mangled Christian social reality imposed on Equiano produced fissures in his theological vision.

A man whose intuitions and longings moved him toward a communal existence was forced to try to imagine Christian community in the face of its deepest social ruptures. The result was a Christian faith that struggled mightily against its social contradiction, yet one that resigned itself to the society constituted by the exchange networks of mercantile capitalism. This Christian faith imagined and sought belonging but was repeatedly thrown back by the dominant racial calculus to a theological isolationism in which God's providential care had to substitute for communal care. There is a difference as well as a connection between providential care and the care of others performed as ecclesial community. However, when providential care is deployed in substitution it indicates an absence, a kind of recapitulation of Gethsemane, of isolated agony where Jesus' disciples failed to help him. But he was sustained in his life mission only by his relationship with his Father, God (Matt 26:36–46). So too Equiano attempts to act faithfully toward God and imagine community in the face of its unrelenting absence. In Equiano's case, visions of providential care had to be stretched to distortion, stretched to cover absurdity after absurdity.

Equiano was keenly aware of the absurdity of faith's performance in the remade world. The biting sarcasm that runs through the narrative is evidence of this. He repeatedly ties the designation of Christian to people whose brutal actions belie this claimed identity. He notes Christian masters who brutally tortured their slave for the slightest offense (108), the ubiquitous rape of women, including very young girls (104), and the theft from slaves who had little or nothing (118, 128, 214). The writer assumed a prophetic position as one who spoke from within the Christian tradition, arguing through its internal logics and utilizing its scriptural wisdom. However, what he was not fully aware of was how far down the absurdity reached into Christianity's performance in the new worlds.[32]

This slow disclosure is understandable given the fabricated moral universe within which he articulated his faith. Contained within the world of white judgment, young Equiano accepted having his life evaluated on the continuum between disobedience and obedience. The African as slave, unlike the sailor, must be made a radically obedient body, one that eats what is given, goes where he is told, submits willingly to rape, works without end, and lives. Good and evil are calibrated to this telos. This white judgment in the construction of good and evil grew out of the form of evaluation administered in the exchange and sale of the African on the shores of Africa, where obedience was joined to market calculation. This meant that the judgment of good and evil tied to black obedience and disobedience overrode considerations of the immorality of black murder and enslavement.[33]

Once Equiano arrived in Montserrat he was sold to Robert King, with whom he would, under the tutelage of King's employee, the captain Thomas Framer, cultivate his skills as a merchant. King's rationale for buying "the slave Gustavus" seemed both convincing and flattering to the young man: "Mr. King, my new master . . . said the reason he had bought me was on account of my good character; and, as he had not the least doubt of my good behaviour, I should be very well off with him. . . . I was very thankful to Captain Doran, and even to my old master, for the character they had given me; a character which I afterwards found of infinite service to me" (99–100). One could interpret Equiano's comments as yet expressing his continued longing for a father figure. But he is articulating a moral sensibility in the midst of a grotesquerie. He attempted to execute this theological sense not only in the middle of slavery but also refracted off the myopic judgments of white masters. That is, he exercised a faint hope of being able to draw out from their evaluative control over his life discursive fragments that would be marketable. He learned that "character" existed for black flesh in the New World as an aspect of use-value, of commodification itself. And he admonished slave masters to treat their slaves well because they in turn would be "faithful, honest, intelligent, and vigorous" in their work, to the benefit of the master (112).

Equiano is a self constituted under the conditions of exchange networks and thus reflects the limitations placed on the imagination for self-fulfillment. One of the most amazing occurrences of these limitations in the narrative is his negotiating the possibility of buying himself back, buying his freedom. King, who was, according to Equiano, by far his kindest master, made him the extraordinary deal that if he could earn through entrepreneurial efforts the exact sum King originally paid for him, he would be allowed to buy his freedom. This is an amazing situation not because of its rarity but because it signifies the best possible relationship between blacks and whites under the conditions of chattel slavery and mercantile capitalism: economic confraternity. It also signifies a stunning narrowing of options for the slave Gustavus—become a "businessman" or remain a slave. The sum of "forty pounds sterling" was agreed on by King and his slave. The slave Gustavus then made every human effort to build up capital. One of the most powerful passages in the narrative is Equiano's description of the day he approached King with the agreed-upon sum and the request that King honor their agreement:

> When we had unladen the vessel, and I had sold my venture, finding myself master of about forty-seven pounds I consulted my true friend, the captain, how I should proceed in offering my master the money for my freedom. He told me to come on a certain morning, when he and my master would be at breakfast together. Accordingly, on that morning, I went, and met the captain there, as he had appointed. When I went in I made my obeisance to my master, and with my money in my hand, and many fears in my heart, I prayed him to be as good as his offer to me, when he was pleased to promise me my freedom as soon as I could purchase it. This speech seemed to confound him; he began to recoil; and my heart that instant sunk within me. "What!" said he, "give you your freedom? Why, where did you get the money; Have you got forty pounds sterling?" "Yes, sir," I answered; "How did you get it?" replied he; I told him, "Very honestly." The captain then said he knew I got the money very honestly, and with much industry, and that I was particularly careful. . . . "Come, come," said my worthy captain, clapping my master on the back, "Come, Robert . . . I think you must let him have his freedom; you have laid your money out very well; you have received good interest for it all this time, and here is now the principal at last. I know Gustavus has earned you more than an hundred [pounds] a-year, and he will still save you money. . . ." My master then said, he would not be worse than his promise; and taking the money, told me to go to the Secretary at the Register Office, and get my manumission drawn up. (135)[34]

Crucial to this event was the mediating necessity of whiteness seen in the actions of Captain Farmer. Farmer's intercession with King with a necessary summation of the economic advantages of the slave Gustavus was the decisive leverage needed to secure his freedom. The irony of this aspect of his journey toward manumission confirms the underlying reality of white control of the networks of exchange. It also confirms the superficiality of the fabricated moral universe within which white judgment functions. The moral self in this situation functions ideologically, calibrated racially as an aspect of the slave–master relation. Without white intervention it was doubtful that the clear faithfulness of Equiano would have been sufficient support for his words, even accompanied as they were with the symbols of exchange, money.

Equiano's honesty in acquiring the money was confirmed by the captain, and with his freedom secured he in reverent gratitude thanked God and thanked his "worthy friends." He then "rose with a heart full of affection and reverence, left the room in order to obey [his] master's joyful mandate [to go obtain manumission documents] . . ." and commented, "As I was leaving the house, I called to mind the words of the Psalmist, in the 126th Psalm, and like him, 'I glorified God in my heart,' in whom I trusted" (136). He continued in the employ of King out of a sense of love and duty, but he began planning immediately how he could return to England and, as he said, "surprise my old master, Capt. Pascal, who was hourly in my mind, for I still loved him, notwithstanding his usage of me" (138). These events in the narrative reveal Equiano's continuing attempt to imagine belonging and relationship beneath the guiding hand of God through relations that are fundamentally diseased and reflective of the remade world.[35]

This is Christianity performed within the horizon of an exchange network. Equiano, as Houston Baker notes, "realizes, in effect, that only the acquisition of property will enable him to alter his designated status *as property*."[36] The profound irony that unfolds in the life of Olaudah Equiano was his realization that the central means through which he would move from property to becoming one who would obtain property was precisely by making his body appear in textual display. He would have to move from one commodity form to another commodity form, from a slave on a ship to a slave in a text. He would secure his transformation by telling his story and thereby re-creating himself in the text just as he had been recreated on the slave ship. In so doing, he would also continue to display his desire to create relationship and to form intimacy.

EQUIANO AS THE SECOND ADAM

The slave ship positions itself next to creation, next to the creating act as creation's recapitulation. It is a moment of metaphysical theft, an ambush of the divine *creatio continua*, the continuing creative act. The creatio continua is first the gracious gift of God's providential care and preservation of the world, a preservation in which humankind participates. If the slave ship is an inversion of that participation, then Equiano will improvise inside that inversion. He will in effect seek to capture the energy of the slave ship and redirect it away from death toward life. By inscribing the horror of the ship inside the writing of his life he will attempt to subject that horror to the power of narration, turning its telos toward a good end, the flourishing of his own life.

The slave ship, however, performs translation, displacement, and disordered creation. It embodies a new story of creation, one in which the first family will be reborn as *familia oeconomicus*. The economic family is not a family structuring its own economic realities, but one being formed by them. The original story is refashioned on the slave ship through the bodies that lay within its holds and the bodies that suffered on deck. The slave ship also captures all other forms of translation: translation of languages, of spaces, of life to death, of innocence to guilt, of joy to unrelenting sorrow. This means that Equiano must also contend with the power and performance of colonialist translation. This proved to be a far more formidable challenge than he understood, because Equiano writes after other words have been spoken and written about black bodies. For Equiano and millions like him, the world he entered was inscribed decisively by others' words regarding his people.[37]

The *Interesting Narrative* was published in 1789, three months before the French Revolution. It followed the important Black Atlantic texts of Briton Hammon, *A Narrative of the Most Uncommon Sufferings and Surprizing Deliverance of Briton Hammon, A Negro Man* (1760); James Albert Ukawsaw Gronniosaw, *A Narrative of the Most Remarkable Particulars in the Life of . . . an African Prince, as Related by Himself* (1772); Phillis Wheatley, *Poems on Various Subjects, Religious and Moral* (1773); Francis Williams, *History of Jamaica* (1774); Ignatius Sancho, *Letters of the Late Ignatius Sancho* (1782); John Marrant, *A Narrative of the Lord's Wonderful Dealings with John Marrant, a Black (Now Going to Preaching the Gospel in Nova Scotia) Born in New York, in North America* (1785); Quobna Ottobah Cugoano, *Thoughts and Sentiments on the Evil and Wicked Traffic of the Slavery and Commerce of the Human Species, Humbly Submitted to the Inhabitants of Great Britain, by Ottobah Cugoano, a Native of Africa* (1787); and also the earlier, little-known but important texts of Jacobus Elisa Johannes Capitein, *Dissertatio politico-theologica, qua disquiritur, Num libertati Christiane servitus adversetur, nec ne?* (1742), and Anton Wilhelm Amo, *De jure Maurorum in Europa* (1729) and *Tractatus de arte sobrie philoso-phandi* (1739).[38]

The *Interesting Narrative* differs from these earlier works in its representational depth in two senses. First, Equiano writes free of the editors that greatly shaped many of the works of his predecessors. He writes beyond an enslaved self, beyond the repression of voice, and beyond the concealment of slavery's horror through emphasis on a sinful self made moral by the intervention of whiteness. He also witnesses the contradictions in Christian culture by disrupting the ideologically evacuated spiritual autobiography.[39] Second, as his premier biographer, Vincent Carretta, notes, Equiano called himself not an African but "the African."[40] He speaks not only for the many (Africans) but also directly to the many (white readers). His goal is to take his readers with him through the journey of his life, not simply as spectators but as those who will by the end of the story claim Equiano as one of their own. Equiano articulates the vulnerability of a human creature in need of relationship in the way he describes his need for acceptance, justice, companionship, and even love: "Soon after this, the blacks who brought me on board went off, and left me abandoned to despair. I now saw myself deprived of all chance of returning to my native country, or even the least glimpse of hope of gaining the shore" (56).[41]

Equiano must make sense of his life no longer in a village configured in ancient space, but on ships configured by global commerce and the calculus of exchange. His narrative is translation. As translated, his narrative is also a product. And Equiano is a businessman. He will offer himself for relationship by offering himself for purchase, not from the hold of a ship but from the free market in a text. Equiano is caught up in the trajectory of English commerce, which was becoming the currency of relationship. During Equiano's lifetime, Britain would eventually rule the Atlantic economic circuit in the eighteenth century and would through that circuit define the lives of millions of Africans.[42] Europeans were not the progenitors of global economic circuits. Yet they built in new and comprehensive ways on that earlier system of world trade so that the commodifying of African bodies flowed seamlessly with the manufacturing and distributing practices of other goods.[43]

The well-known yet crude triangle model for understanding the pathways of Atlantic trade remains helpful as a reminder that the trade circuit determined more than product placement and exchange mechanisms. Textiles, firearms, alcohol, tobacco, and metalware, all of diminishing quality and varied availability, were shipped to West Africa. Africans were traded for these European products and then sent to the Old World and the Americas to work until death. Born of that labor, staple commodities were shipped to the Old World.[44] The circuit constituted the cosmopolitan and the disaporic in their most basic senses. On the one hand, the circuit gestured toward realizing a universal displayed in the possibility of free "peaceful" exchange of goods and services between nations.[45] On the other hand, the extraction of peoples and their surplus labor and goods for profit constituted the deepest sense of exile. Not only would they be peoples in strange lands but their alienated labor would be put to estranged purposes.

Unbridled European consumption and production transubstantiated African bodies. Black bodies juxtaposed to such things as East Indian textiles, Swedish bar iron, Italian beads, German linens, Brazilian tobacco flavored with molasses, Irish beef, butter, and pork, Jamaican rum, and North American lumber announce ownership. In godlike fashion, merchants and traders transformed African bodies into perishable goods and fragile services.[46]

Equiano understood that life beyond slavery will be made possible by the very market that brought him to the New World as property.[47] Thus he seeks by means of his narrative to master the market. A keen reader of the times, as

Carretta notes, "[Equiano] understood that what the abolitionist cause needed now and what readers desired was exactly what he had positioned himself to give them—the story told from the victim's point of view."[48] With an eye to the times, Equiano published his book only a few weeks before William Wilberforce masterfully argued against the Atlantic slave trade in the House of Commons, May 12, 1789.[49] Equiano's behind-the-scenes efforts to bring this publication to life were nothing short of brilliant. Drawing on all the economic survival skills he had honed on slave ships and in slaving ports, working to care for captains and masters alike, Equiano solicited subscribers (that is, investors) for his manuscript, asking for partial advance payment to cover his cost. He also, in an act extremely rare for an author and unheard of for an African writer, kept control of his copyright, thereby always owning his literary self. And most important, he began an entrepreneurial odyssey that wove tightly together abolitionist energy and political activism to his own efforts to thrive in the modern world.

Equiano attracted more subscribers as the number of abolitionists grew. As the abolitionist cause spread, so too did the African take its message with his book throughout the British Isles, initiating what was arguably the first actual book tour. It would be a cheap criticism to call him an economic opportunist; he was simply a shrewd businessman. What is observable in Equiano's actions is far more complex than market reflex. Here one encounters black life forcibly formed inside the market.[50] By keeping each of the nine editions of the book in his constant care and holding complete oversight of his literary project, "acting as his own publisher and principal distributor," Equiano was exposing the echoes of commodified existence, but even more he was lodging within it the protest for intimacy, for acceptance, and relationship for his people and for himself.[51]

It was a subtle but powerful protest, one which first showed itself in the way his face looked out on the world from his book. Unlike any other of his black contemporaries pictured on the cover of their narrative, always looking away from the powerful white gaze, Equiano stared directly at his readers.[52] His black face joined the reader's face, hinting at equality through connection. As noted earlier, Equiano offers the architecture of a hoped-for new kind of intimacy, one between the races. Equiano, however, is forced to imagine intimacy with and against the master–slave relation. The narrative is certainly spiritual autobiography, yet it also draws the reader into a frustrated spiritual longing, an unresolved longing.[53] This means that his narrative carries the demand for humanizing relationships as central to the performance of Christian identity, the very identity claimed by his white readers. It is in the light of this demand that one can understand his comments concerning Israel.

Equiano draws an analogy between Jewish ways of life and those of his own people. They shared purification rites, circumcision, offerings and feasts, the significance of naming, and the "law of retaliation," as he called it. His drawing attention to these cultural analogies sets the reader up for his more serious conclusion: "that the one people had sprung from the other" (43–44). His people came from the Jews, directly from the seed of Abraham. By drawing the black body next to the Jewish body, Equiano suggests a reorientation for his white readers — toward kinship. He then "environmentalizes" race, here understood as skin color. Peoples like the Portuguese, after intermarrying with Africans, became "perfect negroes." Spaniards "darken" after generations in foreign places, and as he says, "surely the minds of the Spaniards did not change with their complexions!" (45). His theological conclusion is powerfully aimed at Europeans: "Let such reflections as these melt the pride of their superiority into sympathy for the wants and miseries of their *sable brethren*, and compel them to acknowledge, that understanding is not confined to feature or colour. If, when they look round the world, they feel exultation, let it be tempered with benevolence to others, and gratitude to God, 'who hath made of one blood all nations of men for to dwell on all the face of the earth; and whose wisdom is not our wisdom, neither are our ways his ways'" (45, emphasis added).

Equiano asserts a portrait of the creation against the false image of superior white/inferior black beings based on intelligence. Following Anthony Benezet's use of the same Scriptures in his *Some Historical Account of Guinea* (1772), he draws together these two counterhegemonic texts, the first from Acts 17:26–27, which challenges notions of Greek superiority, and the second from Isa 55:8–9, which announces the supremacy of God's wisdom and ways above the human mind.[54] Read together these texts suggest a radical equality but, more important, a familial connection for Europeans with their sable brethren. It is also not coincidental that he aligns Jewish identity with the African for his white readership. From the earliest moments of the age of discovery, the question of human origins was an obsession. Having read the theologians John Gill, Granville Sharp, John Clarke, and Hugo Grotius through Clarke, Equiano was doubtless aware of the discussions of Noah's sons and human ancestry.

Protestant Christianity stood in the legacy of biblically generated theories of human origins which focused intense interests on the sons of Noah. Centrally, the discussions circled around the so-called curse of Ham, or more precisely the curse on Ham's progeny, Canaan. That curse was seen by many as the source of blackness and the true justification of enslavement.[55]

Equiano understood that by placing the black body in the womb of Abraham's mate, he circumvented some of that discussion and drew the African into a direct salvific line. This bio-logic would be deployed countless times by future Black Atlantic writers trying to assert a black biblical presence. The point of this biblical presence, for Equiano, was a historical one. It allowed him to make European superiority fully contingent, that is, to undermine its perceived ontological status. European advantage was for him an occasion to be of service to the world. He weaves the story of his white readers into his story, opening up the possibility for them to see their strengths and weaknesses, successes and failures, all the while presenting his story as exquisite human interiority.

The story of his sister brought his readers inside not just his pain of losing his sibling but the brutality women suffered as chattel. Equiano's words, spoken from his adult present to the sister of his childhood past, are within view of the white readers and for their benefit:

> Yes, thou dear partner of all my childish sports! [T]hou sharer of my joys and sorrows! Happy should I have ever esteemed myself to encounter every misery for you, and to procure your freedom by the sacrifice of my own. Though you were early forced from my arms, your image has been always riveted in my heart, from which neither *time nor fortune* have been able to remove it; so that while the thoughts of your suffering have damped my prosperity, they have mingled with adversity, and increased its bitterness.—To the heaven which protects the weak from the strong, I commit the care of your innocence and virtues, if they have not already received their full reward; and if your youth and delicacy have not long since fallen victims to the violence of the African trader, the pestilential stench of a Guinea ship, the seasoning in the European colonies, or the lash and lust of a brutal and unrelenting overseer. (51–52)

This memory with a lesson teaches his white readers the four stages of enslavement. Capture by African traders, life on the slave ship, the mind-bending labor of the colony, and rape await his sister, that is, if she does not meet death along the way. His soliloquy also brings the reader into the tapestry of loss that gives shape to his life. It is exactly the account of loss that centers his famous account of an actual sale of slaves in the slave market: "In this manner, without scruple, are relations and friends separated, most of them never to see each other again. I remember in the vessel in which I was brought over, in the men's apartment, there were several brothers, who in the sale, were sold in different lots; and it was very moving on this occasion to see and hear their cries at parting" (61). The similarity between Equiano's account of 1789 and Zurara's account of 1457 is striking. Both capture the pathos of separation, but Equiano stands in the same position as the slaves observed by Zurara. He is among the enslaved looking out in condemnation—over against Zurara. Unlike the slaves, who looked to heaven speaking an unknown tongue, he speaks with indignation the language of his captors:

> O ye nominal Christians! Might not an African ask you, learned you this from your God? who says unto you, Do unto all men as you would men should do unto you? Is it not enough that we are torn from our country and friends to toil for your luxury and lust of gain? Must every tender feeling be likewise sacrificed to your avarice? Are the dearest friends and relations, now rendered more dear by their separation from their kindred, still to be parted from each other, and thus prevented from cheering the gloom of slavery with the small comfort of being together and mingling their sufferings and sorrows? Why are parents to lose their children, brothers their sisters, or husbands their wives? Surely this is a new refinement in cruelty, which, while it has no advantage to atone for it, thus aggravates distress, and adds fresh horrors even to the wretchedness of slavery. (61)

Equiano's narrative with its powerful protest did draw responses from his white readers. Those responses, however, revealed the deep chasm that existed between the vision of what Equiano hoped would be possible and the vision through which his black body was viewed. The responses did not evaluate the possibility of relationship, but the viability of black humanity gauged through a textual display of intelligence. Take, for example, the review comments about Equiano's narrative by Richard Gough from the *Gentleman's Magazine* of June 1789: "Among other contrivances (and perhaps one of the most innocent) to interest the national humanity in favour of the Negro slaves, one of them here writes his own history, as formerly another of them published his correspondence. . . . These memoirs, written in a very unequal style, place the writer on a par with the general mass of men in the subordinate stations of civilised society, and prove that there is no general rule without an exception. The first volume treats of the manners of his countrymen, and his own adventures till he obtained his freedom; the second, from that period to the present, is uninteresting; and his conversion to methodism oversets the whole."[56]

While Equiano describes in ways heretofore unknown in print the horrors of enslavement, especially on the slave ship from the inner life of a slave, the reviewer finds fault in the quality of the writing—the style is unequal. It is not simply the negativity of the reviewer that is crucial here but also his position as evaluator and his supposed knowledge of the African type. In the *Interesting Narrative* one meets the political struggle of representation in its first, most powerful scenario. Equiano in writing gains no help from the words about black flesh that have gone before him and surrounded him as he wrote. Equiano understands that he must write against the racial image, black and white, write against writing.

This writing against writing was by Equiano's time writing against texts, philosophical, theological, and scientific, that posited black intellectual inferiority by drawing forward the trajectory of comparative anatomy of earlier centuries. Eighteenth-century scientific investigations of the new worlds yielded an even more viciously derogatory portrait of the black intelligence. These classificatory schemas drew the entire known world into grand metanarratives of development. The taxonomies of Carolus Linnaeus (1707–78) in his *Systema Naturae* (1735) and of Johann Friedrich Blumenbach (1752–1840) in his *De generis humani varietate nativa* (1775) and his *Collectis craniorum diversacrum gentium* (1790) are two powerful examples of classificatory systems that placed the comparative practices of the previous centuries on a new level of philosophical and theological speculation.[57]

The alleged intellectual inferiority of the African was working its way into the imaginations of Europeans, as evidenced by the words of Mary Wollstonecraft, who reviewed Equiano's work in 1789. She noted that a "favourite philosophic whim [was to] degrade the numerous nations, on whom the sun-beams more directly dart . . . and hastily . . . conclude that nature, by making them inferior to the rest of the human race, designed to stamp them with a mark of slavery."[58] Yet even her affirming responses illumine the limited reach imposed on Equiano's life story. She concludes that the *Interesting Narrative* may not disprove that philosophic whim, but it does have evidential benefit for Africans: "We shall only observe that if these volumes do not exhibit extraordinary intellectual powers, sufficient to wipe off the stigma [of black inferiority and subhumanity], yet the activity and ingenuity, which conspicuously appear in the character of Gustavus, place him on a par with the general mass of men, who fill the subordinate stations in a more civilized society than that which he was thrown at his birth."[59]

Wollstonecraft's comments support the inclusion of Equiano and those like him in the human community but still reveal at most a middle position for this African, probably below those with extraordinary intellectual powers but yet firmly within the general mass of men. That is to say, Equiano is a usual human of subordinate station, although, as she notes later in her review, he is too pious for her taste. This in effect sounded like what Equiano hoped for by writing his narrative, namely, approved humanity. This, however, was a flawed reward. It was flawed because it was a step further inside the logic of white evaluation, an evaluation that joined the slave market to the book market. Yet even if lower class and too pious for Wollstonecraft, the Christian Equiano is clearly visible through his narrative.

In Olaudah Equiano's masterwork Christian identity and colonial identity speak to one another. Inside this dialogic, Equiano yields space to divine agency and divine speech. In Equiano, God speaks but under constrained conditions.[60] What Equiano dramatizes in his narrative is precisely the vulnerability of real and possible further rejection. Christ's rejection and Equiano's rejection establish the intertextual Christian reality of his narrative. One can understand only this by remembering what Equiano shares with his Savior in his narrative display: they are both the one for the many. Christ is the new creation, the new humanity calling and pleading with the old humanity. Equiano is the racial recreated, the African calling and pleading with the European to accept Africans as human companions. The reality of suffering and possibility of continued rejection looms for both the Christ and the African. The crucial difference is that Equiano also dramatizes the mangled intimacy that flows out of the dialogic between Christian and colonial identities. In this way, Equiano foreshadows some of the greatest possibilities and one of the deepest problems of Western Christian life.

The problem one encounters in Equiano's narrative display of his Christian life is one that intensely focuses the tragedy of Christianity performed within the colonialist imagination. How does one articulate the coming to faith, a life saved by God, in light of having been made a slave and then having been set free from human slavery, that is, in light of a far more determinative transformation of one's life? In this regard, it is crucial that one read his account of salvation in relation to his account of freedom. By holding these two accounts together one can begin to see the dilemma Equiano inherited. He inherited a vision of salvation evacuated of material consequences for identity and for patterns of human belonging. What Equiano envisaged as salvation obtained was not merely captured within mercantile sensibilities, but it carried forward the struggles of his social imagination with its deep sense of loss and its hunger for belonging. Equiano's efforts were marvelous yet contained inside a great tragedy; he was saved, but to whom was he saved?

EQUIANO AND A HOLY PEOPLE DEFERRED

Equiano writes, "[The dangers of my last voyage] . . . caused me to reflect deeply on my eternal state; and to seek the Lord with full purpose of heart ere it be too late. I rejoiced greatly; and heartily thanked the Lord for directing me to London, where I was determined to work out my own salvation, and in so doing, procure a title to heaven; being the result of a mind blinded by ignorance and sin" (179).

The voyage referred to here was to the North Pole, where he served as the personal attendant for the famous inventor Charles Irving. The voyage sought a passageway to navigate as close as possible to the North Pole, but it was unsuccessful and nearly cost the crew their lives. It also led Equiano into a spiritual crisis (161). Before his spiritual crisis and the ensuing spiritual quest for salvation, Equiano had already been baptized in the Anglican church and taught the Scriptures piecemeal within the context of learning his merchant skills. Like so many others, the language of the Scriptures had become his language, and knowledge of the Bible became his obsession.

Scripture patterned Equiano's thought. It did not just give him access to such ideas as the equality of all humanity in the presence of God, but also a way to explicate the world.[61] Equiano did more than simply read his life in the light of Scripture.[62] He, like the many who would follow him, read the entire world into the broad scriptural narrative. He read the world scripturally. The result was a world captured within the broad sweep of biblical history, from sin to salvation to judgment. This scriptural imagination drives the entire narrative and especially his account of his quest for salvation.

Equiano captured in his narrative the power of rendering life theologically. The language of spiritual autobiography sometimes conceals the more profound subject position illumined by this interpretive practice. Such a subject position does not release the self or others to space outside the divine drama. It resists the bracketing of theological reflection from the world created within the master–slave relation: "One Mr. Drummond told me that he had sold 41,000 negroes, and that he once cut off a negro-man's leg for running away.—I asked him, if the man had died in the operation? How he, as a Christian, could answer for the horrid act before God? And he told me, answering was a thing of another world; but what he thought and did were policy. I told him that the Christian doctrine taught us to do unto others as we would that others should do unto us" (104–5). Some commentators would attribute this subject position to an African intellectual framework that operates with theological holisms that shun secular/sacred dualism. It could also be the result of the intensity of the scriptural imagination at work in Equiano. What is important here is the synthetic character of Equiano's imaginative gestures. This propensity to join things that others kept distinct will reemerge repeatedly in expressive cultures of diasporic peoples. It is precisely the position of the black body as a social connector that fosters this thought form. From their emergence from the holds of slave ships, black bodies were positioned between technological advances in the West, economic developments with their concomitant reconfigurations of space, and the multiple discursive practices of Europeans inscribing their New World within the logics of hegemony. These various realities crisscrossed black bodies. Synthetic thinking arose "naturally" out of being forced to contend with the various forms of power interacting on their bodies.

This means that Equiano's drama of conversion already carries inside it a synthetic character. It already holds the actions of God and the vicissitudes of life within the exchange networks created by the master–slave relation. However, it also exposes a soteriological vision robbed of significant transformative possibilities. His vision of salvation touches the ground, but it cannot do anything about the ground it touches because that ground has been recreated racially. The theological idiom he inherited, that of evangelical piety, was not merely an inheritance of a theological past, it was also an innovation of a Protestant/slavery present. That is, it was language being quickly adapted to function on top of the more decisive transformation of the multiple peoples of Africa into black slaves, leaving little room to imagine salvation as the transformation of the social order of things.[63]

If the social order and the processes of commodification are not transformed in relation to the body through salvation, then salvation becomes hyperlocalized to a single relationship: God and the one being saved.[64] One must remember that this is the Christian Equiano recounting his entrance into "a more excellent way." That is, he offers his readers a theological account of his missteps toward understanding what it means to be a Christian. Without a spiritual guide in his search to direct him to salvation, he inquired among the Quakers, Roman Catholics, and Jews, all to no avail. All this was played out against the backdrop of the horrors of slavery and the vulnerability of his own life as a free black. Equiano realized that the social status of a free black was even more precarious than that of a slave because a free black had no legal protections and no master to protect him from assault, robbery, or reenslavement. Fears of dying attended him while he remained in what he called "nature's darkness," that is, the natural state of fallen humanity.

Help for his spiritual quest came in the form of an "old sea-faring man, who experienced much of the love of God shed abroad in his heart" (183), and a dissenting minister of the Church of England who invited him to a love feast. Equiano enjoyed the feast but was frustrated by the participants' clear confidence in their salvation, that is, in "their calling and election from God" (184). His quest at this point in his narrative reveals the anatomy of what would emerge as a classic order of salvation in the slave narratives.[65] This order of salvation refers to the states one experiences in receiving redemption. There is the slow but sure conviction of sin, in which all our efforts to overcome sin and attain salvation become only a greater burden to the soul. This conviction is joined by a sense of abandonment and dread, that is, something similar to the dark night of the soul, and then finally there is the moment of relief and release that accompanies true knowledge of salvation. Equiano's tumultuous experiences culminate on board a ship named Hope bound for Spain. There on board the ship he arrives to "saving knowledge":

> It pleased God to enable me to wrestle with him, as Jacob did: I prayed that if sudden death were to happen, and I perished, it might be at Christ's feet. In the evening of the same day, as I was reading and meditating on the fourth chapter of the Acts, twelfth verse, under the solemn apprehensions of eternity, and reflecting on my past actions, I began to think I had lived a moral life, and that I had proper ground to believe I had an interest in the divine favour; but still meditating on the subject, not knowing whether salvation was to be had partly for our own good deeds, or solely as the sovereign gift of God:—in this deep consternation the Lord was pleased to break in upon my soul with his bright beams of heavenly light and in an instant, as it were, removing the veil, and letting light into a dark place, Isa xxv. 7. I saw clearly, with the eye of faith, the crucified Saviour bleeding on the cross on Mount Calvary: The Scriptures became an unsealed book, I saw myself a condemned criminal under the law, which came with its full force to my conscience. . . . I saw the Lord Jesus Christ in his humiliation, loaded and bearing my reproach, sin, and shame. . . . It was given me at that time to know what it was to be born again. . . . Christ was revealed to my soul as the chiefest among ten thousand. (189–90)

There is a characteristic singularity to the Christian spiritual journey, so one would expect Equiano's account to echo this intensely personal divine work. However, the singularity in his account carries a different valence. His helpers along the journey are given important roles, not by how they guide him but by how they reflect back to him that which he must find for himself. The climax of his search was the knowledge that salvation was a gift from God. He was born again. The place of his conversion, a slave ship, is crucial. The ship is where he became black, became slave, and now it is where he became a "first-rate Christian." The three operations are similar, all riding on white hegemony. The racial and slave transformations precede the Christian and stand at a more decisive level. Equiano, however, drew the first two processes of transformation into the third. He brought the remade world into the world created by the God who saved him: "*Now every leading providential circumstance that happened to me, from the day I was taken from my parents to that hour, was then, in my view, as if it had but just then occurred. I was sensible of the invisible hand of God, which guided and protected me, when in truth I knew it not: still the Lord pursued me although I slighted and disregarded it; this mercy melted me down.* When I considered my poor wretched state, I wept, seeing what a great debtor I was to sovereign free grace. Now the Ethiopian was willing to be saved by Jesus Christ, the sinner's only surety, and also to rely on none other person or thing for salvation. Self was obnoxious, and good works he had none; for it is God that worketh in us both to will and to do" (189–90, emphasis added).

Equiano draws the horrors of his life into theology. The divine hand superintended his life, holding back the forces of death and seeking relationship with him. The self he describes was wholly a soteriological construct, the prideful self, the self constructed of hubris that resisted the mercy and presence of God. At a more decisive level, Equiano certainly aimed at the self that resisted the divine order and rested comfortably in the master–slave relation and the world it had created. Equiano here enters the logics of Christian belonging at its most fundamental christological root. He drew intense connections between himself and the suffering Jesus, whom he envisioned "in his humiliation, loaded and bearing [his] reproach, sin, and shame." Now, "in salvation," he understood that his name Equiano, which meant fortune, signified the personal predestination of a God "that worketh in us both to will and to do" (190). A new self emerged—one that was courageously against the fallen world, *contra mundi*, filled with missionary zeal and clarity of purpose but lacked the fear of death: "I felt an astonishing change; the burden of sin, the gaping jaws of hell, and the fears of death, that weighed me down before, now lost their horror. . . . I viewed the unconverted people of the world in a very awful state, being without God and without hope. It pleased God to pour out on me the spirit of prayer and the grace of supplication, so that in loud acclamations I was enabled to praise and glorify his most holy name" (190–91).

Equiano's account of his conversion was paradigmatic for the salvation testimonies of slaves for generations. However, his spiritual quest with its salvation episode also pointed to a sense of belonging that normalized loss. The loss here is not primarily of family or people, of his mother or sister, of his homeland or a life there. The loss here is an absence of Christianity constituted in community, a Christianity that joins all the people who claim to be Christian. In this regard, loss connotes not memory of a presence now gone missing, but an implied presence centrally woven into Equiano's scriptural imagination and insinuated by his Christian practices. That implied presence could not materialize in the remade world. Equiano entered a Christianity constituted without belonging. So he was left to perform a Christian life filled with the surrogates for that loss, God and the Scriptures: "Every hour a day until I came to London . . . I much longed to be with some to whom I could tell of the wonders of God's love toward me, and join in prayer to him who my soul loved and thirsted after. I had uncommon commotions within, such as few can tell aught about. Now the Bible was my only companion and comfort; I prized it much, with many thanks to God that I could read it for myself, and was not left to be tossed about or led by man's devices and notions. The worth of a soul cannot be told" (191). It may seem counterintuitive to suggest a relationship with God and a strong desire for the Scriptures as surrogate forms, given their constituting centrality for the Christian life. But here one must grasp the deepest tragedy for the formation of Christianity in the racial West: belonging was racialized. Equiano could not overcome this and therefore imagined Christian belonging along the only lines of thought available to him: he belonged to God, and the Scriptures belonged to him. The true worth of his soul was established between those boundaries.

The slave ship solidified a victory over Christianity. Those who descended from the tortured, tainted decks to the pain-filled ports of call, those who ascended from the diseased and fetid holds to be groomed and polished for sale, those who turned bodies into profit and became gentlemen and political leaders, each were tied in bonds of connection which nothing on heaven or earth could separate. Toward the end of his groundbreaking narrative, Equiano offers his white readers a strangely placed vignette: "Soon after my arrival in London, I saw a remarkable circumstance relative to African complexion, which I thought so extraordinary that I shall beg leave just to mention it: A white negro woman, that I had formerly seen in London and other parts, had married a white man, by whom she had three boys, and they were every one mulattoes, and yet they had fine light hair" (220). This brief account seems to come out of nowhere. By this time in the narrative, Equiano is driving toward his abolitionist denouement, showing that the logic of his life renders the slave trade a clearly monstrous injustice. That the slave trade is also hopelessly inefficient and illogical are the judgments he hopes his readers will make for themselves as they enter the final chapter. Yet here he detours them to notice a black woman's body made white, "a white negro woman." She married a white man and together this couple produced three mulattoes, each with "fine light hair" (220). This announcement is not the first time Equiano had been captivated by interracial coupling. Earlier in his narrative he has a similar detour: "While I was in this place, St. Kitt's, a very curious imposition on human nature took place: —A white man wanted to marry in the church a free black woman that had land and slaves at Montserrat: but the clergyman told him it was against the law of the place to marry a white and a black in the church. The man then asked to be married on the water, to which the parson consented, and the two lovers went in one boat, and the parson and clerk in another, and thus the ceremony was performed. After this the loving pair came on board our vessel, and my captain treated them extremely well, and brought them

safe to Montserrat" (119). These two events jut out of the line of the narrative because they do not fit easily into the world he narrates, just as his own interracial
marriage found no place in any of the early editions of his story.[66] The St. Kitts
story captures the contrast between bondage and freedom. Life together for this
couple began not in a church but at sea on their way home to Montserrat. The
fact that returning home meant returning to life as slaveholders seemed not to
draw Equiano's attention. He is captivated by the possibility of love and lovers,
even in the midst of the remade world. The story mirrors much of his own sense
of where his possibilities for freedom and transformation were found—on the
sea. A minimal white Christian presence dots this event, a parson and a clerk
performing a very precise function. This too mirrors much of his Christian walk.
White Christian presence was certainly crucial but completely episodic and not
characteristic of the narrative.

There is far less Christian presence with the shorter vignette near the end of his
story, but it has an eschatological character equally as strong as that of the earlier
story. This is an eschatology of assimilation. The second couple marries and,
like the earlier couple, enters fully into the remade world. The former couple
assimilated economically, and the latter couple assimilated racially. Three boys
born of this couple suggest possible portents—bodies that are clearly black but
look white. Equiano is drawing his white readers to the irrefutable fact that love
and relationship and a future together are possible, but under hegemonic conditions. But these possibilities do not fit easily into his story or the Christianity that
shapes that story. He does, however, suggest near the end of his text the future he
would envision for Britons and Africans, a future consistent with the narrative:
economic confraternity: "If the blacks were permitted to remain in their own
country, they would double themselves every fifteen years. In proportion to such
increase will be the demand for manufactures. Cotton and indigo grow sponta-
neously in most parts of Africa; a consideration this of no small consequence to
the manufacturing towns of Great Britain. It opens a most immense, glorious,
and happy prospect—the clothing, &c. of a continent ten thousand miles in cir-
cumferences, and immensely rich in productions of every denomination in return for manufactures" (235).

Like a merchant missionary, Equiano proposed a relationship constituted by
the exchange networks in which he was formed. His commentators are correct
to find in him capitalist desire that has transmuted his vision of his home and
the many different peoples he encountered into the land of just "black people"
filled with untapped potential for missionary activity and manufactures. Equiano
comes to this hoped-for conclusion as a viable option, a separate and unequal
collaboration, but one that would hold back the power of death by ending the

slave trade. It is his preferred option because his Christianity cannot make anything else possible, either as an option or even as a dream. It could be that our author in the end holds interracial coupling as a dream, a hope. If so, then it is the final surrogacy for Christianity itself because it is a depth of love between peoples that the Christianity he has inherited cannot imagine.[67]

Equiano lived under the stark conditions of assimilation. It could be argued that such conditions make his Christianity itself suspect as simply psychologically forced faith. There is no doubt his is Christianity presented in violence and within European hegemony. And as such it is first cousin to Christianity coercively presented under threat of death. But his Christianity was neither parrot nor parody. The man who styled himself "The African" was of his own desire a Christian, a lover of Jesus. He is a powerful witness not only to the Christian origins of black intellectual life in the modern West, but also to the pained joining of black life to the life of the crucified one. This is not the pain of joining with Jesus, but the frustration and pain of being like Jesus in his rejection. Equiano dramatizes this rejection.

Equiano comes before the advent of the black church and precedes the phenomenal rise of the black preacher. He writes before the genius of the black literary tradition begins to take visible shape, before diasporic expressive cultures will wage war against yet live inside Western intellectual traditions. Equiano will offer up his own courageous salvo. But underlying the before is the Christian. One must recall the Christian not as an act of romantic retrieval in order to demand a reorientation of wayward intellectual trajectories back to the true path of Christian faith. Nor should one recall the Christian in order to cajole appreciation for its resourcing the virtues of Western civilization, Western democracy, and the possibilities of ethical critique. One must recall the Christian for the sake of Christianity itself, recall the Christian in order to capture the pathos of its translation and the grotesquerie of its collective performance.

The Christianity given to "The African" imagined social life racially and therefore executed its intellectual life racially. Olaudah Equiano must speak for his own because his own now designates a possessive vastly more powerful in its imaginative reach and its existential connectivity than any Christian possessive at hand then or now. The Christian possessive here has been dislodged from any significant material connection. Equiano must for the sake of his own people gather them in his mind as one people, black people, and argue as strongly as he can for the end of their displacement, the end of the slave trade. And yet Equiano is pressed to work inside a Christian vision that lacks the ability to imagine multitude, different peoples joined together in love, and thus lacks the desire to reconstitute its life through the many.

He gains a vision of salvation that heightens the sense of belonging to God alone, but it also intensifies the localization of belonging along cultural and racial lines. The poverty of desire continues to live inside Christian intellectual life and especially Christian theology. Its historic colonialist trajectory with its pedagogical imperialism and its epistemic insularity makes the problem difficult to see. The problem is not simply in what or how theologians write, although the writing is a serious problem. The problem is not one of contextuality or insensitivity to situatedness; or of attending to difference, otherness, or alterity in the writing of theological texts; or of determining the true object of theology, God or our perceptions of God, or both. The problem is in imagining whom we theologians belong to as we write, as we think, as we pray. This problem has fundamentally to do with a world formed and continuing to be formed to undermine the possibilities of Christians living together, loving together, and desiring each other. Such a desire is not a narcissistic longing for self to be seen in others, or an indulgent seeking for the comfort of like-minded doctrinal confessors. It is the necessary beginning for overturning the remade world.

Black Atlantic Christianity comes into being with this painful truth. The Christianity it works with is necessary, powerful, and living but not very appealing. It lacks appeal because, enamored of the power and beauty of whiteness, this Christianity presents itself to no one but itself and tragically invites "nonwhite" peoples to do the same. An intellectual life formed in so unappealing a setting becomes crushingly insular. It is exactly the insularity of Christian theology and all its identifiers (for example, orthodox, liberal, conservative, and so on) and the insularity of its Christian contextual responses and all its identifiers (for example, African, Asian, feminist, womanist) that repeatedly show Christians the missed opportunities of Christian intellectual life. I am not dismissing the important parental legacy of Christianity in nurturing key intellectuals of the modern West, and especially intellectuals of the Black Atlantic. But we must not allow this legacy to blind us to the aching absence of a truly Christian intellectual community at the heart of church life in this world. Such a Christian community would reflect in its work the incarnate reality of the Son who has joined the divine life to our lives and invites us to deep abiding intellectual joining, not only of ideas but of problems, not only of concepts but of concerns, not only of beliefs and practices but of common life, and all of it of the multitude of many tongues.

Black Atlantic Christianity has been marked by this absence. Its would-be intellectuals have often had to go it alone, trying to think out through their faith in a world that rejects them, their words, their intellectual contributions, and their faith. It has also been marked by the myriad of intellectuals who, having been raised in the church, have left the church, finding its ways of thinking in the world trapped in a crushing insularity. Many of them had become impatient with its willingness to live life under the conditions of the remade world. Equally poignant has been that other set of black intellectuals who live in the church, stay with the church but in secret silence find its Christianity necessary, powerful, living, but so unappealing. For them, even in the remade world, the intellectual life lives in a space much freer, much more hopeful than their church life. Yet we call them all back to a moment of hope and a moment of power, when a man taken from a place far beyond the recognized world wrote a word that challenged the world.

There is power in the word. The power of the word can break open a world and overturn worldly desire. Olaudah Equiano knew this. He also knew that the world constituted on the slave ship needed to be overturned, even if the overturning he envisioned was a limited one. Limitation most certainly makes him a man of his times. From the attitude of his face on the cover of his famous work, a face that stares directly at the white reader and thereby connotes equality; to his brilliant skills of self-promotion, initiating one of the first book tours; to his genius at cultivating rich and powerful sponsors to underwrite the publication and many editions of the book; to his political savvy in aligning the book and its promotion with the abolitionist cause; to his maintaining the copyrights to his work, he was also perhaps a man ahead of his time. He is crucially important to us in the modern world because he is also a man of our time who uncovers the perils of our remade world and yet spies the possibilities of its unmaking. But he can only quickly glance at those possibilities because, like ships at sea, they disappeared over the endless horizon.

Part III

INTIMACY

5

WHITE SPACE AND LITERACY

Equiano learned to read and write on the small space of a ship and therefore a geographic instability and forced mobility undergirded his intellectual accomplishment. Coupled to this geographic instability, the central resource of his accomplished literacy was the Bible, which played a pivotal role in translating "The African" into English vernacular Christianity and into its domesticity. Reading and writing not only introduced him to a New World but also set him on a path toward a new kind of social performance. Vincent Carretta identifies this as Equiano's desire to be recognized as a gentleman: "[Equiano] subtly and rather quickly offers himself to his audience as the definition of a true gentleman, 'almost an Englishman.'"[1] The African's need for belonging culminated not simply in a nationalist performance but in the presentation of a class consciousness, that of an English gentleman. Equiano exposes to his readers the assimilating character of literacy in the colonialist moment.[2]

It is a literate Equiano who could turn his gaze back to his homeland and see market opportunities, even if couched in heartfelt pleas for national collaboration and confraternity rather than slavery. It is a literate Equiano who joins merchant and missionary interests in the one desire for the abolition of the trade. It is a literate Equiano who articulates a deep piety that is in concert with his intellectual vision. Literacy here is in service to emancipation, but it is also in service to colonialism. One must hold these facts together with the theological accomplishment of the *Interesting Narrative*. Williams Andrews captures an important aspect of that accomplishment when he states, "Equiano's autobiography affirms the power of the narrating persona to create a subjective world that can, in turn, effect change in the discursive realm between text and reader, wherein the white reader could become empowered to read signs outside of himself, i.e., biculturally. Thus Equiano's represents a new kind of black conversion narrative, less simply *about* the narrator than *for* the white reader who needs to learn to read the world redemptively, that is, doubly, inside-out and outside-in."[3]

If Equiano taught his white readers to read the world redemptively by drawing them into his refashioning of the remade world, what were the hidden costs of his literacy? The Christian imaginary that is emerging out of colonialist power naturalized segregationalist mentalities and thereby denied one of its most basic and powerful imaginative possibilities, the deepest and most comprehensive joining of peoples.

One should understand this development within the wider reality of Christianity's assimilation practices. Cultural assimilation and segregationalist mentality are always bound together. The former enables the latter, and the latter always stands in the shadow of the former. This does not mean one should parse segregationalist thinking as the reaction to attempts of cultural assimilation in Christianity. As we have seen in prior chapters, the envisioning of racial and ethnic difference could be seamlessly woven inside assimilation strategies such that the assimilated (that is, Christian) native remained separately and terminally native. Yet far more was at work here than the revelation of patterns of assimilation, resistance, or adaptation.

The emergence of this Christian-colonial way of imagining the world raises a central question: How is it possible for Christians and Christian communities to naturalize cultural fragmentation and operationalize racial vision from within the social logic and theological imagination of Christianity itself? Locating an answer to this question involves drawing from the processes of displacement and translation clearer sight of something genuinely new in the formation of Christianity in modernity, the interpenetration of the vernacularization of Christianity and the production of space.

This new thing began to emerge in the pedagogical imperialist modality of theological reflection in José de Acosta. Visible in Acosta is the historic trajectory of Christian theology's insularity, in which it is drawn into and enclosed in an evaluative form. As noted in chapter 2, pedagogical evaluation in the New World set the context within which the theological imagination functioned. Colonialists disseminated this exaggerated and expanded pedagogical evaluation through a network of relationships that can now be seen more clearly as an exchange network vivified by a capitalist logic.

As we saw in the case of Bishop Colenso, theology encased in evaluative form modulates into an almost unassailable solipsism. The bishop could not, despite his good intentions, moral nobility, and theological seriousness, create a school that was not deeply embedded in the project of colonialist self-reflection in indigenous bodies. As I noted in the treatment of Bishop Colenso, self-reflection was not simply a matter of assimilation: it was also, more tragically, a matter of substantiation. Colenso's mission built upon the disappearance of black bodies and their reappearance in literate form, prepared for the master's use. Literacy in these examples, as in that of Equiano, bound together a Christian world mediated through Scripture to the colonialist world.

Moreover, vernacular translation of the Bible, as we saw in Colenso's case, facilitated the dissemination of the idea of a nation and the expression of cultural nationalisms (I explore this theme below). Translation of the Scripture was the centerpiece of a linguistic process that drew peoples into a new realization of their collective state and new forms of collectivity. As Adrian Hastings points out, vernacular translation marked the transition of a people into nationalist possibilities and marked the Christian Scripture as a source of its new life: "Ethnicities naturally turn into nations or integral elements within nations at the point when their specific vernacular moves from an oral to written usage to the extent that it is being regularly employed for the production of a literature, and particularly for the translation of the Bible. Once an ethnicity's vernacular becomes a language with an extensive living literature of its own, the Rubicon on the road to nationhood appears to have been crossed."[4] Hastings considers "the Bible as prime lens through which the nation is imagined by biblically literate people."[5] Once biblical literacy began centrally to aid the building of national consciousness, the Bible and its important pedagogical trajectory for forming faithful Christian identity became compromised.

MISPLACING SCRIPTURE

This compromise followed along the same lines discerned in Acosta's pedagogical vision. Indeed, the essential character of this compromise was well established in the Jesuit's brilliant synthesis of piety and erudition. Here, biblical knowledge equips piety, and piety draws strength from "religious reading," that is, reading Scripture and other texts within a tradition.[6] Biblical literacy in this regard fosters a sense of communion with God, with other Christians, and with a set of texts illustrative, complementary, and collaborative of the central scriptural texts. Yet the insularity inherent in this process of becoming (biblically) literate was fertile ground for inducing a cultural circularity easily bound to colonialism. Paul Griffiths outlines the coherence necessary for religious reading:

Recall that religious reading requires the establishment of a particular set of relations between the reader and what is read. These are principally relations of reverence, delight, awe, and wonder, relations that, once established, lead to the close, repetitive kinds of reading already described. The questioning of authority and the concern with preliminary issues of method and justification (intellectual attitudes and concerns typical of modernity) make the establishment of such relations almost impossible because of the endless deferral of commitment that such attitudes bring with them. Commitment to some body of works as an endlessly nourishing garden of delights is essential to religious reading; and authoritative direction as to which works are of the right sort is a necessary condition for religious engagement with them.[7]

Griffiths's account of religious reading illumines a basic relation that will be absolutely crucial to grasping the overwhelming power of the vernacular Bible, the deep, intimate connection between particular readers and what is read. It is precisely inside this tender relation that nationalist vision may grow by use of the three aspects outlined in the previous quotation: (1) relations of devotion to and edification from Scriptures written in native dialects, (2) relations of commitment and obedience to Scripture and to those native speakers whose pedagogical authority enables right reading, and (3) metaphorically articulated spatial relations between the particular readers and translated religious texts that become "a familiar place" of nourishing support for right reading. Vernacular translation draws religious reading from within the formation of literate religious communities into a wider theater of identity formation.

The crucial point here is precisely the success of religious readings in the development of the vernacular Bible. As Hastings notes (referring to the English), the vernacular Bible exposed the growing power of literature "in strengthening a common language, installing in all its hearers and readers the idea of nationhood."[8] As in the case of Acosta, traditioned intellectual work enters a new phase of deployment in which such activities as translating Scriptures moves in concert with the translation of space into nation-space. But equally important is the dissemination of pious (Christian) vision into nationalist-vision. Christian piety does not simply become national piety; rather, it informs and energizes a new imaginary literary space.

An interesting example of the ideological transposition of vernacular work that sought to aid biblical literacy was the work of Isaac Watts (1674–1748), the famed English pastor, poet, and hymn writer. In his translation of the Psalms, Watts hoped to present English readers with a more Christianized, common vernacular rendition.[9] His deepest concern was aiding the worship life of Christians by offering a new version of the Psalms, one more useful for singing and one that would "prepare the way for hymnody."[10] Yet Watts also offers a powerful recommendation of Christian reading strategies in service to a nationalist imagination.

Watts did his work at a time when the British Empire was beginning to take the shape that would become familiar to Equiano and, later, to Colenso. Its colonies were multiplying, and it was beginning to reap the spoils of its ventures in commodities. Watts, as a member of the dissenting congregations, was eager to affirm his loyalty to the nation. Watts writes from within the Christian tradition, having received the customary training in theology and the classic languages, Latin, Greek, and Hebrew. Like Acosta, Watts was concerned with forming Christian identity, especially in the worship practices of the church. He was deeply dissatisfied with the versions of the Psalms that had gone before his own because they insufficiently Christianized and strengthened Christian piety. In addition, he thought those renderings did not fully engage the everyday needs of the British people.

In order to accomplish a more comprehensive Christianization, Watts redacted psalms unhelpful to the task at hand. Most important, he replaced the names of Israel and Judah with that of Britain, Jewish kings with those of Great Britain, and some "dark sayings of David" with New Testament themes.[11] In beginning with this fundamental replacement of Israel, Watts drew deeply from the well of supersessionist thinking. But his erasure of Israel carried a more powerful valence than Acosta's. Like Acosta, he placed his own people at the center of the biblical drama, but in Watts one gains a panoramic view of the relation of his Christology to land and nation. Psalm 47 illustrates this. The King James Version reads,

O clap your hands, all ye people; shout unto God with the voice of triumph. [2] For the LORD most high *is* terrible; *he is* a great King over all the earth. [3] He shall subdue the people under us, and the nations under our feet. [4] He shall choose our inheritance for us, the excellency of Jacob whom he loved. Selah. [5] God is gone up with a shout, the LORD with the sound of a trumpet. [6] Sing praises to God, sing praises: sing praises unto our King, sing praises. [7] For God *is* the King of all the earth: sing ye praises with understanding. [8] God reigneth over the heathen: God sitteth upon the throne of his holiness. [9] The princes of the people are gathered together, *even* the people of the God of Abraham: for the shields of the earth *belong* unto God: he is greatly exalted.

Watts offers the following:

O for a shout of sacred joy
  To God the sovereign King!
Let every land their tongues employ,
  And hymns of triumph sing.

Jesus our God ascends on high,
    His heav'nly guards around
Attend him rising through the sky,
    With trumpets' joyful sound.

While angels shout and praise their King,
    Let mortals learn their strains;
Let all the earth his honors sing;
    O'er all the earth he reigns.

Rehearse his praise with awe profound,
    Let knowledge lead the song,
Nor mock him with a solemn sound
    Upon a thoughtless tongue.

In Isr'el stood his ancient throne,
    He loved that chosen race;
But now he calls the world his own,
    And heathens taste his grace.

The British islands are the Lord's,
    There Abraham's God is known;
While powers and princes, shields and swords,
    Submit before his throne.[12]

Watts succeeds in Christianizing the text by transforming the psalm into a witness of "Christ ascending and reigning."[13] He masterfully connects the Christ narrative not only with the opening up of God's election of Israel to the election of the whole world in which "heathens taste his grace," but also with the recognition that the Lord has already claimed the British Isles and its people as his own. This new psalm enacts a Christian people, a British nation as a singular act of divine providence. Furthermore, the psalm invites its readers to join the redemptive journey of God to their specific land and their people. In so doing, it weaves biblical literacy into a clear territoriality.

This is indeed a form of Israel replacement, but it captures one of the most crucial forms of replacement. The multiple biblical stories of ancient Israel's quest for land center on God. The possibility of Israel's sovereignty pivots on the divine will. God stands always between Israel and the land, Israel and its land. If land is absolutely crucial to the identity of a people, then God stood always "in the way," as it were, between Israel and its desire for land, reordering its identity first in relation to the divine word and then to the land. Israel's stories of land gained, lost, and regained disclosed the God of Israel as the creator who "owns" all land

and therefore claimed all peoples. Israel's God is indeed "the King of the whole earth" (Ps 47:7). The revelation of the Creator in and through Israel is the first and foremost point of connection between Israel and all other peoples.

Watts positions Great Britain at this crucial point of revelation, turning Israel's sojourn with God into Britain's own journey. He thereby destroys the trajectory of connection between Israel and other nations. Israel simply models a connection between God and a nation. This important transformation manifests itself in his rendering of Psalm 60. The King James Version and then the Watts version, which was offered for "a day of humiliation for disappointments in war," read as follows:

O God, thou hast cast us off, thou hast scattered us, thou hast been displeased; O turn thyself to us again. ² Thou hast made the earth to tremble; thou hast broken it: heal the breaches thereof; for it shaketh. ³ Thou hast shewed thy people hard things: thou hast made us to drink the wine of astonishment. ⁴ Thou hast given a banner to them that fear thee, that it may be displayed because of the truth. Selah. ⁵ That thy beloved may be delivered; save *with* thy right hand, and hear me. ⁶ God hath spoken in his holiness; I will rejoice, I will divide Shechem, and mete out the valley of Succoth. ⁷ Gilead *is* mine, and Manasseh *is* mine; Ephraim also *is* the strength of mine head; Judah *is* my lawgiver; ⁸ Moab *is* my washpot; over Edom will I cast out my shoe: Philistia, triumph thou because of me. ⁹ Who will bring me *into* the strong city? who will lead me into Edom? ¹⁰ *Wilt* not thou, O God, *which* hadst cast us off? and *thou*, O God, *which* didst not go out with our armies? ¹¹ Give us help from trouble: for vain *is* the help of man. ¹² Through God we shall do valiantly: for he *it is that* shall tread down our enemies.

Lord, hast thou cast the nation off?
   Must we for ever mourn?
Wilt thou indulge immortal wrath?
   Shall mercy ne'er return?

The terror of one frown of thine
   Melts all our strength away;
Like men that totter drunk with wine,
   We tremble in dismay.

Great Britain shakes beneath thy stroke
   And dreads thy threat'ning hand;
O heal the island thou hast broke,
   Confirm the wav'ring land.

Lift up a banner in the field
    For those that fear thy name;
Save thy beloved with thy shield,
    And put our foes to shame.

Go with our armies to the fight,
    Like a confed'rate God;
In vain confed'rate powers unite
    Against thy lifted rod.

Our troops shall gain a wide renown
    By thine assisting hand
'Tis God that treads the mighty down,
    And makes the feeble stand.[14]

Britain is mapped onto the biblical journey of Israel. Israel's history disappears, and the British nation appears as the real history of God with God's people. There is no continuity between Israel's history and that of other nations. All that remains is a kind of parallelism between Israel and Britain. It would be a vast mistake to lose sight of the soteriological effect Watts is properly building on in his vernacular operation. The articulation of a relationship between the God of Israel and that of other peoples is precisely the desired telos of the Christian gospel. However, Watts offers no material connection between that desired telos and the people of Israel. Watts is attempting to more precisely vernacularize the Psalms for the daily spiritual edification of common people. In this regard, he was exquisitely expressing the deep Christian piety that marks his work, which shines through in his beautiful rendering of Psalm 61.

When, overwhelm'd with grief,
    My heart within me dies,
Helpless, and far from all relief,
    To heav'n I lift mine eyes.

    O lead me to the rock
    That's high above my head,
And make the covert of thy wings
    My shelter and my shade.

    Within thy presence, Lord,
    For ever I'll abide;
Thou art the tower of my defence,
    The refuge where I hide.

Thou givest me the lot
Of those that fear thy name;
If endless life be their reward,
I shall possess the same.[15]

Holding Psalms 60 and 61 together, one begins to see how a biblical account of Christian life with God may be construed in such a way as to erase Israel's presence from the text. Biblical literacy enables piety. However, the desire for biblical literacy, when shaped in relation to territoriality, facilitates a nationalist insularity. Here is one of the deepest ironies of vernacular translation: the stronger the connection between Scripture and its rendering in the everyday language of a people, the closer that connection will be with the land and space of a people. Biblical literacy in such a situation easily becomes constitutive of a wider process of spiritual formation that exhausts theological vision inside the task of developing a shared vision of a commonwealth. What undergirds this process is not simply Scripture's translation but the production of national space in and with the vernacular rendering of Scripture.

Watts did not present problems that could have been easily solved if only he offered his readers more historically accurate renderings of the Psalms. He understood literal accounts. He also understood the Jewish matrix of the texts. His point was that such knowledge was irrelevant to the proper execution of a Christian identity in a particular place precisely because such identity never points beyond itself to any other people. Israel was the beginning point, the ethnic *arche* of a process of instantiations of a people living in communion with God. Their imperfect reality in both knowledge of and communion with God was more clearly grasped in Britain. Watts offered Christianity as the propagation of a modularizing process. Christianity engenders models of collectivity, of nation, all beneath the one true kingdom of the Lord Jesus. Note the following verses from Watts's version of Psalm 72 (his Part 2).

Jesus shall reign where'er the sun
Does his successive journeys run;
His kingdom stretch from shore to shore,
Till moons shall wax and wane no more.

[Behold the islands with their kings,
And Europe her best tribute brings;
From north to south the princes meet,
To pay their homage at his feet.

There Persia, glorious to behold,
There India shines in eastern gold;
And barb'rous nations at his word
Submit, and bow, and own their Lord.][16]

Central in this psalm is the positioning of the Pantocrator, the ruling Christ, over all nations.[17] Watts entitled this section of the psalm, "Christ's kingdom among the Gentiles." Nations will each offer up themselves and their gifts to their Lord. But what is missing is a historical process for this submission. In the King James Version of the psalm, Israel's presence offers a point of historic stability for this process. Through Israel the reign of the king over all nations will be realized. Watts could be drawing on an eschatological sensibility in this psalm and calling forward the final reign of the Christ. However, his inserted middle sections suggest a more immanent reading. Indeed, he leaves open the placement of Jesus' reign in order to suggest Great Britain as the launching point for the mission of God.

The result of divine mission, for Watts, is the singular communion of each people with God. There is certainly salvation for everyone and every people. Watts, however, in the way he understood salvation, was a purveyor of privatized religion, of an individualism of the nation that mirrors the individualism of evangelical piety. Again, note Psalm 72, Part 2:

For him shall endless prayer be made,
And praises throng to crown his head;
His name like sweet perfume shall rise
With every morning sacrifice.

People and realms of every tongue
Dwell on his love with sweetest song;
And infant voices shall proclaim
Their early blessings on his name.

Blessings abound where'er he reigns,
The pris'ner leaps to lose his chains;
The weary find eternal rest,
And all the sons of want are blest.

[Where he displays his healing power
Death and the curse are known no more;
In him the tribes of Adam boast
More blessings than their father lost.

Let every creature rise and bring
Peculiar honors to our King;
Angels descend with songs again,
And earth repeat the long Amen.][18]

Watts transforms the salvation of peoples into the salvation of nations. At one
level, this transformation is simply an act of translation (peoples translated as
nations) built on Watts's supersessionist thinking. This would mean that Israel
was a nation, and therefore the salvation brought to the world through Jesus
Christ was a salvation of and for other nations. Yet at another level, once salvation
was imagined territorially it was also imagined racially and drew vernacularization and racial formation into tight collaboration. This means salvation does not
create a new people. *Peoples* are simply saved. This theme is quite powerfully expressed in his rendering of Psalm 67, which he entitled "The nation's prosperity,
and the church's increase":

Shine, mighty God, on Britain shine,
    With beams of heav'nly grace;
Reveal thy power through all our coasts,
    And show thy smiling face.

[Amidst our isle, exalted high,
    Do thou our glory stand,
And, like a wall of guardian fire,
    Surround the fav'rite land.]

When shall thy name, from shore to shore,
    Sound all the earth abroad;
And distant nations know and love
    Their Savior and their God?

Sing to the Lord, ye distant lands,
    Sing loud with solemn voice;
While British tongues exalt his praise,
    And British hearts rejoice.

He, the great Lord, the sovereign Judge,
    That sits enthroned above,
Wisely commands the worlds he made
    In justice and in love.

Earth shall obey her Maker's will,
  And yield a full increase;
Our God will crown his chosen isle
  With fruitfulness and peace.

God the Redeemer scatters round
  His choicest favors here,
While the creation's utmost bound
  Shall see, adore, and fear.[19]

British land, British hearts and tongues all announce British election by God. Not only does the nation, in this supremely important case, Britain, emerge as the plateau from which God envisions and invites the redemption of all peoples willing to look toward "his chosen isle," but language and land surround the Bible. They become the hermeneutical horizon of a scriptural imagination. Literacy enacts territoriality. Territoriality produces space upon which racial being functions. As we saw in chapter 1, the development of racial existence reconfigures identity's relation to place and landscape. In short, the land is first a matter of possession and second, if at all, of signification. Land becomes the space for races. It becomes the occasion for the creation of spaces for multiple peoples.

Biblical literacy was positioned between language and land as a powerful catalyst for the transformation of both and for the formation of peoples as nations. Between these two realities there was little room or energy for a vision that joins, mixes, or fuses peoples and their languages. For Christian theology, literacy bound to vernacular translation (as it emerges in the modern period and as it helped to constitute modernity) had both unlimited reach and limited power for establishing the pedagogical conditions for Christian initiation. On the one side, literacy enabled tremendous missional, even redemptive, ends. Thanks in great measure to the vernacular translation movement, the making of a literate people translated many of them into a Christian world, a world that extended itself into previously unimagined places.

Christianity and especially its theologians rarely failed to understand the importance of literacy. Most theologians, especially Protestants, lived out the idea that reading, writing, and textual production were fundamental to Christian theological vision. Christians were without doubt people of the book, especially at the emergence of colonialism. On the other side, literacy's redemptive possibilities were themselves drawn inside projects of nation building as well as burgeoning performances of class consciousness. This would mean that Christian theology articulated in vernacular literary display would register and reinforce processes of nation and class formation. The strength of salvation's witness in word was sure, but its reach was attenuated and then reframed to fit new purposes and literary spaces.

Watts's psalms exemplified a way of presenting and reading biblical texts that mediated influential nationalist concerns. More crucially, his psalms reveal a constriction of redemptive hope and creation's reality. His supersessionist vernacular loses sight of Israel's story and thereby loses sight of the opening of the world to the disclosure of its creator. He, like so many before and after him, chose instead to lodge the word of witness deeply inside the aspirations of *his* people and in so doing mangled the textual mediation of a good word, a word for *all* peoples. These excerpts from his powerful rendition of Psalm 147, Part 2, bear witness to the aspirations of a people different from biblical Israel:

O Britain, praise thy mighty God,
And make his honors known abroad,
He bid the ocean round thee flow;
Not bars of brass could guard thee so.

Thy children are secure and blest;
Thy shores have peace, thy cities rest;
He feeds thy sons with finest wheat,
And adds his blessing to their meat.

He bids the southern breezes blow;
The ice dissolves, the waters flow:
But he hath nobler works and ways
To call the Britons to his praise.

To all the isle his laws are shown,
His gospel through the nation known;
He hath not thus revealed his word
To every land: praise ye the Lord.[20]

The power and beauty of his verse inscribe his readers inside a compelling portrait of the biblical drama that allows the telos of the Christian life to remain intact, the praise of the one true God. But the pathway to that end has been profoundly altered. God will be praised in and through the establishment of this single people through their language in literary flight, soaring in enunciation of the gospel. His psalm exposes two operations. It gestures toward language unification, and it draws readers' imaginations to the deepest reality of their language; it is now the bearer of God's truth, God's very words. Such a twofold operation carries incredible power to bind a people together as one nation under God.

Hastings says it would be an oversimplification to suggest that vernacular translation, and more specifically the vernacular Bible, was "the sole catalyst for language unification or to claim that the development of a national conscious-ness could not be achieved through other means."[21] In fact, Hastings notes many factors in the creation of the English nation, including wars, weapons, the estab-lishment of territories through naming processes, myths of origin, ecclesiastical organizers and early historians, and vernacular literature.[22] "Nevertheless," he says, "as a matter of fact the correlation between biblical translation and what one may call a national awakening is remarkably close across most of Europe and, quite often, for other parts of the world as well."[23]

More is at stake, however, in the historical building of nations through Chris-tianity's vernacularizing effect than its precise catalytic effect. What is crucial is the interpenetration of the vernacularization of Christianity and the production of space. These two processes must be thought together if one is to begin to see the subversion of Christianity's power and the overturning of its communal tra-jectories. Kept separate in conventional analyses, the two processes can take on a natural, almost evolutionary character, each abiding by its own internal logics. For Christianity and for Christian moderns, the rise of vernacular Christianity shadowed the rise of vernacular space.[24] Vernacular space points to the transfor-mation of indigenous place to commodity space, a space captured by nationalist consciousness yet permeable and open to the constant reconfigurations of its identity. Christianity helped to sire two kinds of space—world literary space and fragmented social space—each helping to generate the other.

BECOMING LITERATE AND FORMING SPACE

At the same time Acosta left Spain for Peru, a cosmographer, a maker of maps, by the name of Juan López de Velasco was ascending to a newly formed office in the Council of the Indies, that Spanish governmental department that had administrative oversight of the colonies in the New World. In 1571, when Velasco became the *cosmógrafo-cronista mayor*, the main cosmographer-chronicler, for the Council of the Indies he inherited the task of fulfilling King Philip II's desire for maps as well as the vocational legacy of his predecessor as cosmographer, Alonso de Santa Cruz (1505–67).[25] King Philip II ruled over the land he had in-herited from his royal ancestors, King Ferdinand and Queen Isabella, the gift of a consolidated and enlarged realm too large to grasp through personal travel and observation. Thus Philip II was a strong believer in the power of images to estab-lish connection. Just as he sent pictures of himself to the far reaches of his realm to touch those he could not touch in person, so he desired maps that would allow him to touch the extension of his world. He had succeeded in establishing maps of his world in Spain. What remained was the attainment of maps of New Spain.

The task of satisfying the king's need to know the space he owned fell to Santa Cruz, who rightly believed that two kinds of description would satisfy the royal hunger, visual description of space and literary description of time in that space. In the words of Barbara Mundy, "Text and image, time and space: together these amounted to a full description of the New World."[26] The descriptions were a very serious matter because economic, political, and ideological concerns hung on the knowledge they comprehended. The New World had been divided under the treaty of Tordesillas (1494) between Spain and Portugal, and both world powers urgently needed longitudinal knowledge of their global share. Santa Cruz quickly discerned that he needed the deep collaboration of cosmographically inclined partners in the New World. He imagined questionnaires that would be the central means of establishing his partners in this knowledge quest and of gathering the knowledge itself. He died before he could realize his plan, leaving among his many papers a preliminary though suggestive effort, a collection of copied maps of the islands of the world with commentary.[27]

Velasco captured the spirit of Santa Cruz and pushed his plan forward. In 1577–78 he placed in the hands of ship captains bound for the New World the instrument he believed would be the catalyst for returning to him the king's desire, a questionnaire that solicited geographic reports from various officials in the New World. This *Relación Geográfica* questionnaire asked New World colonial agents to act as cosmographers by responding to the questions with drawings and written descriptions that showed the Spanish realm. Velasco envisaged rationally depicted geographic and chorographic features that would show the intimate relation between land, sea, and the built colonial environment. He imagined maps that would fully identify colonial sites including the *pueblos de españoles*, the segregated towns for Europeans, the *doctrinas* for native theological education, the mines, the churches, the coastlines, the lagoons, everything from the urban centers to the expansive farms.

Velasco never realized the goal of this desired mapping. Unlike Acosta, he was not present in the New World and therefore depended on the severely uneven interests, energy, and talent of unseen and unknown people. Moreover, he sent his instructions into a world that he did not understand, a world caught between what it was and what it was becoming. His instructions for the report fell into the hands of colonial officials who delegated the mapmaking tasks to a variety of people, including Amerindians. His desired report therefore fell between the colonialist disdain for and suspicion of Amerindians' pictographic writings and the colonials' very high regard for their own printed Spanish language as the central conveyor of truth. Velasco overestimated the cartographic understanding and skill at hand in the New World and moreover was unprepared for the different visions of space embodied in the colonialist and the indigenes. The result was a colossal failure, as noted by the relatively small number of maps produced, representing only a small portion of New Spain and drawn by peoples whose vision of space widely diverged.[28]

The *Relación Geográfica* is significant for my argument not because it shows an important step toward the successful mapping of Spain's New World, but because it gestures toward the comprehensive reformation of space within a vision of ownership. The juxtaposing of indigenous ways of imagining space with European spatial calculations makes the *Relación Geográfica* a remarkable moment in the struggle between two differing visions of the world.[29] Yet it also sheds light on a spatial vernacularizing desire that must be seen next to its social double. Velasco's correspondence to the New World stands next to Acosta's missional activity and the languages that governed that work. When Acosta arrived on the shores of Peru the literary world he had inhabited was shaped by two languages, one of the common people (Spanish) and one of the Catholic Church and its scholars (Latin). As Benedict Anderson notes, the status of Latin as the lingua franca expressed the power of the church: "The astonishing power of the papacy in its noonday is only comprehensible in terms of a trans-European Latin-writing clerisy, *and* a conception of the world, shared by virtually everyone, that the bilingual intelligentsia, by mediating between vernacular and Latin, mediated between earth and heaven."[30] The comprehensive reach of Latin not only indicated Rome's power, but also signaled its monopoly on the channels of official education and scholarship.[31] For theologians, Latin, Greek, and Hebrew constituted the languages of scholarship, yet Latin enabled the "*sacerdotium*— things of faith—to include *studium*," everything concerning the intellectual life.[32] Latin represented a universal and cosmopolitan reality for the church, a language that joined multiple peoples to the thinking of the church. Scholars from diverse ethnic backgrounds were compelled by the church to use Latin as the appropriate linguistic medium for expressing their ideas in texts. Theological treatises wanting to be seen in their important illuminating light had to be written in Latin to be recognized as worthy of serious intellectual attention.

Humanist developments offered an alternative intellectual expression for the use of Latin, Greek, and Hebrew. Acosta and Jesuit scholars in general, like many Catholic and, later, Protestant scholars, sought to incorporate the advantages of humanism into their academic programs. Indeed, the Jesuits and other orders envisioned drawing on humanism to help reform Scholasticism to develop a more robust pastoral theology and spirituality.[33]

Latin was, however, giving way to other languages in the creation of new literary spaces. The change was due not only to the rise of humanistic study but to the convergence of two world occurrences, the Protestant Reformation and the rise of mechanical printing concomitant with capitalist book publishing. Martin Luther's vernacular translations of the Bible not only helped to release the Bible from the Catholic superstructure but also, along with his other writings, stoked the capitalist fire of book publishers.[34] While Latin remained a crucial language of intellectual commerce well into the nineteenth century, as Anderson notes, intellectual commerce informed by book publishers was dramatically shifting toward vernacular markets from the sixteenth century forward:

> The initial market [for book publishers] was literate Europe, a wide but thin stratum of Latin-readers. Saturation of this market took about a hundred and fifty years. The determinative fact about Latin—aside from its sacrality—was that it was a language of bilinguals. Relatively few were born to speak it and even fewer, one imagines, dreamed in it. In the sixteenth century the proportion of bilinguals within the total population of Europe was quite small. . . . The logic of capitalism thus meant that once the elite Latin market was saturated, the potentially huge markets represented by the monoglot masses would beckon. Meantime, a Europe-wide shortage of money made printers think more and more of peddling cheap editions in the vernaculars.[35]

If literary space beyond Latin was emerging in Europe, it was extended and facilitated by the material expansion of Europe itself into Africa and the Americas. Anderson notes that a third factor in the "revolutionary vernacularizing thrust of capitalism" was the deployment of "vernaculars as instruments of administrative centralization" within certain European monarchies.[36] The *Relación Geográfica* stood as a powerful example of such a vernacular administrative instrument.[37] Christianity forced indigenous peoples to enter a Christian world that was linguistically fragmenting as a result of the rise of capitalist-driven vernacularization as well as of the vast expansion of vernacular administrative operations into previously unknown worlds. The significant point here is not the loss of Latin dominance, which represented a supposedly healthy holism that enabled intellectual coherence, but that the mutuality of these occurrences—capitalist-driven vernacularization in the Old World and vernacular expansion tied to colonial expansionism in the New World—revealed a parallelism in its effects on the imagination.

Anderson offered the seminal thesis that print literacy, vivified by print capitalism's vernacular productions, helped people to imagine and to create the nation as limited (that is, bounded in space), as sovereign (that is, possessing freedom), and as a community (that is, having citizenship).[38] Print media, witnessed in the novel and newspapers, presented what he saw as a "profound fictiveness."[39] That is, they presented the idea of "homogeneous, empty time" in which the people of a nation were moving together "down (or up) history."[40] The imagined nation was part of a process of imagining spaces vivified by the Christianized colony that drew all bodies into capitalist calculations. The deepest calculation was of space itself. Colonialism did not create the territorializing of Old World or New World space. It only drew everyday practices into its hyperreality, a reality that reached all the way down into private property and privately owned bodies. Capitalism and colonialism joined to bind territorial vision to people's imaginations so that imagined nation-time, national history, included imagined nationally segregated space.

One must hold together these parallel processes of vernacular formation and vernacular space formation in order to capture the massive growing power of the segregationist mentality. Pascale Casanova writes that by the seventeenth century France emerged as "the dominant literary power in Europe."[41] French intellectuals accomplished supremacy by bringing into French the intellectual, artistic, and rhetorical legacies of the ancients, of Greece and Rome, of Greek and Latin. This remarkable translation of Latin's imperial position and cosmopolitan currency into French happened through the deliberate transposition of Latin's educational and aesthetic trajectories into French.

Latin, through the tutelage and influence of the church, had enjoyed a monopoly in the educational system of France; French students were asked to inhabit a Latin universe in their instruction. However, the growing appeal of vernacularization, no doubt influenced by the Protestant movement and French political aspirations, encouraged an appreciation of the importance of native spoken language. French intellectuals claimed that the "clarity and precision" of Latin could be transposed to the "vital and malleable use of the spoken tongue."[42] This shift would allow a clear focus on the aesthetically appealing aspects of the French language. Thus educational endeavors could be wed to the codifying of the inherent beauties of a people's everyday language.

The idea of this merger of educational work with aesthetic clarification appealed to the ruling classes in France. The men of letters, the elite magistrates, the court nobility, and especially the women of the court nobility joined in the task of cultivating oral performances that would distill a cultivated naturalness of the French vernacular. The result would be a "new oral prose" that would soon break the inertia of Latin scholarly models.[43] If there was a pedagogical struggle with Latin it soon ended in favor of French, not by destroying Latin's power but by drawing that power into the French language itself. Thus, French would emerge as the language of civilization, the language of European aristocracy, that is, the language of universal man.[44]

The significance of the emergence of French literary dominance is that it did not signal a concomitant political dominance; rather, it pointed to a transformation of a theological universal into a secular universal. That is, it pointed to the way in which vernacularization can help solidify national identity and enable transnationalist gestures that point to the transformation of a person or peoples into a universalized state of existence, an anthropology of civilization. By a kind of divine election, the French would contend they had become, against the claims of the Italian humanists, the embodiment of the true humanist modernity. French slowly outpaced the Tuscan dialect and watched as England and Spain joined France as the other literary powers. Spain's power both politically and literarily waned as it moved through the seventeenth century, while French was transformed into the language of literature.[45]

The late seventeenth century saw French reconstitute and then coordinate a global literary space that could be superimposed on all other languages, spoken and written. This literary space was shared with English as one of the most crucial points of opposition to French literary dominance. The struggle between French and English for literary dominance notwithstanding, the crucial point to gather here is the nature and power of vernacular superimposition in the formation of new worlds, literary and spatial. This superimposition in the formation of literary space mirrors the reformation of actual space in the accumulation of land by all the colonial powers.

The seizing of land by colonial powers such as England parallels this superimposition in the conjuring of a new spatial vision of land. This is much more than simply the bringing of land into national territorial spheres. Rather, land itself would be drawn into a new dimensionality that rendered former spatial designations and coordination of ways of life meaningless or at best marginal to the entrance into a civilized sphere of existence. With the Land Survey System suggested by Thomas Jefferson in 1784 and enacted by the Congress of the United States in 1785, Jefferson and others "devised a plan whereby all the vacant unclaimed land in the young republic could be divided into an almost infinite number of squares, each of them a square mile, or 640 acres—more than enough to satisfy the average would-be settler."[46] This grid system became fundamental to the way Americans would imagine actual living space—its divisions, borders, and limits.

The grid pattern of sellable squares of land signified the full realization of property ownership. It also displayed the complete remaking of indigenous land. Now, under the grid system, each space of land could be surveyed and designated for purchase by measurement and location. All native peoples, no matter what their claims to land, no matter what designations they had for particular places, no matter their history and identity with specific lands, landscape, and indigenous animals, were now mapped onto the grid system. As one native, Massasoit, leader of the Wampanoag, stated to a colonist in America much earlier (in 1620), "What is this you call property? . . . It cannot be the earth, for the land is our mother, nourishing all her children, beasts, birds, fish, and all men. The woods, the streams, everything on it belongs to everybody and is for the use of all. How can one man say it belongs only to him?"[47]

From the moment British colonists and others became Americans seized by land greed, such queries fell on deaf ears. Space was reordered mathematically and linguistically, and it thereby was reordered in reality. Thanks to the measuring chain invented by the Englishman Edmund Gunter, the innovative thinking of Thomas Jefferson, the precise refinements to the grid system made by Jared Mansfield, and the fierce struggle for land, a way of thinking about space took shape in America that was primarily concerned not about actual space, but its possible price. The grid system, as the historian Andro Linklater states, was "ideal for buying, trading, and speculating."[48] It was a system in which capitalism and democracy joined arm in arm.[49] But it destroyed the possibility of thinking of identity within land, within place.

This system was tailor-made for a world in which people carried their identities wholly on their bodies. That is, it was tailor-made for New World slavery and for slaveholding societies in which black people joined the land as private property and natives existed as "*resident* 'foreign' nations."[50] Crucial here is the profound work the grid system did from its beginnings to organize Americans' imaginations then and now.[51] This universal effect stands alongside the universalism that was growing out of the preeminence of French in the literary world.[52]

These two forms of universalism, of new property as potentially sellable (that is, as private) and of French literature pointing to a transnational reality, had no apparent connection.[53] In truth, the two forms functioned independently yet harmoniously, collaborating imaginatively. Each would become part of a horizon through which people would imagine the world. They both presented a conceptual imperialism, quietly in operation. The public land survey system deployed in the new nation of America and the literary system that was slowly being deployed globally both expressed the totalizing powers of whiteness. Like the formation of racial vision organized around white bodies, the grid system operated without regard to any specific geographic features. And like the conceptual turnings of whiteness in which tribes and peoples, their stories, their ways of life were charted through the visual logic of their phenotypes and racial classifications, the grid system drew lines through mountains, valleys, rivers, burial sites, and so on. The system allowed for the clear demarcation of white settler lands and so-called Indian lands.

The French ascendency to literary dominance was also about a very distinct demarcation. However, the way in which that demarcation draws from the conceptual legacy of whiteness is more complex. That legacy is woven into the move toward the universal. The French language was not seen as parochial, "but rather as a universal language, which is to say one that belonged to all people and so rose above national interests."[54] French literary space came to stand for intellectual space free of political and nationalist constraint. It was the space of pure humanity grasping its own transcendence.

The power of the French innovation lies in its transformation of the ecclesial trajectory of Latin. The church's use of Latin as the transnational, transethnic resource for intellectual commerce was the immediate backdrop to this new deployment of French. More significantly, because Latin was the discursive home for theology, the literary space it created was the most intensely autonomous, transcendent literary space in existence. Christian theology performed in Latin was one of the most powerful forms of universalized and therefore autonomous literature. It is true that theology drew its life from exegesis of the Scriptures written in Greek and Hebrew; however, the discursive engine for bringing to light the exegetical insights and theological commentaries of theologians, at least in the Western church, was Latin.

It is also the case that the tradition of manuscript reproduction existed at the heart of the church's theological enterprise. Yet from the fifteenth century forward Christian theology was propelled by the growing power of mechanical reproduction, which supplanted manual manuscript reproduction. In like manner, theology entered a powerful reproduction of its literary space. While this movement was not without contest, the lines of contention were shaped primarily by the Catholic–Protestant divide rather than by resistance to the supplanting itself. In fact, the ascendency of French literary space was not a straightforward reproduction of ecclesial-controlled, Latin literary space but a simulacrum drawing on some of its most powerful features. I have mentioned its universalizing and autonomous nature. Within this nature was the implicit use of the ideas of humanity, confraternity, freedom, and reason. Yet all of these themes were stripped of their theological matrix and isolated from the tradition of religious reading. Christian theology followed the ascendency of French literary space, acquiescing to the seeming rightness of its judgments and making use of its power.

The French and with them the British (along with the nascent United States of America) were forming world literary space much as they were creating a new system of weights and measures to help survey land and determine its value.[55] In both cases, they were standing on the same conceptual plateau the church had stood on as it surveyed the world, assessing its needs, potentials, and places for mission and pastoral intervention. From that plateau, a different sense of time and space was regnant, one calibrated eschatologically. This was time and space not bound to the historical occurrences of people and their political vicissitudes. The new literary space took its cues from eschatological time and space:

> Events that "leave a mark" on the literary world have a "tempo" . . . that is unique to this world and that is not—or is not necessarily "synchronous"—with the measure of historical (which is to say political) time that is established as official and legitimate. Literary space creates a present on the basis of which all positions can be measured, a point in relation to which all other points can be located. Just as the *fictive* line known as the prime meridian, arbitrarily chosen for the determination of longitude, contributes to the *real* organization of the world and makes possible the measure of distances and the location of positions on the surface of the earth, so what might be called the Greenwich meridian of literature makes it possible to estimate the relative aesthetic distance from the center of the world of letters of all those who belong to it.[56]

Casanova's comments here capture not only a theological inheritance but also the constitutive ground and location of whiteness. Christian theology, its dogmatic tradition, its doctrinal loci of orthodoxy embodied in the church, in the writings of its theologians, and in its ecclesial practices were a prime meridian for determining the merits or demerits of all intellectual work within its vast international realm. As noted in earlier chapters, ecclesial judgments of who was capable or incapable of learning, articulating, and performing theology were racialized from the first moments of discovery. The fictive meridian of literature was born from the real line of orthodox theological judgment. This is not to say the theological meridian ended with the advent of the new literary center; rather, the theological center began moving toward coordination, if not in some moments synchronization, with the literary center. This is especially the case for European Christian theology in relation to the expressions of its colonial subjects.

What was also at play in the development of this fictive line was a theologically derived aesthetic that determined which literary works were contemporary, participating in modernity as an eternal present as opposed to being out of date, and which works were of universal import rather than provincial. One can see in the formation of world literary space the broad outlines of a prior Christian vision of orthodox literary values. That is, before the advent of world literary space, theologians and their intellectual collaborators wrote texts that followed a similar aesthetic. Those works sought to give witness to the living tradition of Christian reflection and capture a universal applicability, that is, to be useful to the church and its global teaching ministry.

The family resemblance of these aesthetic sensibilities between orthodox literary values and world literary values also carried forward an appreciation for continuity with ancient regimes of language and thought. Casanova says, "The temporal law of the world of letters may be stated thus: *it is necessary to be old in order to have any chance of being modern or of decreeing what is modern.*"[57] The other aspect of this aesthetic dimension, which I explore in more detail later, was its embodiment. Here the implicit question of who would be capable of articulating the modern and the universal, and the different but related question of who most appropriately articulates the modern and the universal, took on racialized responses. Whiteness became the aesthetic anchor for universality's visualization.

The spatial analogy referred to by Casanova has real-world correspondence with the ways the European colonies were organized. As we saw in Equiano's narrative, returning to England was returning to civilization and the locus of its ideas. This spatial organization also constituted an important question for other nations. How would they respond to this Greenwich meridian of literature as well as to the growing centrality of a New World being strongly spatially configured by French and British political and economic interests?

The most important response was powerfully articulated by Johann Gottfried Herder. In the second half of the eighteenth century and at the dawn of the nineteenth century, Herder's thinking gave response to the question of how other nations should consider their (possible) place in world literature. In what Casanova describes as the competition of world literary space, Herder challenged the French order of things by suggesting that each nation carried within itself its own cultural genius. As he famously said in *Another Philosophy of History for the Education of Mankind*, "Every nation has its *center* of happiness *within itself*, as every ball has its center of gravity!"[58] Casanova sums up Herder's achievement in what she called the Herder effect: "By granting each country and each people the right to an existence and a dignity equal in principle to those of others, in the name of 'popular traditions' from which sprang a country's entire cultural and historical development, and by locating the source of artistic fertility in the 'soul' of peoples, Herder shattered all the hierarchies, all the assumptions that until then had unchallengably [*sic*] constituted literary 'nobility.'"[59]

Casanova is right to see an analogy between this development and the vernacular revolution tied to the Reformation. Not unlike the movement that delivered the Bible into the hands of the people, Herder represents the idea that literature arises out of the artistic soul of a people. In the Herder effect, Casanova offers a historical schematic of the development of world literary space. It began with French supplanting Latin, continued with the rise of nationalisms tied to national language and culture, and brought the modern world to the current situation in which decolonization is expanding the literary world. Yet the Herderian response had wider historical resonances than the vernacular revolution of the sixteenth and seventeenth centuries. The outlines of this kind of account of peoples can be found in the perspectives of the colonizers in Africa and the Americas who asked questions regarding the literary capacities of the natives. However, the described immaturity of the indigenes drew negative assessment of their abilities.

Historically, nationalism becomes the spatial analogue to Herder's invention of literary populism. As Anthony Smith notes, the language of sacred homelands draws together belief in the election of particular peoples to particular territories through origin or struggle and the necessary development of their distinctive literature which would reflect this divine sanctioning of their existence.[60] World literary space established a hierarchy within which peoples would struggle for recognition and freedom. World literary space paralleled national, political space and its struggles so that the Herder effect bled its way into the epistemic systems of modern nations and nation-states. The result was the nationalization of literature. Every nation and, in some accounts, every people is now understood to have its own soulfulness, which could be willed into expressive existence by any individual writer or artist in her or his literary work.

The historical trajectory of colonial powers and their formerly dominated peoples continues to shape the "literary inequality of languages."[61] Thus, translation continues to carry the social, political, and cultural power dynamics present from the very beginning of the colonialist moment. Indeed, as we saw in the narrative by Bishop Colenso, translation from oral to written form allowed the Zulu language to constitute cultural nationalist space within a Western framework. Then with the emergence of bilingualism or multilingualism for Nguni language speakers, Zulu people became subject to world literary space at its outermost margins. Colenso, in his desire to capture the universal elements in Zulu thought through the work of translation, also revealed the policing realities inherent in world literary space.

The dilemma of choice set up by world literary space was the dilemma of colonialist existence which continues to affect postcolonialist existence. On the one side "there is *assimilation*, or integration within a dominant literary space [normally of the former colonialist parental power] through a dilution or erasing of original differences," or, on the other, one can seek *"differentiation*, which is to say the assertion of difference, typically on the basis of a claim to national identity."[62] For a writer, choosing to be translated or not carries with it the question of cultural legitimacy and acquiescence to the literary order of things. The position set up for formerly colonized peoples in world literary space depends on their form of dependence on the former colonial powers.[63]

What Casanova has powerfully captured here is the voice of a theological orthodox literary imagination channeled through the historic transformations of vernacular existence. The legitimization process of literary voice is a direct descendent of the legitimization process of theological orthodox voice, especially as it was expressed in the founding colonialist assessments of indigenous peoples' intellectual capacities. By legitimization process, I simply mean the act of being recognized as a theological voice, a theological text useful for speculation, for ecclesial consumption, and for resourcing pastoral imagination. This process determines the entrance into literary existence or nonexistence through official recognition (papal, academic, or ecclesiastical). The offspring of this process showed itself in the colonies from the brutal suppression of indigenous languages all the way to the vicious process of leaving a mother tongue in order to inhabit the civilized literary space of the colonial masters.

Ngũgĩ wa Thiong'o's account of Kenyan children being beaten for speaking their native language in school rather than English points to the farthest reaches of the literary legitimization process, all the way down to the bodies of small colonized children: "One of the most humiliating experiences was to be caught speaking Gĩkũyũ in the vicinity of the school. The culprit was given corporal punishment—three to five strokes of the cane on bare buttocks—or was made to carry a metal plate around the neck with inscriptions such as I AM STUPID or I AM A DONKEY."[64] If these words capture the farthest reaches of literary legitimization, then Frantz Fanon's comments regarding the absolute necessity that black people in the Antilles learn proper French capture its ubiquity. The pull toward literary legitimization in the colonies permeated every step in colonial language acquisition. Fanon noted that to black people learning French constituted the passage from their jungle status, that is, from their blackness, into civilization and whiteness. In commenting on this reality Fanon quotes a poem that registers the stark horror and viciousness of this passage:

Some families completely forbid the use of Creole, and mothers ridicule their children for speaking it.
My mother wanting a son to keep in mind
if you do not know your history lesson

you will not go to mass on Sunday in
your Sunday clothes
that child will be a disgrace to the family
that child will be our curse
shut up I told you you must speak French
the French of France
the Frenchman's French
French French

Yes, I must take great pains with my speech, because I shall be more or less
judged by it. With great contempt they will say of me, "He doesn't even know
how to speak French." In any group of young men in the Antilles, the one who
expresses himself well, who has mastered the language, is inordinately feared;
keep an eye on that one, he is almost white.[65]

Fanon's comments here expose the theological underpinnings of this colonial
literary space. Here, orthodox speech, appropriate speech is French. Heterodox
speech is Creole, broken speech, the "halfway house between pidgin-nigger and
French."[66] Yet theological vision is not only at the foundations of this legitimization process but also merges easily with its social performance. The language of
the church in Fanon's cultural setting, of Mass, of Christian worship, was properly French drawn from the use of proper Latin. The passage into the "oral prose"
of French, the generative reality of its literary space, also illumines the entrance
into theological legitimization.

Christian theology entered this reconstituted non-Latin space with little
protest. Indeed, the writings of almost all Christian theologians since the advent
of literary modernity could be easily mapped through world literary space. On
its one side, Christian theology seeks to determine the relation of its expressions
to the various cultural matrices of nation, language, literature, and the everyday
practices of its peoples. On its other side, Christian theology is trapped in the
revised universalism that feigns the legitimation processes of ancient orthodoxy
while being deeply committed to the literary supremacy and "universal human
genius" of the languages of the central literary powers—French, English, Italian,
German (and sometimes Spanish).[67]

Those theologians who think from within the revised universalism of the world
literary powers are indeed concerned with questions of orthodoxy and the intellectual edification of the faithful. They also recognize organic folkloric connections to theological expressions, yet they would suggest their primary objective
is to discern the continuities of Christian intellectual traditions in current theological expressions. This is an important, well-intentioned concern. But it is a

concern buried inside the hierarchy of languages in world literary space. This means that the center/margin realities of world literature deeply penetrate their evaluations of theology. This is one of the reasons Christian communities and intellectuals outside the meridian of literature (and theology), who have been producing theological literature for centuries, remain virtually unknown and without due consideration. This situation helps to create the myth of a global Christian ecumenicity.

The problem of Christian theology and segregationalist mentalities, however, is not simply a problem of theology's articulation. The difficulties reach down into the very social character of literacy itself and its relation to vernacular space in modernity. Christians are located inside nations and modern nation-states, which means that Christian theology is also located inside a constricting configuration of the social imagination. But the point of confinement is not simply nationalism. The confinement expresses a style of imagining social reality.[68] That style is generated between, on the one side, the historic development of vernacular print capitalism concomitant with the development of world literary space and, on the other side, the formation of vernacular space known as private property. That style is also generated inside the historic advent of whiteness and the racialized world it has produced.[69]

Christianity functioned in the new worlds of Africa and the Americas and in the modern period with one of its most basic pedagogical and communal realities, biblical literacy, diseased and in need of healing. Diseased not in terms of its performance, that is, in enabling the reading of Scripture and the writing of Christian theology and literature, but in the kind of community it imagined—its scope, character, and materiality. Moreover, Christian theology would soon be completely subsumed in the literary order of things, expressing class consciousness and desire and nationalist longings. Biblical literacy therefore entered the world people now inhabit with attenuated power because literacy in modernity already signified a much-mangled space.

One of the most profound historic sites of the mangled space of literacy and the diseased form of imagined community created by it was in the slaveholding society of North America. During the founding years of this new republic, Africans were not allowed to read or write. Understanding this historic reality is crucial for grasping the formation of segregationalist mentalities in operation in Christianity that were unchallenged by Christian theology. The significance of this historic prohibition also shows the complex social dynamics that continue to haunt the Christian social imagination and thwart the formation of Christian community beyond the strictures of nation, language, and peoples.

THE AFRICAN AMERICAN COMPROMISE

A law in South Carolina in 1740 stated the following: "Whereas the having of slaves taught to write, or suffering them to be employed in writing, may be attended with great inconveniences. *Be it enacted,* That all and every person and persons whatsoever who shall hereafter teach or cause any slave or slaves to be taught to write, or shall use or employ any slave as a scribe in any manner of writing hereafter taught to write, every such person or persons shall for every such offence forfeit the sum of one hundred pounds current money."[70]

A law in North Carolina in 1830–31 states,

> Whereas the teaching of slaves to read and write, has a tendency to excite dissatisfaction in their minds, and to produce insurrection and rebellion, to the manifest injury of the citizens of the State: Therefore,
>
> 1. *Be it enacted* . . . That any free person, who shall hereafter teach or attempt to teach, any slave within this State to read or write, the use of figures excepted, or shall give or sell to such slave or slaves any books or pamphlets, shall be liable to indictment in any court of record in the State having jurisdiction thereof; and upon conviction, shall, at the discretion of the court, if a white man or woman, be fined not less than one hundred dollars, nor more than two hundred dollars, or imprisoned; and if a free person of color, shall be fined, imprisoned, or whipped, at the discretion of the court, not exceeding thirty-nine lashes, nor less than twenty lashes.
> 2. *Be it further enacted,* That if any slave shall hereafter teach, or attempt to teach, any other slave to read or write, the use of figures excepted, he or she may be carried before any justice of the peace, and on conviction thereof, shall be sentenced to receive thirty-nine lashes on his or her bare back.[71]

These laws were enacted deep in the heart of the Enlightenment experiment that was the new republic of the United States, a nation with freedom, equality, and human confraternity planted in its ideological soil. More important for my purposes, these laws were enacted during the vernacular transformation of literary space. While literacy was slowly being established as a common gift for the people, here in the midst of modernity were a people denied that very gift.

America began as a slaveholding society, and it is easy to forget that the literacy prohibition presented one of its most blatant communal self-deceptions. The literacy prohibition served a pragmatic function; in states with significant slave populations, such as Alabama, Georgia, Louisiana, Mississippi, North and South Carolina, and Virginia, a literate slave could have argued for her freedom, gained subversive intellectual and social tools, and begun to see herself equal to her master, or even used such tools to plan and organize escape or violent rebellion.

If literacy among slaves went unchecked, the result would be a massive loss in production and a fundamental disruption to the economy.

This pragmatic justification located the feared disruptive possibilities of slave literacy in society writ large. However, it would be more accurate to say that those fears were located essentially in antebellum households. In antebellum America, the household stood at the center of the social world of the new republic, and at the center of the household stood the male landowner. The historian Stephanie McCurry writes of the importance of the household in South Carolina Low Country, but her account reflects American slaveholding society in general: "In South Carolina, as in other slave states, the household was a spatial unit, defined by the property to which the owner held legal title and over which he exercised exclusive rights. But it was much more than that. In societies in which land constituted the chief means of subsistence, title to land historically incorporated claims over the persons and the labor of those dependent on it. The household was thus a social unit as well. Indeed, in antebellum South Carolina households were the constituent units of society, organizing the majority of the population—slaves of both sexes and all ages and free women and children—in relations of legal and customary dependency to the propertied male head, whether yeoman or planter."[72]

The household and its white male head presented the point of intersection between the geographic and literary order of things. From the moment Jefferson's grid system and its related ideas became policy and geographers and land speculators laid claim to the new earth of America, private property became a matter of theological anthropology. The being of (an individual) man and the being of (a particular piece of) land were moving inextricably toward one another as if toward a fundamental, God-given joining.[73]

This ascendency of private property inhered in the original trajectory of colony formation. As we saw with the property developments in Peru, the *encomenderos* exercised tremendous power through landownership and saw the land as an extension of themselves. In America, landownership signaled a different relationship of body to space.[74] The body of the landowner was tied to the land as an extension of the body's vulnerability. This, of course, meant that the land had to be secured and protected from incursion. The opening centuries of the new republic were the story of the growth of property owners' rights. McCurry notes, "'The security of the landowner' assumed the republican mantle. By the end of the antebellum period, common rights [to land], beaten back into privileges and courtesies, were virtually impossible to sustain at law."[75] Yet the most powerful implication of the body–land connection was its effect on the social construction of intimate relations within the household.

Given the foundational role of colony social logics in the New World, it would make sense that the plantation landscape shaped the America landscape. However, the decisive development of this new landscape was that of the house-holder's (that is, landowner's) space as inviolable private space. This made "the authority of the master over [the land] virtually absolute."[76] Whether the land-owner was a planter or yeoman and small farmer, he had complete power over the bodies of those in his household. The boundaries of his land were in fact the boundaries of his body. All those who lived with the owner lived in his body.[77]

The key to grasping the significance of the struggle of slave literacy is land-owner weakness, landowner vulnerability and fear. There were differences between southern and northern households, but they should not be exaggerated. Primarily the differences were that the northern household was not shaped around slave life and labor and the southern household was. Yet the concept of land as private property joined to white male bodies as a sacred right held in both geographies. The household master sought order above all else. In the southern household, order was manifested in obedience and bound to the fear of disorder was the subsequent loss of productivity, which could lead to social or financial disaster or both.

In most cases, household masters understood themselves to be engaged in an unrelentingly Christian and benevolent enterprise. So the prohibition against slave literacy came, in their logic, from the need to protect the vulnerability of everyone, including the slaves themselves. Indeed, the South Carolina law of 1740 against slave literacy was a direct reaction to the Stono Rebellion near Charleston in 1739, in which over twenty whites were killed.[78] Yet the temporal distance between the South Carolina law (1740) and the North Carolina law (1830) not only indicates how social prohibitions reflect and help constitute the perceived natural order, but also gestures toward a compelling vision of the created order itself.[79]

The temporal distance between these two laws and the social order out of which they arose indicate a perceived naturalness of slave illiteracy and unnaturalness of literate slaves. Literacy laws remained in effect through the Civil War, which meant that prior to slavery's end multiple generations grew up, lived, and died within the reality of black illiteracy. African slaves fought against this natural order of things. Equally important, a challenge to this natural order of things came from within white Christianity itself. There was great ambivalence among slaveholding families about whether it was their Christian duty to teach their slaves to read and write for the sake of learning the Bible because learning the Bible was central to cultivating Christian faith.

If slaveholding society desired to be seen as democratic, slaveholding households wanted to be seen as Christian. This helped to establish the political struggle over slave literacy that would continue as a significant area of contention among whites right through the Civil War. On the one side were the abolitionists and other missionary-minded Christians (often those who owned slaves) deciding it was their Christian duty to teach slaves to read Scripture. Reading would condition the slave to accept his social lot, his place in society provided by God, and furthermore (it was argued) the revolutionary leaders of the young country believed that the health of any democracy depended upon universal literacy.

Opposing the abolitionists and the slave owners who were teaching slaves to read were the civic officials and slave owners who thought it a very bad idea. This opposition group had found a clear connection between literate slaves and the rise of slave revolts. All the so-called rebel slave leaders had some measure of learning and had made what the slaveholders thought was horrible use of their knowledge. In fact, many slaves who learned to read and write wrote inflammatory materials and seemed to gravitate to the apocalyptic materials in the Scriptures. The fanatical, Scripture-inspired words of the slave rebel leader Nat Turner served as an example to buttress antiliteracy sentiment: "And about this time I had a vision—and I saw white spirits and black spirits engaged in battle, and the sun was darkened—the thunder rolled in the Heavens, and blood flowed in streams—and I heard a voice saying, 'Such is your luck, such you are called to see, and let it come rough or smooth, you must surely bare [*sic*] it.'"[80]

What came into being with literate slaves, from the perspective of antiliteracy proponents, was often some supposed wild form of interpretation of an imminent divine judgment upon the society. One of the most infamous antiliteracy proponents was State Senator Whitemarsh Seabrook of South Carolina, who "claimed that anyone who wanted to acquaint the slave with the whole Bible was fit for 'a room in the Lunatic Asylum.'"[81] However, literacy advocates were not convinced by Seabrook-like arguments; indeed, they believed that correct interpretation of the Bible in the very process of teaching slaves to read would overcome the problems noted by people like Seabrook.

Slaves had to be taught how to read the Bible, just as all Christians had to be initiated in appropriate hermeneutic practices. Centrally this was done by being schooled in the very practices of the church. Many teachers of the slaves invested heavily in the ancient practice of catechizing would-be adherents to the gospel. The "instruction of the Negroes" became a major area of reflection for lay and professional theologian alike. Often noted but seldom understood is the theological significance of the reworking of catechisms to suit a slaveholding context. The catechisms constructed by the famous instructor of slaves Rev. Charles Colcock Jones (1804–63) serve as an example of this theological operation. One section of a catechism is rendered as follows:

Q. Who only is perfectly good in himself, and does good to us and to all creatures?

A. God . . .

Q. Tell me some of God's goodness to you.

A. He gives us father and mother, meat and drink, and clothes to wear; and when we are sick he makes us well.

Q. Is it not great goodness in God to make us live in a Gospel land, and to give us his holy word?

A. Yes . . .[82]

Certain biblical themes were emphasized over others, for example, obedience, service, loyalty, humility. A portion of one catechism states,

Q. 37 When Negroes become religious, how must they behave to their masters?

A. The *Scriptures* in many places command them, to be honest, diligent and faithful in all things, and not to give saucy answers; and even when they are whipped for doing well, to take it patiently and look to God for their reward . . .

Q. 39 Which do you think is the happiest person, the master or the slave?

A. When I rise on a cold morning and make a fire, and my master in bed; or when I labour in the sun, on a hot day, and my master in the shade; then I think him happier than I am.

Q. 40 Do you think you are happier than he?

A. Yes: When I come in from my work; eat my hearty supper, worship my maker; lie down without care on my mind; sleep sound; get up in the morning strong and fresh; and hear that my master could not sleep, for thinking on his debts and taxes; and how he shall provide victuals and clothes for his family, or what he shall do for them when they are sick—then I bless God that he has placed me in my humble station; I pity my master, and feel myself happier than he is.

Q. 41 Then it seems every body is best, just where God has placed them?

A. Yes the *Scriptures* say, if I am called being a slave, I am not to care for it; for every true Christian, is Christ's free man, whether he be bound or free in this world.

Q. 41 How can you be free and bound both?

A. If Jesus Christ has broke the chain of sin, and freed me from the curse of the law, and the slavery of the devil, I am free indeed, although my body and services may be at the command of another. [emphasis added][83]

To see that such catechisms were mind-controlling devices is to overlook a much more significant reality of this practice. While control of the slaves is a matter of concern, it is control of their reading of the Scriptures that is at issue in catechesis. Another manual of slave instruction brings this point to light:

Who gave you a master and a mistress?
God gave them to me
Who says that you must obey them?
God says that I must.
What book tells you these things?
The Bible. [emphasis added][84]

Again and again the Scripture is surrounded by interpretation so that the slave is led to the text chained in and to a discourse of white hegemony. In this discourse, Christian doctrine and practice found their place in the practice of interpretation. They were woven together to civilize the slave and secure slaveholding society by means of the text. What this procedure showed at a basic level was that doctrine and church practice together were the necessary tools for accessing the meaning of Scripture.

In effect, the act of interpretation concerned itself with determining the scope of reading Scripture and thereby sought to determine the scope of biblical authority in the nature of faith for the slave.[85] Whereas for the slaveholder (and even for those whites opposed to slavery) the authority of the Bible stood as the unmediated foundation of Christian life and doctrine, for the slave the Bible was offered only in conjunction with the interpreting word of the slave master. In truth, however, the number of household masters or members prepared or willing to engage in this level of theological education and pedagogical instruction of slaves was small. Most simply followed antiliteracy sensibilities and kept literacy a guarded secret. Many slaves, however, sought and gained access to the secret. They were driven in this dangerous and risky effort by knowledge of literacy's power in helping them achieve freedom and in many cases by the desire to know the Scriptures for themselves. What ensued was the great struggle for black (biblical) literacy in America. Slaves used ingenious means to learn to read and write as much as they could. From tricking unsuspecting children in the household to teach them their ABCs, to brokering deals with wide varieties of social outcasts, to picking up bits and pieces of information by watching other members of the household, slaves were always on the hunt for knowledge.

Heather Andrea Williams notes that most enslaved people had to "'steal' an education."[86] They would covertly meet early in the morning or late at night, in the woods or other secluded places, hidden from sight in order to gather together their slender threads of knowledge or to learn from someone who had precious knowledge of how to read and write. An important time for these covert operations was Sunday mornings, when the white families went to church. As a slave in Person County, North Carolina, said, "When my master's family were all gone away on the Sabbath, I used to go into the house and get down the great Bible, and lie down in the piazza, and read, taking care, however to put it back before they returned."[87] All these efforts were undertaken at great risk. If caught, slaves might be beaten, whipped, mutilated, sold, or see their family members sold.

Slaves' determination to read and write and their postbellum children's determination to build educational institutions and secure their intellectual growth and survival is an important and crucial story in itself. My concern, however, is not primarily with the majestic heroism of black literacy efforts (though they are indeed majestic), but with the deeper tragedy that attended this occurrence and that continues to mark ecclesial life. The greater tragedy is located in the central structure of social life in the new republic. There in racialized spaces literacy signified fragmentation. The slave learning to read and write had to work in secret. When slaves sought biblical literacy, in that too they were forced to enact strategies of assembly (*ekklesia*) that bound the ways they imagined their freedom (if not also their survival) to reading alone and apart. Here was a compromise of epic significance, a young (black) church forced to read alone in fear of violence and death. Where biblical literacy was guided by white slaveholding society, it was a profoundly racialized reading. The Bible was read within racial difference, and racial difference was read into the Bible.

What is true of the communal distortions of biblical literacy was also true of the development of worship in America: however, segregated worship practices are a step further along and indicate complex realities to be explored later. But one must not lose sight of the impotence of Scripture to enact community at this historical moment. Moreover, it is precisely the spatial dynamics of New World existence in the colonies that fostered biblical literacy's ineffectiveness. As we saw in the first chapter, the land disappeared as identity-facilitator and reappeared as private property facilitated by the racial landscape and determined by whiteness. In the formative years of the United States, geographic-based identity was turned on its head. Rather than a peoples' identity coterminous with its landscape and its realities—water, trees, seasons, animals—the land was identified with its white male owner. This was also an overturning of the imagination in which the ability of Scripture to help people reimagine the world was severely limited.

The Bible was constrained within hierarchical literary space that was enclosed in fundamentally distorted geographic space. What connected these spaces was the racial imagination that permeated both the creating and shaping of perception and helped to vivify both spaces. The result was fragmentation, not simply one affecting the Bible but also one effected by the performance of Scripture itself in these mangled spaces. This fragmentation was the ground for a distorted individuation—people envisioning themselves as distinct groups within Christianity itself. Simply put, they were not the people of God but peoples of God. I am not referring here to the continuation of various cultural practices, memory, and story, which when articulated became the basis for the actual distinction between peoples. What is at play here is the constraining of the goal for the embodiment of Christian community.

There is yet another crucial aspect to the phenomenon of segregated mentalities. To capture this additional aspect requires returning, in a sense, to the household of the slave master. The tragedy of New World biblical literacy is part of the tragedy of fragmentation, but it is also the problem of the enclosure of identity to racialized bodies. However, as I showed with the southern household, there was a geographic expansion of identity around the body of the master, the body of whiteness. Herein lay the other aspect of the problem that helped to generate segregated mentality within Christian imagination, that is, a world forced inside the intimacy of white existence.

LIVING INSIDE THE WHITE HOUSE

Starting in 1863, slavery ended and the literacy prohibitions were ignored and then repealed. But the deeper cognitive and social structures that gave rise to them accumulated. What accumulated over time was the extension of whiteness over space itself, layered with each generation of landowner, enacting a racialized spatial geography.[88] To be a slave in America was to be subject to white flesh. This subjection not only dictated the channels of human relationship but also affected how relationships were perceived. While slaves and masters had intimate relationships, slaves always sensed the fragility of those relationships, knowing they could be sold with little or no notice. This fragility held in place by white power left little doubt in the minds of slaves about who was at the center of the relationship: "Through care and discipline, slaves' bodies were physically incorporated with their owner's standards of measure. . . . From an early age, enslaved children learned to view their own bodies through two different lenses, one belonging to their masters, and the other belonging to themselves."[89]

The "owner's standards of measure"—this sublime phrase hints at the slave masters' complex practices of slave evaluation tied to one single goal, utility. The lens through which the masters looked at the slaves and taught slaveholding society to look at black flesh was one of use-value. How useful is black flesh? Was the black body docile, friendly, loving, industrious, and positive? or was it malicious, rebellious, deceitful, lazy, and haughty? I am careful to say "body" and not "person," because black flesh was first a commodity.[90]

The interior life of the black body was never the guiding concern of slave society. The guiding concern was the black body's performance. Constant, consistent, excellent performance could allow some black bodies to rise to the level of person in the eyes of white masters, but such personhood was puppet-like, held up only by consistent performance. The interior life of white flesh, on the other hand, had to be the slaves' most central concern. For any slave living in close proximity to white flesh, life itself depended on understanding and immediately discerning every mood, manner, and motion of white people. In her novel *The Bondwoman's Narrative* (the first novel written by a black, North American female slave), Hannah Crafts displays the practice of understanding white people found in so many later slave narratives.[91] Hannah tells the reader that as she was being sold by Mrs. Henry to Mrs. Wheeler she understood deeply the difference between these two mistresses. She arrived at such knowledge as a matter of survival and carried it into every interaction with the two women. Mrs. Henry was an honorable, deeply loving woman; Mrs. Wheeler was not. The disparities between the two women, unremarkable to others, were clearly discerned by Hannah because her welfare, her very life, depended on it.

Slaveholding society put these horrific patterns of cultural intimacy in place. The plantation established the contours of a house in which white intimacy set the stage and the play of all other forms of cultural intimacy. All who came to the (colonial) house of intimacy formed out of race and slavery had to live in that house. There was resistance, cultural resistance. If the house could not be torn down, then rooms could be occupied. These rooms, these cultural enclaves, could exist in the house. Black slaves and all immigrant groups could occupy rooms and (even if only for brief periods) step out of the corridors of white intimacy and into private spaces of cultural belonging.

This structuring reality associated with white bodies is a fundamental aspect of the architecture of distorted cultural intimacy in the modern West. Through its powerful antecedents in the crucial markers of world literary dominance, the novel and newsprint, to its presentations in Western art forms, to its current realities, white bodies, in print media, in electronic visual media, are presented as the bearers of humanity, the interpreters of human capacities and possibilities. White bodies function as the archetype of humanity, and all other bodies are drawn into an unrelenting comparison. The comparison is just as often covert as it is overt, as in the advertising and cosmetic industries, which continue to configure the standard images of models within white body type (for example, skin tone, facial features, manner of dress, and other aspects of their visual presentation). Or one could consider the production of the genre of science fiction films and television shows which overwhelmingly imagine not only advanced intelligence but standard intelligence too as centrally white. Aliens are overwhelmingly projected as mirroring white humanoid existence.[92] Apparent in the ubiquitous media is cultural approximation, a logic that announces one doesn't have to be white to have what some white Western bodies have. You simply need to approximate what these white bodies have in consumptive mood, manner, and dress, that is, the material realities that accompany "humans living well." The architecture here is subtle but very powerful.[93]

I am talking about longitudinal effects, and that explains the metaphor of architecture. Any house can be filled with new people and new practices, but the very shape of the house and where things are positioned exert a deep and abiding influence on those who live in the house. It is exactly the architecture of white intimacy that must be seen in relation to the global realities of immigrant mobility and migration. Arjun Appadurai notes that the imaginations of multiple postcolonial peoples have been expanded beyond indigenous "art, myth, and ritual."[94] In effect their imaginations have been displaced from the earth, from specific land, and joined through electronic media to realities of mobility and migration endemic to current material life under capitalism.

People now imagine their lives over vast expanses of space, and in fact many live their lives over those extended spaces. They must now "move and drag their imagination for new ways of living along with them."[95] Tied to this development is the mobility of electronic media itself. People all over the world consume mass media, and this provokes a number of responses, including "resistance, irony, selectivity" but, most important, "agency."[96] Consumption is crucial because consumption globally understood entails the constitution of agency. As Appadurai says, "Where there is consumption there is pleasure and where there is pleasure there is agency."

Peoples, especially former colonial subjects, are now subject to the interpenetration and expansion of their lives and their ways of life in completely unanticipated ways. Not only must they envision life over vast expanses, but they must witness that very envisioning process itself taken up and held inside advertising practices and the creation of consumer desire. Their local existence is no longer simply local but covered with transnational relations of production and reproduction. Their everyday actions are no longer self-generated but collaborative with the fetish of the consumer that pulls their actions into patterns of behavior and forms of desire congenial to their perceived needs and goals. Moreover, they are given newly imagined possibilities for life that have no necessary connection to their cultural traditions, but that present themselves in a far more compelling and evangelistic way.

Appadurai's account of the importance of mobility and migration bound up inside processes of consumption and production is helpful for grasping the postcolonial situation. However, there is a wider, deeper problem that escapes his analysis, a problem that often escapes analyses of immigrant existence in the West.[97] At one level, he has not sufficiently theorized racial existence as part of the global imaginary terrain, and therefore, at a second level, he has not fully grasped the historical trajectories that centrally constituted the current global situation. Appadurai has made an important observation regarding the space that is America: "In raising the issue of the *postnational*, I will suggest that the journey from the space of the former colony (a colorful space, a space of color) to the space of the postcolony is a journey that takes us into the heart of whiteness. It moves us, that is, to America, a postnational space marked by its whiteness but marked too by its uneasy engagement with diasporic peoples, mobile technologies, and queer nationalities."[98]

Appadurai's recognition of whiteness is accurate but inert and much too localized. While he is right to capture America as a space profoundly marked by whiteness, he seems unaware of its geographic breadth and historical depth. Moreover, Appadurai grasps no relation between the dimensions of global economic and cultural flows and the architectonics of racial existence. However, it is virtually impossible to make adequate sense of the constant turnings of consumer image formation, fantasy production, and imagined ways of better life without understanding the spatial performance of whiteness.[99]

In a very telling comment reflecting on his own identity and its social marking in the streets of America, Appadurai wanders into some aspects of the flexibility of racial existence: "My own complexion and its role in minority politics, as well as in street encounters with racial hatred, prompt me to reopen the links between America and the United States, between biculturalism and patriotism, between diasporic identities and the (in)stabilities provided by passports and green cards. . . . As I oscillate between the detachment of a postcolonial, diasporic, academic identity (taking advantage of the mood of exile and the space of displacement) and the ugly realities of being racialized, minoritized, and tribalized in my everyday encounters, theory encounters practice."[100] Appadurai in this moment of re-flection entered into a social dynamic much wider than street-level racial classi-fication or its relation to other forms of identity and their constituting sites. He encountered the trajectory of the racial imagination, local yet flexible enough to capture all peoples within racial existence—between black and white. What one encounters in Appadurai is a kind of postlapsarian racial vision. He enacts a racial vision even as he attempts to circumvent it.[101] He builds his analysis of globaliza-tion from within acceptance of the historic processes of displacement as natural, as a historical given. This is not to say he ignores, accepts, or approves of the his-torical processes of colonialism. And he is not unaware of the deep connections of people and places. In fact, Appadurai is quite critical of the anthropological vision that confines peoples to particular spaces as inseparable objects of cultural analysis. Indeed, he is committed to the idea that "groups are no longer tightly territorialized, spatially bounded, historically unselfconscious, or culturally homogeneous."[102] This is a fairly obvious observation, yet it is beside the point I wish to make. The central issue here is the fundamental disruption and trans-formation of the relationship of people to place, to land. In Appadurai's thesis, as in the dominant identity theories at play in the world today, land constitutes primarily relations of possession and production, while bodies individual and collective constitute primarily relations of identity. The deeper structures that connect these two constituting realities are rarely considered or understood.

The mobile, transitory nature of cultural life, especially that of former colonial subjects, that he surmises is a new thing is in fact very old. It is the result of colo-nialist processes of land displacement. His concept of ethnoscapes, for example, suggestive for analyzing practices of cultural migration and redeployment, rele-gates cultural identity wholly to the body. What this means is that Appadurai is not sufficiently aware of the racial landscape facilitated by the historical infiltrat-ing realities of whiteness.[103]

Whiteness was a central facilitating reality of the social world of the slave ship, giving birth to a protocosmopolitanism in service to black enslavement, which solidified a flexibility of racial existence that continues to operate today. What is far more crucial at this point is to grasp the constitution of cultural intimacy inside of whiteness.

Modern processes of consumption need to be understood historically as situ-ated next to the formation of whiteness.[104] White images established and in many cases continue to establish the possibilities and character of pleasure tied to the consumption of product, manner, mood, or mentality. Like a ripple in a pond, the initial form and placement of those images may have sunk below the surface, but they emit strong temporal and spatial effects. For example, the body form of the model used to sell goods and services globally is in large measure profoundly shaped by a European aesthetic.

My point is the givenness of this cultural form and its interactions with the machinations of whiteness. The issue here is not how a cultural form may be changed, adapted or adopted by former colonial subjects, but how whiteness may reassert itself as the *arche* of its universal values, the arbiter of its deepest internal logics, and the energizing image and prototype of its proper moral trajectory.[105] For example, whiteness may be signified and white bodies deployed as the embodiment of the highest ideals of sport right on top of its local indigenized embodiments, even if those local performances are seen as magnificently unprecedented.

All one has to do in this regard is look at such sporting sites as (American) football, baseball, hockey, soccer, track and field, or basketball to see this constant operation. Although nonwhite athletes are often celebrated as a particular sport's best players at a given moment, what surrounds those exclamations is a discursive network indebted to the historic racial formations of whiteness. This means that whiteness can be and often is signified inside the acclamation of black and other minority athletes—(white) players of (supposedly) lesser ability but (clearly implied) greater heart, courage, discipline, honesty, and integrity are identified as the embodiments of the sport's fundamentals and of its highest principles, even if they lack the natural talent of the black athlete.[106] This discursive network very powerfully echoes aspects of the master–slave relation in which judgments of people carry a profoundly racial valence and in which disciplinary and surveillance regimes seem oddly similar to those of antebellum chattel slavery procedures that were clearly intensely invasive. This is not a matter of increased media attention or of the responsibilities of role models. This has to do with the discursive patterns of describing, analyzing, and evaluating black bodies and behavior patterns operative throughout the entire economic ecology of sport.[107]

This architecture of distorted cultural intimacy may not be easily discerned because it is disseminated over vast distances and intricately woven into electronic media. It exists in old and not-so-old television shows produced in the West and seen around the world. There are lessons, both social and moral, taught every week in these shows by white characters who recognize the problems, propose the solutions, realize human weakness, grasp human strength, understand hopes and dreams, and discern truth and lies—performing humanity. The social and moral landscape belongs to the white characters.

One can grasp this architecture in the multibillion-dollar film industry that blankets the world with white images as the central embodiments of humanity.[108]

If one looks deeply into this power its fundamental characteristic becomes manifest: white flesh presents intimacy and invites everyone else to enter. This presenting of intimacy through white flesh displays intimacy's architecture, intimacy's house, and invites approximations of white flesh in manner, mood, persona, and appearance. This architecture is discernable in advertisements that suggest new possibilities of pleasure. While most people may not look like the models presented in the media, everyone can have their effect by buying what they sell. But the model is not simply a mediator of the commodity; the model, even if non-European, most often is a white approximation, his or her features and gestures of appearance flowing in some measure back to European archetypes.

Equally important, one can discern this architecture in the constitutions of social space in which the land is constantly narrated as isolated fragments of private property wholly distinct from peoples' identities. The only conceptuality strong and wide enough to anchor in a comprehensive way the many identities of people in relation and interaction with one another is race, subtly but unmistakably signified by its always present but unspoken facilitator, whiteness.[109]

Much is at risk in the expansion of peoples and their cultural forms over vast spaces and in their penetration by aggressive capitalist-generated media. If cultural recapitulation is a possibility, the greater possibility is cultural dissolution. Here, Africans in the Diaspora, indigenous peoples of the Americas and the Pacific islands, Africans on the continent of Africa are all powerful witnesses to the struggle against cultural decomposition into commodity fragments as well as to the fight to assert narrative existence in the face of far more powerful storytellers. The question facing the modern world is whether there is a form of cultural joining and cultural interaction that does not depend on or enact the dissolution trajectories of modern global economies and cultures or set in place desperate and destructive xenophobic responses to these overwhelming forces.

SEEING MANGLED SPACE

If Christianity is just such an alternative form of cultural joining and interaction, then Christian communities and their theologians will have to reckon with their legacy of ecclesial failure. Thus I return to the question offered at the beginning of this chapter: How is it possible for Christians and Christian communities to naturalize cultural fragmentation and operationalize racial vision from within the social logic and theological imagination of Christianity itself? My goal in this chapter in addressing this crucial question was twofold: first, to move current conversations beyond the superficial emotive responses that fail to analyze the historic social dynamics within which contemporary subjectivities continue to be formed and operationalized; and second, to open the possibilities of a new optic that allows people to see the spatial dimension of segregationalist mentalities. That spatial dimension must be seen not primarily as a product of behavior (that is, peoples isolate themselves along cultural difference), but as the dual operation of the way the world is imagined and the way social worlds constitute the imagination.

If Christianity is going to untangle itself from these mangled spaces, it must first see them for what they are: a revolt against creation. This recognition turns toward a far more grounded vision of a doctrine of creation. A Christian doctrine of creation should not be articulated as though it is first an academic dissertation about divine power and ownership or human stewardship of the earth or about theoretical possibilities of the exact nature of human origins or about the precise relationship between biblical accounts of creation and the actual cosmic order of material existence. A Christian doctrine of creation is first a doctrine of place and people, of divine love and divine touch, of human presence and embrace, and of divine and human interaction. It is first a way of seeing place in its fullest sense. Christianity is in need of place to be fully Christian. One of the first factors in rendering the Scriptures impotent and unleashing segregated mentality into the social imagination of Christians was the loss of a world where people were bound to land. Through this loss the complex revelation of God's relation to land and people fell on deaf ears. The moment the land is removed as a signifier of identity, it is also removed as a site of transformation through relationship. Of course, the colonialist moment was about transformation and relationships, yet both were marked by death.

The right transformation I am referring to here is Christian faith receiving its heretofore undiscovered identities, which are found only through interaction with the social logics of language, landscape, and peoples. The right relationships I am referring to here are those that invite new patterns of life woven through and by means of the deep structures of Christian faith slowly opened through ongoing interpretation and struggle. Those relationships involve deep joining, the opening of lives to one another in love and desire. This is the erotic nature of the body, of materiality, of Christian existence. At heart, there was an important aspect of the connection between creation and redemption that probably never seemed to take hold in the Christian imagination.

As the church entered the colonialist moment, what should have been in place was nowhere to be found. What was missing was the central social reality that constituted a new people in the body of Jesus—their joining to Israel, and the power of that joining on the social imaginary of Christian life. If Christian existence stands on nothing greater than the body of one person, then it could be that the only way for Christian communities to move beyond cultural fragmentation and segregated mentalities is to find a place that is also a person, a new person that each of us and all of us together can enter into and, possibly, can become.

6

THOSE NEAR BELONGING

The question of how one should imagine space is by far one of the most complex questions facing the world today. Space continues to be ever further enclosed inside the economic and political calculations of nation-states and corporations. Yet how one imagines space is inseparably bound to how one imagines peoples and their places in the world. Although the history of Christians in the colonial West shows the difficulty of people imagining space and peoples together, Christianity itself offers hope of their joining.[1]

To capture this new possibility I return to an old theological question. How are the people of God constituted? How is their identity established, given the boundaries that attend group identities today, whether they be nations, ethnicities, or peoples? Who are the people of God? Attempts to define the people of God always open up deeper confusion.[2] If space and race go together in the making of modern peoples, then what would be involved in the spatial and racial unmaking of modern peoples, that is, the remaking that should be the constitution of Christian people? This question poses a seeming impossibility, the transformation of social imaginations shaped in the fragmenting of place as private property and the slicing of human existence in racial vision. While neither race nor space is an easily abandoned imaginary,[3] the constitution of the people of God points to a remaking that could move the world away from historical uprootedness and discontinuity.[4] Walter Brueggemann offers some of the key notions involved in this remaking: "Biblical faith begins with the radical announcement of discontinuity which intends to initiate us into a new history of anticipation. It challenges and contradicts a consciousness of land loss and expulsion as false consciousness. That is not the way life is intended to be or can finally be, because the power of anticipation rooted in the speech of God overwhelms the power of expulsion. A new history begins in that discontinuity and initiation."[5]

Uprootedness coupled with anticipation of something new, discontinuity coupled with continuity, land loss and expulsion coupled with rerootedness — these notions point to the themes that have shaped my examination: displacement, translation, and intimacy. They also point to the actual frame of reference within which one must imagine the constitution of the people of God: Israel, the hermeneutic horizon on which one comes to understand not only the deeper significance of displacement, translation, and intimacy, but also the possibilities of a rerootedness, continuity, and life-giving newness.[6] Up to this point, I have operated with a nonspecific referent for the designation "Israel." I have had in mind throughout this book both biblical Israel or, as one theologian designates it, "canonical Israel" and living Israel, the Israel that is Judaism, the practitioners of its living faith, as well as the communities of memory that claim deep and abiding familial connection to Abraham, Isaac, and Jacob and their God.[7] I have also had a view of Israel as an ethnic, cultural, even racial reality.[8]

Christianity and Christian theology are unintelligible without Israel. While very few Christian writers and Christian communities have historically disputed this, Christians have interpreted Israel as an antiquated element in the wider revelation of the Christian God who has elected a new people, the Christians.[9] An increasing number of theologians recognize the problem of supersessionism for Christianity and are now reading the theological traditions of the church in light of acknowledging this historical shortcoming.[10] So it is an important advancement in Christian theological imagination to return to Israel, recognizing its continuing importance to Christian existence.[11] However, the deeper challenge is whether Christian theology can explain how Israel is important to Christian existence. Indeed, Christian theologians have yet to capture the depth of the supersessionist problematic as it expressed itself in the New World of colonialism.[12]

There was already in place with the colonialist entrance in the new worlds of the Americas and Africa a failure of recognition equal to their failure to recognize the complexity and majesty of life marked by place. This failure of recognition was far more than simply forgetting Israel by claiming that Christian *communitas* surpassed their common life. This failure was more than poor knowledge of history or memory loss. The historic failure of recognition brings Christians to the threshold of Israel's existence with a basic, life-altering question: How did we get here in the first place? where is here? The here is outside Israel, outside the conversation between biblical Israel and its God, outside the continuing conversations living Israel has with that same God. Gentiles, the *goyim*, are outside Israel, lacking intimate knowledge of the ways and struggles of life inside.[13] Yet to even know that we are outside, that we are Gentile, that we are not addressed in the conversations of biblical Israel with its God is already to admit an entrance. Someone allowed us to draw close enough to hear that there was a conversation going on between God and a people in the first place.

To recapture the original situation of Gentile existence one must address what amounts to the racial unconscious that continues to shape Christian readings of biblical Israel and Christian interaction with living Israel.[14] In approaching biblical Israel (hereafter simply referred to as Israel), one must attend to the overarching intertextual dynamics at play when one reads what one theologian calls the church's "standard canonical narrative" of Israel.[15] By recapturing the original situation out of which Gentile Christian faith must always think and imagine itself, one also captures the powerful social analog that emerges from the recreation of humanity in Jesus Christ. The first step is remembering Gentile existence.[16]

WRITTEN INTO THE LAND OF ISRAEL

Christians arrived to Scripture through the mediation of a person, Jesus of Nazareth, and we Christians care about Israel's Scriptures because they tell us about the Savior of the world. But at another level, Jesus' life positions us at the door of Israel, its stories, its practices, its interactions, its hope, and its dreams. Even if we don't want to look, even if we don't know what we are looking at, even if we don't know what to do with what we are looking at, we still must see Israel even as we behold Jesus.

Several crucial angles of perception are involved: (1) we are Gentile readers reading the biblical narrative that is the story of Israel; (2) we are Gentile readers positioned to read the story of Israel as a result of the life of Jesus; (3) we are Gentile readers who should perceive living Israel through the lens provided by biblical Israel; (4) we are Gentile readers who should read our own existence by the lens provided by the Jewish Jesus. These angles of perception all presuppose a fundamental spatial reality—we read existence from within Israel's space.

When we read the Scriptures we are entering the space of Israel. It is first a space constituted through literacy with an entrance enabled through translation. As we enter the story of Israel we are being drawn into their land, their hoped-for place and their life in that space. Yet what constitutes that space is centrally neither land nor literacy, but God. Israel's story opens to all people not simply the very nature of humanity, but the drama of peoples in the presence of the living

God. With breathtaking power, biblical Israel performs humanity. The stories of biblical Israel also set the stage for God, drawing our attention through nothing less than a rupture in our knowledge. Israel's God ruptures the way peoples imagine their collective existence, reorganizing what they know about God and how they should understand themselves in their land and in the world. If we exist in a world constituted by Israel's God, then we exist not merely as readers of Israel's story but as participants in that story. It is exactly Christian inability to maintain the reader–participant bond that creates problems in how we understand the representative power of Israel's story for us.

Jesus introduced us to a God who promised to Israel the land of its ancestors—Abraham, Isaac, and Jacob—and the eternality of its Davidic kingdom. God's revelation was bound to Israel's life, which meant Israel's journey toward becoming a landed people was the drama through which God announced divine intentions for the entire creation. This was a drama in which we found out that Israel's God, YHWH, is the creator of all. The terror of this revelation only intensifies once it is seen in its powerful placement inside Israel:

> For ask now about former ages, long before your own, ever since the day that God created human beings on the earth; ask from one end of heaven to the other: has anything so great as this ever happened or has its like ever been heard of? Has any people ever heard the voice of a god speaking out of a fire, as you have heard, and lived? Or has any god ever attempted to go and take a nation for himself from the midst of another nation, by trials, by signs and wonders, by war, by a mighty hand and an outstretched arm, and by terrifying displays of power, as the LORD your God did for you in Egypt before your very eyes? To you it was shown so that you would acknowledge that the LORD is God; there is no other besides him. From heaven he made you hear his voice to discipline you. On earth he showed you his great fire, while you heard his words coming out of the fire. And because he loved your ancestors, he chose their descendants after them. He brought you out of Egypt with his own presence, by his great power, driving out before you nations greater and mightier than yourselves, to bring you in, giving you their land for a possession, as it is still today. So acknowledge today and take to heart that the LORD is God in heaven above and on the earth beneath; there is no other. (Deut 4:32–39)

The priority of Israel noted in this biblical text and best captured in the idea of divine election was not simply a historical marker establishing a point of reference for a God who would very soon quickly transcend any real connection to Israel. The election of Israel, as has been articulated in many strains of the Christian tradition, is a matter of divine grace, divine initiative. It is not dependent on any intrinsic characteristics of Israel. In fact, Israel is created out of election. As Jon Levenson notes, Israel's history is first its theology. It exists only by the will of God: "It is significant that the Torah's promise to Abraham predates the existence of a people Israel, which indeed comes into being only as a result of YHWH's mysterious grace and the equally mysterious but edifying obedience of Abraham. By making the theology earlier than the people, the Torah underscores 'the necessity of viewing the greatness of the nation in light of the greatness of her God.' Indeed Israel exists only because of God's choice, and apart from God, it has no existence at all. . . . Israel has no profane history, only a sacred history, a history of redemption, of backsliding and return, punishment and restoration."[17]

The idea of Israel's election, however, quickly destabilized inside Christian thought. The fact that Israel's election was a matter of prevenient grace, of divine initiative, came to signify the freedom of God from Israel, detachable from Israel and thereby attachable to other peoples. With the colonial moment, the idea of election entered the currencies of the new transatlantic economic order with its burgeoning nationalist operations energized within vernacular biblical translation. Divine election bound to the church trickled down to its various nation-state subjects, so that their prosperity and unchallenged power yielded an irrefutable conclusion: we are chosen by God. In truth, the election of Israel never significantly entered into the social imagination of the church. Israel's election has not done any real theological work for Christian existence.

Israel's election, however, announces more than the disclosure of divine freedom. It also disrupts the connection of all peoples to their gods, drawing their attention to this drama. Israel's life in its land will be the stage upon which the Creator will speak to the creation. Unfortunately, by emphasizing divine freedom in Israel's election, Christian theology was able to decouple divine disclosure from the specifics of Israel's life and land and thereby help make possible a novel reading of Israel—not as God's people but as an ethnic group.[18]

The reading of Israel as an ethnic group remains a powerful imaginary. This means that the modern sensibility of land as possession (by a people) shapes the way Christians continue to read the standard canonical narrative. In this schema, Israel, as a coherent (even multicultural) ethnic group, journeys in search of a land to possess by any means necessary. Such a reading can only turn Israel's election into ethnic ideology.[19] However, if one can resist this modernist sensibility, one might discern in some of the key identity-constituting moments of their journey to the promised land the unfolding of a different process of identity formation for Israel centered in God's involvement with them.[20]

The alternative to reading Israel ethnically is not reading Israel idealistically. Indeed, one could easily see not just one Israel in Scripture but many Israels corresponding to their historic moments. One could also immediately register the danger of the notion of election given its historically situated social and political problems. If the deployment of a notion of election was problematic for modern nations formed from the colonialist moment, why would that same notion not be just as problematic when witnessed on the pages of the Bible?[21] Yet this is precisely where biblical Israel's life in its multiple historical displays and a notion of election are intended to create problems. Reading Israel's story is intended to be disruptive, especially for Gentile existence. Given human existence on the other side of the refashioning of the world, and the formation of modern peoples, Christians live with a powerful temptation to resist or domesticate Israel's story and the God depicted therein. However, if we domesticate this story we risk losing sight of the important work God was doing in Israel, which has direct implications for human existence.[22]

Centrally, YHWH repositioned the importance of land for Israel. Through the story of Israel, God stands between them and the land, constantly showing divine sovereignty over the land as its creator. God announced the divine intentions to Moses to fulfill the promise made to his ancestors, Abraham and Sarah, on ground made holy by divine presence and holy fire. YHWH presented the land as subservient to the divine will. If there is a close connection between people and land out of which come material culture and the identity created therein, then YHWH challenged the identity of Israel formed in Egypt. This was done through disruption of place and the disorientation of its signifying capabilities. Israel's God challenged the identity formed in the place of bondage by disrupting the deep connection of people with the land. In so doing, God brought into judgment and ultimately into submission the powerful claim of that land upon Israel's being.

One can see this in the way the story describes the disruption: God mutilated every aspect of life in the land of Egypt. The so-called ten plagues, or the signs and wonders, or, as Carol Meyers designates them, the "nine calamities and the one plague," inflicted on Egypt are intended to force Pharaoh to free Israel. They are aimed at breaking the connection of identity to land by challenging faith in the land to sustain life through human powers.[23] Through these signs and wonders God challenges Egypt, the superpower of the ancients.[24] Yet more to the point, they deconstruct a matrix of identity bound to specific practices in a particular place. The characteristics of this absolute disruption are visible in the loss of life-sustaining Nile water to the profound interruption of daily life with the oppressive and overwhelming presence of frogs, gnats, and flies. That disruption continued with the loss of life-sustaining food by the death of livestock, and the presence of boils on the Egyptians and their animals. The land itself could not yield food for the Egyptians with the coming of the thunder and hail, the locusts, and the darkness. Finally, God challenged the most central ancient symbol of prosperity in a land—the emergence of the first fruit, the firstborn. By killing the firstborn of Egypt, both humans and animals, YHWH signaled that life in the land was completely under divine power. No future is possible without the creator of life. Yet if these events were signals to hardhearted Pharaoh, they were also powerful witness to Israel that its God stood between them and the land, forever reordering their connection to place.

This aspect of the story of Israel reveals a God who draws death and violence into the divine sphere of influence, drawing death into a circle of contest.[25] Death asserts its power through the hands of the Egyptians, showing itself as the absolute arbiter between peoples. The power of death through violence divides the powerful from the powerless, the victors from the victims. Death refashions peoples, weaving its power into their collective being through memories of its horrifying display. But the God of Israel reveals that death and violence are less powerful than God's divine will.

This revelation intensifies the problem of a violent God, making of it an epistemological crisis. However, in order to recognize Israel's God as an epistemological crisis for us we must consider another crucial aspect of Israel's story, the journey to and in the promised land. Freed from Egyptian bondage, the children of promise sojourned toward its fulfillment. But from the beginning they displayed the struggle of reorientation, of entering a new relationship with land and a new identity. From Mount Sinai, through the revelation of the law, through the rehearsal of the covenants, through the eruptions of disobedience, the story reveals a God who stands between the land and Israel.

This God enfolds the holy people in the truth that YHWH, not the land, is the giver of life; YHWH, not the land, defines their identity; YHWH imparts into their collective life the divine *dabarim*, the divine word and demands they live by that word. Divine word certainly precedes land. But word and land are bound together as the realities that constitute the stage of life for Israel. They live between the word spoken and the land given. Torah and land flow out of the divine will for Israel. Their story shows a demanding God who yet sustains their life even in the wilderness and through their times of disobedience. Christian theology has rightly discerned the representative nature of Israel's journey. Israel is not simply a people coming into full existence in the presence of the living God, but the human creature in sojourn with the Creator God, striving to hear, obey, and live.

This representative character, however, also extends to the other peoples who surround Israel in the story. Here is precisely where Israel's God presents a moment of crisis for us. The narrative brings us to a God who demands that Israel invade, occupy, and slay the inhabitants of the promised land. From almost any angle of vision this act looks like the workings of statecraft.[26] The representative character of Israel's life with God suggests, however, a different angle of perception not simply for their acts of conquest but for the divine demand of obedience.[27] If the story of Israel's life in the land is first the ideological justification for conquest, then its representative character is simply a matter of repetition. That is, Israel represents yet another example of the ways in which peoples use God to justify their greed, desire, and ambition in using violence to impose their will on other peoples. But if the representative character of Israel's life with God entails the encircling of violence, drawing it into an ever-tightening sphere of divine sanction, then something quite powerful is taking place in Israel: YHWH is seizing the reins of violence and bringing it into subjection to the divine word.

This, however, is not yet the full reality of the representative character of Israel at play here. There was a profound scandal for other peoples slowly being formed in the story of Israel. Israel's God drew an irrepressible distinction between the elect and those outside Israel. The distinction was not first a boundary of difference but a marking of entrance. Indeed, the distinction between the elect and nonelect, between those of Israel and those not of Israel, is not easily discerned in the Scripture. The issue, however, in terms of representation is not the question of distinct identity—who is Israel or who is not Israel?—but the question of distinct space: where is Israel to be found or where is Israel not to be found? All those who entered Israel's land entered the space of God's claim. It may seem an intellectual sleight of hand to call the Canaanites' land Israel's land, but divine presence is the central interpretive element in the story. The land changed possessors, but more decisively the land served as the occasion for the disclosure of its Creator. In this place of God's claim, life or death hung in the balance.

If Israel's God was the one true God, then only this God gives life and takes it away. For those outside Israel and for all Gentiles, the horror of violence was not weakened by this revelation, and the stench of death was no less pungent. No justification for Israel's conquests could be given. Israel's very existence questioned every other alleged theocracy. Inside the space of Israel, no one could stand in judgment of the Creator or the Creator's demands for life or death. There was no ethical space, no plateau of moral truth on which to stand in judgment of Israel's actions. Such a space was already occupied by Israel's God. However, the deepest aspect of this scandal received scant attention in the history of the church's theologies: Gentiles may never claim for themselves what was true only for Israel.

The theological justification for conquest was an unrepeatable act.[28] What was repeatable, however, was the clear implication for Gentiles: YHWH announced divine claim from the land of Israel on all land and all peoples. Of course, the story of Israel in the land is far more complex than simply the divine announcement of ownership. The story was also the stories of internal strife, conflict, violence, and oppression patterned to some measure through divinely sanctioned social hierarchy, patriarchy, and slavery. Their story is also the story of human failure in the struggle of faithfulness to the covenants with the sorrows of land loss—exile, oppression, and occupation. The struggle for biblical Israel was one of identity. As T. F. Torrance noted, it was the struggle to live into their destiny and calling as God's people, rather than to enter the logic of being just another people trying to establish its eternal existence, an ethnic Gentile destiny.[29] We have failed to read Israel's story as in part a struggle against internalized Gentile identity precisely because we have read their story as Gentiles who have forgotten that we read as Gentiles. Thus, we have misapprehended our participation in the story. We have failed to see their story as the struggle for the emergence of a people beyond the agonist vision of ethnic destiny.[30] Thus, reading Israel's life is also profoundly reading our own unacknowledged plea for help and the unanticipated answer from God.

Israel suffers because they are not Gentiles. Torrance suggests three senses in which they suffer. First, Israel suffers through the illumination of their sin and faithlessness. Second, Israel suffers because the light of righteousness cast on it by YHWH reflects outward upon other peoples. If Israel is a light to other nations, it is a light that occasions unwanted exposure. Third, Israel suffers because other nations reject Israel's theological claims for the sake of their own gods.[31] Torrance's threefold sense of Israel's suffering is a highly suggestive reading of a more complex and multileveled history of Israel's interactions with its neighbors and other peoples.[32]

Israel presents a reorientation of truth for Gentiles. Israel's life was not simply an example of human life but the very ground on which God inscribed the nature of our lives.[33] At the threshold of Israel's land, in the presence of Israel's God, the story of every people ruptures, cracks open, revealing a second layer, an underlying layer of reality bound to this God. This second layer of reality was there all the time, yet it remained hidden apart from the revelation in Israel of the Creator who made covenant and whose character was slowly being exposed over the vast landscape of Israel's odyssey.

What we know of our collective selves, of our peoples, and of our ways of life is not eradicated in the presence of Israel's God, but that knowledge is up for review. Indeed, some of the stories, practices, and fragmented memories that lay hidden in the shadows of our peoples must now be moved to the center of life. Other truths of our people, time-honored, irrefutably powerful, aiming toward eternality are irretrievably weakened in the presence of Israel's God. However, we are confronted with that God not as the One who thundered divine word from Mount Sinai, but as the One who cried in a manger and on the lap of his mother, Mary.

JESUS, THE ONE FOR THE MANY

Jesus is Jewish, and it is a sad and grotesquely ironic reality that the supersessionist moment in Christian theology was enabled through Christian reflection on Jesus Christ. Rather than focus on the christologically based mangling of Israel, I will retrieve the organic connection between Israel, Jesus, and Gentile existence. I want to deepen our reading of Israel from an alternative subject position: as Gentile readers of the Jesus story. By taking this alternative subject position, I am to a certain extent bypassing some of the prevailing issues and interpretive architectonics of contemporary New Testament study, such as issues of historicity in relation to the life and sayings of Jesus.[34]

The life of Jesus, like all of life, is open to multiple interpretations.[35] Indeed, this multiplicity of interpretation is not of necessity a problem but is inherent in the revelation of a God who speaks to and with the human creature. However, ideological uses of Jesus begin with the fundamental decoupling of Jesus from Israel's life. The story of Jesus becomes, through ideological deployment, a social cipher for any and every redemptive vision of a people. There is, of course, an intrinsic applicability of his life, an important connection for all humanity. But the way to that connection requires that we turn our attention back to his relationship with Israel. In so doing we must resist the temptation to read Jesus as though we are his disciples before we are Gentiles. As Gentile readers who lack precise intimate knowledge of the Torah, the ability to discern the differences of voices in Israel, and the history of listening and obeying, we are positioned to see what an outsider can see, namely, God speaking.

Jesus' election witnessed in Mary becomes the stage on which Israel's God will make known the intensity and depth of the Holy One's journey with Israel and God's great love for the elect people.[36] From the womb of a virgin, God will announce a reality of newness placed in the midst of Israel's conventional cultural realities. The scandal of this claim is bound tightly to the scandal of Israel's existence as the people of God. Jesus' election is not an election next to or in competition with the election of Israel, but an election in the heart of Israel's space, displaying the trajectory of the Holy One toward communion with the elect.[37]

Just as Israel's election ruptures Gentile space (and time)—breaking open knowledge and reorienting truth—so does Jesus' election bring to Israel a rupture. This rupture, however, is not the destruction or eradication of Israel's knowledge, its theological truth. This rupture breaks open their story and reveals a deeper layer for how Israel should understand birth, family, and lineage. Jesus is both Son of David and the Son of God. The God who created the first family Israel is now in Israel recreating the family. This reading of the organic connection of Jesus and Israel could be construed as a collapse of Israel into Jesus and a loss of the distinct reality of Jewish life inside a Christian theological vision. However, such a conclusion would have to bypass not only our rehearsal of the inherent logic of the scandalous reality of Israel itself in Jesus, but also the trajectory of Jesus' work. He comes for Israel, for Israel's sake in the world.

Jesus is Israel for the sake of Israel. We can see his recapitulation of Israel not only from the initial announcements of his election with Mary and the biblical accounts of the beginning aspects of his life, but from his journey in the wilderness.[38] Dietrich Bonhoeffer captured the social implications of Jesus' temptations.[39] Bonhoeffer suggested that our temptations are not our own, but of Jesus' body and its members. The implications of this stunning insight are far-reaching.[40]

Jesus in the wilderness is Israel in the wilderness. From within the urgency of need and facing the exhaustion of energy and life without sustenance, Jesus faces the fears of all peoples. Jesus in his temptation is enacting the social realities not only of Israel but of all peoples—the hopes, dreams, fears, and desires of all peoples. In this wilderness, the true power of the tempter can be seen only if one imagines the seduction of the many, not simply a single sojourner through life.[41] The tempter offers Jesus what every people wants, especially peoples oppressed and despised, especially people caught in the urgency of need and held in the gripping fear of the exhaustion of energy and life without resources.

The temptation is fundamentally one of an isolating self-sufficiency that heeds no other voice and that needs no other voice than the internal voice that speaks only what would be good and right for the survival of a people. Every people, every nation wants to be self-sufficient, to feed its own, to turn its stones into bread. And Jesus was told to enter this self-sufficiency, to allow the urgency of need to determine his course of action, his obedience. "Obey me and follow my advice," he is told. His response, however, builds from the central truth of Israel in the land. They are not sustained simply in the face of any urgency by the land but by the words of God. The second temptation then builds from the first.

The tempter presses Jesus to prove the divine care of his life, proof of holy protection. With this temptation, the Word of God is deployed to support the test. This is the longing of all peoples to be safe and secure, to be freed from danger, to be supported on all sides by angels, to see their collective existence as ordained by God and secured by the divine will.[42] Collective existence, the existence of a socially imagined community only intensifies the knowledge of our weakness in the presence of forces we cannot control. Jesus, however, once again invoked Israel's story and deepened it in the moment of its invocation. He speaks the holy name in intensified commitment of his life to God's care. He will not test his father and his God.

At the third temptation, the devil parades his power, showing the nations already bound to his deception and under his power.[43] The devil, the prince of this world, enacted a direct line to worldly power through himself. Now, he presents to Jesus a straight shot and a short route to world victory. This is a temptation too powerful to pass up for almost any people. If given the chance, any people would want to rule the world and guide all other peoples in its own national vision of the true, the good, and the beautiful. Any people could rationalize its purpose for world domination and leadership—for the sake of world safety, world peace, for the good of every people, we must lead. Every people wants to stand on the world stage "in splendor," as a global player, and not be ignored, mistreated, or disrespected. Jesus' response is a flat denouncement of Satan's power.

If the one danger is to collapse Israel's life into Jesus, then the reciprocal danger may be to rob Jesus of his own temptations. The gospel story does in fact give us the temptations of this one man, the temptations of Jesus. They are his temptations, the temptations of his own body and of his life. But he did not wander into the wilderness for his own sake. He was driven by the Spirit into the wilderness. He was driven in the journey of all peoples to reestablish the reality of Israel's faithfulness for the sake of the world. And here is where one can discern the intertextual realities of Gentile existence: Jesus is alone in the wilderness, but we are there with him.

We are there in failure, as the ones who have succumbed to temptation. Again and again we have fallen, joined gladly in alliance with the tempter's desires. The temptation narrative does not underwrite a Manichean vision of an eternal, divine struggle against evil. The narrative draws us to the awful condition of our collective weakness, yet the wilderness struggle and victory anticipates a possibility: a people joined to the body of Jesus who can overcome the temptations of evil.

Jesus' ministry was aimed at the lost sheep of Israel, not at the goyim, not to us. This is a reality of his story that never truly did its work in the social imagination of Christians. Israel was constantly read as a permeable reality of the gospel story, allowing us to completely read through Israel to imagine divine direct address to us, the Gentiles. However, to weaken the connection of Jesus to Israel is also to miss the actual mode of connection he draws to us. The story itself gives us the clues to our presence. We are the ones who believe the word of God to Israel. We were present in the story of Israel but we are also present in the Jesus story. We are those outside of Israel who ask for a gift intended for Israel. We ask for Jesus' help.[44]

We are in the story through a prohibiting word to his disciples, "Go nowhere among the Gentiles, and enter no town of the Samaritans" (Matt 10:5b). We are in the story in the form of humble requests, for example, as the centurion who, recognizing, even if through the lens of military hierarchy, the distance between himself and Jesus, asks Jesus to heal his servant (Luke 7:1–10). We are also in the story as desperate pleas for help, as with the Canaanite woman (Matt 15:21–28), which rehearses for us the dynamic of Israel and the Gentiles, yet with a profound difference.

The story of the Canaanite woman is especially provocative as it carries with it the clear sense not only of Israel's election, but also of the undomesticated God of Israel, one who cannot be approached except on the terms established by the divine word. The Canaanite woman pleads for her daughter's deliverance from the evil one, and the disciples have little patience with her plea. Here is where the incessant supersessionist tendency shows itself in our constant habit to confuse our subject position in this powerful story.

The colonialist moment helped to solidify a form of Christian existence that read this text as though we were standing with Jesus looking down on the woman in her desperation, when in fact we, the Gentiles, are the woman, not we, a generic humanity, but we, those who are outside Israel. The fact that this is a woman interceding for her daughter should not escape our reflection. It is precisely from within the logic of this gendered social hierarchy that we may begin to see the path that draws us to the body of Jesus. This path does not escape the horror of this woman's debasement in front of Jesus and his disciples, but intensifies it.

All peoples become the Canaanite woman and her tormented daughter. It would be a profound theological mistake to seek to escape the ugliness of this episode or its clear intertextual connection to the priority of Israel. We must enter fully into its scandal. All peoples face a future under the assault of the tormentor, and all peoples are in need of the deliverance Jesus brings. Jesus' initial response to the woman is the prohibition—his gifts are of Israel and for Israel, not for (Gentile) dogs.[45] The Canaanite woman stands in for all Gentiles who would presume on the grace of God. Yet, more important, she marks the path forward.

She takes onto her lips the words of Israel. She enters their story, reciting their words of worship, "Have mercy on me, Lord, Son of David." She is not pretending to be Israel. She is to be counted among the goyim and she knows it. Her daughter is of the goyim, and she knows it. Yet she recognizes that even those outside of Israel may benefit from the gifts of God for Israel. Through the faith of Israel in their God her daughter is freed from the tormentors and healed. The path marked out by this nameless woman in the story is the way of Gentile inclusion.

Jesus' Israel-centrism is bound to a power that will break it open. If he draws into himself the social hierarchies of his people and among his people, he also displays the power to release people from them. We see in him the sharing in our realities for the sake of our healing. As Gregory of Nazianzus stated, "That which he has not assumed, He has not healed; but that which is united to His Godhead is also saved."[46] He recapitulates the reality of Israel in a fallen world in order to overcome the power of the world in Israel. By calling Israel to receive the presence of their God through his teachings, he is also asking them to witness to its absolute embodiment in him. And the Gentiles from the centurion to the Canaanite woman overhear. Gentile inclusion is born out of this overhearing. The overhearing, however, comes with a price.

A separation is occurring with Jesus, a breaking of political arrangements and social bonds and a tearing asunder of allegiances.[47] His hearers are offered a choice: remain as you are or follow him. Jesus is offering an alternative way forward for Israel. Yet to know that way will require the greatest of sacrifices in Israel. The children of Israel must choose to form a new family in Israel. Jesus will challenge the very foundations of social life by challenging the power of the kinship network, which organized the central social, economic, and geographic realities of life in Israel.[48] Jesus entered fully into the kinship structure not to destroy it but to reorder it—around himself. Again, the story in Mark points to this shaking of the familial foundations. He announces that his family will be those who do the will of God (Mark 3:21–22, 31–35).

Jesus reveals a wholly new determination for the life of a child of the covenant. He is defined by his people, yet determined by his God. He is one with their story, but he has become the new storyteller. This is the ground from which the Christian idea of the triune identity grows, yet it is crucial to see how this ground was being ruptured and reoriented. The world of his people will be turned upside down if they enter inside his words. This will be the new inside Israel that cannot be placed inside old interpretation—new wineskins are demanded for new wine (Mark 2:22; Matt 9:17; Luke 5:37–38).[49] The more specific implication of the new is the reconfiguration of patterns of belonging around Jesus himself. He presents a new intensity of covenant love greater than the power of death, love that leads to new life. This new must be chosen. It requires social death for the sake of new life (Matt 10:32–39).[50]

Jesus does not intend the destruction of Israel, only its rebirth in him. But he must be chosen, and the choosing demands that those in Israel cross the "killing field" of kinship. If Joshua at the entrance to the promised land demanded that the households of Israel choose to serve YHWH as his household would do, now Jesus demands that those in the land of Israel choose this new household with God his father. To break the power of death, the power of the kinship network would have to be rerouted through the very life of the Son of God. Jesus did not seek to destroy kinship, to undermine its defining power rooted in story, memory, and cultural practice. Rather, he drew it to a new orientation, a new determination. The family must follow him. The one family must follow from him—flow from his life as its new source.[51]

The kinship network in Israel would now be profoundly qualified. Jesus came first—not husband or wife, not mother, father, sister, brothers, not familial obligations and demands, not cultural conventions, and not social responsibilities. If the strongest bonds of relationship were qualified through commitment to Jesus, then the entire socioeconomic and political structuring processes deeply woven inside these bonds came into qualified view and ultimately unrelenting challenge.

Jesus drew a new communion together in Israel. This new communion carried of necessity the distinctive marks of his scandal.[52] To follow him, to even at times be seen with him required awkward, painful, and even dangerous negotiations with one's primary alliances and allegiances, familial, cultural, social. This is why the rabbi Nicodemus came to Jesus at night (John 3:1). The point here is that there is a social and cultural instability engendered by involvement with Jesus before there is the formation of a new coherent community.

There is a communion taking place in the gathering of listeners to Jesus. For some the desperation of life, the torment of the evil one, and the signatures of death drove them to seek out his words and his power. Others sought the deliverance of Israel, its emergence as a self-determining political power, and freedom for authentic, unadulterated worship of the one true God, the God of Israel. Others simply heard that something new and unheard of was at work in Israel, and old hopes and dreams might be planted in fresh soil. So they sought out Jesus, and in the seeking, in the straining to hear and see him, they were forced to stand together. Those who under normal circumstances would never be together must be together to find Jesus of Nazareth, to hear him and gain from him their desires. Jesus, in forming a new Israel in the midst of Israel, positioned himself as the new source of desire.

Not negating their desire, he drew it more deeply toward himself. Jesus, as it were, captured the power of consumptive practices to form collectives and imagine the social by positioning himself as the object of desire, individual and collective. He was the bread that must be eaten. He was the source of living water that must be asked for. Jesus placed his body between the many and their desires. Indeed, he understood unordered desire as being bound to Gentile existence.[53]

In contrast to nations trapped in the chaos of desire, his body was intended to break the power of the tempter who played in the desires of the many. Jesus positioned his body between Israel and the world, between Israel and Gentile (ethnic) existence, and called the people of God into the scandal of choosing him and thereby choosing a new reality of kinship. Such a call was heard throughout the valley of the shadow of death, and the Gentiles came, having heard that bread was being given. Even if it was meant only for the children of Israel, they could in fact have some of the crumbs.

Rather than follow a historical construct that posits the Jesus movement as simply a reform movement in Judaism or follow a vernacularization thesis that isolates the gospel message into its essential components, which were then reseeded in the cultural/ethnic matrices of various peoples, Roman, Hellenistic, and so forth, I suggest an advent of a new form of communion with the possibility of a new kind of cultural intimacy between peoples that might yield a new cultural politic.

THE POSSIBILITY OF INTIMACY FOR THE MANY

Christian identity pivots on the resurrection of the same Jesus who presented himself to Israel as its reconstitution. The story of Jesus never leaves Israel. This is not the denial of the universality of Jesus' life. However, universality, as we have seen throughout this book, is a highly dangerous concept that, bound to the legacies of supersessionism and whiteness, did and continues to do strange things to the story of Jesus.[54] I suggest a commitment not to an abstract idea of the universal or even of the universal applicability of Jesus, but to follow Jesus' own trajectory toward the many in Israel and through Israel to the many in the world.

The resurrected Jesus described a future for the disciples that would solidify the reconfiguration of kinship and establish the ground for the reformation of social life in Israel. There in Jerusalem they were to wait for his Father, who was also their Father, to baptize them in the Spirit. This was the promise of the continuation of communion. In response to this announcement the disciples asked a crucial question for any people whose leader intends to reconstitute the fortunes of his people: "Lord, is this the time when you will restore the kingdom of Israel?" (Acts 1: 6b).

The disciples rightly understood what the resurrected Jesus meant for Israel's fortunes—the reign of its God was now visible in the world through his Son who had overcome death. Thus, their question is exactly right. Is now the time when you will overturn the world order through Israel? They assumed that Jesus' victory over death must ultimately mean victory for Israel over the Roman Empire. They rightly sensed in Jesus a new thing emerging in Israel, its rebirth in him. Thus, the Spirit of the Father would be given, and Jesus would be glorified as the inauguration of a new age for Israel.

If in fact the book of Acts presented an idealized vision of the beginning of the church, then the coming of the Spirit upon the disciples in Acts 2 failed to offer great ideological service for any hopes of world dominance. Indeed, the presence of the Holy Spirit presents a profoundly counterhegemonic reality in which the sign of the Spirit's coming is language imposition (Acts 2:2–12). Furthermore, the presence of the Spirit drew the followers of Jesus into the language systems of other peoples. The sign of the new age was the disciples of Jesus speaking the languages of other peoples.

What joined these diverse peoples together was their faith in the God of Israel. They are "devout Jews from every nation under heaven" (Acts 2:5). This is indeed an auditory miracle—they each hear their native sound. Yet, if we see this only as a miracle of hearing, then its embodiment in the disciples of Jesus becomes inconsequential; that is, it simply prepares the ground for an abstract universal. What the day of Pentecost would then mean is that the message of Jesus may be translated into every tongue, its universal applicability assured by the Holy Spirit. In such a paradigm of interpretation, the sign of the new age would be embodiment without joining. Each people would hear the gospel and glorify God in their own way, in their own language. Unfortunately, this continues to be the dominant reading of the miracle of Pentecost.[55]

If, however, one recalls the significance of language for entering the world of another, then the work of the Spirit in Israel begins to signal a powerful new reality of relationship. Here the disciples dramatize not simply the miracle of hearing and the claim of the God of Israel on all peoples, but, more significantly, they dramatize the joining of bodies and lives in the worship of the God who was witnessed by Jesus. The speaking of another's language signifies a life lived in submersion and in submission to another's cultural realities. Nothing is as humbling as learning the language of another in which the very rudiments of daily life must be identified in the signification system of another people. Such learning inevitably involves learning either directly or indirectly the land out of which the language came to life in the operation of everyday practices. Language is bound to landscape as the essential context of identity.

The disciples performed a gesture of communion, a calling to all peoples that the Spirit of God would have them join together, and together they would worship the God Jesus reveals. Just as Jesus, driven by the Spirit into the wilderness, enacted the reality of the many in facing the tempter for us, so on the day of Pentecost the Spirit descended on the disciples and drove them into the languages of the world to enact the joining desired by the Father of Jesus for all people. This is the coming of the one new reality of kinship. This is not only the continuation of Jesus' work of forming the new Israel in Israel, but the full disclosure of the desire of Jesus for the entire world. This in effect is the Creator reclaiming the world through communion.

In Jesus, Israel's election does a stunning work by opening the possibilities of boundary-shattering love between strangers and enemies. The election of Jesus turns Israel's election outward. This election enabled desire to be formed between Jew and Gentile, a desire that drew them together in longing for him and in turn invited them to desire one another. It is precisely on the disciples who awaited the beginning of Israel's new age as a world power that the Spirit presses this gesture of communion. This was indeed the rebuilding of Israel.[56]

Those who heard the words of cultural intimacy on the day of Pentecost were invited to act on the meaning of this event. They must choose Jesus and be baptized in his name. The narrative in Acts shows that this early church event remained fundamentally in Israel, so that the first disciples did not realize the ramifications of speaking the languages of others. Such wider implications were muted, given the overarching reality of the Jewish identity of those listening. Indeed, one learns in this story that this moment of language acquisition did not necessarily mean relationship or communion, for language acquisition, as is well known, may serve (and in many cases has served) as a means of cultural imposition and destruction more often than as a means of communion.

The disciples would begin to see these wider implications only as the Spirit of God continued to impose on them gestures of communion. One of the most important episodes in the book of Acts beyond the episode of the day of Pentecost was the vision and action of Peter in Acts 10 and 11, which culminate in the first church council noted in chapter 15. This dynamic story, often sterilely referred to as the event of Gentile inclusion, reveals not merely the word of salvation in Jesus taking root among Gentiles, but also a new order of relationship for Jews and Gentiles coming into being rooted in the life of Jesus.

A vision from God prepares Peter to enter the space of Gentile existence. Peter, in a moment of spiritual intimacy, of *ekstasis*, of being "out of himself" in a trance, is brought by the Spirit of God to the threshold of receiving into himself a new reality, Gentile life. In the vision, God places in front of him food prohibited by ancient command and demands he prepare the food and eat it. The vision draws Peter not into negation of Torah but into reception of the most intimate kind. That which God offers him (Gentile food, signifying Gentile existence, Gentile difference) he must take into himself as vital to his existence. The vision prepares Peter to receive a devout God-fearer named Cornelius, a Gentile—a centurion who had patterned his life according to the theological practices of Israel. Indeed, Acts 10 is first and foremost set as the story of Cornelius in which Peter acts as its inner logic. The vision from God and the subsequent instruction from the Spirit of God guides Peter to the household of Cornelius, where Peter utters the seminal words that announce a new trajectory for Israel: "And as he talked with [Cornelius], he went in and found that many had assembled; and he said to them, 'You yourselves know that it is unlawful for a Jew to associate with or to visit a Gentile; but God has shown me that I should not call anyone profane or unclean. So when I was sent for, I came without objection. Now may I ask why you sent for me?'" (Acts 10:27–29). Even at this moment Peter is unclear why the Spirit of God had brought him to this space and time. Slowly, as Cornelius informed Peter of his own vision in which God told Cornelius to contact Peter, did he begin to sense the new thing God was doing in and through Israel: "I truly understand that God shows no partiality, but in every nation anyone who fears him and does what is right is acceptable to him" (Acts 10:34–35). From this point in the story Peter rehearsed the drama of Jesus—his words and his life sent to Israel for its deliverance and the reordering of the world through his reign. This story in Acts then turns to what was completely unanticipated by Peter and the disciples who accompanied him but was intensely implied from the moment they chose to follow Jesus and entered the reality of the Spirit's imposition: "While Peter was still speaking, the Holy Spirit fell upon all who heard the word. The circumcised believers who had come with Peter were astounded that the gift of the Holy Spirit had been poured out even on the Gentiles, for they heard them speaking in tongues and extolling God. Then Peter said, 'Can anyone withhold the water for baptizing these people who have received the Holy Spirit just as we have?' So he ordered them to be baptized in the name of Jesus Christ. Then they invited him to stay for several days" (Acts 10:43–48). Peter and the other "circumcised believers" were astounded. They witnessed a moment of divine repetition in which the Spirit for a moment reversed the subject position of Israel and the Gentiles and made Israel recipients of the gesture of communion. The Spirit drew the Gentiles into the language of others just as had been done with the disciples. Israel, signified in Peter and the other Jewish believers, hears the Gentiles "speaking in tongues and extolling God" (Acts 10:46).

God was also making real the implications of Gentile election: they stood in the presence of Israel and called back to them a sharing in communion with the God of Jesus in the Spirit. The one communion in the Spirit illumines the obvious for Peter: "Can anyone withhold the water for baptizing these people who have received the Holy Spirit just as we have?" (Acts 10:47). Together they shared in the baptism in Jesus, and the deepest transgression of cultural boundaries was solidified in that moment.

Now Peter, in accordance with the work of the Spirit, received the invitation from the Gentiles "to stay [with them] for several days" (Acts 10:48). This invitation, this simple gesture, symbolized a trajectory of new belonging enacted by the Spirit. Yet none of this was of Peter's own accord. This event was fundamentally counterhegemonic, holding within itself the potential to reorder the world. If a centurion and his household could be drawn into a new circle of belonging, then its implications for challenging the claims of the Roman state were revolutionary. If Israel could be drawn into a new circle of belonging, then the implications for how it might envision its renewal and restoration were equally revolutionary. If a world caught in the unrelenting exchange system of violence was to be overcome, then here was the very means God would use to overcome violence—by the introduction of a new reality of belonging that drew together different peoples into a way of life that intercepted ancient bonds and redrew them around the body of Jesus and in the power of the Spirit.

The disciples and Jewish believers in Jerusalem, however, were not ready for the revolution of the intimate signaled by the events in Cornelius's home. Gentile conversion engendered a crisis for the people of God. How would common life for the Jewish followers of Jesus be defined vis-à-vis these Gentile believers? In Acts 15 the church sought clarity on this question by rehearsing the essential characteristics of covenant identity in Israel. Some suggested that continuity of identity was rooted in the polity of God's people, Israel. They argued therefore that Gentiles must be circumcised, "according to the custom of Moses [or they cannot] be saved" (Acts 15:1). Paul emerges in the book of Acts as one of the key characters in the narrative. In Acts 15 his was a crucial voice in the discussion, and he represented along with Peter and others an alternative consideration for the Gentiles. Peter, speaking the mind of what would be the consensus, suggested that Gentiles not be brought into the intricacies of Jewish polity.

The power of this decision grew from the central insight Peter gained from the Spirit's work in and with him as well as from the testimonies of Paul and Barnabas regarding Gentile conversion: "And God, who knows the human heart, testified to them by giving them the Holy Spirit, just as he did to us; and in cleansing their hearts by faith he has made no distinction between them and us" (Acts 15:8–9). James affirmed Peter's recommendation, suggesting that Gentile conversion was in continuity with ancient prophetic utterance. The prophet Amos saw the rebuilding of Israel bound together with the turning of the Gentiles to their God.

Thus the decision was to recommend to the Gentiles a posture toward the world that mirrored the posture of Israel. So in their letter to these Christians, the council of Jerusalem required Gentiles to shun the markings of a pagan world (Acts 15:28–29).

On the one hand, these pastoral recommendations present a breathtaking assault on the ethnocentrism that was embedded in Israel's perspective on the Gentiles. However, on the other hand, Peter's comments also indicate the disciples' inability to enter fully the trajectory of intimacy intrinsic to this new spatial dynamic of faith in Jesus. The limitation meant that Peter and the disciples as depicted in Acts 15 could at best only imagine parallel theological universes in which the Gentiles imitated Israel's *contra mundi* posture as the fundamental signature of their newfound faith in the God of Israel through Jesus Christ.[57] This limitation in their social imagination also meant they did not yet grasp the trajectory of the Spirit's work in their lives. It was the Spirit of God who was driving Israel toward the Gentiles in the space constituted by Jesus' body. It was the Spirit who drove the Gentiles toward Israel and into the languages of other peoples. In Acts 8, it was the Spirit who drove the Jewish believer Philip to join himself to the chariot of an Ethiopian eunuch who was trying to understand Torah. There Philip explained Torah, introducing the eunuch to Jesus, and then Philip baptized him. These actions of the Spirit have often been interpreted in disembodied ways, so that the placement of the message (about Jesus) becomes the only point.

The Spirit's actions do not imply a God interested in inserting divine word without communion. The disciples understood that the advent of Torah constituted social space in which God's people would live together under divine command. The ongoing ministry of Jesus in the Spirit was found precisely in the drawing of peoples together around his words. There would be in such an endeavor no vision of a floating message dropped into the language of other peoples outside of Israel. The disciples did not imagine a form of life together in which Gentile life could be enfolded into their life of obedience to the Torah and their life of obedience could be enfolded into Gentile existence. They did not see a Spirit-led process of bilingualization inherent in the speaking of other tongues as their future. This meant they did not imagine the reformulation of ways of life (Jew and Gentile) established in the spatial reality created by Jesus himself.

It would be a mistake to call this a sinful failure on the part of the disciples in Acts 15. It was simply the exposure of the tremendous challenge toward intimacy created by the presence of the Spirit of God.[58] It would, however, not be a mistake to say that the church has failed to capture this trajectory coming out of the New

Testament toward communion. The tragedy here is cumulative. If the struggle toward cultural intimacy was not faced by the church as inherent to the gospel itself, despite the constant work of the Spirit to turn Israel and Gentiles peoples toward one another, then over time the only other option was the emergence of a Christian segregationalist mentality. The best Christian theology has been able to suggest this side of the epochs of conquest and the Shoah is a return to the original social imaginary of the earliest church groping to articulate separate yet faithful existence, a theological Jim Crow existence for Jews and Christians.[59] Christian theologians are still unable to capture the spatial implications of life with the Jewish Jesus, that is, a Spirit-directed joining of peoples constituting a new space for Israel, but drawing out of Israel a new identity for both Jew and Gentile. In effect, there would be a rebirth of peoples in the expression of a new cultural politic.[60]

A NEW CULTURAL POLITIC

In his letter addressed to the Gentile church at Ephesus, Paul recounts the original situation of the Gentiles in relation to Israel and then elaborates on the changed reality created by the life of Jesus (Eph 2:1–10).[61] He notes that death indicates more than the inevitable reality of each individual. Death points to the captivity of all peoples to a world of violence and unrelenting contention.[62] We are captured in a destructive kinship network vivified by the spirit of the evil one that signifies us as "children of disobedience." Our desires lack a central re-demptive focus, and we are as peoples subject to the power of the evil one. But the mercy and love of God are revealed in Jesus, who became a new space of existence for us. We are made alive in him and "raised up with him and seated . . . with him in the heavenly places." From this new space our history forward will take a new direction as witness of the immeasurable riches of God's grace and kindness for us in Christ Jesus. The multiple histories of peoples continue in this new spatial reality but are now situated in the story of Israel:[63] "So then, remember that at one time you Gentiles by birth, called 'the uncircumcision' by those who are called 'the circumcision'—a physical circumcision made in the flesh by human hands—remember that you were at that time without Christ, being aliens from the commonwealth of Israel, and strangers to the covenants of promise, having no hope and without God in the world" (Eph 2:11–12).

The power of this account of Gentile status radically undermined any distinc-tion Gentiles held for themselves vis-à-vis other peoples. It is the ultimate decon-structive statement regarding Gentile ethnocentrism. If Jesus constitutes a new space for Jew and Gentile existence, then in that new space a common life must ensue that allows the formation of a new identity. Space here is both a relational practice and that which is created by a relation between Israel and Gentiles: "But now in Christ Jesus you who once were far off have been brought near by the blood of Christ. For he is our peace; in his flesh he has made both groups into one and has broken down the dividing wall, that is, the hostility between us. He has abolished the law with its commandments and ordinances, that he might create in himself one new humanity in place of the two, thus making peace, and might reconcile both groups to God in one body through the cross, thus putting to death that hostility through it" (Eph 2:13–16). The spatial dynamic metaphorically at play here is of spaces (for example, temple space or land) separated but now joined by the removal of a fundamental boundary. This transformation of the space from two to one implies the transformation of peoples from two to one. This does not happen simply in the removing of the boundary but in the reconfiguration of living space itself around a new center. If there is a moment at the heart of Christianity in which something is superseded it may be found precisely here.

It is not the usurpation of the people of God, Israel replaced by the church, but of one form of Torah drawn inside another, one form of divine word drawn inside another form — that is, the word made flesh. If Torah was inseparably connected to the living of life in the promised land, then Torah's transformation into the living word of God in Jesus continues its central purpose. Just as Torah formed Israel's identity, establishing human life in the presence of God, so Jesus intends the formation of new humanity in his presence, listening to his speaking through the Spirit. This new biracial humanity, Jew and Gentile (metaphorically speaking), would be the basis for peace. Jesus marked an alternative path away from violence and toward peace through his own body, in which he constituted a new space of reconciliation. In a powerful inversion of the power of death, Paul claims that Jesus, through his death, put to death hostility.

A space built on Jesus of Nazareth and the claim that he is indeed Israel's Messiah, their Christ, is a space that cannot protect itself from any critique or ridicule. It is a space open to the nations and their desire. It announces a kinship network that cannot be verified but only enacted through discipleship and living together in communion with God. On the one side, this network of kinship exists as a painfully weak space that positions itself as a site of Israel and for Israel. It is a network that presents interlopers as family and strangers as kin who claim their connection only through the voice of a single one in Israel, Jesus. His life is the slender thread that holds Gentiles inside Israel as authentic not exclusive inheritors of its legacies.

On the other side, this network of kinship exists in abiding tension with other kinship networks that demand adherence. This new network must face the power of naming and claiming inherent in any world of kinship. The identities being formed in this new space are constantly challenged by worlds of kinship that see Jesus and anyone who follows him only "according to the flesh" (2 Cor 5:16). That is, these worlds see people only within the structures of cultural belonging and its concomitant social and political commitments. They see people only through the binary of adherence or betrayal of culture, nation, or people. These worlds generate unrelenting resistance to the possibility of living life formed in and through new discursive systems and spatial rearrangements. That is, these worlds resist their recreation, a new creation (2 Cor 5:17).

The worlds of kinship can easily exact a terrible price from those who dare challenge their absolute determination of life. They may draw on the tempter's violent power to kill the one who has joined to the body of Jesus in this new space. They may, through the fear of either physical death or social death, constantly seek to undermine the reformation of identity in this new communion. This new space has no inherent power to prevent their threats. In fact, the new space, when viewed from the longevity, stability, and power of the old worlds of kinship, never looks as safe, secure, or honorable as the old places of identity and belonging. The space of Jesus' body carries forward the characteristics of his body, a body that was, as Isa 53:2 states, of "no form or majesty that we should look at him, nothing in his appearance that we should desire him." Jesus was the "rejected cornerstone" (Luke 20:17). He was the one whose presence gave no confidence of a future that peoples could build on.

Life inside this new space, then, carries uneasiness and even a discomfort as those within it attempt to negotiate powerful cultural claims of kinship. It is in the face of these tensions that Paul's declarations of a new citizenship (Eph 2:19) indicate profound risk taking for anyone who wishes to claim identity in the new space, that is, to claim being Christian. This claim, in light of its risk, points to the essential nature of the new cultural politics inaugurated by Jesus' life and announced by the Spirit. This new cultural politic is a complex new configuration of social alliance and political allegiance bound up in life together with the many. The implications of this new space in which a new cultural politic emerges are breathtaking.

Imagine a people defined by their cultural differences yet who turn their histories and cultural logics toward a new determination, a new social performance of identity. In so doing, they enfold the old cultural logics and practices inside the new ones of others, and they enfold the cultural logics and practices of others inside their own. This mutual enfolding promises cultural continuity measured only by the desire of belonging. Thus the words and ways of one people join those of another, and another, each born anew in a community seeking to love and honor those in its midst.

The new people formed in this space imagine the world differently, beyond the agonistic vision of nations and toward the possibility of love and kinship. Aesthetics preceding ethics, these disciples of Jesus love and desire one another, and that desire for each other is the basis of their ethical actions in the worlds of allegiances and kinships. This enfolding is done not through isolated individual bricolage, but in the everyday realities of life together with others. Moreover, this enfolding process issues in a new network of kinship that transgresses life-threatening and life-diminishing boundaries. It also upsets the particular ideological arrangements of nations, peoples, and corporations, enabling resistance to the temptations of all peoples toward violence in pursuit of their survival, safety, and world power.[64]

What characterizes the communion of this new space is not the absence of strife, contention, or division but its complete capture. Just as Jesus drew into himself the energy of a violent world in order to heal that energy and turn it toward the good, so the communion envisioned by his body draws into itself the agon of peoples in order to turn strife into desire. This communion also helps us envision a relationship between living Israel and the church built on more intimate possibilities.[65]

The church is always turned toward Israel by its very life. If, in fact, the church has come to be precisely through the witness of Israel to the world through Jesus, then by implication Israel by its life always witnesses the true God, a witness forever acknowledged and received by the church. Therefore, the church stands between living Israel and its witness to the world. Living Israel stands between the church and its witness to the world as the reality that makes the church's witness intelligible. The organic connection between Israel and church is simply Jesus, the space that joins and the space that draws.

Both church and Israel witness to the world of the one true God. The communion that constitutes Christian life and identity should echo something strangely identifiable in living Israel. It should echo not a stolen imitation of the original but prophetic utterances now embodied—of many Gentiles drawn toward the "dwelling of David" (Acts 15:16) in order to learn of the Lord and his ways. Such an echo should provoke an invitation for relationship and never a compelling demand, unless in the midst of it the Spirit speaks to the many in Israel, saying, "Go join yourself to them." Given the history of Christian existence, this is an invitation not much offered and justifiably an echo rarely heard.

If Christian social imagination is ever going to be turned back toward the possibilities of communion, then it must be brought back into the original relationship—of Israel and the Gentiles. But by this return I am not simply affirming interreligious dialogue between Judaism and Christianity, although such dialogue is close to the heart of the matter. A painful hollowness characterizes much Jewish–Christian interreligious dialogue precisely because it builds on the naturalization of the racial imagination. Until we clearly reckon with the awesome power of the racial calculus deeply embedded in the theological vision of the Western world, no amount of exacting exegesis, careful theological clarification of doctrinal differences, or parsing of the connections or distinctions between Jewish and Christian historical liturgical trajectories will bring us to the deepest possibilities of communion.[66]

The return to the original relationship of Jews and Gentiles is blocked by the advent of whiteness and its deeply embedded social performances in the pedagogical, economic, and cultural relations of the Western world. The return I envision brings us back to bodies, and the formation of racialized bodies. We must think through to the utter limits of the racial calculus to expose its deepest fault lines. We must do this in order to tear open racial identity so as to reveal the original relation—exposing it afresh to our social imaginations. If whiteness became the facilitating reality, as that form of identity inside of which all other identities could be imagined, then walking away from or renouncing or questioning existence within white identity is no simple matter. There are, however, two bodies inscribed in the racial calculus that exists in a crucial position in relation to its utter limits and its fault lines, the (racialized) Jewish body and the black body. The way forward for a renewed Christian social imagination will be greatly aided by meditating on the racialized bodies of blacks and Jews in modernity. Such a meditation would allow us to peer through the cracks of the modern racial calculus and discern fragments of the original situation of Israel and Gentiles, of Israel and a Gentile church, of the Jewish body and the Gentile body joined.

JEW, BLACK, AND INTERRACIAL

The implicit though powerful question that emerges from the historical transformation of peoples into races was, where does one fit in the racial imagination?[67] By their being virtually consigned to the lowest rank of race—those furthest removed from salvation, transcendence, or humanity—the black body presented the shame concealed inside whiteness, its bloody journey to power.[68] If the black body presented the truth of racial existence, the racialized Jewish body presented its lie, the usurpation of a deep theological truth, of election, of covenant, and the concealment of the actual state of things—we (Gentiles) have no hope and are without God in the world.

Black body and Jewish body did indeed fit inside the racial imagination, yet there was from the beginning a problem with their fit. "Blacks" and all reckoned as like them entered racial space but showed themselves incapable of complete transformation into whiteness. Even by generating powerful approximations through dress, language, habit of mind and body, and miscegenation they remained black. Black bodies by their very presence exposed the edge of racial covering, its pure will to power. This exposure was rarely interpreted as such; rather, it supposedly indicated deep and abiding failure of black being, its pathology.

Unfortunately, the only bodily presence within the racial imagination powerful enough to affirm the black body's exposure of the edge and to in fact expose the truth beneath that covering was itself being placed under the same cover. The Jewish body also exposed an edge by exposing a false theology that energized the racial imagination, a Christian vision of election drawn inside whiteness and performed through European colonial power. Jews' failure to fit within the racial imagination was not simply on account of their racial appearance or of their religion, but owing to something deeper. Their lives bound to Torah and its powerful echoes of Israel's priority sharpened fundamental differences from European Christian civilization, creating ruptures in the racial imagination that could not be easily closed. Jonathan Schorsch in *Jews and Blacks in the Early Modern World*, a study of Sephardic Jews, notes that whiteness became a powerful tool of social inclusion for Jews: "The specific usefulness of Whiteness for Jews inhered in the fact that Jews could include themselves in the dominant culture as Whites in a way they could not as non-Christians. . . . Whiteness provided entrée into the dominant class to Jews who believed they belonged there by dint of the quality and antiquity of their civilization; such was their hope, in any case."[69] This hope stood in stark contrast to the realities of the Iberian racial caste system, with its virulent and infectious Spanish obsession with *limpiezas de sangre*, purity of blood. For the Spanish Jewish Diaspora spread throughout the colonialist world, the fear of being identified with the black body informed their eager participation in discursive practices that affirmed the "constellation of significations surrounding Whiteness [which] linked it to noble status, purity, and good looks."[70] Schorsch suggests that Jews participated in the colonialist refashioning of the world even as they carried forward deep anxieties about their abilities to remain hidden inside whiteness: "In seventeenth-century Sephardic Amsterdam . . . the intellectual, emotional, and *theological prioritization* of Whiteness, worries about perceived Jewish Blackness, increasing colonial opportunities and mind-sets, and the anxiety of some congregants over the visibility of Black and mulatto slaves within their own community led to an increased application of Black/White discourse" (emphasis added).[71]

Schorsch's important insight points to the slow, steady surrender to the theological power of whiteness and how it became determinative of the true (intelligence), the good (morality), and the beautiful (aesthetics). Much more, however, is at play here than the pathos of assimilation. The Jewish body and the black body signified the space of struggle for the overturning of the racial imagination and the reassertion of the theological framework necessary for the generation of an authentic Christian social imagination. Yet this central truth was never grasped. However, the space of struggle remained, not hidden but not clearly identified as a salvific possibility, the reassertion of a new reality of communion with God. That space is currently characterized by three kinds of relations between blacks and Jews—the sociopolitical, the literary-artistic, and the exilic—each of these currently suffers a lack of serious theological meditation, but each carries the potential of exposing the identity of the one whose despised flesh is the salvation of the world and the true but hidden desire of all nations.

THE SOCIOPOLITICAL SPACE

As the nineteenth century drew near its end and the twentieth century dawned, blacks and Jews entered into the dominant conversation that defined and continues to define their interactions and perspectives on each other: the discourse on survival. By this period, the legacies of atrocities and the shadow of death hung over their social spaces like circling vultures. Blacks and Jews became convinced that the Enlightenment project gave them reason to believe that social uplift and political engagement bound to assimilationist strategies held the key to their flourishing.[72] The end of slavery saw, for the first time, the children of African slaves conceiving life on the trajectory toward whiteness.

Although the reality of racial identity was powerful, many within black communities believed that the possibilities of the nation-state contained the tools to break down the oppression of blacks. This belief, fueled by the idea of American equality, stood in contrast to the idea that the only way to overcome racial identity was to take on the realities of white identity as best one could.[73] White identity was the common denominator, definer, and the ground-leveling reality upon which blacks could be judged solely by their abilities.

The most obvious yet most complex obstacle to growing the emulation tactical branch and its assimilationist tree was that blacks could not find uncontaminated soil in which to plant the tree. The power of the racial imagination permeated the American landscape both figuratively and literally. Thus, blacks struggled mightily against the centuries-old overgrowth of mental and visual images of black inferiority rooted in extremely powerful optic and discursive practices. One of the most powerful categories of images was the black minstrel.[74]

Assimilationism was not working well for Jewish Americans either. David Levering Lewis notes that during this time "what Jewish and Afro-American elites principally shared was not a similar history but an identical adversary—a species of white Gentile."[75] The America of this period confronted black and Jewish bodies with a racism and anti-Semitism seemingly joined at the hip. What the civil rights movement meant was the most powerful counterattack on both racism and anti-Semitism that was simultaneously the most absolute surrender to the theological vision of the racial imagination.

The civil rights era brought recognition that there were now in place enough black people and Jewish supporters within some structures of power to lobby for structural changes in the nation-state. The power of the civil rights movement lay in its ability to manipulate the process of re-presentation and thereby appeal to the themes of white American self-identification, that fairness and equality are at the very heart of who we, as Americans understand ourselves to be.[76] The power of the civil rights movement for blacks and Jews lay in the fact that for a brief moment the movement tapped into the space existing between the black body and the racialized Jewish body. Each shook the racial imagination, sending ripples through the social imaginary of America that continue to widen to this day.

The deep commitment of many Jews to the civil rights movement did not mean a placidly collaborative history of joint social engagement by the two communities. Indeed, the political engagements of blacks and Jews before, during, and after the civil rights movement indicate an important and oftentimes intense argument over their respective dilemmas and destinies in America. Yet many Jews supported the civil rights movement because they implicitly understood what was at stake in it for them.[77] Unfortunately, the vision of the movement was quickly drawn into the supersessionist logic of whiteness and fashioned in the form of a truly American schema. In this schema, what made America was the American ability to judge a person on his true inner reality as opposed to the external factors of race, cultural history, or ethnic tribe. How one performed in America was the true measure of the person, a performance gauged by the logic of capitalism.

The civil rights movement's raison d'être came to be the affirmation of a white fiction: that America was from the beginning the new Israel, a place of opportunity, of empty spaces, where people could by their own merit and hard work move forward in life in new and creative ways. And this self-revelation of America is always ready to break forth in the minds of Americans, and this is what makes America the experience, America the experiment in democracy, so great. This particular discursive arrangement that slowly but surely wove itself inside prevailing accounts of the civil rights movement is born of survival, anguish, and hope.[78] But it resists a deeper theological power that lay dormant yet within arm's reach, a power concealed in and often to the black church (in its multiple forms) and living Israel. That power resides precisely between social existence and social death and is bound to an abiding question: what would give us life now and forever? It is indeed the question of life eternal and not merely survival on the American landscape that fuels the social hope of the collective black body and the Jewish body, and the black church and living Israel. That social hope cuts through the racial imagination and gestures toward its transcendence. Such gestures have been powerfully and beautiful expressed in the second kind of relational space between blacks and Jews, the literary-artistic.

THE LITERARY-ARTISTIC SPACE

If one were going to speak of an American artistic soul, he or she would have to imagine that soul as shaped between black and Jewish bodies. Their artistic performances unleashed a power and a freedom that became not only central to the intoxicating spirit of America but also compelling to a wide swath of immigrants seeking to discern the American identity and approximate it.

The literary art of black and Jewish writers in America, especially since the dawn of the twentieth century, was indeed a matter of self-expression refracted through complex and dangerous modes of self-representation.[79] The realities of suffering, struggle, and marginality created a context within which they could display the contours not only of their humanity, but of humanity itself. Black and Jewish writers, from within the specificities of their lives and sometimes their lives together, painted portraits of the human condition. Such portraits invited readers to see themselves reflected in the pages of texts, and in this way black and Jewish existence could be imagined as a suitable carrier for anyone's self-understanding or even someone's self-expression.[80] Indeed, they established a kind of mysticism between the black and Jewish body, naming it as a mysterious space generative of the dreams of humanity, as the writer Isaac Rosenfeld showed in his autobiographical novel, *Passage from Home* (1946): "Why was he a Negro and I a Jew? Why not the other way around? Or both of us Negroes or both Jews? There was something between us that neither of us might grasp, some understanding of which we had only the dimmest impression; who knew what this was, or what the design was into which we had been cast? The connections between things were too fine to be discovered."[81] Writers did venture to discover that connection, always marking it as an elusive center, a center worthy of endless investigation and exploration. One of the most powerful explorers of that mystical nexus was James Baldwin. He saw the density of the connection in both its theological and racialized dimensions. Consider this passage from his essay

"The Harlem Ghetto," from 1948, in which he captured the linkages between black Christians and Jews: "The Negro identifies himself almost wholly with the Jew. The more devout Negro considers that he *is* a Jew, in bondage to a hard task-master and waiting for a Moses to lead him out of Egypt. The hymns, the texts, and the most favored legends of the devout Negro are all Old Testament and therefore Jewish in origin. . . . The birth and death of Jesus, which adds a non-Judaic element, also implements this identification. It is the covenant made with Abraham again, renewed, signed with his blood. . . . The images of the suffering Christ and the suffering Jew are wedded with the image of the suffering slave, and they are one: the people that walked in darkness have seen a great light."[82]

Baldwin, because of his Christian background, saw the relationship between racial and theological identities for blacks and Jews. In his essay "Negroes Are Anti-Semitic Because They're Anti-White" (1967) he captured the deep connection of whiteness to Christianity and how the complexities of white identity operated within black and Jewish relationships: "If one blames the Jew for having become a white American, one may perfectly well, if one is black, be speaking out of nothing more than envy."[83] Baldwin, however, like many writers, did not surmise the implications of the deeper resonance of that mystical-theological connection.

Michael Alexander, in his brilliant study *Jazz Age Jews*, explored the ways in which Jewish actors and musicians took on the racial identity of others, in this case blacks. Alexander sees most profoundly that this was done as a theological act: "In blackface, Al Jolson became a symbol through which Eastern Jewry in America understood itself. To a people who imagined itself fundamentally as Other, a Jew painted as an African American was an image of magisterial striking power. To the Jews in America, its symbolic power must have compared with that of the prophet Ezra, swallowing a Torah scroll in an age when to be a Hebrew meant to embody the Law. That comparison is not made glibly or without the counsel of the Yiddish journalist who thought Jolson's burnt cork had superseded the talis. . . . The people of the book have also become the people of the fringe. Marginalization has become a core component of American Jewish identity."[84] If Jewish identity could be signified through the artificial re-presentation of black identity, then it exposed a power of vicarious existence, to will one's voice to be heard within another's voice, to shade another discourse behind the bright light of a dominant one.[85] One should not press this ability too strongly within the derogatory reality of minstrelsy and in the social habit of presenting black flesh as grotesque flesh.[86] The larger reality here speaks on the one side to the ability of Jewish identity through the arts to re-present racial identity—white, black, or other—as a theological act signifying Jewish existence, and on the other side to the ability of black identity through those same arts to take the givens of racial identity and refashion them as expressive elements within black life.[87] Together these powers form the ability to call forth the image of humanity in its complexity.

One of the most powerful examples of this is the formation of American jazz. Jazz was decisively shaped at the intersection of the creative powers, social vicissitudes, and racial struggles of blacks and Jews. The history of jazz is in fact the history of the creation of a Jewish/black immigrant improvisational space within which one could not only survive in America but also refashion it into a creative extension of oneself. Jazz music developed and moved forward through extended kinship networks of blacks and Jews that crisscrossed and intersected at different moments in which there was unprecedented cross-pollination of ideas and some genuine hybridization of racial identities.

A history of the inner life of jazz from the vision of the space constituted between black and Jewish bodies has yet to be written. Consider the importance of Tin Pan Alley, the home of some of the most important Jewish writers of American music (for example, Gus Kahn, Irving Berlin, and George Gershwin) and the source of many foundational jazz standards; and the significance of the caring Jewish surrogate family for the young Louis Armstrong, the undisputed creative font of modern jazz improvisation.[88] One could also think of the collaborative relationships that gave birth to so many musical stars, as when the clarinetist and bandleader Artie Shaw, the son of Russian Jewish immigrants, hired Billie Holiday and, later, Roy Eldridge; or the collaborations of another Jewish clarinetist and bandleader, Benny Goodman, when he hired the African American Fletcher Henderson as a pivotal arranger for his band and drew from the talents of a number of other African American arrangers, such as Mary Lou Williams.[89] One could consider as well the founding of the incredibly important Blue Note Records by two German-Jewish immigrants from Nazi Germany, Alfred Lion and Frank Wolff, who collaborated with, documented, and recorded a vast array of black jazz luminaries, too numerous to even begin to identify.[90]

As is obvious from this brief though not inconsequential listing, the collaboration extended into the performance itself, establishing a vision of improvisation that is not primarily of an individual musician imbued with the spirit of modernism engaged in a wholly democratic and creative performance, producing musical pieces *ex nihilo*. Rather, jazz performance from its origins presented artistic interpretive traditions and communities of interpretation moving in and out of one another. Jew and black interfaced on the rough seas of representation, drawing other peoples and their cultural expressive traditions out onto the choppy waters, and in the process signifying both their existence as bodies engaged in

emancipatory performances.[91] While Jewish and black musical expressive traditions indicate a challenge to the racial imagination, they also point to the power
of the racial imagination to forge even tighter essentialist chains between artistic
expression and racial type.[92]

For my purposes, however, the significance of literary-artistic expression is
that it draws power from word and voice, yet it cannot capture sight of whose
word and voice it draws power from. It dances in the awesome reality of vicarious existence, but it has not entered the depths of that representative reality that
stands beyond the human constituted within the strictures of the racial imagination. There, in the depths of that representative reality, one gains sight of the
possibility of a new humanity that draws the expressive traditions of all peoples
to a new space of communion, a holy city not made by hands. Most important,
this historically collaborative literary-artistic expression presents an opportunity
for the church (and especially the black church) and living Israel to explore
together why each sings the songs of Zion in strange lands. That is, it opens up
the possibility of exploring together the implications of the formation of identities through the worship of the God of Israel considered against the backdrop of
the racial imagination. Rather than dialogue that simply reflects on Christian
and Jewish liturgical traditions, there is a history of collaboration between Jewish
and black artists that exposes profound theological conversational possibilities.
That possible theological conversation may yet yield sight of a truly Pentecostal
reality—the speaking of the language of another by the power of the Holy Spirit.
However, it is exactly the singing of songs in strange lands that leads finally to
the deepest kind of relation characterizing the space between Jewish and black
bodies, the relation of exile.

THE EXILIC SPACE

Woven through the relations, both sociopolitical and literary-artistic, is the
reality of exile. Exile here is not primarily the absence of a land or of a space,
but of home, of a place constituted in peace, safety, and prosperity. Exile in this
regard is a matter of consciousness, born of the long histories of scattered existence.[93] This need for place born of Diaspora existence is not only a material one
but a conceptual one for blacks and Jews. Both enter the challenge of narrating
their lives and histories in the face of suffering and the unrelenting continuous
dance with violence and death. If most people on the American social landscape
are aware of the Shoah and the Atlantic slave trade, the horrors of these historical realities have been sequestered into museumlike intellectual exhibitions
that people simply move through to be reminded of the generalities of human
evil, the depths of suffering, and the indomitability of the human spirit. Yet they

announce legacies of ongoing struggle which demand, especially for blacks and Jews, the hard work of making sense of the absurdities of their situations. Christianity and Judaism thus share in a profound challenge of presenting theological identities that speak to the deepest realities of black life and Jewish life.

This is an exceedingly difficult task because of the complex, ongoing struggles that attend the inheritors of these troubled sojourns and also because of the strange career of Christianity's effects on both. Indeed, many blacks and Jews look impatiently at Christianity and Judaism, respectively, asking very serious questions about and sometimes of God. This is not simply a matter of needing a theodicy for their peoples or a compelling account of their histories to situate concretely their struggles. What might be at play here is the possibility of a theological narration of life bound to a theological identity that is compelling. Such a compelling narration wed to a robust and powerfully articulated spiritual identity that presses deeply into the inner logics of black and Jewish life remains an elusive goal.

Few have captured an insight similar to that of the Jewish theologian Peter Ochs, who said that living Israel must learn to read and study Scripture in light of the Shoah and learn to write theology by "reexamin[ing] Scripture through the witness of Torah scholars who survived the Shoah, who studied Torah during and after the Shoah."[94] Ochs's insight could be echoed for Christian scholars, who must learn to reflect theologically with those who bore and continue to be marked by the deepest effects of the colonialist moment.[95] The need for Christians to learn to reread Torah alongside living Israel, attending carefully to Christianity's deep involvement in the Shoah, follows compellingly from examining the tragic legacy of the colonialism. Learning to reread Christian existence and relearn Torah, however, stand in contrast to the emergence of a twofold problematic faced by both living Israel and the black church. On the one hand blacks and Jews face the formation of cultural nationalisms that imagine theological identity wholly contained inside ethnic identity. On the other hand we face complex pedagogical challenges. Those challenges are different, to be sure, but they share the same taproot of trying to narrate theological identity within and sometimes against historical accounts that question the efficacy of belief. Again Ochs captures the situation for living Israel:

(a) We Jews know the God of Israel as the God of history through the way we study Scripture from out of our immediate communal and historical context.

(b) However, long before the Shoah, modern Jews fell out of the habit of reading Scripture this way, *as* Scripture (or Torah), and read Scripture instead

as a record of what they considered "past events" and "traditional beliefs." But neither past events nor traditional beliefs contained any precedents for knowing God from out of the context of Shoah, as total destruction.
(c) After the Shoah, the theologians of modern Judaism were therefore unprepared to consider the God of Israel the God of *this* history of Israel; they therefore tended either to speak of Israel independently of God, or to speak of God independently of Israel *in* history. In fact, Jews do not yet know the identity of the God who was God during the Shoah, because they have not yet studied Scripture from out of the context of that terrible time.[96]

If Jewish theological pedagogy faces a challenge within this twofold problematic exacerbated by the horror of the Shoah, then the black church carried forward a theological pedagogy that has been thwarted by a historical reality: It has limited social reach. Black Christians sought to make sense of a colonialist world in which Christian practices, including theological reflection, had limited import in effecting change in that world. Despite their limitations, Christian practices were useful for the uplifting of the race, the sustaining of hope, and the cultivation of joy in the midst of sorrow and frustration. But, as we saw with Equiano, Christian pedagogy lived and grew in very tight spaces.

The constant reminder that a robust Christian pedagogy made little difference in the social situation profoundly challenged theology's importance. This meant that a Christian pedagogic regime's ability to exert decisive power on the intellectual imaginations of blacks has always been severely complicated. Born of a racially bifurcated and socially hampered Christian pedagogy, a Christian intellectual life has always been a difficult road to mark out for black Christians. Black intellectuals raised in the church and entering the academy entered with a sense of Christian pedagogy's importance but its limitation. That limitation connected to racial segregation, and white supremacy became deeply coupled with theology's marginalization in modernity. The effect has been an ever-widening intellectual and spiritual bifurcation.

This bifurcation has made it difficult for black intellectuals to reconcile the unabated character of black suffering and public displays of black piety. If all intellectual work must eventually come to the fiery brook of violence, suffering, and death, then black and Jewish intellectual life never moves too far out of sight of these realities. Sight, in this regard, is the crucial issue. How do blacks reconcile what we see with what we believe? African and African Diaspora Christianity, for example, exposes what some consider a growing absurdity: what does it mean to say, as some historians, sociologists, and theologians do, that the center of Christianity is now in Africa (and Latin America), when Africans are dying at a monstrous rate through violence, hunger, disease, and natural disasters, the blows of which could be softened?[97]

The African (church) situation exposes deep but undertheorized connections to black Christian life around the world and the global economic situation. The sense of absurdity that connects African Christians to all black Christians might be stated in a question: how can there be in black communities growing churches, robust attendance, and vital piety coupled with intractable, cancerous social conditions? Most people in America know very well many of the ways in which black people in this country live out the disproportions, from crimes experienced and convicted of to diseases carried and left uncured, from low salaries earned to informal social benefits denied. Yet an analogous disproportion attends the Christianity of black peoples. We are in greater numbers earnest, faithful, compliant, hopeful, attending Christians.[98] These disproportions confront a Christian intellectual witness with a serious task of interpretation.

The situation for Jewish intellectual life, intellectual life deeply informed by Torah, is equally, if not more, complicated. The rise of the Jewish nation-state now profoundly articulated through Zionism created a challenging context for the articulation of a theological identity. Faithfulness to the Torah appears to be joined to the problem of ethnic violence, death, and the temptation of worldly power.[99] Thus, the question for living Israel and the church is not, how do we form faithful people, but what does it mean to form faithful people, given the complex social situations for our theological pedagogies?

The need to establish a powerful theological pedagogic vision that reaches deep into the social imagination of a people is not a new one and certainly not one limited to blacks and Jews. However, their exilic existence decisively marks the modern situation, naming a pedagogical challenge for theology, Jewish and Christian, unmatched by its social intensity. Indeed, God sought to address exilic existence by bringing the people of God into the desert and through the wilderness that they might learn the truth of their existence—they are not *ethnoi*, but *laos*. The truth of this lesson required that it be repeated. There was a man, born of Israel, who faced the needs of all peoples for the sake of many and who offers to Israel and to the Gentiles a similar word, you are not *ethnoi*, but my *laos*.

By carefully attending to the realities of modernity constituted around and signified by the black and Jewish body Christians might be able to gather what they are in desperate need of, namely, a clear, unobstructed view of a redemptive word spoken to Israel and the Gentiles. However, the significance of these bodies will be fully understood only as Christians allow black and Jewish situations to illumine the white body and the constructing realities of whiteness. The irony of the history of Jewish–black relations is that in the midst of sociopolitical and literary-artistic collaborations and with a parallel sense of the challenges of exilic existence, both groups have yet to reflect together deeply about the reality of Jesus' body, why this body figures into our histories and for many of us haunts us daily. Instead, the body of another has remained at the center of our relational imagination, the body of a powerful, white, Western man, the image of self-sufficiency, social power, and self-determination. If Jewish–black relations are marked by the absence of serious reflection on the body of Jesus, then Jewish–Christian theological dialogue is marked by the absence of serious reflection on that racial body, the body of the centered white man.

THE IMAGINED SPACE

If the deeper theological conversation ever begins to happen, then maybe there can be an interreligious dialogue for Christians and Jews that draws them to the real risks of faith, a risk found only in the space of possible joining, and a destiny marked by love. We are in need of a vision of the journey of faith imagined as the joining of peoples now separated by violence, poverty, or race. Where, however, is this space of joining and of communion? Is it only mental space, space conceived but never lived? Is it only a possibility? Given the constant displacement of peoples from land and the ever-increasing transformation of land into private property in the social imaginations of many peoples, it seems that a space of communion that binds people to place, whether new or old, can be only a dream, a possibility.

If place has become in our thinking, that is, in the thinking of peoples deeply touched by the multiple legacies of the colonialist moment, nothing more than the raw materials of potential development, of the constant turnings of spaces inside commodified existence—from residential sectors, to business sectors, to religious sectors, to education sectors, or back to "natural habitats"—then we can refer to the space of joining and communion only as having a possible corner inside commodified space. Yet if the space of joining and of communion is not first a possibility but a reality unrealized inside the identities and potential relationships between different peoples who have been convinced of the power of Jesus' life, then this space may become a profoundly visible place on surprising spaces that give sight of a different world.

The space of communion is always ready to appear where the people of God reach down to join the land and reach out to join those around them, their near and distant neighbors. This joining involves first a radical remembering of the place, a discerning of the histories and stories of those for whom that land was the facilitator of their identity. This must be done to gather the fragments of identity that remain to learn from them (or at least from their memory) who we might become in that place. This must also be done to discern the ever-present processes of commodification and transformation of place. We must learn the history of a place that has entered into the state of transition, because therein lies our point of departure for imagining a future by remembering a past. Yet such learning helps prepare us for interface with the processes of commodification and transformation. Such processes must constantly be engaged, analyzed, and sometimes resisted so that land is never simply released to capitalism and its autonomous, self-perpetuating turnings of space inside commodity form.

This joining also involves entering into the lives of peoples to build actual life together, lives enfolded and kinship networks established through the worship of and service to the God of Israel in Jesus Christ. Such kinship networks would, of necessity, come into contention with the permeation of class and economic stratification inherent in the transformation of land into private property. The space of communion draws into itself the social divisions enacted by and facilitated through that stratification in order to overcome them. The identities being formed in the space of communion may become a direct challenge to the geographic patterns forced upon peoples by the capitalistic logic of real estate. We who live in the new space of joining may need to transgress the boundaries of real estate, by buying where we should not and living where we must not, by living together where we supposedly cannot, and being identified with those whom we should not. Thus the new space may betray the logics of geographic commodity form by drawing local communities and their myriad of designations (for example, residential, business, commercial, and so on) into a wider, even global kinship network.

For us in the racial world, the remade world, a crucial point of discipleship is precisely global real estate. Where we live determines in great measure how we live. Where we agree to the spatial configurations of land inevitably means a tacit agreement to the racial formation of the world. We must enter the struggle of land acquisition, space and place design, targeted housing development, buying, and selling which constantly reestablishes and strengthens segregationist mentalities and racial identities.[100] We must, for example, disrupt the smooth formation of global real estate brokers and entrepreneurs formed in a process that deepens the logic of displacement and tightens the connection of space to commodity form, yielding the further naturalization of distinct living spaces for peoples with varying degrees of capital.[101] Our imaginations must be drawn to new possibilities of living arrangements that capture our freedom in Christ and turn them toward desiring a journey of joining enabled and guided by the Spirit of God.

For some, my account of Jesus-space and of communion will seem idealistic, a denial of Christian failure and the realities I rightly pointed toward in the previous chapters. If my account of space looks like an idealist account, it is precisely because it is an account held in stark contrast to the utter inversion of the Israel/Gentile relation. If my account of communion looks like an ideologically naïve ideation, it is because the very fragments of memory of Gentile existence have been altered and reconfigured to make room for other identity-facilitating realities. In the remade world born of the colonialist moment, Christian possibilities of communion and cultural intimacy have been subverted to draw all people toward an existence marked by the reversal of its telos. In this regard, my account of space and communion seems at odds with the order of things precisely because a perverted version of space and communion drawn from Christian logics pervades many parts of the world. My hope is for a joining of peoples not only to each other but also to the God who calls them to touch his body. For some, this deeply erotic image is disturbing. But it should be far less disturbing to us than bodies that never embrace, that never walk together on a moonlit night awaiting the dawn of a new day.

CONCLUSION

A different story of race needs to be told, one that helps people grasp the depth and power of racial perception. Many theorists and historians are trying to tell the story of race beginning, of the origins of a concept of race. Some believe race conceptuality has its determinative origins in the Enlightenment and in modernity. For my part, I join the chorus of voices that spy out racial formation before the Enlightenment, before common notions of modernity's beginnings, and in the earliest moments of modern colonialism. Yet I want to draw attention not simply to a medieval beginning of racial vision but also to a theological beginning. There is more here in this beginning and in my position than an alternative beginning of the race story. The story of race is also the story of place.

Geography matters for race as well as for identity, vision, and the hope of how one might live life. It is this deep connection between place and identity that will be difficult for many to grasp because people have been formed in a world in which such connections are only imagined, only fictions enabled solely by volition and market desire, the parents of private property. We cannot go back to a different world, the world where animals, landscape, and people together form an identity, collective and individual. But the first task of this text was to try to illumine the power of the racial imagination as exactly a power that draws its life from copying a centered existence between animals, landscape, and peoples. That power found expression through theological voice that gave shape to racial anthropology and nurtured its power to stand in for landscape in its facilitating characteristics.

There is no mystery to race. But until we reckon with its substitution for place and place-centered identity, its power will remain and remain mysteriously ever renewing with each generation of race-formed children. In truth, it is easy to imagine a time and a day in which race will not matter. Indeed if one has enough money, race does not matter now. If one is born in a particular place, with particular opportunities, educational, economic, social, political, even cultural, race can be rendered nondeterminative for one's social horizon, economic imagination, and cultural reflections. But as I have sought to show here, the elimination of race is beside the point. The world has been changed, and the earth has been taken from us—or should I say continues to be taken from us and given back to us changed, transformed into a mass of potential. Thus our lives, even if one day freed from racial calculations, suffer right now from a less helpful freedom, freedom from the ground, the dirt, landscapes, and animals, from life collaborative with the rhythms of God's other creatures and from the possibilities of imagining a joining to other peoples exactly in and through joining their lives on the ground.

In effect, a postracial future, if imagined inside the current order of things, will be only a continuing reflex of the commodification and transformation of space. That is, it would be peoples freed to be anything they wish, enabled by marketability and consumer-identity building possibilities. I don't say this to engender an unrelenting pessimism but to point to the need for a slower, more carefully imagined postracial future. That future requires an intense consideration of the formative power of whiteness. As I have shown in this text, whiteness must be analyzed not simply as substantiation of European hegemonic gestures but more precisely in its identity-facilitating characteristics, its judgment constituting features, and its global deployments of embodied visions of the true, the good, and the beautiful. To analyze whiteness requires nothing less than a theological consideration.

Theology, however, needs a different narration. I have offered that different narration in three aspects. First, it was crucial to locate a theological account of the colonialist moment. Postcolonial theory has drawn great wisdom from the disciplinary wells of philosophy, literary studies, sociology, history, feminist theory, and anthropology, to name only a few sources, but the decisive trajectories that flow out of the theological imagination of the West remain an untapped resource for deliberation. What is needed, however, is not primarily a historical account of the phenomenon of theology at the *arche* of colonialism, for example, the medieval theological character of colonialist imagination; rather, theological reflection itself can aid in our analysis of the world that has come upon us. It can also reveal the redemptive elements buried inside the colonialist operation, elements that truly can open up possibilities of a new world beyond the tragedy of the remade one. Theology in this regard is indeed filled with hope but also analytical, enabling a clearer grasp of the machinations of death and the demonic at work in the world. Theological reflection also opens up the possibility of a conversation that has yet to happen: a Christianity born of the colonialist wound speaking to itself in its global reality, pressing deeply inside the miracle of its existence, battered, bruised, marginalized, yet believing, loving, Christian. For better or worse, many of those whom Fanon called the wretched of the earth became and are in fact Christians. Yet the postcolonial has yet to encounter this Christianity—Catholic, Protestant, Pentecostal, syncretistic—and consider its struggles, sometimes reflecting the death of the colonial imagination and at other times showing new life, new possibilities gesturing toward the joining.

Second, it was also important to begin to restore to theology a richer sense of its identity from the colonialist moment forward. Sadly, Christianity and its theologians live in conceptual worlds that have not in any substantive way reckoned with the ramifications of colonialism for Christian identity or the identity of theology. The intellectuals whom theological education in the West produces continue to have a massive gap in their conceptual imaginations. The historical trajectory that shapes the curriculum of most seminaries focuses intensely on the early church, its New Testament and Christian antiquity origins, culminating in the deliberations of the councils, then moves to the high medieval period, turns steadily toward the Reformation, moves quickly through scholasticism, circles around key figures of the Enlightenment, and then lands on contemporary theological figures and movements, with some attention to missions and "contextual voices and problems." The problem here is not curricular coverage but how curricular sensibilities betray the concealment of modern identity formation with its constant social performances of detachment, distorting translation, and failed intimacy.

I yearn for a vision of Christian intellectual identity that is compelling and attractive, embodying not simply the cunning of reason but the power of love that constantly gestures toward joining, toward the desire to hear, to know, and to embrace. Such an identity articulates its judgments, its discernments, its prohibitions, even its risky negations of social forms and practices deeply inside the gestures of joining and longing. Here theology elicits life patterns that mirror God's own seeking of the creation and of the creature turned away from the divine voice. More important, such a theological identity enters imaginatively into various social forms and imagines the divine presence joining, working, living, and loving inside boundary-defying relationships. This kind of Christian intellectual identity depends on a conceptual recalibration that draws direction from its crucial originating trajectory, the relation of Gentiles to Israel.

Third, it was absolutely necessary that I narrate Christian identity from within the Gentile–Jewish relational matrix and specifically the epistemological implications of Gentile existence for the social performance of Christianity. But it was also necessary to capture the deep connections between the loss of that sense of identity and the conceptual problems arising inside Christianity within the colonialist moment. Only by analyzing this mutual enabling of a supersessionist sensibility coupled with visions of life from within white supremacist imaginings can one begin to discern the precise nature of Christian hubris performed in its educational and aesthetic expressions. That Christian hubris gave life to a destructive form of joining, in effect, to borrow from Bonhoeffer, a *sicut deus* form of communion in place of an *imago dei* form of communion. Its characteristics are tragic:

- Rather than a way of life that illumines the God of Israel as the reality between land and peoples, colonialism established ways of life that drove an abiding wedge between the land and peoples.
- Rather than a vision of a Creator arising through the hearing of Israel's story bound to Jesus who enables peoples to discern the ways their cultural practices and stories both echo and contradict the divine claim on their lives, the vision born of colonialism articulated a Creator bent on eradicating peoples' ways of life and turning the creation into private property.
- Rather than the possibility of new identity rooted in the resurrected Son of God, an identity that draws definition from our cultural realities yet is determined by a new reality of love and belonging, colonialist new identity meant unrelenting assimilation and the enfolding of lives and cultural practices inside processes of commodification.
- Rather than a process of transformation that involves the enfolding of peoples and their ways of life inside one another through communion with the triune God, the goal being a social performance that announces a way of peace and love in a visibly boundary-transgressing kinship network, we have been transformed into racial identities. Our racial identities enfold imagined connections to land inside our individual bodies and construct racialized boundaries and racial kinship. Our interactions with one another and the land weave through these racial patterns of displacement profoundly and announce social performances guided by a racial imagination.
- Rather than a vision of new life in Jesus Christ as the emergence of a new space of communion in Israel for the sake of all peoples and the reconfiguration of their social imaginations, we received a vision informed by colonialist logic of new life in Jesus Christ being wholly consumed in the social imaginations of nations. Christianity then comes to belong to peoples and is not tied in any meaningful way to Israel. Such Christian vision is also devoid of its spatial and geographic dimensions.

- Rather than a pattern of discipleship that moves forward from the trajectory of Pentecost, that is, of entering into the lives of others in submission and tutelage — learning their language — for the purpose of binding lives together, our interactions with peoples are informed through segregationalist mentalities. In addition, our interactions with land are guided by capitalist networks of exchange. These networks enfold all peoples within the binary logic of global production and consumption, the goal being that logic's endless repetition.
- Rather than the emergence of spaces of communion that announce the healing of the nations through the story of Israel bound up in Jesus, spaces situated anywhere and everywhere the disciples of Jesus live together, we are now the inheritors and perpetrators of a global process of spatial commodification and social fragmentation. These processes are performed within the class and economic calculations of global real estate. They force local communities to reflect global networks of exchange in regard to private property that echo colonialism's racial hierarchies and divisions.

If it is true that race and theology require this kind of narration in order to grasp some of our current difficulties, then what remains is to see how these different narrations might help facilitate a different social imagination. I anticipate some resistance to the fundamental claim of this work, that Christian social imagination is diseased and disfigured. In making such a claim I am not saying that the church is lost, moribund, or impotent. Rather, I want my readers to capture sight of a loss, almost imperceptible, yet articulated powerfully in the remaining slender testimonies of Native American peoples and other aboriginal peoples. This loss points not only to deep psychic cuts and gashes in the social imaginary of western peoples, but also to an abiding mutilation of a Christian vision of creation and our own creatureliness. The loss is nothing less than the loss of a sense of our own creatureliness. I want Christians to recognize the grotesque nature of a social performance of Christianity that imagines Christian identity floating above land, landscape, animals, place, and space, leaving such realities to the machinations of capitalistic calculations and the commodity chains of private property. Such Christian identity can only inevitably lodge itself in the materiality of racial existence.

A social imagination that begins to take place seriously begins to grasp the textures of the social in a comprehensive way. At one level, I hope to open up a new dialogue between disciplines that rarely interact — geography, theology, postcolonial theory, race theory, ecology, Native American studies, and so forth. In this regard, I hope for a conversation between those deeply involved in the formation of space and those concerned with identity formation — urban planners, ecologists, scientists, real estate brokers, developers joined in conversation with theologians, ethicists, literary and postcolonial theorists, sociologists, anthropologists, and historians. I also carry great hope for a new more serious conversation between Jews and Christians. At another level, my hope is more than academic. By attending to the spatial dynamics at play in the formation of social existence, we would be able to imagine reconfigurations of living spaces that might promote more just societies. Such living spaces may open up the possibilities of different ways of life that announce invitations for joining. Of course, our imaginations have been so conditioned by economically determined spatial strictures that increasingly different peoples do in fact live next to each other and remain profoundly isolated. Thus spatial reconfiguration must stand within a wider analysis and intervention into the ways identity formation has been channeled away from place.

To change one's way of imagining connection and one's way of desiring joining is no small thing. Yet I am convinced that such a change is not only necessary but now stands before human communities as the only real option for survival in a world of dwindling natural resources and tightening global economic chains of commodification. To imagine along the direction I suggest in this book would be nothing less than a theological act, indeed, as I suggest, a Christian act of imagining. And if, as I believe, Christian life is indeed a way forward for the world, then it must reemerge as a compelling new invitation to life together.

NOTES

INTRODUCTION

1. Milton C. Sernett, *Bound for the Promised Land: African American Religion and the Great Migration* (Durham: Duke University Press, 1997); James N. Gregory, *The Southern Diaspora: How the Great Migration of Black and White Southerners Transformed America* (Chapel Hill: University of North Carolina Press, 2005). An incredibly important text in this regard is William H. Chafe et al., eds., *Remembering Jim Crow: African Americans Tell about Life in the Segregated South* (New York: New Press, 2001).
2. Toni Morrison, *Beloved* (New York: Plume Book, 1998), 30.
3. The claims of a Native American lineage are the stuff of legend in many quarters of African American life; however, both the claims and the real history are worth much more exploration. See William Loren Katz, *Black Indians: A Hidden Heritage* (New York: Aladdin Paperbacks, 1997).
4. John Edgar Wideman, *Hoop Roots: Playground Basketball, Love, and Race* (New York: Houghton Mifflin, 2003).
5. Pierre Bourdieu, *Pascalian Meditations* (Stanford: Stanford University Press, 1997). Bourdieu writes that the scholastic disposition "implies (active or passive) ignorance not only of what happens in the world of practice, and more precisely, in the order of the *polis* and politics, but also of what it is to exist, quite simply, in the world" (15). What I observed was the inability of these would-be Christian intellectuals to see, understand, and even begin to imagine the profound realities of connectedness and belonging exposed in the act of theologizing, in inhabiting Christian intellectual form. In contrast, their formation facilitated what Bourdieu (following Heidegger) called "the forgetting of Being," that is, it gave them permission to forget their historical existence and the social conditions that make possible their continuing existence as a scholar. More extensively, this forgetting allowed them to perform the intellectual

life encased within racial agency, imagining the problems of Christian theology in the form of scholastic subjectivity. Bourdieu suggests that there is a form of scholastic subjectivity that lives within "a theodicy of [its] privilege" (25). This scholastic subject gives himself or herself to an embodied apology for reducing their sense of participation in identity-structuring processes that carry historical trajectories of oppression that they might otherwise call into question.

6. Richard John Neuhuas, *American Babylon: Notes of a Christian Exile* (New York: Basic Books, 2009); R. R. Reno, *In the Ruins of the Church: Sustaining Faith in an Age of Diminished Christianity* (Grand Rapids: Brazos Press, 2002); Rowan Williams, *Lost Icons: Reflections on Cultural Bereavement* (Edinburgh: T & T Clark, 2000); Gavin D'Costa, *Theology in the Public Square: Church, Academy, and Nation* (Malden, Mass.: Blackwell, 2005); Jeffrey Stout, *Democracy and Tradition* (Princeton: Princeton University Press, 2004).

CHAPTER 1. ZURARA'S TEARS

1. Gomes Eanes de Azurara, *The Chronicle of the Discovery and Conquest of Guinea*, 2 vols. (London: Hakluyt Society, 1896–99), 79–80. Hereafter cited as Zurara, *Chronicles of Guinea*. Translation of *Crónica Dos Feitos de Guiné*, 2 vols. (Lisbon: Agência Geral Das Colónias, 1947). Hereafter cited as Zurara, *Crónica Dos Feitos de Guiné*.

2. Peter Russell, *Prince Henry "the Navigator": A Life* (New Haven: Yale University Press, 2001).

3. Zurara, *Chronicles of Guinea*, 80.

4. Edgar Prestage, *The Chronicles of Fernão Lopes and Gomes Eanes de Zurara* (Lisbon: Watford, 1928).

5. Virginia de Castro e Almeida, ed., *Conquests and Discoveries of Henry the Navigator: Being the Chronicles of Azurara* (London: George Allen and Unwin, 1936). Hereafter cited as Zurara, *Conquest of Ceuta*. Cf. Russell, *Prince Henry*, 5.

6. Zurara, *Chronicles of Guinea*, 80–81.

7. I am aware of the problematic nature of deploying the term *African* as a substantial identity marker. Such a designation at this time is anachronistic, supplying a geographic holism that in fact did not exist then and does not exist now. However, I am claiming a conceptual holism with this designation that I hope captures the formation of an unrelenting derogatory gaze that is very much historically situated and clearly visible. Thus, the astute reader, having meditated on V. Y. Mudimbe's pathbreaking work, could take issue with me. However, I ask such readers to allow me what appears to be an essentialism, trusting that I am aware of the constructive/discursive "reality of the African." V. Y. Mudimbe, *The Invention of Africa: Gnosis, Philosophy, and the Order of Knowledge* (Bloomington: Indiana University Press, 1988). Also, see his *The Idea of Africa* (Bloomington: Indiana University Press, 1994).

8. To note only a few, it is cited not only in Russell, *Prince Henry*, 242, but also in Robin Blackburn, *The Making of New World Slavery: From the Baroque to the Modern, 1492–1800* (London: Verso, 1997), 103–5; Scott L. Malcomson, *One Drop of Blood:*

The American Misadventure of Race (New York: Farrar Straus Giroux, 2000), 150–52; Hugh Thomas, *The Slave Trade: The Story of the Atlantic Slave Trade: 1440–1870* (New York: Touchstone, 1997), 21–22; and David Brion Davis, *Inhuman Bondage: The Rise and Fall of Slavery in the New World* (Oxford: Oxford University Press, 2006), 95.

9. Zurara, *Chronicles of Guinea*, 81.

10. Ibid., 81–82.

11. Ibid., 82–83.

12. Zurara, *Crónica Dos Feitos de Guiné*, 124. He states, "Eu te rogo que as minhas lagrimas nom sejam dano da minha consciencia, ca nem por sua ley daquestes, mas a sua humanidade constrange a minha que chore piedosamente o seu padecimento, E se as brutas animallyas, com seu bestyal sentyr, per huũ natural destinto conhecem os dampnos de suas semelhantes, que queres que faça esta minha humanal natureza, veendo assy ante os meus olhos aquesta miseravel companha, nembrandome que som da geeraçom dos filhos de Adam!" Russell's comments, in *Prince Henry*, on Zurara's narrative at this point are telling. "What is unusual about Zurara's description is that it describes in much detail an actual auction of African slaves in Lagos and does so in terms which not only show an ability to understand the human misery involved but set out to draw the reader's attention to it. . . . Zurara unexpectedly explains that, since the captives were human beings and the children of Adam just as he was, it was natural that their suffering should move him to tears when he came to write about this event," 243.

13. Zurara, *Chronicles of Guinea*, 81.

14. Zurara, *Crónica Dos Feitos de Guiné*, 124–25. He states, "No outro dya, que eram viij. dyas do mes dagosto, muito cedo pella manhaã por rezom de calma, começarom os mareantes de correger seus batees, e tirar aquelles cativos pera os levarem, segundo lhe tora mandado; os quaaes, postos juntamente naquelle campo, era hũa maravilhosa cousa de veer, ca antre elles avya alguũs de razoada brancura, tremosos e apostos; outros menos brancos, que queryam semelhar pardos; outros tam negros come tiopios, tam desafeiçoados, assy nas caras como nos corpos, que casy parecia, aos homees que os esguardavam, que vyam as imagees do imisperyo mais baixo." Black bodies were believed to image the physical effects of life in Hell. Russell, *Prince Henry*, 243. Also see James H. Sweet, "The Iberian Roots of American Racist Thought," *William and Mary Quarterly* 54:1 (Jan. 1997): 143–66, 154.

15. Benjamin Braude, "The Sons of Noah and the Construction of Ethnic and Geographical Identities in the Medieval and Early Modern Periods," *William and Mary Quarterly* 54:1 (Jan. 1997): 103–42. Also see Davis, *Inhuman Bondage*, 48–76.

16. Nancy F. Marino, ed., *El Libro del Conoscimiento de Todos Los Reinos [The Book of Knowledge of All Kingdoms]* (Tempe: Arizona Center for Medieval and Renaissance Studies, 1999).

17. Russell, *Prince Henry*, 124–26. Russell suggests that they knew the French text, *Le Canarien*, which draws from the *Libro del conoscimiento,*

18. Marino, *Libro del Conoscimiento*, 61.

19. Ibid., 83–84.

20. Invoke the word *identity* today and you run the great risk of being misinterpreted, no matter what follows that invocation. As Stuart Hall noted, "There has been a veritable discursive explosion in recent years around the concept of 'identity.'" See Stuart Hall, "Who Needs Identity?" in Stuart Hall and Paul du Gay, eds., *Questions of Cultural Identity* (London: Sage, 1997), 1. Unfortunately, an explosion may connote either destruction or fruitfulness and, depending on scholarly perspective, identity discussions lead inevitably to one or the other. This chapter is not an exploration of the precise nature of identity formation, its vicissitudes, possibilities, or problems of articulation. I am concerned, instead, with the dilemma of identity articulated by Hall and others. That is, an articulation of identity formation must somehow offer an "account of discursive and disciplinary regulation [together] with an account of the practices of subjective self-constitution." (Hall, *Questions of Cultural Identity*, 13. Also see his "New Ethnicities," in *Stuart Hall: Critical Dialogues in Cultural Studies*, eds. David Morley and Kuan-Hsing Chen [London: Routledge, 1996], 441–49). I am certainly not attempting in this chapter to engage in such an articulation. Rather, I am suggesting indirectly that such attempted accounts must be rethought in light of a different construal of the problem of subjectivities, especially racial subjectivities.

21. Russell, *Prince Henry*, 242. Although Bartolomé de Las Casas certainly characterized Prince Henry as an evil power.

22. *Zurara, Conquest of Ceuta*, 77–80.

23. "Bull Romanus Pontifex, January 8, 1455," in *European Treaties Bearing on the History of the United States and Its Dependencies to 1648*, vol. 1, ed. Frances Gardiner Davenport (Washington: Carnegie Institution of Washington, 1917), 13–26, 20–21.

24. Ibid., 22.

25. Claiming this as an antiessentialist moment may seem counterintuitive, if not bordering on anachronistic. Critiques of essentialist thinking are normally aimed specifically at racialisms, that is, the beliefs in racial essences. We have not arrived at the racial categories formed through the scientific and anthropocentric discourses of the seventeenth through the nineteenth centuries. But we are witnessing here a far more powerful and determinative theological operation, one which blows by the distinctive realities of peoples.

26. Ibid., 21.

27. Ibid.

28. Ibid., 23. The key phrase repeated from the *Dum diversas*, June 18, 1452, indicates the right to enslave; however, slavery is enclosed in the actions of land appropriation. This is indicated by a number of verbs—"invadendi, conquerendi, expugnandi, et subjangandi"; then we find, "illorumque personas in perpetuam servitutem redigendi," cited in *European Treaties*, 17.

29. This struggle against Islam would culminate for this pope in the great social trauma he and Christendom would experience, the sacking of Constantinople by the Turkish armies. It is a vulnerable pope, one who has escaped an assassination plot but who is nearing death, who writes this bull. These realities help contextualize the papal endorsement of perpetual slavery (*perpetuam servitutem*) for the church's enemies, which has appropriately been the focus of much analysis. See P. G. Maxwell-Stuart,

Chronicle of the Popes (London: Thames and Hudson, 2006), 145–46; James Muldoon, "Papal Responsibility for Infidel," in *Canon Law, the Expansion of Europe, and World Order* (Aldershot, UK: Ashgate, 1998), 168–84.

30. Christopher Columbus, "Account of the Third Voyage. La Historia Del Viaje Qu'el Almirante Dom Cristóval Colón Hizo La Tercera Vez Que Vino a Las Indias Quando Descubrió La Tierra Firme, Como Lo Embió a Los Reyes Desde La Isla Española," in *Accounts and Letters of the Second, Third, and Fourth Voyages*, ed. Paolo Emilio Taviani, Consuelo Varela, Juan Gil, and Marina Conti, pt. 1 (Roma: Istituto Poligrafico e Zecca dello Stato, Libreria dello Stato, 1994), 69, 71.

31. Rotem Kowner, "Skin as a Metaphor: Early European Racial Views on Japan, 1548–1853," *Ethnohistory* 51:4 (Fall 2004): 751–78, 752.

32. Columbus, "Account of the Third Voyage," 85.

33. Ibid.

34. C. R. Boxer, *The Christian Century in Japan, 1549–1650* (Berkeley: University of California Press, 1967), 31. Also cited in Kowner, "Skin as a Metaphor," 753.

35. Columbus, "Letter 6," in *Accounts and Letters of the Second, Third, and Fourth Voyages*, 359. See Valerie I. J. Flint, "Columbus and His Christian World," in *The Imaginative Landscape of Christopher Columbus* (Princeton: Princeton University Press, 1992), 182–214. Also see Felipe Fernández-Armesto, *Columbus* (Oxford: Oxford University Press, 1991).

36. Boxer, *The Christian Century in Japan*, 74. Also see Josef Franz Schütte, *Valignano's Mission Principles for Japan*, vol. 1, pts. I and II (St. Louis: Institute of Jesuit Sources, 1980). English translation of *Valignanos Missionsgrundsätze für Japan, I Band: Von der Ernennung zum Visitator bis zum ersten Abschied von Japan (1573–1582) 1 Teil: Das Problem (1573–1580)* (Roma: Edizioni di Storia e Letteratura, Via Lancellotti 18, 1951).

37. Boxer, *The Christian Century in Japan*, 94.

38. C. R. Boxer, *The Church Militant and Iberian Expansion 1440–1770* (Baltimore: Johns Hopkins University Press, 1978), 23. Boxer reports that the derogatory term *nigger* was a commonly found designation in reports about troublesome Japanese. One official describes them as follows: "estes negros são diabólicos em seu governo." (Cf. *The Church Militant*, 130).

39. Dauril Alden, "Recruitment for an Enterprise: The Pertinacity of Eurocentrism," in *The Making of an Enterprise: The Society of Jesus in Portugal, Its Empire, and Beyond, 1540–1750* (Stanford: Stanford University Press, 1996), 255–97; Jerome Friedman, "Jewish Conversion, the Spanish Pure Blood Laws and Reformation: A Revisionist View of Racial and Religious Antisemitism," *Sixteenth Century Journal* 18:1 (Spring 1987): 3–30; Jonathan M. Elukin, "From Jew to Christian? Conversion and Immutability in Medieval Europe," in *Varieties of Religious Conversion in the Middle Ages*, ed. James Muldoon (Gainesville: University of Florida Press, 1997), 171–89.

40. Schütte, *Valignano's Mission Principles for Japan*, vol. 1, pt. I, 131–32. Also cited in Alden, *The Making of an Enterprise*, 56.

41. Ibid., 131. Also cited in Alden, *The Making of an Enterprise*, 56.

42. Boxer, *The Christian Century in Japan*, 8ff.

43. Ibid., 80.
44. Ibid., 131.
45. Bernard Lewis, *Race and Slavery in the Middle East: An Historical Enquiry* (New York: Oxford University Press, 1990). Sweet, "The Iberian Roots of American Racist Thought," 145–50.
46. Sweet, "The Iberian Roots of American Racist Thought," 147. Sweet notes, "The Muslim world expected blacks to be slaves."
47. Ibn Khaldūn, *The Muqaddimah: An Introduction to History* (Princeton: Princeton University Press, 2005), 117. Also cited in Sweet, "The Iberian Roots of American Racist Thought," 147.
48. Sweet, "The Iberian Roots of American Racist Thought," 148.
49. A. J. R. Russell-Wood, *The Portuguese Empire, 1415–1808: A World on the Move* (Baltimore: Johns Hopkins University Press, 1998).
50. Schütte, *Valignano's Mission Principles for Japan*, vol. 1, pt. II, 93.
51. Ibid., 93, 119. Schütte states, "The giant figure of the visitor and the dark-skinned Negro who accompanied him as servant were objects of special interest," 93. This description is stated quite matter of factly by Schütte, and the story of the "slave examination" is in a footnote. Both of these statements indicate the irony that is deeply embedded not only in the medieval missionary enterprise but also in the historical accountings of it. Also see Michael Cooper, *Rodrigues the Interpreter: An Early Jesuit in Japan and China* (New York: Weatherhill, 1974). Cooper mentions a slave who was asked to sing and dance for a Japanese official. He states, "Hideyoshi then asked that a Negro in the ship's party should dance and sing for him, and was much pleased by his performance," 95. Cf. George Elison, *Deus Destroyed: The Image of Christianity in Early Modern Japan* (Cambridge: Harvard University Press, 1988).
52. Calvin Luther Martin, *The Way of the Human Being* (New Haven: Yale University Press, 1999). Hereafter cited as Martin, *Human Being*.
53. Ibid., 26.
54. Ibid., 13. To what extent Martin hopes for any kind of restoration is unclear. More important, he clearly understands and articulates the tragedy of land loss in a remarkable way. As we will see in subsequent chapters, the possibility of return is closed to us. However, we may, I believe, envision a future of land connection that begins to speak to the problems of racial identity.
55. Ibid., 56.
56. Philip J. Deloria, *Playing Indian* (New Haven: Yale University Press, 1998); Eva Marie Garroutte, *Real Indians: Identity and the Survival of Native America* (Berkeley: University of California Press, 2003); James Clifton, ed., *The Invented Indian: Cultural Fictions and Government Policies* (New Brunswick: Transaction Publishers, 2003); Shepard Krech III, *The Ecological Indian: Myth and History* (New York: W. W. Norton, 1999).
57. In subsequent chapters I will return to the history of the myth of the noble savage and the profoundly theological character of its historical performance; however, what is at play here is not indebted to that history, though that history is indeed inescapable. See Ter Ellingson, *The Myth of the Noble Savage* (Berkeley: University of California Press,

2001); John F. Moffitt and Santiago Sebastián, *O Brave New People: The European Invention of the American Indian* (Albuquerque: University of New Mexico Press, 1996).

58. Deloria, *Playing Indian*, 5 (emphasis added). Deloria and Garroutte capture in very different ways the dilemmas of Indian identity, given the history of America. However, neither is able to calibrate landscape into their thesis in such a way as to render visible the deeper problem for identity in modernity. Identity "floats" and is politically unstable not simply because of white hegemony, but because of the ways in which white hegemony is embodied not simply in bodies but in the land itself.

59. Deloria, *Playing Indian*, 187. This powerful phrase comes from Renato Rosaldo, *Culture and Truth: The Remaking of Social Analysis* (Boston: Beacon, 1993).

60. Martin, *Human Being*, 34.

61. Ibid., 35.

62. Ibid., 25. Also see Calvin Martin, "The American Indian as Miscast Ecologist," *History Teacher* 14:2 (Feb. 1981): 243–52.

63. Martin, *Human Being*, 25.

64. Ibid., 33.

65. I am not invoking here something like the infamous anthropologist E. B. Tylor's vision of animism or his equally derogatory vision of primitive "survivals." Cf. E. B. Tylor, *Primitive Culture: Researches into the Development of Mythology, Philosophy, Religion, Language, Art, and Custom* (New York: Holt, 1889); Martin D. Stringer, "Rethinking Animism: Thoughts from the Infancy of Our Discipline," *Journal of the Royal Anthropological Institute* 5:4 (Dec. 1999): 541–55, esp. 542–43.

66. Martin, *Human Being*, 69. The appearance of place joins the appearance of persons. The vision of personhood joins the vision of all other animals. This aesthetic does not announce idealized beauty or goodness. It announces abiding necessary relationship.

67. Ibid., 42. It is precisely this sense of absence, of unawareness that needs careful historical accounting as part of the history of Christianity. This is why Philip Sheldrake's otherwise fine text, *Spaces for the Sacred: Place, Memory, and Identity* (Baltimore: Johns Hopkins University Press, 2001), does not capture the depth of what is at stake in Christian appropriation of space and a theology of place.

68. Martin, *Human Being*, 168. As Martin notes, the most devastating and enduring impact of Western interlopers on the American continent and its indigenes was to "furnish . . . it all in fear."

69. S. A. Mousalimas "The Divine in Nature: Animism or Pantheism?" *Greek Orthodox Theological Review* 35:4 (1990): 37170. Martin, *Human Being*, 121–22.

71. Ibid., 124–25.

72. Calvin Martin, "The Metaphysics of Writing Indian–White History," in *The American Indian and the Problem of History*, ed. Calvin Martin (New York: Oxford University Press, 1987), 3–26.

73. Elizabeth Marshall Thomas, *The Old Way: A Story of the First People* (New York: Farrar Straus Giroux, 2006). Hereafter cited as Thomas, *The Old Way*.

74. Robert J. Gordon, "A Kalahari Family," *Visual Anthropology Review* 19:1 and 19:2

(Spring-Summer 2003): 102–13. Edwin N. Wilmsen, "A Kalahari Family Named Marshall," *Visual Anthropology Review* 19:1 and 19:2 (Spring-Summer 2003): 114–27.

75. Elizabeth Marshall Thomas, *The Harmless People* (New York: Vintage, 1989).
76. Thomas, *The Old Way*, (Emphasis added) 6.
77. Johannes Fabian, *Time and the Other: How Anthropology Makes Its Object* (New York: Columbia University Press, 1983). Also see his *Anthropology with an Attitude: Critical Essays* (Stanford: Stanford University Press, 2001).
78. Fabian, *Time and the Other*, 19.
79. Ibid., 18.
80. Ibid., 23.
81. Ibid., 25.
82. Ibid., 29.
83. Ibid., 30–31.
84. Ibid., 31.
85. Ibid.
86. Fabian, *Time and the Other*, 32.
87. Thomas, *The Old Way*, 25.
88. Ibid., 62.
89. Ibid., 71–79.
90. Ibid., 79.
91. Ibid., 98–99.
92. Ibid., 18.
93. Ibid., 207.
94. Ibid., 165–66.
95. Ibid., 46.
96. The idea of "sharing a world" culturally speaking is a complex one. Here I do not mean this in the sense of a Wittgensteinian language game or a Lindbeckian cultural-linguistic framework. See George Lindbeck, *The Nature of Doctrine: Religion and Theology in a Postliberal Age* (Philadelphia: Westminster Press, 1984); *The Wittgenstein Reader*, ed. Anthony Kenny (London: Blackwell, 1994); Rush Rhees, *Wittgenstein's On Certainty: There–Like Our Life* (London: Blackwell, 2005); Norman Malcolm, *Wittgenstein: A Religious Point of View?* (New York: Cornell University Press, 1993)
97. Thomas, *The Old Way*, 278.
98. Ibid., 279.
99. Fabian, *Time and the Other*, 41.
100. Ibid.,
101. Thomas, *The Old Way*, 278.
102. Ibid., 283.
103. Ibid., 285.
104. Ibid., 295.
105. Polly Wiessner, "Owners of the Future? Calories, Cash Casualties and Self-Sufficiency in the Nyae Nyae Area between 1996–2003," *Visual Anthropology Review* 19:1 and 19:2 (Spring-Summer 2003): 149–59. Wiessner offers a very insightful account of the

current situation of the Ju/hoansi of the Nyae Nyae. They continue to be plagued by governmental interventions shaped by mythologized visions of their former way of life.

106. Edwin Wilmsen, in "A Kalahari Family Named Marshall," offers a sympathetic critique of John Marshall's work, yet he is also clear about the great danger in speaking about the "Bushman" in racialist discourse. "Any conception that posits a person's objective condition to be *natural* rather than *historical* is racialist," 120. Here he is quoting Johannes Fabian. Cf. Fabian, "Hindsight," in *Anthropology with an Attitude*, 103–17. He also quotes Michael Brown's list of three key elements of racialist discourse: "(1) a naturalist's catalogue of human types; (2) an unforgiving, ahistorical perspective on the human experience; (3) an evolutionary view of the relationship between those who have adapted to nature and those who have adapted nature to themselves," 120. (Michael Brown, "The Viability of Racism: South Africa and the United States," *Philosophical Forum* 18:10 [1986]: 254–69). However, what is at stake here is less the essentialist problematic than the inability to see how the transformation of the land is calibrated to the relocation of bodies into racial (i.e., ethnic [no longer localized] space).

107. Keith H. Basso, *Wisdom Sits in Places: Landscape and Language among the Western Apache* (Albuquerque: University of New Mexico Press, 1996). Also see *Senses of Place*, ed. Steven Feld and Keith H. Basso (Santa Fe: School of American Research Press, 1996).

108. Basso, *Wisdom Sits in Places*, 31.

109. Ibid., 32.

110. Ibid.

111. Ibid.

112. Ibid., 33.

113. Ibid.

114. Ibid., 33.

115. Ibid., 14–16.

116. Ibid., 30.

117. Ibid., 50–51.

118. Ibid., 52.

119. Ibid., 24.

120. Ibid., 58–59.

121. Ibid., 61.

122. Ibid., 38–39.

123. Ibid., 39.

124. Ibid., 34.

125. Ibid., 71.

126. James Wilson, *The Earth Shall Weep: A History of Native America* (New York: Grove, 1998). Also see Paula Mitchell Marks, *In a Barren Land: The American Indian Quest for Cultural Survival, 1607 to the Present* (New York: HarperCollins, 1998); Judith Nies, *Native American History* (New York: Ballantine, 1996); Peter Nabokov, *Native American Testimony*, rev. ed. (New York: Penguin, 1999); Cathy N. Davidson and Ada

Norris, eds., *Zitkala-Sa: American Indian Stories, Legends, and Other Writings* (New York: Penguin, 2003); Eliza McFeely, *Zuni and the American Imagination* (New York: Hill and Wang, 2001); Frederick Turner, ed., *The Portable North American Indian Reader* (New York: Penguin, 1974); Charles A. Eastman (Ohiyesa), *From the Deep Woods to Civilization* (Lincoln: University of Nebraska Press, 1977).

127. N. Scott Momaday, "The Man Made of Words," in *Indian Voices: The First Convocation of American Indian Scholars* (San Francisco: Indian Historian Press, 1970), 49–84.

128. *The Conquest of America: The Question of the Other* (New York: Harper and Row, 1984), 43ff.

129. (Edinburgh: T & T Clark, 1957), 257–321.

130. Eberhard Jungel, *God's Being Is in Becoming: The Trinitarian Being of God in the Theology of Karl Barth—A Paraphrase* (Grand Rapids: Eerdmans, 2001).

131. Barth, *Church Dogmatics*, II/1, 311 (emphasis added).

132. Found in *For This Land: Writings on Religion in America* (New York: Routledge, 1999), 241 (emphasis added). The intellectual testimony of Vine Deloria Jr. has yet to receive the serious consideration from Christian theologians it deserves. Both his work and his life bring serious questions to not only the nature of Christian theology but the nature of the theological academy in the Western world. We also lack a substantive, comprehensive biography of this important religious intellectual.

133. Toni Morrison, *Playing in the Dark: Whiteness and the Literary Imagination* (Cambridge: Harvard University Press, 1992), 48.

134. Ibid., 59.

135. Throughout this chapter I have avoided voicing the idea that there are multiple subjectivities of racial existence, that is, that there are multiple ways of being white and of being black. Indeed, some readers of this argument will have concluded very early that I am working with what appears to be a monolithic vision of whiteness, or an essential concept of whiteness, rather than fully historicizing whiteness as it is deployed in different ways at different times for different purposes. I agree that there are multiple subjectivities of racial existence. However, articulating that multiplicity often carries with it fundamental problems. The articulations of those racial subjectivities (being white in this way or being black in that way) offer weak accounts of their origins and continuing power. More important, the articulations are fully captured within the reality of displacement so that they operate solely as visions of individuated signifiers even if referring to specific groups. When the act of signification is narrowly construed in this way it leaves few hermeneutic options. Either we carry forward a constructivist focus seeking to determine how people imagine their racial existence, moving in focus from the machination of ethnic or racial groupings all the way down to individual antinomian improvisations of racial or antiracial life; or we could focus on strategic essentialized deployments of racial existence to promote political or social agency and empowerment. Both of these options miss the point.

136. Edward F. Fischer, "Cultural Logic and Maya Identity: Rethinking Constructivism and Essentialism" (with comments and replies from Quetzil E. Castañeda, Johannes Fabian, Jonathan Friedman, Charles Hale, Richard Handler, Bruce Kapferer, and

Michael Kearney), *Current Anthropology* 40:4 (Aug.-Oct. 1999): 473–99. Fischer's essay and the replies are telling in that they all recognize the problem when anti-essentialist critique is deployed against native peoples' self-descriptions. Such deployment is unmasked for what it is—imperialist imposition of modernist freedom for self-creation, a freedom which is shallow in its political wisdom. For his part, Fischer attempts in this essay to make use of Bourdieu's vision of a cultural logic to move beyond what he envisions as essentialism and constructivism to a more organic use of both in indigenous identity formation. The majority of his responders are not persuaded by his proposal. Ironically, Fischer is grasping for a way of "thinking the land" as crucial to identity, but his central concern with essentialism and constructivism, that is, with discourse, closes off his imagination from capturing the ways the ground is a signifier for peoples.

137. I am not saying that analyzing the ways of whiteness is an unimportant endeavor. However, thus far the endeavor reflects the central conceptual problem I am considering in this text. I identify at least four forms of analysis that are gaining ascendancy: (1) Whiteness as a mode of agency in class formation: Here whiteness comes into view as an identity form born as the peasants of the Old World enter the New World and begin their movement toward social stability and economic advantage. This mode also entails important body juxtaposing vis-à-vis indigenes and slaves. See Theodore W. Allen, *The Invention of the White Race*, 2 vols., vol. 1: *Racial Oppression and Social Control*; vol. 2: *The Origin of Racial Oppression in Anglo-America* (London: Verso, 1994); David Roediger, *The Wages of Whiteness: Race and the Making of the American Working Class* (London: Verso, 1991). Also see his *Colored White: Transcending the Racial Past* (Berkeley: University of California Press, 2002); and *Towards the Abolition of Whiteness* (London: Verso, 1994); Deborah Posel, "Race as Common Sense: Racial Classification in Twentieth-Century South Africa," *African Studies Review* 44:2, *Ways of Seeing: Beyond the New Nativism* (Sept. 2001): 87–113; Dana D. Nelson, *National Manhood: Capitalist Citizenship and the Imagined Fraternity of White Men* (Durham: Duke University Press, 1998). (2) Whiteness as a symbolic order: White identity in this calculus forms within a host of networked perceptions that organize sets of social performances and cultural practices. Again, juxtaposing is important—the objects of perception (nonwhite bodies) and the imperial act of perceiving are keys to this analysis. See Alfred J. López, ed., *Postcolonial Whiteness: A Critical Reader on Race and Empire* (Albany: State University of New York Press, 2005). Also see his "Whiteness and the Colonial Unconscious," in *Posts and Pasts: A Theory of Postcolonialism* (Albany: State University of New York Press, 2001), 85–119; Kalpana Seshadri-Crooks, *Desiring Whiteness: A Lacanian Analysis of Race* (London: Routledge, 2000); Sarah Nuttall, "Subjectivities of Whiteness," *African Studies Review* 44:2, *Ways of Seeing: Beyond the New Nativism* (Sept. 2001): 115–40. (3) Whiteness as "self" perception. Here, white identity forms in the act of making visible all common human characteristics, attributes, and virtues. White identity is the invisible signifier of everyday experiences. It supplies the normal narratively and is thereby a form of governmentality. It gives voice to the intimate and is a way of seeing and looking inside ourselves to our essential realities. See Todd Vogel, *ReWriting White: Race, Class, and Cultural Capi-*

tal in Nineteenth-Century America (New Brunswick: Rutgers University Press, 2004); Valerie Babb, *Whiteness Visible: The Meaning of Whiteness in American Literature and Culture* (New York: New York University Press, 1998); Ira Bashkow, *The Meaning of Whitemen: Race and Modernity in the Orokaiva Cultural World* (Chicago: University of Chicago Press, 2006); Vron Ware and Les Back, *Out of Whiteness: Color, Politics, and Culture* (Chicago: University of Chicago Press, 2002); Birgit Brander Rasmussen et al., *The Making and Unmaking of Whiteness* (Durham: Duke University Press, 2001). (4) Whiteness as positional alchemy: Being or becoming white, in this analysis, has to do with being placed — spatially, socially, economically, politically, and linguistically — in proximity to a constellation of nonwhite bodies in such a way as to render a different judgment of identity for the person so placed. Here the ideas of movement and position both materially and analogically are keys to white identity. One can become white by approximations and by proximity. The form of analysis locks into the perception of traveling visual markers of whiteness, markers that may cross cultural spaces. See Matthew Frye Jacobson, *Whiteness of a Different Color: European Immigrants and the Alchemy of Race* (Cambridge: Harvard University Press, 1998); Noel Ignatiev, *How the Irish Became White* (New York: Routledge, 1995); Grace Elizabeth Hale, *Making Whiteness: The Culture of Segregation in the South, 1890–1940* (New York: Vintage, 1998); Jennifer Cuglielmo and Salvatore Salerno, *Are Italians White? How Race Is Made in America* (New York: Routledge, 2003). None of these texts precisely matches simply the particular form of analysis outlined above. However, the general direction of analysis may be located in these various essays and chapters. Of course, many should rightly be placed in multiple forms of analysis. What joins these four forms of analysis are the importance at multiple levels of perception coupled to discursive practices, and a realization of the comparative moment and the racial complementarity at work in the formation of whiteness. These forms of analysis are surely fruitful and capture in important ways what is at stake in the powerful operations of whiteness and the complexities of racial imaginings. I draw on all of them at various points in order to situate the deeper problems of the theological imagination in forming the new racial world order. However, what also joins these forms of analysis is their failure to grasp the wider horizon on which racial ways come to life. They are intellectual meditations that are, to use Basso's phrase, "geographically adrift." These are theories of whiteness and race that are unaware of the scope of the racial refashioning of human and spatial ecology that was the New World order. It is racial vision trapped in the refashioning itself. A way forward requires seeing a theological operation masked in a spatial revolution.

138. Martin Heidegger, "Building Dwelling Thinking," in *Basic Writings* (New York: Harper SanFrancisco, 1993), 349.

CHAPTER 2. ACOSTA'S LAUGH

1. Claudio M. Burgaleta, *José de Acosta, S.J. (1540–1600): His Life and Thought* (Chicago: Loyola Press, 1999). John W. O'Malley, *The First Jesuits* (Cambridge: Harvard University Press, 1993).

2. O'Malley, *The First Jesuits*, 15.

3. Ibid., 27.

4. Ibid., 244.

5. Terry Pinkard, *Hegel: A Biography* (Cambridge: Cambridge University Press, 2000), 50.

6. O'Malley, *The First Jesuits*, 223–24. Two of his plays, *Jephthah Sacrificing His Daughter* written in 1555, at the age of fifteen, and *Joseph Sold into Egypt*, written one year later, were widely celebrated in his community.

7. Burgaleta, *José de Acosta*, 15–21.

8. Bernice Hamilton, *Political Thought in Sixteenth-Century Spain: A Study of the Political Ideas of Vitoria, De Soto, Suárez, and Molina* (Oxford: Clarendon, 1963).

9. José de Acosta, *De Procuranda Indorum Salute* (Scotland: Mac Research 1995–96), 1: vi. Hereafter cited as *De Procuranda*.

10. MacIntyre, *Whose Justice? Which Rationality?*(Notre Dame: University of Notre Dame Press, 1988), 178–79.

11. Alasdair MacIntyre, *After Virtue* (Notre Dame: University of Notre Dame Press, 1984). Also see his *Ethics and Politics: Selected Essays*, vol. 2 (Cambridge: Cambridge University Press, 2006), 3–82. Also his *Three Rival Versions of Moral Enquiry: Encyclopedia, Genealogy, and Tradition* (Notre Dame: University of Notre Dame Press, 1990). John Horton and Susan Mendus, eds., *After MacIntyre* (Notre Dame: University of Notre Dame Press, 1994). Bruce W. Ballard, *Understanding MacIntyre* (Lanham, Md.: University Press of America, 2000).

12. Herbert McCabe, *God Still Matters* (New York: Continuum, 2002), 199–211. David B. Burrell, *Freedom and Creation in Three Traditions* (Notre Dame: University of Notre Dame Press, 1993). Stanley Hauerwas, *The Peaceable Kingdom: A Primer in Christian Ethics* (Notre Dame: University of Notre Dame Press, 1983). Also see *The Hauerwas Reader* (Durham: Duke University Press, 2001). Jeffrey C. K. Goh, *Christian Tradition Today: A Postliberal Vision of Church and World* (Grand Rapids: Eerdmans, 2000). Tracey Rowland, *Culture and the Thomist Tradition: After Vatican II* (London: Routledge, 2003). J. B. Schneewind, "MacIntyre and the Indispensability of Tradition," *Philosophy and Phenomenological Research* 51:1 (March 1991): 165–68.

13. MacIntyre, *Whose Justice? Which Rationality?* 355.

14. Ibid., 361–62.

15. Ibid., 354.

16. Jeffrey Stout, *Democracy and Tradition* (Princeton: Princeton University Press, 2004), 118ff. Modernity, however, its presence, power, or absence, is not the central focus of this chapter. I focus in this chapter on the reformation of Christian theology and Christian intellectual life at the hands of theologians such as José de Acosta.

17. Indias Occidentales was the desgination for the new world by Acosta and a number of other theologians, philosophers, and merchants.

18. Pedro de Cieza de León, *The Discovery and Conquest of Peru* (Durham: Duke University Press, 1998). James Lockhart and Stuart B. Schwartz, *Early Latin America: A History of Colonial Spanish America and Brazil* (Cambridge: Cambridge University Press, 1983).

19. Sabine MacCormack, "Pachacuti: Miracles, Punishments, and Last Judgment: Visionary Past and Prophetic Future in Early Colonial Peru," *American Historical Review* 93:4 (October 1988): 960–1006, esp. 969.

20. Ibid., 968.

21. Elinor G. K. Melville, *A Plague of Sheep: Environmental Consequences of the Conquest of Mexico* (Cambridge: Cambridge University Press, 1997), 4–5. Although Melville's study takes Mexico as its object of analysis, the environmental effects she notes are present throughout the areas of New World conquest by the Spanish and the Portuguese, especially my area of concern, Peru.

22. Peter Flindell Klarén, *Peru: Society and Nationhood in the Andes* (New York: Oxford University Press, 2000), 34.

23. Christine Hunefeldt, *A Brief History of Peru* (New York: Facts on File, 2004), 45.

24. Sabine MacCormack, *Religion in the Andes: Vision and Imagination in Early Colonial Peru* (Princeton: Princeton University Press, 1991), 249.

25. Hunefeldt, *A Brief History of Peru*, 53.

26. Michel de Certeau, *The Practice of Everyday Life* (Berkeley: University of California Press, 1988), 34ff.

27. Robert Himmerich y Valencia, *The Encomenderos of New Spain, 1521–1555* (Austin: University of Texas Press, 1991). Jack A. Licate, *Creation of a Mexican Landscape: Territorial Organization and Settlement in the Eastern Puebla Basin, 1520–1605* (Chicago: University of Chicago, 1981), 23–39. Here, what is modern comes into view through the rapid change of spatial logics, the redistribution of bodies, and the repositioning of social patterns all in service of Spanish interests. This sense of modern, unlike the later Kantian articulation of Enlightenment, focuses on practices of totalizing geographic upheaval. But like Kant's articulation of Enlightenment, this sense of modern is a denial of authority, in this case, native authority, because native authority is precisely that which must remain under tutelage, as Kant himself will in his own time come to believe and powerfully articulate.

28. Bartolomé de Las Casas, *A Short Account of the Destruction of the Indies* (New York: Penguin, 1992), 39.

29. Sabine MacCormack, "Demons, Imagination, and the Incas," in *New World Encounters*, ed. Stephen Greenblatt (Berkeley: University of California Press, 1993), 113.

30. Tzvetan Todorov, *The Conquest of America: The Question of the Other* (New York: Harper Torchbooks, 1984), 33. The *encomienda* follows what Todorov discerns as the logic of Columbus in preferring land over people and in positing a hermeneutic in which "human beings have no particular place."

31. Melville, *A Plague of Sheep*, 6.

32. Ibid., 39–40. Melville's powerful account does not refer to the geographic specifics of Peru. However, the effects she describes are clearly applicable to the world Acosta entered and in which he performed his theological vision.

33. Ibid., 115.

34. See fig. 10, Lockhart and Schwartz, *Early Latin America*, 70.

35. Ward Stavig, "Ambiguous Visions: Nature, Law, and Culture in Indigenous-Spanish

Land Relations in Colonial Peru," *Hispanic American Historical Review* 80:1 (Feb. 2000): 91.

36. Walter D. Mignolo, *The Idea of Latin America* (Oxford: Blackwell, 2005), 89. This is what will develop later into what Mignolo designates so powerfully as *Latinidad*.

37. Jerome Friedman, "Jewish Conversion, the Spanish Pure Blood Laws and Reformation: A Revisionist View of Racial and Religious Antisemitism," *Sixteenth Century Journal* 18:1 (Spring 1987): 3–30. Also see Jonathan Schorsch, *Jews and Blacks in the Early Modern World* (Cambridge: Cambridge University Press, 2004), 50ff.

38. C. R. Boxer, *The Church Militant and Iberian Expansion, 1440–1770* (Baltimore: Johns Hopkins University Press, 1978), 38.

39. Magnus Mörner, *Race Mixture in the History of Latin America* (Boston: Little, Brown, 1967), 22. Mörner writes, "The Spanish Conquest of the Americas was a conquest of women."

40. Cited in Todorov, *The Conquest of America*, 48–49.

41. This is Todorov's language.

42. See figures 11 and 12, Lockhart and Schwartz, *Early Latin America*, 130. Also see J. H. Elliott, *Empires of the Atlantic World: Britain and Spain in America, 1492–1830* (New Haven: Yale University Press, 2006), figure 15: "Andres de Islas. Four Racial Groups (1774)."

43. David Cahill, "Colour by Numbers: Racial and Ethnic Categories in the Viceroyalty of Peru, 1532–1824" in *Journal of Latin American Studies*, Vol. 26, No. 2. (May, 1994): 336. Cahill notes that it is not clear to what extent this nomenclature functioned heuristically to organize social vision. However, the greater significance of such racial calculations is their indication of the power of whiteness to stabilize identity.

44. José F. Buscaglia-Salgado, *Undoing Empire: Race and Nation in the Mulatto Caribbean* (Minneapolis: University of Minnesota Press, 2003).

45. Lockhart and Schwartz, *Early Latin America*, 108. As the authors note, "In the first generation the parish was included within the *encomienda*, integrated with, dependent upon, and subordinate to it, rather than parallel."

46. Ibid., 109.

47. Susan Migden Socolow, *The Women of Colonial Latin America* (Cambridge: Cambridge University Press, 2000), 42.

48. Burgaleta, *José de Acosta*, 29.

49. Michel de Certeau, *Heterologies: Discourse on the Other* (Minneapolis: University of Minnesota Press, 1986), 69.

50. Cited in Luis N. Rivera, *A Violent Evangelism: The Political and Religious Conquest of the Americas* (Louisville: Westminster John Knox, 1992), 20. Also see Benjamin Keen, *Essays in the Intellectual History of Colonial Latin America* (Boulder: Westview, 1998), 177.

51. Keen, *Essays in the Intellectual History of Colonial Latin America*, 121. Keen notes that "the discovery of America and its peoples posed . . . serious challenges to traditional authority," scientific, philosophical, and theological. However *challenge* may not be the best word for what is at play here. One might consider *upheaval* a better word

because *challenge* suggests an awareness of the necessary rearticulations of bodies of knowledge thrust on intellectuals by the sheer immensity of the new worlds.

52. Ibid., 120ff. Also see Anthony Grafton, *New Worlds, Ancient Texts: The Power of Tradition and the Shock of Discovery* (Cambridge: Belknap, 1992). Keen and other scholars have suggested that the other authority that moved to the front was experience itself. It is true that the experiences of New World travelers affected Old World theorization. However, the experiences of the New World were never separate from the traditioned rationalities that were the necessary vehicles that brought those experiences to articulation. Old World textual authorities were not being challenged so much as they were being altered through separation and clarification of their connection to the actual observable world.

53. José de Acosta, *Natural and Moral History of the Indies* (Durham: Duke University Press, 2002), book 2: chapter 9, 88–89. Hereafter cited as *Historia*, bk./chap. Also see *Historia Natural y Moral de las Indias* (Madrid: Historia 16, 1987), 141.

54. Acosta also wrote a catechetical text in the New World, *Doctrina Christiana y Catecismo para Instrucción de los Indios*. Examination of this text is beyond the scope of my treatment of Acosta. See Burgaleta, *José de Acosta*, 146–49.

55. Acosta, *Historia*, 5–6.

56. Thayne R. Ford, "Stranger in a Foreign Land: José de Acosta's Scientific Realizations in Sixteenth-Century Peru," *Sixteenth Century Journal* 29:1 (Spring 1998): 20.

57. MacIntyre, *Whose Justice? Which Rationality?* 358.

58. Ibid., 362.

59. Acosta, *Historia*, 100n3. Walter D. Mignolo provides commentary throughout this edition of the *Historia*.

60. Mignolo, *The Idea of Latin America*, 17.

61. Ibid., 36.

62. Keen, *Essays in the Intellectual History of Colonial Latin America*, 121.

63. Karl W. Butzer, "From Columbus to Acosta: Science, Geography, and the New World," *Annals of the Association of American Geographers* 82:3, *The Americas Before and After 1492: Current Geographical Research* (September 1992): 543–65. Saul Jarcho, "Origin of the American Indians as Suggested by Fray Joseph de Acosta (1589)," *Isis* 50:4 (December 1959): 430–38.

64. Charles O. Frake, "Cognitive Maps of Time and Tide Among Medieval Seafarers," *Man* 20:2 (June 1985): 254–70; E. G. R. Taylor, "The Early Navigator," *Geographical Journal* 113 (Jan.-June 1949): 58–61.

65. Mignolo, *The Idea of Latin America*, 8.

66. Walter Mignolo, "Commentary on José de Acosta's *Historia Natural y Moral de las Indias*: Occidentalism, the Modern/Colonial World, and the Colonial Difference," in Acosta, *Historia*, 467. Mignolo captures this problematic when he states, "Acosta's work . . . contributed to building an epistemic imaginary in which Amerindian knowledge did not count as sustainable. It was only considered an object of description and the work of the devil."

67. Acosta, *Historia*, 236.

68. Ibid., 181.
69. Anthony Pagden, *The Fall of Natural Man: The American Indian and the Origins of Comparative Ethnology* (Cambridge: Cambridge University Press, 1982), 153. Indeed, the modern vision of religion began its strange career precisely at the birth of colonialism. This modern concept of religion is deployed often without being aware of its origins in the racial reasoning of Iberian conquest.
70. MacCormack, *Religion in the Andes*, 264.
71. MacCormack, "Demons, Imagination, and the Incas," 115.
72. Ibid., 114 (emphasis added).
73. Ibid., 115. Also see Lynn Sikkink and Braulio Choque M., "Landscape, Gender, and Community: Andean Mountain Stories," *Anthropological Quarterly*, 72:4 (October 1999): 167–82.
74. David L. Graizbord, *Souls in Dispute: Converso Identities in Iberia and the Jewish Diaspora, 1580–1700* (Philadelphia: University of Pennsylvania Press, 2004). Graizbord focuses on a time period a bit beyond Acosta, but the theological vision that is at work is precisely the one that shaped Acosta's understanding of Israel and Jewish converts.
75. MacCormack, *Religion in the Andes*, 265–66.
76. Kenneth Mills, *Idolatry and Its Enemies: Colonial Andean Religion and Extirpation, 1640–1750* (Princeton: Princeton University Press, 1997), 3–74.
77. MacCormack, "Demons, Imagination, and the Incas," 102–3.
78. Lewis Hanke, *All Mankind Is One: A Study of the Disputation Between Bartolomé de Las Casas and Juan Ginés de Sepúlveda in 1550 on the Intellectual and Religious Capacity of the American Indians* (DeKalb: Northern Illinois University Press, 1974).
79. Bartolomé de Las Casas, *In Defense of the Indians* (DeKalb: Northern Illinois University Press, 1992), 221–48.
80. MacCormack, "Demons, Imagination, and the Incas," 119.
81. Ibid., 120.
82. Todorov, *The Conquest of America*, 189.
83. Ibid., 189–90.
84. Ibid., 189.
85. Friedrich Schleiermacher, *On Religion: Speeches to Its Cultured Despisers*, trans. and ed. Richard Crouter (Cambridge: Cambridge University Press, 1996). Also see David E. Klemm, "Culture, Arts, and Religion," in *The Cambridge Companion to Friedrich Schleiermacher*, ed. Jacqueline Mariña (Cambridge: Cambridge University Press, 2005), 251–68.
86. MacCormack, *Religion in the Andes*, 266.
87. Daniel Castro, *Another Face of Empire: Bartolomé de Las Casas, Indigenous Rights, and Ecclesiastical Imperialism* (Durham: Duke University Press, 2007); Rivera, *A Violent Evangelism*, 180ff. Although Las Casas came to denounce black slavery and deeply regret his early comments that recommended black slavery in place of Indian forced servitude, he kept a black slave at least thirty years longer than an Indian slave; as Todorov notes, "Yet we know that in 1544 he still possessed a black slave (he had

released his Indians in 1514), and we still find expressions of this sort in his *History*: 'Surely the blindness of those people who first came here and treated the natives as if they were Africans was something to marvel at,'" *The Conquest of America*, 170.

88. Bernard McGrane, *Beyond Anthropology: Society and the Other* (New York: Columbia University Press, 1989). The demonic operation, once it was detected, revealed for Acosta the underlying cultural and social inferiorities that made demonic manipulation possible in the first place. This meant that objectively determined cultural inferiority was a theological invention rooted in the discernment of the possibilities of demonic manipulation. Acosta made use of the transparency he created. He could read through the religious practices to see the demonic and then read through the demonic to see their cultural weaknesses and inferiorities. At the same time, he could narrate Spanish superiority and presence in the New World as two realities of divine providence. With this operation, Acosta was performing the modern white theological gaze.

89. José de Acosta, *De Procuranda Indorum Salute: Pacificacion y Colonizacion*, ed. L. Pereña et al., 2 vols. (Madrid: Consejo Superior de Investigaciones Científicas [CSIC], 1984), 1:60.

90. Pagden, *The Fall of Natural Man*, 163.

91. José de Acosta, *De Procuranda Indorum Salute: Pacificacion y Colonizacion*, 60, 62.

92. McIntosh, *De Procuranda*, 1:5.

93. Ibid.

94. Ibid., 1:6.

95. Ibid.

96. Pierre Bourdieu, *The Logic of Practice* (Stanford: Stanford University Press, 1990), 53. Also see his *Outline of a Theory of Practice* (Cambridge: Cambridge University Press, 1977). David Swartz, *Culture and Power: The Sociology of Pierre Bourdieu* (Chicago: University of Chicago Press, 1997).

97. Rolena Adorno, "The Depiction of Self and Other in Colonial Peru," *Art Journal* 49:2, *Depictions of the Dispossessed* (Summer 1990): 110–18.

98. Acosta, *De Procuranda Indorum Salute: Pacificacion y Colonizacion*, 108.

99. Indeed, *De Procuranda* received papal approval for its publication only after some of its content was censored and edited out, content that was critical of how the Indians had been or were being treated. McIntosh, in his introduction to *De Procuranda* (13–15), notes the text written in Peru was censored in Spain in the following sections: chaps. 1, 4, 11, and 18 of book 2 and chap. 21 of book 6 were removed; chaps. 5, 7, 9, 11, and 17 of book 3 were greatly cut and edited. In those censored sections Acosta is critical of soldiers, *encomenderos*, *corregidores*, and especially priests for the murder, harsh treatment, exploitation, and horrible witness of Christianity that had been inflicted on the Indians. Take, for example, censored comments on the tribute demanded of the Indians. "Who could have watched a scene like that of a few days ago without feeling pain in one's heart nor fail to shed tears, for the sobbing and cries of these unhappy Indians? They grieved and wept bitterly over the fact that we had placed on them more severe tribute, while at the same time obliging them to work on forts and provide provisions for the directors and inspectors of works. These people forcibly stripped the

Indians of their lambs and even their old clothes and imposed upon them such bitter tribute that even the most hardened and inhuman spirits amongst us were moved by their state. We also observed how the leaders of their communities received thrashings and were beaten in public, with rods, in front of their own people. . . . Spaniards! Is this how you treat your servants? And, on top of that you have the gall to say they are not really servants at all! Is this what we call 'the easy yoke of Christ'"? (*De Procuranda,* III: 9). The extent to which Acosta saw, understood, and critiqued the oppressive behavior of the empire toward the native peoples is important but secondary to his reconfiguration of theology.

100. Swartz, *Culture and Power,* 108. Swartz, summarizing an aspect of the thought of Bourdieu, helps identify Acosta's intellectual performance here as manifestations of the "dispositions of habitus," which "represent *master patterns* of behavioral style that cut across cognitive, normative, and corporal dimensions of human action." These master patterns are "objectively 'regulated' and 'regular' without being in any way the product of obedience to rules," and they "may be accompanied by a strategic calculation tending to perform in a conscious mode." See Bourdieu, *The Logic of Practice,* 53.

101. Matt 28:19.

102. Michel Foucault, "Truth and Power," in *Power/Knowledge: Selected Interviews and Other Writings, 1972–1977* (New York: Pantheon, 1980), 109–33.

103. Joseph Rouse, "Power/Knowledge," in *The Cambridge Companion to Foucault,* ed. Gary Gutting (Cambridge: Cambridge University Press, 1994), 92–114.

104. Michel Foucault, "The Subject and Power," in *Essential Works of Foucault, 1954–1984,* vol. 3: *Power,* ed. James D. Faubion (New York: New Press, 1994), 326–48. Also see his *Technologies of the Self: A Seminar with Michel Foucault,* ed. Luther H. Martin et al. (Amherst: University of Massachusetts Press, 1988).

105. Foucault, "The Subject and Power," 333.

106. Ibid., 334.

107. Saint Anslem, *Monologion and Proslogion with Replies of Gaunilo and Anslem,* trans. Thomas Williams (Indianapolis: Hackett, 1996); Augustine, *Confessions,* trans. Garry Wills (New York: Penguin, 2006); Denys Turner, *The Darkness of God: Negativity in Christian Mysticism* (Cambridge: Cambridge University Press, 1998), 50ff.; Eleonore Stump and Norman Kretzmann, *The Cambridge Companion to Augustine* (Cambridge: Cambridge University Press, 2001), 171ff.; Carol Harrison, *Augustine: Christian Truth and Fractured Humanity* (Oxford: Oxford University Press, 2000); Karl Barth, *Anselm: Fides Quaerens Intellectum: Anselm's Proof of the Existence of God in the Context of His Theological Scheme* (London: SCM, 1960).

108. Michel Foucault, *Discipline and Punish: The Birth of the Prison* (New York: Vintage, 1977), 138.

109. Acosta, *De Procuranda Indorum Salute:* vol. 2, *Educación y Evangelización,* 108: "Apud barbaras fœminas pudor tam deest, ut nihil hac parte a pecude distent; imo vero cum pecudes pudore non superent, libidine superant. Quis igitur ex tanto incendio sospes exibit nisi quem gratia divina protexerit et quotidiana carnis mortificatio vallaverit?"

110. McIntosh, *De Procuranda*, 2:36.
111. Natural Law as applied to the Indians, as in the work of Francisco de Vitoria, *De Indis et De Ivre Belli Relectiones*, ed. Ernest Nys (Washington: Carnegie Institution of Washington, 1917).
112. Adrian Hastings, *The Church in Africa, 1450–1950* (Oxford: Clarendon, 1994), 74–75. The Church historian Adrian Hastings said of Iberian encounters and inter-actions with African societies, they (Iberian and African) shared a similar vision of the connection of landscape and the sacred. The same may be applied to other New World peoples. "There was a profound sense of divine participation in the landscape, whereby nature was invested with a kind of innate sensitivity to the sacred—a sort of animism, if one dare use the word, as much Iberian as African. The religious sensibili-ties, then, of sixteenth-century Iberians as much as of pagan Africans were absolutely pre-Enlightenment, and close cousins to one another. Africans would not be too con-scious of moving into a different intellectual world by going from one to the other. You were, at least at first, doing no more than embracing a new name and source of superior power, almost as a village in Spain embraced a new saint, a new relic from Rome."
113. Mignolo, *The Idea of Latin America*, 8.
114. Gustavo Gutiérrez, *A Theology of Liberation* (Maryknoll, N.Y.: Orbis, 1973). See Roberto S. Goizueta, "Gustavo Gutiérrez," in *The Blackwell Companion to Political Theology*, ed. Peter Scott and William Cavanaugh (Malden, Mass.: Blackwell, 2004), 288–301.

CHAPTER 3. COLENSO'S HEART

1. George W. Cox, *The Life of John William Colenso, D. D., Bishop of Natal*, 2 vols. (London: W. Ridgway, 1888); Jeff Guy, *The Heretic: A Study of the Life of John William Colenso, 1814–1883* (Pietermaritzburg: University of Natal Press, 1983); Wyn Rees, ed., *Colenso Letters from Natal* (Pietermaritzburg: Shuter and Shooter, 1958); Peter Hinchliff, *John William Colenso: Bishop of Natal* (London: Thomas Nelson, 1964).
2. Samuel Taylor Coleridge, *Aids to Reflection and the Confessions of an Inquiring Spirit* (London: George Bell, 1904), 120; hereafter cited as Coleridge, *Aids to Reflection and the Confessions of an Inquiring Spirit*.
3. Guy, *The Heretic*, 23.
4. Coleridge, *Aids to Reflection and the Confessions of an Inquiring Spirit*, 115–16.
5. F. D. Maurice, *Reconstructing Christian Ethics: Selected Writings*, ed. Ellen K. Wondra (Louisville: Westminister John Knox, 1995), xi. Also see J. N. Morris, *F. D. Maurice and the Crisis of Christian Authority* (Oxford: Oxford University Press, 2005), 46–53.
6. Morris, *F. D. Maurice and the Crisis of Christian Authority*, 169.
7. John Wright and Carolyn Hamilton, "Traditions and Transformations: The Phon-golo—Mzimkhulu Region in the Late Eighteenth and Early Nineteenth Centuries," in *Natal and Zululand from Earliest Times to 1910: A New History*, ed. Andrew Duminy and Bill Guest (Pietermaritzburg: University of Natal Press, 1989), 63; this

edited volume hereafter cited as *Natal and Zululand*. Carolyn Hamilton and John Wright note, "The penetration of external trade, once begun, can thus be seen as having set in motion a self-reinforcing process of political centralization and social stratification."

8. Julian Cobbing, "The Mfecane as Alibi: Thoughts on Dithakong and Mbolompo," *Journal of African History* 29:3 (1988): 487–519, esp. 492–98; Carolyn Anne Hamilton, "'The Character and Objects of Chaka': A Reconsideration of the Making of Shaka as 'Mfecane' Motor," *Journal of African History* 33:1 (1992): 37–63.

9. David Welsh, *The Roots of Segregation: Native Policy in Colonial Natal, 1845–1910* (Capetown: Oxford University Press, 1971), 31–42, 47–66.

10. John Wright, "Political Mythology and the Making of Natal's Mfecane," *Canadian Journal of African Studies/Revue Canadienne des Études Africaines* 23:2 (1989): 272–91, 273–280. Also see Warren R. Perry, *Landscape Transformations and the Archaeology of Impact: Social Disruption and State Formation in Southern Africa* (New York: Kluwer Academic/Plenum, 1999). Wright summarizes the seminal thesis of Cobbing, who questioned the so-called Mfecane theory according to which the Zulu kingdom was the central cause of upheaval in the region immediately prior to the arrival of Europeans. Other scholars have challenged some of Cobbing's findings. See J. B. Peires, "Paradigm Deleted: The Materialist Interpretation of the Mfecane," *Journal of Southern African Studies* 19:2 (June 1993): 295–313; Elizabeth A. Eldredge, "Sources of Conflict in Southern Africa, c. 1800–30: The 'Mfecane' Reconsidered," *Journal of African History* 33:1 (1992): 1–35; also see Carolyn Anne Hamilton, "The Character and Objects of Chaka," 37–63.

11. John Lambert, *Betrayed Trust: Africans and the State in Colonial Natal* (Scottsville, South Africa: University of Natal Press, 1995), 9–10.

12. Beverley Ellis, "The Impact of White Settlers on the Natural Environment of Natal, 1845–1870," in *Enterprise and Exploitation in a Victorian Colony: Aspects of the Economic and Social History of Colonial Natal*, ed. Bill Guest and John M. Sellers (Pietermaritzburg: University of Natal Press, 1985), 71–98. Also see Lambert, *Betrayed Trust*, 9–69.

13. Norman Etherington, *Preachers, Peasants, and Politics in Southeast Africa, 1835–1880: African Christian Communities in Natal, Pondoland and Zululand* (London: Royal Historical Society, 1978), 24–46; also see his "Christianity and African Society in Nineteenth-Century Natal," in *Natal and Zululand*, 275–301.

14. R. E. Gordon, *Shepstone: The Role of the Family in the History of South Africa, 1820–1900* (Cape Town: A. A. Balkema, 1968), 86.

15. Guy, *The Heretic*, 198.

16. Ibid., 42.

17. Ibid., 45.

18. Norman Etherington, "The 'Shepstone System' in the Colony of Natal and beyond the Borders," in *Natal and Zululand*, 171.

19. Ibid., 172.

20. Ibid., 174.

21. Ibid., 175. Etherington states, "Africans . . . paid for . . . the salaries of all government

officials, all the hospitals, all the gaols, all the grants to white schools, all the ammunition bought by the government, all the money spent on colonial defence, the postal services, roads, streets, bridges, and the Legislative Council which levied the taxes. In other words, while Africans suffered taxation without representation, white settlers enjoyed representation virtually without taxation."

22. John William Colenso, *Ten Weeks in Natal: A Journal of a First Tour of Visitation among the Colonists and Zulu Kafirs of Natal* (Cambridge, U.K.: Macmillan, 1855), 45.

23. Colenso, *Ten Weeks in Natal*, 45–46.

24. Vukile Khumalo, "The Class of 1856 and the Politics of Cultural Production(s) in the Emergence of Ekukhanyeni, 1855–1910," in *The Eye of the Storm: Bishop John William Colenso and the Crisis of Biblical Inspiration*, ed. Jonathan A. Draper (London: T & T Clark, 2003), 209–14, 222–23. Also see Vukile Khumalo, "Ekukhanyeni Letter-Writers: A Historical Inquiry into Epistolary Networks(s) and Political Imagination in Kwazulu-Natal, South Africa," in *Africa's Hidden Histories: Everyday Literacy and Making the Self*, ed. Karin Barber (Bloomington: Indiana University Press, 2006), 118–20.

25. Rees, ed., *Colenso Letters from Natal*, 39.

26. Colenso's son Francis recounts his father's efforts in learning isiZulu: "His mastery of the Zulu tongue was the reward of stubborn work, of sitting with natives who could not speak a word of English, day after day, from early morn till sunset, till they as well as [he] were fairly exhausted . . . and when they were gone still turning round again to [his] desk to copy out the results of the day." Qtd. in Patrick Kearney, "Success and Failure of 'Sokululeka': Bishop Colenso and African Education," in *The Eye of the Storm*, 202.

27. Guy, *The Heretic*, 66–67.

28. The biblical scholar Jonathan Draper, following the insight of Jean and John Comaroff, calls this "a liminal space." Jonathan A. Draper, "Hermeneutical Drama on the Colonial Stage: Liminal Space and Creativity in Colenso's Commentary on Romans," *Journal of Theology for Southern Africa* 103 (March 1999): 13–32, 15. Also see Jean and John Comaroff, *Of Revelation and Revolution: Christianity, Colonialism, and Consciousness in South Africa*, vol. 1 (Chicago: University of Chicago Press, 1991); *Of Revelation and Revolution: The Dialectics of Modernity on a South African Frontier*, vol. 2 (Chicago: University of Chicago Press, 1997).

29. Etherington, *Preachers, Peasants, and Politics*, 42.

30. Ibid., 115–79; Lambert, *Betrayed Trust*, 34–35. Also see Michael McKeon, *The Secret History of Domesticity: Public, Private, and the Division of Knowledge* (Baltimore: Johns Hopkins University Press, 2005), 3–48, 110–61.

31. *Three Native Accounts of the Visit of the Bishop of Natal in September and October, 1859, to Umpande, King of the Zulus*, ed. and trans. John William Colenso (Pietermaritzburg: Vause, Slatter, 1901). Also published in English in John William Colenso, *Bringing Forth Light: Five Tracts on Bishop Colenso's Zulu Mission*, ed. Ruth Edgecombe (Pietermaritzburg: University of Natal Press, 1982), 163–205.

32. Magema M. Fuze, *The Black People and Whence They Came: A Zulu View*, ed. A. T. Cope, trans. H. C. Lugg (Pietermaritzburg: University of Natal Press, 1979).

33. See Hinchliff, *John William Colenso*, 54ff. Also see Cox, *The Life of John William Colenso*, 1:212ff.

34. B. B. Burnett, *Anglicans in Natal* (Durban: Churchwardens, St. Paul's, 1953), 45–46; cited by Hinchliff, *John William Colenso*, 68.

35. John William Colenso, *St Paul's Epistle to the Romans: Newly Translated, and Explained from a Missionary Point of View* (New York: D. Appleton, 1863); hereafter cited as Colenso, *Romans*.

36. See note 4.

37. Andrew Walls, *The Missionary Movement: Studies in the Transmission of Faith* (Maryknoll, N.Y.: Orbis, 2000), 66. Walls states, "As systems, and ultimately the collective labels for systems which we call the world religions, have slipped into the place of ungodly people in the interpretation of Romans 1, so Christianity, also conceived as a system, has sometimes slipped into the place of the righteousness of God. The true system has been opposed to false systems condemned there. It has sometimes, but not always, been realized that 'Christianity' is a term formally identical with the other labels; that it certainly covers as wide a range of phenomena as most of them; that, if the principalities and powers work within human systems, they can and do work within this one. Man-in-Christianity lies under the wrath of God just as much, and for the same reasons, as Man-in-Hinduism."

38. John William Colenso, *Natal Sermons: A Series of Discourses Preached in the Cathedral Church of St. Peter's, Maritzburg*, 1 (London: N. Trübner, 1867), 39, qtd. in Guy, *The Heretic*, 169.

39. David Chidester, *Savage Systems: Colonialism and Comparative Religion in Southern Africa* (Charlottesville: University Press of Virginia, 1996), 18–20.

40. Ibid., 94.

41. Ibid., 124.

42. John Lambert notes that the nineteenth century saw the steady deterioration of life for Africans in Natal as they were constantly moved, through settler terrorism and administrative manipulation, from lands desired by white settlers. He states, "Even for those Africans who were able to recreate a semblance of homestead life on new land, the impact of their removal from land intimately associated with their past and with ancestral spirits would have involved a traumatic change in lifestyle, one to which it would have been difficult to adapt," *Betrayed Trust*, 177.

43. Jonathan Sheehan, *The Enlightenment Bible: Translation, Scholarship, Culture* (Princeton: Princeton University Press, 2005). I am endebted to my colleague Jay Kameron Carter for introducing me to this important text.

44. Ibid., xii.

45. Ibid., 4.

46. Ibid., 17.

47. Ibid., 18.

48. Ibid., 24.

49. Ibid., 85. In highlighting that distancing among Pietist translation-scholars of the eighteenth century, Sheehan exposes the irony at work in their endeavors: "By moving the Bible beyond the hegemony of theology, Pietists opened it up to the dispersive media of the Enlightenment."

50. Ibid., 91.
51. Ibid., 171–72, 217.
52. Ibid., 217.
53. Ibid., 249.
54. Ibid., 251–53; also see Guy, *The Heretic*, 101–3.
55. Sheehan, *The Enlightenment Bible*, 252–58.
56. Ibid., 252–53. Also see Raymond Williams, *Culture and Society, 1780–1950* (New York: Columbia University Press, 1958).
57. Franklin E. Court, *Institutionalizing English Literature: The Culture and Politics of Literary Study, 1750–1900* (Stanford: Stanford University Press, 1992), 78, qtd. in Sheehan, *The Enlightenment Bible*, 255.
58. Colenso, *Romans*, iii.
59. Ibid., iv.
60. Ibid.
61. Jonathan A. Draper, "Colenso's *Commentary on Romans*: An Exegetical Assessment," in *The Eye of the Storm*, 116–17.
62. Colenso, *Romans*, 15–16.
63. Ibid., 41.
64. Ibid., 33.
65. Ibid., 42–43. The following two quotations are also taken from these pages.
66. Ibid., 45. Draper's account of Colenso's vision of righteousness is instructive: "Colenso interpreted 'the righteousness of God' to refer not to the nature of God, nor to any act by which human beings make themselves righteous before God, not even the act of faith, but to the gift of righteousness which God gives to humans in his Son. . . . In his Zulu translation of Romans, Colenso was able to capture this understanding with the passive verbal form, *ukulungiswa okungoNkulunkulu* ('the being made right which is from God')," "Colenso's *Commentary on Romans*," 117.
67. Colenso, *Ten Weeks in Natal*, 253.
68. John William Colenso, "On the Efforts of Missionaries among Savages," *Journal of the Anthropological Society of London* 3 (1865): ccxlviii–cclxxxix, ccli.
69. Colenso, *Romans*, 50.
70. Draper, "Colenso's *Commentary on Romans*," 117.
71. Colenso, *Romans*, 56.
72. Ibid., 59.
73. Ibid., 113. Also cited in Draper, "Colenso's *Commentary on Romans*," 120.
74. Colenso, *Romans*, 117.
75. Ibid., 108.
76. Guy, *The Heretic*, 81.
77. Ibid., 82.
78. Colenso, *Romans*, 113.
79. Colenso, "On the Efforts of Missionaries among Savages," cclxvii–cclxviii, qtd. in Guy, *The Heretic*, 77.
80. I am not suggesting that Bishop Colenso or his rightly famous family members did not develop important relationships and attachments with African peoples. Indeed,

his family members are crucially important for understanding South Africa/Zulu history in colonialism. See Jeff Guy, *The View across the River: Harriette Colenso and the Zulu Struggle against Imperialism* (Charlottesville: University Press of Virginia, 2002); Frances Colenso, *My Chief and I, or, Six Months in Natal after the Langalibalele Outbreak; and, Five Years Later: A Sequel* (Pietermaritzburg: University of Natal Press, 1994).

81. Colenso once wrote quite movingly of having been able "to sit down, hour by hour, in closest friendly intercourse with natives of all classes, and in the spirit of earnest, patient research, with a full command of the native language, [to] have sought to enter, as it were, within the heart, and search for the secret characters of light, which may be written by God's own finger there." Qtd. in Guy, *The Heretic*, 77. Thus I am not denying the reality or at least the possible desired confraternity of Colenso with the native peoples, but this is a far cry from any vision of cultural submission and transformation. The strategies of colonial domestication were unrelenting and always present.

82. Qtd. in Hinchliff, *John William Colenso*, 115. Also see Robert Gray, *A Statement relating to facts which have been misunderstood and to questions which have been raised in connexion with the consecration, trial, and excommunication of the Right Rev. Dr. Colenso*, 2 vols. (London: Rivingtons, 1867).

83. Qtd. in Ronald B. Nicholson, "Other Times and Other Customs: A Storm in a Victorian Teacup?" in *The Eye of the Storm*, 173. Charges 1 through 4 reflect positions expressed in his Romans commentary. Charges 5 through 9 lack clear connection to Colenso's thought, and some scholars suggest that where in fact Colenso might have agreed with the general direction of these statements he would not have stated things so crudely. As some commentators have noted, the ideas expressed in charges 5 to 8 are closer to the positions of contemporary biblical scholars.

84. Colenso, *Romans*, 183.

85. Ibid. Colenso realized in such a situation that he could not in good conscience believe in the "everlasting torment after death, of all impenitent sinners and unbelievers, including the whole heathen world."

86. Guy quotes the famous assessment of Colenso by Owen Chadwick, who said Colenso "had no sense of history, no idea how to criticise documents, no wide reading, and no profundity of mind," *The Heretic*, 174.

87. John Willinsky, *Learning to Divide the World: Education at Empire's End* (Minneapolis: University of Minnesota Press, 1998), 58. In the face of native questions, Colenso unveiled an intellectual habit that marks theology from the colonialist moment, especially from the nineteenth century. Colenso turns indigenous voices into occasions for theological solipsism. Willinsky suggests that with colonialism "the world-as-picture becomes the educational privilege of the West, closely tied to its colonizing and civilizing mission."

88. Ibid., 78. "Travel, as a way of finding oneself through a greater knowledge of the other, brings us to perhaps the busiest of intersections between education and imperialism."

89. W. Winwood Reade, "Efforts of Missionaries among Savages," *Journal of the Anthropo-*

logical Society of London 3 (1865): clxiii–clxxxiii, clxv. Reade states, "In plain words, I found that every Christian negress was a prostitute, and that every Christian negro was a thief. The missionaries allow that no moral change in their parishioners is perceptible to the naked eye. But said one of them to me, you cannot measure the amount of moral influence which our teachings exercise. He was quite right. You cannot."

90. Colenso, "On the Efforts of Missionaries among Savages," cclxxix.

91. Ibid., cclxxx. His use of the letter was clearly also apologetically aimed at Bishop Gray's claims of the cancerous effects of his teachings. However, what is most important for us is the translating operation that is in effect in his performance before the Anthropological Society of London.

92. Qtd. in Guy, *The Heretic*, 101.

93. Matthew Arnold, "The Bishop and the Philosopher," in *Essays, Letters, and Reviews by Matthew Arnold,* ed. Fraser Neiman (Cambridge: Harvard University Press, 1960), 45–68; hereafter cited as Arnold, "The Bishop and the Philosopher," in *Essays.* Originally published in *Macmillan's Magazine* 7 (Jan. 1863): 241–56. Also see Jeff Guy, "Class, Imperialism and Literary Criticism: William Ngidi, John Colenso and Matthew Arnold," *Journal of Southern African Studies* 23:2 (June 1997): 219–41.

94. Guy, *The Heretic*, 188. Guy's comments here are very instructive. Colenso "was ridiculed, deprived and buried not because his book was *incompetent* but because it was *effective* . . . every attempt had to be made to discredit the author and the work. It is here, in the whole complex inter-relationship between ideas and power and privilege that Colenso's defeat as a biblical critic had to be located. It was not long before the Church of England came to accept that theories of literal interpretation and scriptural inerrancy could not be upheld. But of course it was 'the Church' that came to that conclusion; those who directed its thinking, not an individual colonial bishop with a mathematical training and eccentric views on the virtues of blacks."

95. Qtd. in Jeff Guy, "Class, Imperialism and Literary Criticism," 219, where he cites the newspaper *The Natal Witness,* 1863, as the source.

96. Arnold, "The Bishop and the Philosopher," in *Essays,* 63.

97. Terry Eagleton, *Criticism and Ideology: A Study in Marxist Literary Theory,* rev. ed. (London: Verso, 2006), 109.

98. Colenso, "On the Efforts of Missionaries among Savages," cclxvi.

99. A. F. Walls, "Review of 'The Heretic: A Study of the Life of John William Colenso 1814–1883,' by Jeff J. Guy," *Journal of Religion in Africa* 19:3 (October 1989): 282–85, 284. Andrew Walls, in following the general historical assessment of Colenso, unfortunately fails to see the wider colonialist operation displayed in Colenso's intellectual projects. As a result, he minimizes the ecclesial and political significance of Colenso's troubled biblical scholarship and his work as a translator. He states, "It is hard not to lament that the man with such command of Zulu language and such access to Zulu sources spent all that labour boning up on German and conducting a vendetta with the author of the Books of Chronicles. Yet Colenso's career as Biblical critic arose from his work as a Bible translator, and was launched by a Zulu, his co-translator William Ngidi. There is irony in this, for subsequent African Christianity has been very little exercised by Ngidi's type of question, and very little interested in Colenso's type of

scholarship or its results. Was he driven forward in his literary labours by the miniature colonial universe? Did he feel that as the public symbol of the Church he was personally responsible for everything to be said or done everywhere in the name of the Church?"

100. Qtd. in Gordon Mitchell, "A Moment in the 'Long Conversation' between African Religion and Imperial Christianity: William Ngidi and John Colenso," in *The Eye of the Storm*, 255–63, 260. This development is the beginning of the question of theological contextuality—the use or uselessness of theology to indigenous people in answering their questions. The question of theological contextuality is rooted in the ways in which the native, in this case the African, was made useful for European theological and political struggles. Utility begat utility. If we find in Colenso's translation of Ngidi's letter a parroting effect, it is equally a symptom of hegemony and a sign of the beginnings of segregated theological mentalities. If his relationship with William Ngidi was the occasion for Colenso to pursue his own theological interests, so too would it soon be the case for William Ngidi. Indeed, William Ngidi would later leave the mission, attempting to recite native cultural practices through a Colenso-like Christian vision. I am not suggesting that Ngidi's efforts mirror Colenso's white theological self-absorption. Rather, Ngidi performed an emergent contextual theology. These are two theological endeavors, separate but equal. My argument may seem to some counterintuitive, given Colenso's appreciation for some Zulu thought patterns, especially their names for God. Indeed, Colenso held out the possibility that someday African cultivation would signal a new level of interaction with the white race. As Colenso states, "We know not what may be the special work of the African. . . . Perhaps we may yet have to find that we 'without them cannot be made perfect'—that our nature will only exhibit all its high qualities when it has been thoroughly tried in the case of cultivated black races, as well as white. And surely with our own experience before us we cannot presume to assert that the human family will never be benefited by light reflected even from the thinkers of Zululand." However, Colenso registers the possibility of native positive effect on whites as a byproduct of a completed assimilation process.

101. Lamin Sanneh, *Translating the Message: The Missionary Impact on Culture* (Maryknoll, N.Y.: Orbis, 1989), 7; Lamin Sanneh, *Encountering the West: Christianity and the Global Cultural Process* (Maryknoll, N.Y.: Orbis, 1993); Lamin Sanneh, *Whose Religion Is Christianity? The Gospel beyond the West* (Grand Rapids: Eerdmans, 2003); Lamin Sanneh, *Religion and the Variety of Culture: A Study in Origin and Practice* (Valley Forge, Penn.: Trinity Press International, 1996). Not only does his work fly in the face of conventional colonial historiography, but also his thinking moves against the grain of the standard postcolonialist critiques of missionary involvement with colonialism.

102. In this regard, Sanneh and Walls share a very similar vision. Walls, *The Missionary Movement in Christian History*. Also see his *The Cross-Cultural Process in Christian History: Studies in the Transmission and Appropriation of Faith* (Maryknoll, N.Y.: Orbis, 2002).

103. Sanneh, *Translating the Message*, 9. Or, more precisely, his reading begins by placing

Israel itself within a historical dynamic, one which Sanneh sees as theological. The expansion of Christianity would mean that Jews would be relativized and Gentiles destigmatized "under the radical pluralist dispensation demanded by God's absolute sovereignty."

104. Ibid., 25.
105. Ibid., 28.
106. Ibid., 29.
107. Ibid.
108. Ibid.
109. Ibid., 31.
110. Ibid., 32.
111. Ibid., 105. Sanneh states that the practices, "the means and methods of mission," carried an inherent logic that potentially dislodged colonialist ideology. It is precisely this way of reading history that makes Sanneh a deeply transgressive historian. He often ignores the boundaries between history and theology, deploying theological rationales at the precise moments when conventional historiography would demand either immanent critique or local teleologies.
112. Ibid., 106.
113. Ibid., 202.
114. Marilyn Robinson Waldman, Olabiyi Babalola Yai, and Lamin Sanneh, "Translatability: A Discussion," *Journal of Religion in Africa* 22:2 (May 1992): 159–72, 165. Sanneh empowers his critics, Marilyn Waldman and Olabiyi Babalola Yai, who point out that Sanneh deemphasizes the intrinsic solidarity between Christianity and mission on the one hand and colonization and Westernization on the other hand.
115. Ibid., 169.
116. Ibid. Also see Lamin Sanneh, "'They Stooped to Conquer': Vernacular Translation and the Socio-Cultural Factor," *Research in African Literatures* 23:1, *The Language Question* (Spring 1992): 95–106. Sanneh does not sufficiently historicize the reality of unequal exchange in the history of missionary translation. Waldman and Babalola Yai also correctly capture the problems with Sanneh's undertheorized (and nonhistoricized) concept of cultural revitalization through vernacular translation. As Babalola Yai states, "Are we to believe that just because our cultures, which [Sanneh] characterizes as 'hitherto obscure cultural systems' (are) 'being thrust into the general stream of universal history', they are *ipso facto* thereby revitalized? Is it not also the case that Christianity circumscribed translation to religious discourse and discouraged the translation of other texts deemed profane, thereby introducing a religious versus profane cleavage which lacked significance in many African cultures?" Ibid., 167.
117. In some ways, Sanneh stands within a more mature postcolonialist position, one that theorizes the possibilities of resistance, creativity, and flourishing even in the midst of oppression.
118. Walls, *The Missionary Movement*, 27–28.
119. Ibid., 7.
120. Ibid., 47.
121. Ibid., 17–18.

122. Ibid., 44. The gospel, what he metaphorically calls the Jesus Act, like an act in a play on a stage, can only be heard through the linguistic medium familiar to us and under the conditions of multiple "sightlines," that is, multiple vantage points that are common to all human beings.

123. Ibid., 51. Discipleship of a nation or a people begins with this intercourse of Christ (mediated through missionary presence) with the thought patterns of a people. Not merely the thought patterns but also "the patterns of relationship within that nation, the way the society hangs together, the way decisions are made." Such a process of intercourse takes generations and finds its embodiment in a people's progeny.

124. Ibid., 47.

125. Indeed, what I said earlier of Sanneh, as a postcolonialist thinker, might also be said of Walls, albeit with a lighter valence. In this regard, it is ironic and yet telling that the *oeuvre* of Sanneh and Walls fails to attract its deserved attention. Postcolonialist and subaltern theorists continue to ignore Sanneh, while conventional theologians continue to ignore both Sanneh and Walls. For the former, Sanneh's work is too positive in its assessment of Christianity; for the latter, the work of both is too radical in its repositioning of theology itself. That being said, however, there are problems with their visions of translation that rightly give a variety of postcolonial theorists and theologians reason for pause.

126. Both authors are focused on language for an additional reason. They are very concerned about the alternative theological visions of Islam and Judaism, which allow less flexibility in translation and would be, in Sanneh's words, far more culturally diffusive and culturally centric. I appreciate this concern, but the particularity of Israel and Jesus requires a thicker, more complex vision of mediation than Sanneh and Walls allow.

127. Guy, *The Heretic*, 197.

128. Ibid., 202.

129. Ibid., 209.

130. Ibid., 242.

131. Ibid., 243.

132. Ibid., 275.

133. Ibid., 287, with quotations from Colenso's preface in C. Vijn, *Cetshwayo's Dutchman; Being the Private Journal of a White Trader in Zululand during the British Invasion,* ed. and trans. J. W. Colenso (London: Longmans, Green, 1880), xii.

134. Guy, *The Heretic*, 286.

135. Colenso, *Bringing Forth Light*, 193–94.

CHAPTER 4. EQUIANO'S WORDS

1. Vincent Carretta, *Equiano, the African: Biography of a Self-Made Man* (Athens: University of Georgia Press, 2005), 7ff. Paul E. Lovejoy, "Autobiography and Memory: Gustavus Vassa, alias Olaudah Equiano, the African," *Slavery and Abolition* 27:33 (December 2006): 317–47, 321ff. Whereas Lovejoy defends Equiano's claim to African birth, Carretta disputes it. See Vincent Carretta, "Response to Paul Lovejoy's

'Autobiography and Memory: Gustavus Vassa, Alias Olaudah Equiano, the African,'" *Slavery and Abolition* 28:1 (2007). Whether he was actually born in Africa or, as the literary scholar Carretta suggests, in South Carolina may be an important matter as we consider the effect of his narrative, but what is far more important for us at this moment is not where he was born, but when and where he lived.

2. Nick Hazlewood, *The Queen's Slave Trader: John Hawkyns, Elizabeth I, and the Trafficking in Human Souls* (New York: William Morrow, 2004), 68.

3. Cited in Hazlewood, *The Queen's Slave Trader*, 66.

4. Marcus Buford Rediker, *The Slave Ship: A Human History* (New York: Viking, 2007), 347ff. Also see Robin Blackburn, *The Making of New World Slavery: From the Baroque to the Modern, 1492–1800* (London: Verso, 1997), 383–98. Kenneth Morgan and Economic History Society, *Slavery, Atlantic Trade and the British Economy, 1660–1800*, New Studies in Economic and Social History (Cambridge: Cambridge University Press, 2000), 12–24.

5. Olaudah Equiano, *The Interesting Narrative and Other Writings*, ed. Vincent Carretta (New York: Penguin, 2003), 191.

6. Angelo Costanzo, *Surprizing Narrative: Olaudah Equiano and the Beginnings of Black Autobiography* (New York: Greenwood, 1987), 28.

7. Joseph Calder Miller, *Way of Death: Merchant Capitalism and the Angolan Slave Trade, 1730–1830* (Madison: University of Wisconsin Press, 1988), 48–49.

8. Miller, *Way of Death*, 47.

9. Ibid. As Joseph Miller notes, "Control over the 'means of production' in its highest human form brought deference rather than storehouses filled with spoiling fish or rotting grain."

10. Ibid., 50.

11. Ibid., 66. As Miller notes, one must recognize the spreading effect of Europe's system of exchange for what it was, an attempt to bind "Africans' dependents [to] Europeans' wares."

12. Ibid., 94–95.

13. Ibid., 57–60.

14. Ibid., 149.

15. Violence and death were their most tormenting companions. The Diaspora, the cosmopolitan, and the African international will come to signify a legacy of resourcefulness and a constellation of practices of resistance. Yet one must slow down enough in recollecting this tragic part of human history to remember the deeper theological tragedy of a Diaspora. That tragedy begins with the march itself.

16. Dietrich Bonhoeffer, *Creation and Fall: A Theological Exposition of Genesis 1–3* (Minneapolis: Fortress, 1997), 113. Translation of *Schöpfung Und Fall: Theologische Auslegung von Genesis 1–3* (Chr. Kaiser Verlag München, 1989). On the slave ship, humanity is delivered up to a false god who creates a false humanity. It all presents the *curvatus in se*, the human creature turned in on itself. Bonhoeffer speaks of the Fall most provocatively as the emergence of the *sicut deus*, the formation of the creature without limits, "humankind similar to God in knowing-out-of-its-own-self about good and evil . . . and acting-out-of-its-own-resources, in its aseity, in its being alone." Redi-

ker tells of a sailor who named the first two slaves gathered on his ship, a couple, Adam and Eve. Remaking indeed. Rediker, *Slave Ship*, 3.

17. Ibid., 57–58.

18. Ibid.

19. Emma Christopher, *Slave Ship Sailors and Their Captive Cargoes, 1730–1807* (New York: Cambridge University Press, 2006); Marcus Buford Rediker, *Between the Devil and the Deep Blue Sea: Merchant Seamen, Pirates, and the Anglo-American Maritime World, 1700–1750* (Cambridge: Cambridge University Press, 1987); Margaret S. Creighton and Lisa Norling, *Iron Men, Wooden Women: Gender and Seafaring in the Atlantic World, 1700–1920*, Gender Relations in the American Experience (Baltimore: Johns Hopkins University Press, 1996).

20. Rediker, *Slave Ship*, 261.

21. Ibid., 259; Christopher, *Slave Ship Sailors*, 91ff. The officers of the slave ship—the captain, chief mate, and surgeon—stood atop its social order. Under them were the sailors, workers of many tongues and from diverse peoples, all joined together for the sake of gaining money. Beaten, afflicted, but wage-earning, these men organized themselves against the abuses of the upper classes. They did this sometimes in open mutiny and at other times in protest at port, giving us the origin of the term *strike* for sailors who struck, or took down, the ship's sails. As Emma Christopher notes, the modern notion of freedom has sailor revolt and protest as one of its strong progenitors.

22. Ian Baucom, *Specters of the Atlantic: Finance Capital, Slavery, and the Philosophy of History* (Durham: Duke University Press, 2005), 24. Baucom writes of time as not passing but accumulating. Drawing on the wisdom of Walter Benjamin, and with a view toward Giovanni Arrighi's masterful book, *The Long Twentieth Century*, Baucom notes that "for Benjamin, time accumulates in things, even, or particularly, those commodified things whose commodification entails not only the assignation of an exchange value but the willed repudiation of the time stored within them." Baucom's paraphrasing of Benjamin's deeply theological insight helps one grasp the accumulation that is presented by the ecology of the slave ship. On the slave ship time repeats itself, not in an eternal cycle but in the inertia of social orders that drew human beings into either forced servitude or the enabling of forced servitude. This was, of course, no choice whatsoever.

23. I shall return to the idea of the accumulation of time marked by bodies when I consider Israel and Africa, black and Jewish bodies, in the final chapter, but at this point I want to point out the African body for its function in this operation. It is the reason for the many. While the many were for the enslavement of the one, I am not suggesting special or unique status for the suffering of the African slave. As I noted in chapter 1, the African establishes in her or his body the cohesiveness of a fallen social order. Beneath cosmopolitan possibilities lies tormented black flesh. This will be the pattern of the long centuries of the societies that contained and followed the life of the slave ship. Here is a tragically mocking election that exists inside Christianity's wider misappropriation of Israel's election—African slaves will be the people by whom many nations will shape their social orders and through whom many will grow rich and

powerful. This election (like Israel's election) will establish the hermeneutic horizon through which one can understand this recreation. But before I turn to the specifics of the recreation of the world inhabited by black slaves we must grasp the superficiality of the cosmopolitan as it comes to inhabit our consciousness from the advent of the Atlantic slave ship. The many, though financially enabled by the one, become sad improvisations of the one, the one enslaved multiplicity of African peoples. They are an unhappy though genuine diversity echoing a diverse population screaming in deepest anguish in the holds of slave ships. This superficial cosmopolitanism was the inevitable result of the market-driven relations born of the Atlantic slave market.

24. Rediker, *Slave Ship*, 276.
25. Ibid., 220. Captain John Newton understood enslavement as a process bathed in brutalization. He states, "A savageness of spirit, not easily conceived, infuses itself . . . into those who exercise power on board an African slave-ship, from the captain downwards. It is the spirit of the trade, which, like a pestilential air, is so generally infectious, that but few escape it."
26. Christopher, *Slave Ship Sailors*, 187. Christopher states, "Sailors hardly needed the authorization of their employment to mistreat their female captives. It was partly because of their captors' overtly masculine character that the slave women simply had different experiences of the transatlantic crossing than their male equivalents. Demarked by their gender from the start, they were commonly left unshackled because they were considered good-natured or docile, and because it left them more at the mercy of the crew. Many of the experiences were wholly female. They conceived children, had miscarriages, gave birth, and had their children taken from them. The rhythms of life continued aboard a slave ship, set surreally against the looming spectre of death."
27. William D. Piersen, "White Cannibals, Black Martyrs: Fear, Depression, and Religious Faith as Causes of Suicide among New Slaves," *Journal of Negro History* 62:2 (1977): 151.
28. Rediker, *Slave Ship*, 9. As Rediker notes, these tools indicated one of the three identities of a slave ship: it was a war machine (because of its cannons), a factory for the making of slaves, and a mobile prison.
29. Ibid., 260. Also see D. B. Chambers, "Ethnicity in the Diaspora: The Slave-Trade and the Creation of African Nations in the Americas," *Slavery and Abolition* 22:3 (2001).
30. Carretta, *Equiano, The African*, 37.
31. Ibid., 45.
32. Ibid., 185.
33. Surely captains and crews had a sense of the evil of the slave ship itself and of the trade. It could be argued that the very fact that they "sensed its evil" even as they swallowed it testifies to the human knowing, the moral sense, to ethical conscience. Yet this is exactly the point of human failure, to claim to know and yet be unable to do the good is, as the apostle Paul tells us, humanity in sin (Rom 7:13–20). Equally important, this inability reaches into human misperceptions and constructions of good and evil. The power, born of slavery, of white judgment over black bodies endured because it existed within a theological register. White judgment over black behavior yet endures because

it draws its life from potent discursive fragments produced at the intersection of moral discourse, the market, and the prison. This was enabled by the slave ship.

34. Houston A. Baker, *Blues, Ideology, and Afro-American Literature: A Vernacular Theory* (Chicago: University of Chicago Press, 1984), 37. Baker notes that this narrative gives one an "ironically mercantile ascent by the propertied self from the hell of 'commercial deportation.'" It offers a graphic 're-invention' of the social grounding of the Afro-American symbolic act par excellence." It shows us the Black Atlantic origins in a slave economics "that *must be mastered* before liberation can be achieved." Baker captured the limited situation within which Equiano had to argue for his freedom.

35. Wilfred D. Samuels, "Disguised Voice in the Interesting Narrative of Olaudah Equiano, or Gustavus Vassa, the African," *Black American Literature Forum* 19:2 (1985). Also see Katalin Orban, "Dominant and Submerged Discourses in the Life of Olaudah Equiano (or Gustavus Vassa?)," *African American Review* 27:4 (1993). Samantha Manchester Earley, "Writing from the Center or the Margins? Olaudah Equiano's Writing Life Reassessed," *African Studies Review* 46:3 (2003). Wilfred D. Samuels envisions Equiano's literary performance as a series of disguises formed to walk the tightrope of racist assumptions constructed with the racial identities of his white readership and meant to address abolitionist needs. Samuels is certainly on fertile ground in drawing attention to the powerful role of white readers in the literary process, its commodification, production, and assessment. But Equiano lives in the self he creates. He seeks to inhabit the world he suggests. This is a matter not only of desire but also of constraint. His self-narration, tied as it was to his self-promotion, subjected him to new levels of surveillance and contest of his words. Such a situation required him to live what he said under the constraints of slave society. I could at this moment, following Samuels, draw a distinction between the author and the person, between Equiano writing for a white readership and the man *in concreto* and thereby suggest his strategic deployment of such ideas as friendship, joy, and happiness for the benefit of his readers. However, such a distinction is not helpful. This is the one Equiano trying to make sense of his world as a Christian. But he is working at a significant disadvantage.

36. Baker, *Blues, Ideology, and Afro-American Literature*, 35.

37. I must refer imprecisely to "Equiano's people" because with him we arrive at the racial generic—African, black. When his words enter the remade world, they are made to signify for all black flesh.

38. With the exception of Anton Wilhelm Amo's *De jure Maurorum in Europa*, which is now lost, most of these texts are now widely available in various anthologies and in republished editions. See J. E. J. Capitein and Grant Richard Parker, *The Agony of Asar: A Thesis on Slavery by the Former Slave Jacobus Elisa Johannes Capitein, 1717–1747* (Princeton: Markus Wiener, 2001). J. E. J. Capitein, *Dissertatio Politico-Theologica De Servitute Libertati Christianae Non Contraria* (Lugduni Batavorum: Apud S. Luchtmans, 1742), microform.

39. William L. Andrews, *To Tell a Free Story: The First Century of Afro-American Autobiography, 1760–1865* (Urbana: University of Illinois Press, 1986), 46–47.

40. Carretta, *Equiano, The African*, 294.

41. This is why hermeneutic strategies that focus on gestures of resistance or assimilation in his narrative miss the deeply human and deeply Christian character of the work.

42. Giovanni Arrighi, *The Long Twentieth Century: Money, Power, and the Origins of Our Times* (London: Verso, 1994), 51.

43. "Europe's rise was substantially assisted by what it learned from other, more advanced cultures—at least until Europe overtook and subdued them." Janet L. Abu-Lughod, *The World System in the Thirteenth Century: Dead-End or Precursor?* (Washington: American Historical Association, 1993). Also see Janet L. Abu-Lughod, *Before European Hegemony: The World System A.D. 1250–1350* (New York: Oxford University Press, 1989).

44. Morgan and Economic History Society, *Slavery, Atlantic Trade and the British Economy, 1660–1800,* 13. Also see Herbert S. Klein, *The Atlantic Slave Trade,* New Approaches to the Americas (Cambridge: Cambridge University Press, 1999). Blackburn, *The Making of New World Slavery,* 219ff.

45. Immanuel Kant, *Kant: Political Writings,* Cambridge Texts in the History of Political Thought (Cambridge: Cambridge University Press, 1991), 41–53. Also see Gillian Brock and Harry Brighouse, *The Political Philosophy of Cosmopolitanism* (Cambridge: Cambridge University Press, 2005).

46. Tzvetan Todorov, *On Human Diversity: Nationalism, Racism, and Exoticism in French Thought* (Cambridge: Harvard University Press, 1993), 90ff. Racial formation comes to life between these global processes of consumption and production. Between these twin processes, everything was brought within new comprehensive practices of accumulation.

47. Elizabeth Jane Wall Hinds, "The Spirit of Trade: Olaudah Equiano's Conversion, Legalism, and the Merchant's Life," *African American Review* 32:4 (1998): 635. Also see Geraldine Murphy, "Olaudah Equiano, Accidental Tourist," *Eighteenth-Century Studies* 27:4 (1994). Equiano was in a very real sense formed on a slave ship and all that the ship signified—slavery, commerce, and individualism. As Elizabeth Jane Wall Hinds notes, Equiano's narrated self is decisively capitalist: "[Equiano's narrative] demonstrates one extreme of Enlightenment individualism constructed by an expanding capitalist marketplace in the last half of the eighteenth century. As a merchant, Equiano enters imaginatively into a public, free-market 'structure of feeling,' a marketplace and legalistic psychology through which the individual becomes an actor in a public spectacle of exchange relations, and consequently exchanges individual subjectivity for a perceived market object status designed to ensure success." His narrative reveals what she calls "a fourfold self" consisting of "a slave, a merchant, a juridical subject and a [Christian] convert" (636). For Hinds, Equiano is captured by the "commercial paradox he inhabited while still a slave. The ironic slave-and-merchant matrix of Equiano's identity is not resolved by his conversion but reproduces the split subjectivity he has inhabited all along" (639). Hinds has persuasively shown the deep interpenetration of merchant and Christian sensibilities in Equiano; however, they do not present a duality; rather, they indicate the Christian enfolded inside the merchant or, more precisely, Christian relations constituted within the economic circuit.

48. Carretta, *Equiano, The African,* 270.

49. Ibid., 277.
50. Joseph Fichtelberg, "Word between Worlds: The Economy of Equiano's Narrative," *American Literary History* 5:3 (1993): 460. Fichtelberg captures this dilemma when he states, "Has Equiano somehow distanced himself from the motives that produced enslavement, or has he simply found new footing on old ground? Is it possible to disown one's governing discourse? To ask the question in this manner is to make more acute the conflict between the narrator's desire for freedom and the discourse that produced him—to make this text a paradigm not only of African-American textuality but of all writing as it struggles within and against ideology."
51. Carretta, *Equiano, The African*, 302.
52. Ibid., 290ff.
53. W. Jeffrey Bolster, "An Inner Diaspora: Black Sailors Making Selves," in Ronald Hoffman et al., *Through a Glass Darkly: Reflections on Personal Identity in Early America* (Chapel Hill: University of North Carolina Press, 1997), 419–48.
54. Cited in Carretta, *Equiano, The African*, 319.
55. Benjamin Braude, "The Sons of Noah and the Construction of Ethnic and Geographic Identities in the Medieval and Early Modern Periods," *William and Mary Quarterly* 54:1 (Jan. 1997): 103–42.
56. Cited in the critical edition of Olaudah Equiano and Werner Sollors, *The Interesting Narrative of the Life of Olaudah Equiano, or Gustavus Vassa, the African* (New York: Norton, 2001), 297.
57. Carolus Linnaeus and Johann Friedrich Gmelin, *Systema Naturae Per Regni Tria Naturae, Secundum Classes, Ordines, Genera, Species, Cum Characteribus, Differentiis, Synonymis, Locis*, Ed. XIII, aucta, reformata / ed. (Lugduni: apud J.B. Delamollière, 1789). Johann Friedrich Blumenbach et al., *On the Natural Varieties of Mankind/De Generis Humani Varietate Nativa* (New York: Bergman Publishers, 1969). Johann Friedrich Blumenbach et al., *The Anthropological Treatises of Johann Friedrich Blumenbach* (London: Longman, Green, Roberts, Green, 1865).
58. Cited in the critical edition of *The Interesting Narrative*, ed. Werner Sollors, 297.
59. Ibid., 296–97.
60. Dietrich Bonhoeffer and Manfred Weber, *Meditations on the Cross* (Louisville: Westminster John Knox, 1998), 11–12. As Bonhoeffer notes, "Jesus . . . is the Christ who is rejected in suffering. Rejection robs suffering of any dignity or honor. It is to be suffering void of honor. Suffering and rejection are the summary expressions of Jesus' cross. Death on the cross means to suffer and to die as someone rejected and expelled." It is an established fact that the slaves identified with the suffering Christ. Equiano's narrative offers one of the historic groundings of this identification. This identification with Jesus' suffering and death is not to the exclusion of his life. It is precisely the vicissitudes of Christ's life, specifically his calling to his people and his rejection, that background Equiano's identification. Here the vicissitudes of rejection are both past and present.
61. Potkay, Costanzo, and Aravamudan all note that Equiano's reading strategies echoed ancient church practices of spiritual interpretation. Adam Potkay, "History, Oratory, and God in Equiano's Interesting Narrative," *Eighteenth-Century Studies* 34:4 (2001);

Srinivas Aravamudan, *Tropicopolitans: Colonialism and Agency, 1688–1804* (Durham: Duke University Press, 1999), 233–88; Srinivas Aravamudan, "Equiano Lite," *Eighteenth-Century Studies* 34:4 (2001): 616. Also see Roxann Wheeler, "Domesticating Equiano's Interesting Narrative," *Eighteenth-Century Studies* 34:4 (2001). Adam Potkay, "Olaudah Equiano and the Art of Spiritual Autobiography," *Eighteenth-Century Studies* 27:4 (1994). Potkay wants the religious to play an organizing role in Equiano interpretation. Potkay also wants Equiano read within Christendom, that is, within a tradition of social influence in the construction of Western civilization and its literature. In this way of reading, Equiano becomes another voice affirming the decisive role of Christianity in the canon formation of central Western texts. Potkay's concern over reading Equiano within Christianity's siring of a Western literary canon leads him to dismiss as wrongheaded a postcolonial reading of this historic figure. Potkay may be justified in reading Equiano within Western Christendom as one of its literary reflexive expressions, but such a reading or such a recommended reading engenders judgments of superficiality. And those judgments are justified. Thus Srinivas Aravamudan finds Potkay's recommendations on reading Equiano shortsighted and deadening. For his part, Aravamudan does recognize the importance of Equiano's Christianity, but he, like several other postcolonial literary theorists, contends that "religious salvation is not the be-all and end-all for [Equiano's narrative]" (616). Aravamudan is correct to see in Potkay's recommended reading "a recipe for ideological evacuation" (617). However, neither Potkay nor Aravamudan can offer a sense of the tangled Christian imagination at work, forming its world in the torturous situation of a remade world. The deeper theological tragedy that attends Equiano's narrative is beyond the purview of either scholar.

62. A richer analysis of Equiano's scriptural reading strategy is beyond the scope of this chapter; however, suffice it to say that much more is going on here than deployment of practices of ancient church spiritual exegesis. Costanzo, Potkay, and Aravamudan quite correctly identify the family resemblance and even the genetic coding in Equiano. But his use of Scripture enacts a far more comprehensive scriptural vision than they account for. See Allen Dwight Callahan, *The Talking Book: African Americans and the Bible* (New Haven: Yale University Press, 2006). Also see Henri de Lubac, *Medieval Exegesis*, 2 vols. (Grand Rapids: Eerdmans; Edinburgh: T & T Clark, 1998).

63. It is beyond my purview to consider the history of soteriological discourse in relation to the rise of Protestantism and the rise of New World chattel slavery. My point here is simply one of conceptual reorientation—the language of salvation in evangelical piety, as was the case for other ecclesial idioms that spoke of salvation during Equiano's day, was being brought into the orbit of the production of slaves. The civilizing processes of New World peoples occupied Christian social imagination.

64. One could consider this the incipient individualism that began to reshape soteriological vision in eighteenth- and nineteenth-century Protestant churches. But it is not my concern at this juncture to consider the problems or promise of the repositioning of soteriology around the individual. My concern about hyperlocalization is focused on neither the problem of individualism in Christian modernity nor particular doctrinal developments in the articulation of an *ordo salutis*, that is, the order of salvation. In-

stead, I draw attention to Equiano's spiritual quest as performing a surrogacy for the absence of a material display of Christian belonging.

65. Clifton H. Johnson, *God Struck Me Dead: Voices of Ex-Slaves* (Cleveland: Pilgrim, 1993).

66. Carretta notes, "From the fifth edition of his narrative on he mentions his marriage in April 1792 to the white Englishwoman Susanna Cullen to demonstrate that the story of his own life anticipates on the personal level the bicultural union he calls for between nations," *Equiano, The African*, 329.

67. Equiano, in an open letter printed in *The Gentlemen*, responded to the notorious racist James Tobin, who in print played on white fears of miscegenation. Equiano suggested that instead of the concealed practice of rape and immoral interracial sexual relations, interracial marriages ought to be encouraged: "[Moses] established marriage with strangers by his own example—The Lord confirmed them—and punished Aaron and Miriam for vexing their brother for marrying the Ethiopian—Away then with your narrow impolitic notion of preventing by law what will be a national honour, national strength, and productive of national virtue—Intermarriages!" "Gustavus Vassa: Letter to James Tobin," reprinted in *The Interesting Narrative*, ed. Werner Sollors, 199. Also see Carretta, *Equiano, The African*, 258–59.

CHAPTER 5. WHITE SPACE AND LITERACY

1. Vincent Carretta, *Equiano, the African: Biography of a Self-Made Man* (Athens: University of Georgia Press, 2005), 328. Equiano described himself as "almost an Englishman" in Olaudah Equiano, *The Interesting Narrative of the Life of Olaudah Equiano, or Gustavus Vassa, the African: Written by Himself*, vol. 1 (London: T. Wilkins, 1789), 132.

2. Carretta, *Equiano, the African*, 320–21. Carretta suggests that Equiano's sense of his higher social standing could have been tied to his claimed elevated African lineage. This meant that his natural higher status was equivalent to being a gentleman in England.

3. William L. Andrews, *To Tell a Free Story, the First Century of Afro-American Autobiography, 1769–1865* (Urbana: University of Illinois Press, 1986), 60.

4. Adrian Hastings, *The Construction of Nationhood: Ethnicity, Religion, and Nationalism* (New York: Cambridge University Press, 1997), 12.

5. Ibid.

6. Paul J. Griffiths, *Religious Reading: The Place of Reading in the Practice of Religion* (New York: Oxford University Press, 1999).

7. Ibid., 68. Griffiths has in mind more than simply the Bible in his account of religious reading; he understands these elements as positive aspects necessary for the reversal of modern consumerist reading strategies. Consumerist reading strategies are ways of reading that build on a flight from authority and toward moral autonomy in which the individual constructs his or her own moral and religious vision piecemeal. I appreciate Griffiths's concern and his deployment of a MacIntyrian program to reintroduce religious reading into the modern scholarly universe; however, his account of religious

readings must be read against the Iberian theological universe as it formed in its colonialist sites. It is precisely those sites that display piety and erudition in reading biblical texts encased in imperialist form. This is the missing narrative in the rise of biblical exploration from the colonialist moment forward.

8. Hastings, *The Construction of Nationhood*, 24.

9. Isaac Watts and Calvin College. Christian Classics Ethereal Library. "The Psalms and Hymns of Isaac Watts with All the Additional Hymns and Complete Indexes," http://www.ccel.org/ccel/watts/psalmshymns.html. Hereafter cited as Watts, *The Psalms and Hymns of Isaac Watts,*

10. Arthur Paul Davis, *Isaac Watts: His Life and Works* (London: Independent, 1948), 199.

11. Ibid.

12. Watts, *The Psalms and Hymns of Isaac Watts*, 88.

13. Ibid.

14. Ibid., 109–10.

15. Ibid., 110.

16. Ibid., 133 (square brackets in original).

17. John M. Hull, "From Experiential Educator to Nationalist Theologian: The Hymns of Isaac Watts," *Panorama: International Journal of Comparative Religious Education and Values* 14:1 (Summer 2002): 97–98. Hull suggests that Watts's inserted middle sections (noted by the brackets) regarding tribute and India's gold alluded to the increasingly lucrative Indian imports. There is no doubt that Britain's increased economic growth serves as one subtext for Watts's imaginative psalms.

18. Watts, *The Psalms and Hymns of Isaac Watts*, 133.

19. Ibid., 121–22.

20. Ibid., 280–81, omitting verses 3–4.

21. Hastings, *The Construction of Nationhood*, 24.

22. Ibid., 53–54.

23. Ibid., 24.

24. John Brinckerhoff Jackson, *A Sense of Place, a Sense of Time* (New Haven: Yale University Press, 1994), 65.

25. Barbara E. Mundy, *The Mapping of New Spain: Indigenous Cartography and the Maps of the Relaciones Geográficas* (Chicago: University of Chicago Press, 2000), 17.

26. Ibid., 15.

27. Ibid., 16.

28. Ibid., 25–27.

29. Walter D. Mignolo, *The Darker Side of the Renaissance: Literacy, Territoriality, and Colonization* (Ann Arbor: University of Michigan Press, 1995), 281ff. Also see Ricardo Padron, *The Spacious Word: Cartography, Literature, and Empire in Early Modern Spain* (Chicago: University of Chicago Press, 2004)

30. Benedict Anderson, *Imagined Communities: Reflections on the Origin and Spread of Nationalism* (London: Verso, 1999), 15–16.

31. Pascale Casanova, *The World Republic of Letters* (Cambridge: Harvard University

Press, 2004), 48. The expression "linguistic servitude" is quoted from Marc Fumaroli, "The Genius of the French Language," in *Realms of Memory*, ed. Lawrence D. Kritzman, trans. Arthur Goldhammer, 3 vols. (New York: Columbia University Press, 1998), 3:558. Casanova writes in her account of the development of literary space, "Latin exercised almost complete control over existing intellectual resources and thus imposed . . . a genuine 'linguistic servitude.'"

32. Casanova, *The World Republic of Letters*, 48.

33. Ibid., 49. Casanova might be overstating the case in claiming that "European humanism . . . represents an early instance of the emancipation of the literate world from the control and domination of the church." What is certainly the case and more central to my concern is that humanism, with the facilitation of the church, helped to constitute "emerging intellectual spaces" centered around other vernaculars, first with the Tuscan dialect and then with French.

34. Jonathan Sheehan, *The Enlightenment Bible: Translation, Scholarship, Culture* (Princeton: Princeton University Press, 2005), 14ff.

35. Anderson, *Imagined Communities*, 38.

36. Ibid., 39–40.

37. The important yet relative independence of this history of vernacularization from the formation of the literary world is noted not only by Anderson but also in the work of Anthony D. Smith, *Chosen Peoples* (Oxford: Oxford University Press, 2003); Anthony D. Smith, *Myths and Memories of the Nation* (Oxford: Oxford University Press, 1999).

38. Anderson, *Imagined Communities*, 5–6.

39. Ibid., 33.

40. Ibid., 26.

41. Casanova, *The World Republic of Letters*, 54.

42. Ibid., 60–61.

43. Ibid., 61.

44. Ibid., 67–68.

45. Ibid., 64.

46. Jackson, *A Sense of Place, a Sense of Time*, 3–4.

47. Qtd. in Andro Linklater, *Measuring America: How an Untamed Wilderness Shaped the United States and Fulfilled the Promise of Democracy* (New York: Walker, 2002), 44.

48. Ibid., 174.

49. Ibid., 175. Also see the classic study by Payson J. Treat, *The National Land System, 1785–1820* (New York: E. B. Treat, 1910). Also crucial is the magisterial work by C. Albert White, *A History of the Rectangular Survey System* (Washington: U.S. Department of the Interior, 1983).

50. Governor Robert H. Morris of Pennsylvania, as quoted in Earl S. Pomeroy, *The Territories and the United States, 1861–1890* (Philadelphia: University of Philadelphia Press, 1947; reprint, Seattle: University of Washington Press, 1969), 95; qtd. in Donald William Meinig, *The Shaping of America*. Vol. 1: *Atlantic America, 1492–1800* (New Haven: Yale University Press, 1986), 393.

51. White, *A History of the Rectangular Survey System,* includes an inscription on a stone marker in East Liverpool, Ohio, marking the beginning of the grid (rectangular survey) system, that states, "1112 feet south of this spot was the 'point of beginning' for surveying the public lands of the United States. There, on September 30, 1785, Thomas Hutchins, first Geographer of the United States, began the Geographer's Line of the Seven Ranges," ii. Also, see Linklater, *Measuring America,* 1–6.

52. Casanova, *The World Republic of Letters,* 68. Casanova states, "French came to be generally established, without the assistance or cooperation of any political authority, as a common language—the language of cultivated and refined conversation, exercising a sort of jurisdiction that extended to all of Europe. Its cosmopolitan character is evidence of the curious 'denationalization' of French, whose dominance, never recognized as national, was accepted instead as international. . . . [French was] the vehicle of a symbolic supremacy whose ramifications were long to be felt, never more plainly than at the moment when Paris emerged as the universal capital of literature and began to administer its 'government' . . . over the entire world," 68.

53. One could speculate on a connection through Thomas Jefferson. It was Jefferson who came up with the idea of a grid system of rectangles with specific measurements for dividing the New World called the United States. And it was Jefferson who reported for envoy duty in France immediately after serving on the committee through which his ideas were articulated. In France he found congenial intellectual partners, most notably Marie-Jean Antoine Nicolas de Caritat, the Marquis de Condorcet, famed mathematician, philosopher, and influential advocate of the French Enlightenment. In Jefferson, Condorcet found an intellectual soulmate and friend who, like him, believed that a new uniform system of measurement for space, for property, could be found and based on science, which would remove all injustice and embody the highest ideas of the Enlightenment. Condorcet, who was at the time of Jefferson's five-year sojourn in France the secretary of the Académie royale des Sciences, shared Jefferson's democratic thinking about private property and the scientific approach to the measurement of space; he also believed in the universal applicability of the French ideas of humanity, justice, reason, and equality.

54. Casanova, *The World Republic of Letters,* 72.

55. Linklater, *Measuring America,* 102.

56. Casanova, *The World Republic of Letters,* 88.

57. Ibid., 89.

58. Johann Gottfried von Herder and Ioannis D. Evrigenis, *Another Philosophy of History and Selected Political Writings* (Indianapolis: Hackett, 2004), 29. Also see John H. Zammito, *Kant, Herder, and the Birth of Anthropology* (Chicago: University of Chicago Press, 2002).

59. Casanova, *The World Republic of Letters,* 76–77.

60. Anthony D. Smith, *Chosen Peoples,* 131–65.

61. Casanova, *The World Republic of Letters,* 133.

62. Ibid., 179.

63. Ibid., 256. That dependence, Casanova notes, may be political, which is both linguistic and literary, or linguistic, which is primarily literary, or only literary. What leads to visi-

bility and literary existence is in some way entering *littérisation*, which is "any operation—translation, self-translation, transcription, direct composition in the dominant language—by means of which a text from a literarily deprived country comes to be regarded as literary by the legitimate authorities," 136.

64. Ngũgĩ wa Thiong'o, *Decolonising the Mind: The Politics of Language in African Literature* (London: James Currey, 1986), 11.

65. Frantz Fanon, *Black Skin, White Masks*, trans. Charles Lam Markmann (New York: Grove, 1967), 20–21.

66. Ibid., 20.

67. Casanova, *The World Republic of Letters*, 154. Casanova captures this revised universalism when she states, "The notion of universality is one of the most diabolical inventions of the [literary] center, for in denying the antagonistic and hierarchical structure of the world, and proclaiming the equality of all the citizens of the republic of letters, the monopolists of universality command others to submit to their law. Universality is what they—and they alone—declare to be acceptable and accessible to all."

68. Anderson, *Imagined Communities*, 6.

69. Ibid., 134.

70. Qtd. in Heather Andrea Williams, *Self-Taught: African American Education in Slavery and Freedom* (Chapel Hill: University of North Carolina Press, 2005), 207.

71. Cited in ibid., 206.

72. Stephanie McCurry, *Masters of Small Worlds: Yeoman Households, Gender Relations, and the Political Culture of the Antebellum South Carolina Low Country* (New York: Oxford University Press, 1995), 6.

73. Ibid., 9.

74. See my essay "Speaking in Tongues: Language, Nationalism, and the Formation of Church Life," in *On Being Christian—and Human: Essays in Celebration of Ray S. Anderson*, ed. Daniel J. Price et al. (Eugene: Wipf and Stock, 2002).

75. McCurry, *Masters of Small Worlds*, 13.

76. Ibid., 11.

77. Elizabeth Fox-Genovese, *Within the Plantation Household: Black and White Women of the Old South* (Chapel Hill: University of North Carolina Press, 1988), 64. Elizabeth Fox-Genovese noted, "Southerners participated in the unfolding bourgeois culture, including the ideologies of spheres, motherhood, and domesticity, but they interpreted and applied those ideologies according to their own social and gender relations." The sphere at issue here was the sphere of male sovereignty over his land and all the bodies upon it. Also see Elizabeth Fox-Genovese and Eugene D. Genovese, *The Mind of the Master Class: History and Faith in the Southern Slaveholders' Worldview* (Cambridge: Cambridge University Press, 2005).

78. Williams, *Self-Taught*, 13.

79. Pierre Bourdieu, *Outline of a Theory of Practice* (Cambridge: Cambridge University Press, 1977), 164. This vision of the accurate order of things is what Pierre Bourdieu called the *doxa*. The doxic mode is the unarticulated perception of what is believed to be the natural world created by the arbitrary actions of actors and structures within a given social order. He states, "Every established order tends to produce . . . the natural-

ization of its own arbitrariness. Of all the mechanisms tending to produce this effect, the most important and the best concealed is undoubtedly the dialectic of the objective chances and the agents' aspirations, out of which arises the *sense of limits*, commonly called the *sense of reality*, i.e., the correspondence between the objective classes and the internalized classes, social structures and mental structures, which is the basis of the most ineradicable adherence to the established order."

80. "Appendix: The Text of *The Confessions of Nat Turner: As Reported by* Thomas R. Gray (1831)," in *William Styron's Nat Turner: Ten Black Writers Respond*, ed. John Henrik Clarke (Boston: Beacon, 1968), 102. Also see Gayraud S. Wilmore, *Black Religion and Black Radicalism: An Interpretation of the Religious History of Afro-American People* (Maryknoll, N.Y.: Orbis, 1983), 64–65.

81. Janet Duitsman Cornelius, *When I Can Read My Title Clear: Literacy, Slavery, and Religion in the Antebellum South* (South Carolina: University of South Carolina Press, 1991), 40–41.

82. Taken from *A Catechism of Scripture Doctrine and Practice, for Families and Sabbath Schools, Designed also for the Oral Instruction of Colored Persons*, cited in Donald G. Mathews, "Charles Colcock Jones and the Southern Evangelical Crusade to Form a Biracial Community," *Journal of Southern History* 41 (August 1975): 311.

83. Cited in Riggins R. Earl Jr., *Dark Symbols, Obscure Signs: God, Self and Community in the Slave Mind* (Maryknoll, N.Y.: Orbis, 1993), 41; cf. Forrest G. Wood, *The Arrogance of Faith: Christianity and Race in America from the Colonial Era to the Twentieth Century* (Boston: Northeastern University Press, 1990), 39–83.

84. Wood, *The Arrogance of Faith*, 72.

85. Donald G. Mathews, "Charles Colcock Jones." Also see Timothy L. Smith, "Slavery and Theology: The Emergence of Black Christian Consciousness in Nineteenth-Century America," *Church History* 41 (December 1972): 497–512. Cf. Luther P. Jackson, "Religious Development of the Negro in Virginia from 1760–1860," *Journal of Negro History* 16 (1931): 168–239.

86. Williams, *Self-Taught*, 20.

87. Cited in ibid., 21.

88. By using the word "accumulate" I return to an idea first explored in the discussion of Equiano. There I drew on Walter Benjamin's notion of time accumulating in commodified things. In this regard, I am suggesting that there was an accumulation of time in the land itself and in its relationship to its owner. In a sense, we moderns remain in the long nineteenth century with spaces woven into a complex racialized process of formation and reformation. See Ian Baucom, *Specters of the Atlantic: Finance Capital, Slavery, and the Philosophy of History* (Durham: Duke University Press, 2005), 17ff.

89. Walter Johnson, *Soul by Soul: Life inside the Antebellum Slave Market* (Cambridge: Harvard University Press, 1999).

90. Johnson states in *Soul By Soul*, "That was commodification: the distant and different translated into money value and resolved into a single scale of relative prices, prices that could be used to make even the most counter-intuitive comparisons—between the body of an old man and a little girl, for example, or between the muscular arm of

a field hand and the sharp eye of a seamstress, or, as many nineteenth-century critics of slavery noted, between a human being and a mule," 58.

91. Hannah Crafts and Henry Louis Gates, *The Bondwoman's Narrative* (New York: Warner, 2002). Also see Henry Louis Gates and Hollis Robbins, *In Search of Hannah Crafts: Critical Essays on the Bondwoman's Narrative* (New York: Basic Civitas, 2004).

92. For some, the inclusion of science fiction and its artful performances may seem trivial. However, a multibillion-dollar industry bound up inside global distribution networks with production efforts that have no end in sight demand a very serious consideration. Indeed, it is precisely the collective display of fantasy production energized by white male desire that is presented in much Western science fiction. Important lessons regarding the architecture of white intimacy remain to be learned from an analysis of this crucial site of the imagination.

93. Herman Gray, *Watching Race: Television and the Struggle for "Blackness"* (Minneapolis: University of Minnesota Press, 1995); Herman Gray, *Cultural Moves: African Americans and the Politics of Representation* (Berkeley: University of California Press, 2005); Howard Winant, *The New Politics of Race: Globalism, Difference, Justice* (Minneapolis: University of Minnesota Press, 2004).

94. Arjun Appadurai, *Modernity at Large: Cultural Dimensions of Globalization* (Minneapolis: University of Minnesota Press, 1996), 5.

95. Ibid., 6.

96. Ibid., 7.

97. The problem here is a failure to recognize the racial architecture of cultural intimacy. In order to see this problem one must reverse the suspicion of a racial reductionism that believes it confines social and political analysis to consider primarily race. Rather, the issue at stake here is to capture a Christianity-based trajectory that constitutes the stage upon which peoples enact social forms. See Iain Chambers, *Migrancy, Culture, Identity* (London: Routledge, 1994); Ronald Niezen, *A World Beyond Difference: Cultural Identity in the Age of Globalization* (Oxford: Blackwell, 2004); Ruben G. Rumbaut and Alejandro Portes, eds., *Ethnicities: Children of Immigrants in America* (Berkeley: University of California Press, 2001); Ellen Alexander Conley, *The Chosen Shore: Stories of Immigrants* (Berkeley: University of California Press, 2004); Sandhya Shukla, *India Abroad: Diasporic Cultures of Postwar America and England* (Princeton: Princeton University Press, 2003).

98. Appadurai, *Modernity at Large*, 159.

99. Ibid., 31. To be sure, Appadurai understands the historic place of the United States in the global production of images, but he has too quickly imagined that America's place has been superseded by global processes themselves: "The United States is no longer the puppeteer of a world system of images but is only one node of a complex transnational construction of imaginary landscapes. The world we live in today is characterized by a new role for the imagination in social life." America as a conglomeration of state apparatuses is not the master controller of a world system of images. This is exactly right. However, it is precisely the texture of a world system of images that Appadurai has too quickly moved past in his analysis.

100. Ibid., 170.

101. Bourdieu, *Outline of a Theory of Practice*, 164. He states, "Every established order tends to produce . . . the naturalization of its own arbitrariness."

102. Appadurai, *Modernity at Large*, 48.

103. As I noted in my analysis of the slave ship, its crucial place in the remaking of the world anticipates global realities of media usage and migration. Indeed, the slave ship already witnesses the expansion of identities over vast distances, the redeployment of the imagination to do identity formation work, and the active interaction of people, cultural realities, technology, finance, information, and ideology. Drawing on the work of a number of cultural and social theorists, Appadurai created a basic framework that he believes will help us understand the "fundamental disjunctures between economy, culture, and politics" (ibid., 33). He did this by suggesting we examine the relations among five aspects of "global cultural flows": (1) *ethnoscapes*—the landscape of persons who constitute the shifting world in which we live: tourists, immigrants, refugees, exiles, guest workers, and so on; (2) *mediascapes*—the distribution of electronic capabilities to produce and disseminate information, mixing news, politics, and fantasy; (3) *technoscapes*—the global configuration of technologies and technologists; (4) *financescapes*—the [rapid] movement of global capital; and (5) *ideoscapes*—an assortment of images and ideas and terms drawn from the Enlightenment, often embedded in the political struggles and ideologies of the state and counterideologies of various movements orientated toward grasping state-level power (ibid., 33–36). His play on the notion of landscape is intentional in that he is conjuring up a basic perspectivism. The "scapes" represent the different "angles of vision" and different subjectivities through which actors play out the imagined worlds suggested by the material operations of ethnic groups, the media, technology, global finance (and markets), and ideologies and their complex interactions. These imagined worlds are inside imagined communities. The power of Appadurai's ingenious theoretical constellation is that he has taken hold of macroprocesses and bound them tightly to micropersonal processes. The weakness of this constellation is that *landscape* is a metaphor pointing to a profound disruption and destruction that Appadurai has not seen and whose results he has therefore naturalized.

104. Ibid., 84. Appadurai understands consumption as a practice tied to repetition and habituation (and not simply to imitation or opposition) for the sake of cultivating "an ethic, aesthetic, and material practice of the ephemeral." *Ephemerality*, as he uses it in this regard, refers to the fleeting realities of pleasure that in order to be sustained require a body disciplined, yet malleable enough to see and seek its realities through regularized practices of consumption. However, the racial habitation at play here is precisely in the possibilities of approximating pleasure.

105. Ibid., 111–12. Appadurai's example of the game of cricket is important because it shows the refashioning of a cultural space by former colonial subjects. I cannot do justice here to his analysis of how cricket was in Indian contexts gradually unyoked from its Victorian value framework. But he offers an account similar to the way vernacular translation of the Bible drew Scripture into the cultural logics of a people, allowing them to claim the text as their own. He states, "How did cricket, a hard cultural

form tightly yoking value, meaning, and embodied practice, become so profoundly Indianized, or, from another point of view, de-Victorianized? Because in the process of its vernacularization (through books, newspapers, radio, and television) it became an emblem of Indian nationhood at the same time that it became inscribed, as practice, onto the Indian (male) body." This may be true, yet it is precisely the question of cultural unyoking that requires a more deliberate and communal analysis. Indeed, one must consider the embodiments of sports' highest ideas and virtues and who consistently determines and displays these precise virtues in public space.

106. John M. Hoberman, *Darwin's Athletes: How Sport Has Damaged Black America and Preserved the Myth of Race* (Boston: Houghton Mifflin, 1997).

107. William C. Rhoden, *The Rise, Fall, and Redemption of the Black Athlete* (New York: Crown, 2006).

108. Also see Winant, *The New Politics of Race*, 129ff. Also see Gargi Bhattacharyya, John Gabriel, and Stephen Small, *Race and Power: Global Racism in the Twenty-First Century* (London; New York: Routledge, 2002), 28ff.

109. I am not saying that whiteness determines reality in ways that eradicate agency, resistance, or creativity. Nor am I discounting other cultural realities that displace, supersede, or lie outside the machinations of whiteness. Nor am I saying that the only social dynamic at play is a struggle between diversity and whiteness. That would be far too simplistic and nowhere near the point of the matter. I am pointing to deeply embedded characteristics in our social imaginations that remain in operation and go unchallenged by Christianity.

CHAPTER 6. THOSE NEAR BELONGING

1. Even today one of the great challenges facing Christians is how to imagine their space. It has been much easier for Christians to imagine their time and live in their time. At a very basic level, the vast majority of Christians would agree that they live between the ascension of Jesus the Christ and his second coming, the *paraousia*. Most Christians can grasp this Christ-shaped time, even if they never speak of it in formal theological language or understand the implications of such a vision of time for how they should live. But space, that is, the spatial dimensions of their existence in faith, eludes many, if not most. Yet if life inside Christ-shaped time means at the very least a different evaluative process of time used, time lived, and time experienced, then what accompanies this time for Christians is also life in space constituted in and through Jesus Christ. There is then a new possibility for Christians to see themselves in and with that new sense of space.

2. I am not saying that the question of identity is unimportant. Indeed, it emerges fairly quickly once one begins to consider the historical process through which Christian community comes into existence. However, starting with the identity question orients our thinking toward group distinction. What normally follows from gauging the identity perimeters of the people of God is a second troubling set of questions regarding the pluralities of this identification. If Christians are the people of God, aren't Jews the other people of God? If there are two peoples of God, why aren't there more peoples

of God, peoples of other religious traditions? One important answer to these kinds of questions has been that the term "people of God" carries a theological definition peculiar to Christians and Jews. This kind of response, however, bypasses the problem raised when one starts with distinction and definition. That starting point leads to boundary formation, which may easily be conceptualized socially, culturally, and, in the end, racially.

3. Henri Lefebvre, *The Production of Space* (Malden, Mass.: Blackwell, 1991), 52. Lefebvre states, "Any 'social existence' aspiring or claiming to be 'real', but failing to produce its own space, would be a strange entity, a very peculiar kind of abstraction unable to escape from the ideological or even the 'cultural' realm. It would fall to the level of folklore and sooner or later disappear altogether, thereby immediately losing its identity, its denomination and its feeble degree of reality." The significance of Lefebvre's insight for us is precisely in helping us draw the connection between racial existence and the constitution of spatial existence supportive of that very existence.

4. Paul Gilroy, *Against Race: Imagining Political Culture Beyond the Color Line* (Cambridge: Belknap Press of Harvard University Press, 2000), 12–13. Paul Gilroy reminds us that race is not an easily abandoned imaginary. He states, "For many racialized populations, race and the hard-won, oppositional identities it supports are not to be lightly or prematurely given up. These groups will need to be persuaded very carefully that there is something worthwhile to be gained from a deliberate renunciation of race as the basis for belonging to one another and acting in concert. They will have to be reassured that the dramatic gestures involved in turning against racial observance can be accomplished without violating the precious forms of solidarity and community that have been created by their protracted subordination along racial lines."

5. Walter Brueggemann, *The Land: Place as Gift, Promise, and Challenge in Biblical Faith* (Minneapolis: Fortress, 2003), 15–16.

6. Hans Georg Gadamer, *Truth and Method* (New York: Continuum, 2004).

7. Robert Jenson, "Toward a Christian Theology of Judaism," in Carl E. Braaten and Robert W. Jenson, *Jews and Christians: People of God* (Grand Rapids: Eerdmans, 2003), 2ff.

8. However, as I suggest in this chapter, it is precisely the power of this essentialized view of Israel that disrupts a reading of biblical Israel and hinders a theological appreciation for Judaism. This is not to say I deny the existence of ethnic Israel, of Jewish people; rather, the troubled history of ethnicity will be factored into my treatment of Israel so as not to reinvent the very problem we are trying to overcome, namely, the inability to see the theological significance of Israel, both biblical Israel and living Israel.

9. This is the heart of supersessionism—Israel is a historical moment reflective of a narrow ethnocentric theological vision that has been transcended with the coming of the Christ. As we saw with Bishop Colenso's reflections, Israel presented an impoverished law—works theology rooted in blood and soil. Colenso's work exemplified the idea of Israel as theological antique. To his credit, Colenso tried to put his supersessionist vision to good antiracist use by calling into question Israel's election and by implication the election of any single people. For Colenso, the universal love of the Father-God enacts the brotherhood of humanity, thereby trumping any priority of Israel.

10. Tikva Simone Frymer-Kensky, ed., *Christianity in Jewish Terms* (Boulder: Westview, 2000); R. Kendall Soulen, *The God of Israel and Christian Theology* (Minneapolis: Fortress, 1996); Scott Bader-Saye, *Church and Israel after Christendom: The Politics of Election* (Boulder: Westview, 1999); Michael Wyschogrod and R. Kendall Soulen, *Abraham's Promise: Judaism and Jewish–Christian Relations* (Grand Rapids: Eerdmans, 2004).

11. It has become an inescapable conclusion that the Holocaust would not have happened without a German Christian community permeated with a ferocious supersessionism that helped to fuel hatred of Jewish people. Cf. Robert P. Ericksen and Susannah Heschel, *Betrayal: German Churches and the Holocaust* (Minneapolis: Fortress, 1999); Doris L. Bergen, *Twisted Cross: The German Christian Movement in the Third Reich* (Chapel Hill: University of North Carolina Press, 1996); Claudia Koonz, *The Nazi Conscience* (Cambridge: Belknap, 2003); George L. Mosse, *Germans and Jews: The Right, the Left, and the Search for a "Third Force" in Pre-Nazi Germany* (Detroit: Wayne State University Press, 1987).

12. Supersessionism, to be sure, is a problem that precedes the epochs of discovery. Multiple points of origin for this problem could be suggested that (a) begin with the earliest writings of the church, that is, in the New Testament itself (see James D. G. Dunn, *Jews and Christians: The Parting of the Ways, A.D. 70 to 135: The Second Durham-Tübingen Research Symposium on Earliest Christianity and Judaism* [Durham, September 1989] [Grand Rapids: Eerdmans, 1999]), or (b) look toward the earlier post–New Testament thinkers (see Daniel Boyarin, *Border Lines: The Partition of Judaeo-Christianity* [Philadelphia: University of Pennsylvania Press, 2004]), or (c) consider the so-called Constantine shift from a small persecuted church to a state-supported church (see John Howard Yoder, Michael G. Cartwright, and Peter Ochs, *The Jewish-Christian Schism Revisited* [Grand Rapids: Eerdmans, 2003]), or (d) discern tensions that grow out of the rapid spread of Christianity and the concomitant rise of Christian vernacularization (see Kenneth R. Stow, *Jewish Dogs: An Image and Its Interpreters: Continuity in the Catholic-Jewish Encounter* [Stanford: Stanford University Press, 2006]). Tracing the multiple possible seeds of supersessionism, although an important endeavor, lies beyond my purview. My concern lies within the thick tangles of the problem as it grows in the colonialist soil and is nourished by the racial imaginaries of modernity and fragmented space. We saw that Colenso learned to read Israel racially much as he read the Zulus. This ability to read Israel as a race alongside other races was a profound achievement not simply of supersessionist strategies but of the racial imagination. Specifically, Israel was read inside whiteness. As we noted in chapter 1, once Israel could be read inside whiteness, whole new possibilities of subverting their election opened up. What adds to the difficulty of the supersessionist problematic is that it draws its original power from the very serious tension that emerges out of Christianity's central claims regarding Jesus Christ. Those tensions are authentic and present a fundamental challenge to Jewish self-understanding. No critique of supersessionism can avoid this deeper point of real conflict that must be acknowledged. We can, however, draw an important distinction between that conflict, that is, the parting of the ways between Christianity and Judaism, and supersession-

ism. More important, we can tease out from the original tension another aspect of its significance for understanding Israel's importance. Indeed, I want in this chapter to capture some sense of the basic aspects of that tension in hopes of recasting it as a dissonance that calls for a resolution and not a supersessionist response.

13. My use of the term "goyim" is not meant to signify a racist or derogatory gesture but to mark a fundamental distinction in terms of a way of life. It is an epistemic and a sociological and, most important, a theological deployment.

14. In this regard, I draw on a notion of unconsciousness following the conceptual trajectory articulated in Fredric Jameson's seminal text, *The Political Unconscious: Narrative as a Socially Symbolic Act* (Ithaca: Cornell University Press, 1981). Jameson states, "It is in detecting the traces of that uninterrupted narrative [of class struggle and warfare], in restoring to the surface of the text the repressed and buried reality of this fundamental history, that the doctrine of a political unconsciousness finds its function and its necessity," 20. My concern is not in following the Jamesonian project but in drawing it toward a different, uninterrupted narrative, of God with Israel, of Jews and Gentiles in the body of Jesus and the racial resistance and submersion of that narrative.

15. Soulen, *The God of Israel and Christian Theology*, 25–108.

16. My goal in this final chapter is to unearth a fundamental ecclesial process, that is, how peoples come to exist in a new way—as the people walking with God. In so doing, I shall approach themes that have flowed through the entire text but without their fuller explanation or definition. The first theme is the importance of Israel to Christian identity. The second theme is the nature of the communion that was repeatedly gestured toward as a social desideratum. If Christians and Christian communities are ever going to engage the stronger ramifications of the performance of their faith as community, then one must slowly begin to reimagine Gentile existence as a theological starting point for imagining Christian community. It is important to clarify what concerns are not in view at this point. I am not concerned with questions of ecumenicity, that is, with questions regarding the relationship between various communions within Christianity. Addressing the theological fragmentation within the global community of Christian faith remains a very important question; however, I want to approach theological fragmentation in another key and from another angle. I am not downplaying the schisms that have plagued the church for more than a millennium. What I have displayed throughout this book are profoundly theological matters as serious as the ecclesial fragmentation that plagues the global church. We cannot, however, arrive at the kind of ecumenical dialogue that may yield unification as long as wider processes of cultural fragmentation remain unaddressed as theological problems. In order to address this fragmentation as a theological problem, the identity question must be repositioned. It must be placed inside the larger question of the constitution of the people of God.

17. Jon Levenson, "The Universal Horizon of Biblical Particularism," in Mark G. Brett, ed., *Ethnicity and the Bible* (Leiden; New York: Brill, 1996), 152–53. I am indebted to Amanda Beckenstein Mbuvi for pointing this important essay out to me. See Amanda

Beckenstein Mbuvi, "Belonging in Genesis: Biblical Israel and the Construction of Communal Identity" (Ph.D. diss., Duke University, 2008), 6.

18. Ethnicity, while a powerfully useful idea for designating people groups, takes its modern cues from the racial imagination. Specifically, the idea of ethnicity allows one to imagine the collective identities of peoples tangentially related and sometimes completely unrelated to specific land and landscapes. Ethnicity comes to designate a people by their products, stories, rituals, practices, memories, and so forth, and is often tied implicitly to their racial characteristics. The idea of ethnicity performs a softer surrogacy for land than race. It allows one to capture a sense of the fluidity of peoples in space while not taking their actual space into a strong calculation of identity. By emphasizing their products, ethnicity is able to localize identity in ways that make conceptual room for private property. This means one can imagine people in space, yet see them as fundamentally independent of the very space they inhabit. Ethnicity, in this sense, is a modern invention. However, its antecedents can be discerned precisely in the subversion of Israel's election. See Kenan Malik, *The Meaning of Race: Race, History and Culture in Western Society* (New York: New York University Press, 1996); Werner Sollors, *Beyond Ethnicity: Consent and Descent in American Culture* (New York: Oxford University Press, 1986). Both Malik and Sollors are aware of the problem with ethnicity in terms of its racializing function. It remains, however, a powerful way of conceptualizing difference even for those theorists aware of its entanglement. See *Race, Nature, and the Politics of Difference*, ed. Donald S. Moore, Jake Kosek, and Anand Pandian (Durham: Duke University Press, 2003).

19. For a powerful example of this schema, see his classic work, Norman K. Gottwald, *The Tribes of Yahweh: A Sociology of the Religion of Liberated Israel 1250–1050 B.C.E* (London: SCM, 1980). Also see J. David Pleins, *The Social Visions of the Hebrew Bible: A Theological Introduction* (Louisville: Westminster John Knox, 2001).

20. The central hermeneutic principle that informs my argument at this point is that Jewish existence must always be read theologically; that is, biblical and living Israel must be thought of as though God absolutely matters in their constitution and in their existence. Any modernist reading of Jewish existence that ignores God draws itself and Israel into a strange identity cul-de-sac. As Emil Fackenheim stated, "The modern expulsion of God from the human world made Jewish existence problematic. . . . The moment the living God became questionable, Jewish existence became questionable. The Jew had to embark on the weary business of self-definition." Quoted in Katya Gibel Azoulay, *Black, Jewish, and Interracial: It's Not the Color of Your Skin, but the Race of Your Kin, and Other Myths of Identity* (Durham: Duke University Press, 1997), 135.

21. Joel S. Kaminsky, *Yet I Loved Jacob: Reclaiming the Biblical Concept of Election* (Nashville: Abingdon, 2007).

22. It is a crucial matter that we understand the *dabarim* of YHWH (the word of the Lord) as addressing Israel in respect to its journey toward and in the land. I have argued that the identity of a people is bound to their land. This means that the fundamental equation for premodern collective identity (that is, collective identity before colonialist

land seizure and its commodity transformation) includes landscape and its specifics, animals, seasons, and so forth. It also means that the story of Israel with its land is the story of God establishing the identity of a people. In order to understand the implications of this divine operation, one must not only resist the modernist habit of imagining ethnicity, but also imagine a spatial dynamic to divine revelation.

23. Carol L. Meyers, *Exodus* (Cambridge: Cambridge University Press, 2005), 71ff.

24. Walter Brueggemann, *Theology of the Old Testament: Testimony, Dispute, Advocacy* (Minneapolis: Fortress, 1997), 504.

25. Meyers, *Exodus*, 94. This connection between death, violence, and God has always been a disturbing connection for many Jewish and Christian readers of Israel's story. Carol Meyers suggests that an ideological reading of the text as an ahistorical creation of an Israel "struggl[ing] to find and maintain her distinctive identity in the fluid cultural waters of the ancient Near East" may lessen the force of this depiction of a violent, mass-murdering God. However, before one commits oneself to an ethnic reading of Israel, it is important to recognize what God in the story is doing with violence and death.

26. Norman C. Habel, *The Land Is Mine: Six Biblical Land Ideologies* (Minneapolis: Fortress, 1995). Norman Habel suggests that there are at least six land ideologies present in the Hebrew Bible, each functioning in different modulations to announce Israel's right to occupy the land. Habel's reading suggest the following: (1) the royal ideology, teased out from 1 Kgs 3–10 and the select Psalms, sees the land as the source of wealth given by God to the monarch; (2) the theocratic ideology, drawn primarily from Deuteronomy, envisions the land as conditional grant given by God; (3) the ancestral household ideology, found in the book of Joshua, sees the land as family lots given by God to the faithful ones of Israel; (4) the prophetic ideology, seen in the prophet Jeremiah, holds that the land is YHWH's personal *nachalah* (inheritance) to be shared by the chosen people; (5) the agrarian ideology, reflected in Lev 25–27, holds that the land is bound to YHWH and the rhythms of life centered around Sabbath-keeping; and (6) the immigrant ideology recognized in the Abraham narratives sees the land as host country promised by God to the ancestor Abraham, who without violence shared the land with its historic inhabitants.

27. Habel's point in discerning these ideological strands in the biblical narrative is to show how a theological vision can be woven into an ideological position to justify the invasion and occupation of a desired land. Habel's reading of the story of Israel reflects the aftermath of colonialism's horror. His reading strategy is patently contextual. He draws a direct line from the theologically flavored ideologies of modern collectivities back to Israel's multiple historical justifications of conquest. Habel wrote this text with the history of colonialist occupation in Australia in mind. He was keenly aware how the biblical narrative could be used to support the taking of native lands. Indeed, he resists drawing conclusions regarding land use today, preferring to offer a cautionary tale regarding the use of Israel's story to underwrite any divinely sanctioned land possession. There is little doubt that Habel rightly sees a justification for violence in the story of Israel that sets the stage for its massive redeployment by modern nations. However, the way toward resisting the redeployment of this ideological justification is

to establish a specific theological limitation. This was only for Israel, and any further claim to it, even by Israel, was collapsed onto Jesus himself. That is, Jesus presents a way forward from violence for Israel and the entire world.

28. This, of course, constitutes a counterreading to important voices in the Christian tradition. It is exactly the possibilities of the repetition of Israel-like conquest that suggest the deepest supersessionist logic, because such claims in effect perform an Israel replacement in that God speaks and commands (or allows) war for the sake of establishing a reality of redemption in a particular place. See, for example, "Francisco de Vitoria," in Oliver O'Donovan and Joan Lockwood O'Donovan, eds., *From Irenaeus to Grotius: A Sourcebook in Christian Political Thought* 100–1625 (Grand Rapids: Eerdmans, 1999), 609.

29. Thomas F. Torrance, *Theology in Reconstruction* (Eugene: WS Publishers, 1996), 196ff; Thomas F. Torrance, *The Mediation of Christ* (Colorado Springs: Helmers and Howard, 1992).

30. My use of "ethnic" in this sense is a designation not of identity but of collective orientation and collective imagination. What people could possibly imagine life beyond the *agon*, that is, the eternal struggle for dominion and power? Certainly, not all peoples could be described as warring, power-hungry tribes, yet no people is eternally secured from feeling the effects of such peoples or being infected by the desire to secure its own future through conquest of others. Our participation in Israel's story is precisely as the subtext, the intertextual reality that informs Israel's textual performance.

31. Torrance, *The Mediation of Christ*, 7ff. With the first sense of suffering, Torrance does not seem to be reiterating the Protestant idea that the law was an unbearable burden for Israel. Rather, his point is the disciplining realities of the divine presence in Israel. God judges every aspect of Israel's life. Under the light cast by the *dabarim*, Israel's sins cannot be hidden, and they demand a response from YHWH, their covenant partner. Suffering in this sense is on the order of rebuke, chastisement, and discipline with the fearful reminder that YHWH is capable of punishing Israel. Here Israel's suffering illumines humanity's shortcomings in the presence of God. Our waywardness comes into view in Israel's struggles of faithfulness. We also see what God desires from the Gentiles—repentance and obedience. This is the vicarious nature of Israel's life within the commandments of God. That vicarious nature continues with the second sense of its suffering. Israel suffers because they expose our (Gentile) sin. The exposure of ways of life that Israel's God deems unacceptable could only enlist responses of defensiveness against or, more dangerously, hatred of Israel. The story of Israel reveals a people hated by other nations because Israel's life bore witness to divine prohibitions among the Gentiles. Yet, once exposed there was no turning back, only a turning away from the light of Israel. This suffering because of hatred ties to a third sense of suffering for Israel. Israel's life lived in life-giving discipline provided by the wisdom of the Torah was also a guide to other nations. The one true God is revealed in Israel, and each day Israel by its quotidian practices showed to other peoples how one must live in obedience to God. Yet obedience exposes disobedience. The expression of love for YHWH can also expose the competition between this God and the gods of other nations. Why should other peoples abandon their gods for this God? Why should the demands of

the Hebrews' God be important to them? It is precisely this dynamic that illumines the nature of theological hatred of the other, that is, of Israel.

32. Of course, one can only reflect on Israel's suffering in light of the horror of the Shoah. Indeed, the theological complexity of that event of Jewish suffering is only heightened in the light of this threefold sense of biblical Israel's suffering. See Robert Gibbs, "Suspicions of Suffering," in *Christianity in Jewish Terms*, ed. Frymer-Kresky, 224. The Jewish philosopher Robert Gibbs offers helpful distinctions in the way one might envision Jewish suffering. He suggests this suffering may be viewed as representative, subordinating, or totalizing. The sense of representative suffering aligns with Christian views of Israel's suffering as specifically vicarious, an instance of suffering for the entire world. This representative sense differs from a subordinating view in which Jewish suffering is simply a part of a historical and global reality of human suffering. In this regard, he suggests, Jewish suffering "loses any meaning without reference to the whole."

33. Gibbs, "Suspicions of Suffering," 225. The totalizing view stands in exaggerated relation to the subordinate view. The totalizing view makes Jewish suffering instrumental. The totalizing view makes "Jewish suffering . . . part of religious suffering, maybe even a vital organ, and it is justified when we grasp how the whole world forms a totality and needs suffering in order to achieve its unity" (224). Subordinate and totalizing views of Jewish suffering fail precisely because they refuse to recognize the asymmetry of Jewish suffering. Gibbs says that "it is not just particular suffering that represents the suffering of the whole world, but *our* particular suffering. *Who* suffers is a vital aspect of interpreting representative suffering."

34. N. T. Wright, *Jesus and the Victory of God* (Minneapolis: Fortress, 1996); Dale C. Allison, *Jesus of Nazareth: Millenarian Prophet* (Minneapolis: Fortress, 1998). These important standard texts treat the questions of historicity, that is, the historical Jesus questions, with great theological care. However, my concerns do not follow such treatments.

35. The relationship between the historical Jesus and ancient Christian communities of interpretation remains an important hermeneutic concern in New Testament scholarship. That concern, however, often gets articulated in ways that completely ignore this crucial reality of the (Gentile) subject position of the readers. In this regard, I must recall Sheehan's account of the formation of the Enlightenment Bible and Casanova's account of the emergence of the (colonialist) literary world order. New Testament scholarship by and large continues to function in the arena constituted between these two developments. See Jonathan Sheehan, *The Enlightenment Bible: Translation, Scholarship, Culture* (Princeton: Princeton University Press, 2005); Pascale Casanova, *The World Republic of Letters* (Cambridge: Harvard University Press, 2004).

36. Karl Barth and Geoffrey William Bromiley, *The Doctrine of Reconciliation: Church Dogmatics*, 4:1 (Edinburgh: T&T Clark, 1956). The Christian theological themes of a virgin birth and the oneness of the Son with the Father, the Son of God as of the same substance with God his father (*homoousion tō patri*), flow out of a deep conviction that Christians have seen the election of God in flesh in Israel and it is Jesus.

37. See Hos 11: 1–2; Matt 2: 13–15; Exod 4: 22–24.

38. Matthew 4: 1–3a.

39. Dietrich Bonhoeffer, *Creation and Fall: A Theological Interpretation of Genesis 1–3* (New York: Macmillan, 1959); Eberhard Bethge, *Dietrich Bonhoeffer: Man of Vision, Man of Courage* (New York: Harper and Row, 1977), 409ff. In the spring of 1937 over the course of several days Bonhoeffer guided a group of former seminarians in a Bible study reflecting on the temptation of Jesus. These former seminarians were part of the Confessing Church that stood against the Nazi regime.

40. One should resist the tendency to read the temptation narratives of Jesus as an exercise in discerning one's own individual temptations. In such an exercise, my own temptation is juxtaposed to Jesus' temptation. What Bonhoeffer's insight makes possible is a way to return one's vision of Jesus' temptation to Israel and its implications for Gentile existence. (Matt 4: 3–4)

41. Bonhoeffer, *Creation and Fall*, 103–4. Here in the wilderness is a new exposition and a new revealing: the tempter comes. In the wilderness where Israel fell before the tempter, Jesus must stand before the great destroyer and tempter of all peoples. As Bonhoeffer notes, "In distinction from the temptation of Adam and all human temptations the tempter himself comes to Jesus. . . . Whereas elsewhere he makes use of creatures, here he himself must conduct the struggle. This makes it clear that in the temptation of Jesus it *is a matter of the whole* (emphasis added).

42. (Matt 4: 5–7) Jesus' life is in (hypothetical) danger. This is the worst kind of danger because it knows no bounds, no beginning and no ending. It is the danger that is inextricably tied to the fear of the unforeseen, the anxiety over the sufficiency of internal strength to face external enemies, and it is therefore tied to theological tests. See Bonhoeffer, *Creation and Fall*, 105. Bonhoeffer states the case powerfully: "Jesus' answer sets the God's Word against God's Word, but in such a way that there is no fatal uncertainty, and so that truth is set against lies. Jesus calls this temptation a temptation of God. He will remain only by his Father's Word; that suffices him."

43. Bonhoeffer, *Creation and Fall*, 105. Bonhoeffer is insightful when he notes that in this temptation, "Satan fights with his very own weapons. There is no more veiling, no more dissimulation. Satan's power matches itself directly against the power of God. Satan hazards his ultimate resources. His gift is immeasurably big and beautiful and alluring; and in return for his gift he claims worship."

44. By Gentile presence I am not focused on the architectural logic of the writers of the Gospels in which some texts (for example, the Lukan narrative, which was probably written with a Gentile audience in mind) support Gentile inclusion, while others (such as the Matthean narrative) were clearly written in full recognition of Jewish distinctiveness. In this regard, I am not concerned with the question of the intended audience of various New Testament texts. Rather, I am drawing attention to the spatial logic articulated in the actions of Jesus in relation to Gentiles.

45. Karl Barth, *The Doctrine of Reconciliation: Church Dogmatics* 4:1 (Edinburgh: T&T Clark, 1958), 170. His words are, as Barth notes (following the insight of Luther), the divine "no" that conceals the divine "yes."

46. Philip Schaff et al., *Cyril of Jerusalem, Gregory Nazianzen* (Peabody, Mass.: Hendrickson, 1994), 440.

47. Ched Myers, *Binding the Strong Man: A Political Reading of Mark's Story of Jesus* (Maryknoll, N.Y.: Orbis, 1988), 167. The religious elite who benefited from that order objected to him and designated Jesus an agent of Beelzebul, of Satan, because he upset the sociopolitical order of things. Jesus' response, as the biblical scholar Ched Myers notes, turns the accusation back against the religious elites. It is they who are the agents of the evil one by fitting Israel's religious life comfortably into the hegemonic sociopolitical system. Myers states, "Jesus . . . turned the tables completely upon his opponents [the scribal class]: it is they who are aligned against God's purposes. To be captive to the way things are, to resist criticism and change, to brutally suppress efforts at humanization—is to be bypassed by the grace of God."

48. K. C. Hanson and Douglas E. Oakman, *Palestine in the Time of Jesus: Social Structures and Social Conflicts* (Minneapolis: Fortress, 1998), 19ff.

49. Myers, *Binding the Strong Man*, 159. Ched Myers notes that in Mark this new wine for Israel will be revealed "as the genuine social practice of nonviolent love."

50. Orlando Patterson, in his seminal text *Slavery and Social Death: A Comparative Study* (Cambridge: Harvard University Press, 1982), notes that the life of a slave is characterized by what he terms social death; that is, the slave is without voice, distinction, and is in a constant state of alienation. Social death forms one of the essential markers of slave existence. The others include natal alienation and dishonor. Patterson's account of slavery illumines the nature of the risk involved in publicly identifying with Jesus of Nazareth. Indeed, it helps one make sense of Paul's account of Jesus as existing in the form of a slave.

51. Jesus could not have postured himself toward Israel in this way if in fact this new orientation was not already a reality in him. Herein lay the great mystery and a great power articulated from within the Christian vision of the eternal relationship between the Father and the Son in the Spirit. Jesus said leave parents and the determining processes inherent in kinship life because he displayed the power to recapitulate the reality of belonging through his own body. Just as violence and death found their first home in kinship with the killing of Abel by Cain, so now Jesus would destroy the power of violence and death at work in families.

52. Gerhard Lohfink, *Jesus and Community: The Social Dimension of Christian Faith* (Philadelphia; New York: Fortress; Paulist, 1984), 56. In this regard, community may be too strong a designation as we find, for example, in the seminal work of the theologian Gerhard Lohfink, *Jesus and Community*, whose thesis that Jesus sought to establish a contrast-society is very persuasive. Lohfink states, "Jesus understood the people of God which he sought to gather as a *contrast-society*. This in no way means that he envisioned the people of God as a *state* or a *nation*, but he did understand it as a community which forms in its own sphere of life, a community in which one lives in a different way and treats others in a different way than is usual elsewhere in the world. We could definitely describe the people of God which Jesus sought to gather as an *alternative* society. It is not the violent structures of the powers of this world which are to rule within it, but rather reconciliation and brotherhood." While this account is persuasive and fundamentally correct, it reaches for a cohesiveness that is premature

given the realities of scandal that surround Jesus. He was seen by many as a madman whose theological vision was deeply suspect.

53. Matt 6: 31–34.

54. Daniel Boyarin and Jonathan Boyarin, "Diaspora: Generation and the Ground of Jewish Identity," in Daniel Boyarin, *A Radical Jew: Paul and the Politics of Identity* (Berkeley: University of California Press, 1994).

55. Ben Witherington, *The Acts of the Apostles: A Socio-Rhetorical Commentary* (Grand Rapids: Eerdmans; Carlisle, U.K.: Paternoster, 1998); Beverly Roberts Gaventa, *The Acts of the Apostles* (Nashville: Abingdon, 2003); Justo L. González, *Acts: The Gospel of the Spirit* (Maryknoll, N.Y.: Orbis, 2001); Ernst Haenchen, *The Acts of the Apostles: A Commentary* (Philadelphia: Westminster, 1971).

56. My language of gesture is not meant to turn the speaking of tongues into a mere symbol for a natural process of translation, thereby undermining a Pentecostal hermeneutic. Rather, gesture means here an intentionality to move the disciples by the presence of the Spirit toward a new imaginative possibility of the gathering of Israel in the presence of God.

57. There was real content to this *contra mundi* posture for Gentiles because it required them to denounce and resist involvement with pagan ritual, which was no small matter in the ancient world. Such ritual was woven into the fabric of daily life for many, and it was the central source of economic existence for even more. However, this limitation in the social imagination of the Jewish believers is understandable given not only their status as a religious minority within the Roman Empire, but also now as a religious sect within that religious minority. They were perceived as an unstable and chaotic movement that carried the real danger of upsetting the social order and disrupting multiple religious communities.

58. Indeed, one could fruitfully read the remaining chapters of Acts, which are centrally the odyssey of Paul, as the exposure of the struggle of two ways of life, Jew and Gentile, being irreversibly drawn together through the revelation of Jesus, God's only Son. From the introduction of Timothy in Acts 16, the "biracial" child of a Jewish mother and a Greek father, as Paul's mentee and assistant, to the constant attacks he endured from both Jews and Gentiles, to his exhausting attempts to convince both Jews and Gentiles of the new way to be found in Jesus, we see the Spirit of God laying bare the complex depths of resistance to the joining of peoples in a new way of life that would upset the social order. We also gain clues to how the Spirit-constituted gesture of communion might be worked out in the joining of peoples who would experience both continuity and discontinuity in various aspects of their cultural and social realities.

59. The vision in Christian theology today for separate but equal (theological) existence for Jews and Christians and all other Christian peoples arises out of an important attempt to address the legacies of conquest and violence as well as the desire to show appreciation and respect for cultural difference. There is also the desire to respect the integrity of and the continuation of Jewish theological tradition on the one hand and on the other hand the various cultural traditions of different Christian communities. These are notable desires; however, they must be situated in both the historical tra-

jectory of life turned toward communion established by Jesus through the Spirit and the continuing trajectory of the reformation of identity through the processes of displacement and colonialist translation. Christian theology has the unique challenge of articulating a joining of peoples through the spatial reality constituted by the life of Jesus that overcomes the agon between peoples. This must be done, however, in full awareness of the socioeconomic processes that perpetuate an agonistic social imagination and even now continue to undermine the possibilities of that joining. Thankfully, the Apostle Paul gave us even more clues to aid in this articulation.

60. We must keep in mind that neither Jew nor Gentile here refers to a cultural monolith but to a complex variety of peoples. Thus the joining of peoples fosters the mixture of peoples and their ways of life in such a way that cultural continuity is disclosed in cultural discontinuity and cultural discontinuity is disclosed in cultural continuity.

61. Pheme Perkins, *Ephesians* (Nashville: Abingdon, 1997); Pheme Perkins, "The Letter to the Ephesians: Introduction, Commentary, and Reflections," in *New Interpreter's Bible* (Nashville: Abingdon, 2000), 11:349–466. Pauline authorship of Ephesians remains a disputed question: however, for my concerns Pauline authorship is not the crucial matter. There is more scholarly agreement that this letter reflects the outgrowth of Paul's insights and may even be, if indeed Pauline, written by a mature Paul in whom these insights grew through years of life in and in between Jewish and Christian communities. Regardless, these words are significant here in the way Paul (whose name I will use for the sake of simplicity and semantic clarity) captures the Gentile situation. The urgency of these ideas is even more compelling if one considers them in light of my earlier exegesis of the temptations of Jesus and the captivity of the nations.

62. Markus Barth, *The Broken Wall: A Study of the Epistle to the Ephesians* (Chicago: Judson, 1959).

63. Recall Henri Lefebvre's threefold idea of space as perceived, conceived, and lived. As noted in chapter 5, Lefebvre offered a way of grasping the creation of space in three modes: (1) *spatial practice*, which is the material environment, (2) representations of space, which are conceptual models we use to guide our practice, and (3) spaces of representation, which are the lived social relations of users to the environment. Space in this regard is not simply the container of activity but an activity itself, not simply a place of relation but a relation itself. Physical, mental, and social spaces are interdependent and mutually constitute one another. Lefebvre's insight into the nature of space helps one capture the wider implications of Paul's vision of communion between Jews and Gentiles and for the very nature of cultural intimacy. I am less concerned here with rehearsing Paul's elaborate discussions of the salvation of Israel or the nature of the law and its relation to Jew and Gentile or his searing critique of the Christian Judaizers. Rather, my compelling consideration is looking at the new reality constituted by the life of Jesus for Jews and Gentiles.

64. By this account I am imagining a reversal of the trajectory of the intimate established by colonial relations. That trajectory established the social imaginary as bound to an intimacy established by whiteness performed through a Western episteme and its aesthetically powerful deployment of discursive systems. In such a schema, all the peoples of the world imagine cultural continuity or discontinuity or both through the

dictates of use-value within particular global economic arrangements. See Ann Laura Stoler, *Carnal Knowledge and Imperial Power: Race and the Intimate in Colonial Rule* (Berkeley: University of California Press, 2002); Elizabeth A. Povinelli, *The Empire of Love: Toward a Theory of Intimacy, Genealogy, and Carnality* (Durham: Duke University Press, 2006); John Armstrong, *Conditions of Love: The Philosophy of Intimacy* (New York: W. W. Norton, 2003).

65. Torrance, *Theology in Reconstruction*, 197–99. Another crucial implication of this new space is the reacknowledgment of Christian existence inside Israel. T. F. Torrance noted that Jesus is the head of the church and the messiah of Israel (at the same time). By his statement Torrance captured what he called the organic connection between Jesus and Israel and between Jesus and the church. This connection, if taken seriously, yields a nonsupersessionist way of envisioning the life of the church as always bound up in a word for Israel.

66. It is a tragic but profound truth that there has been no significant conversation between Christian and Jewish theologians about race, the racial imagination, or whiteness. Whiteness is the given of identity that permeates the interreligious theological texts of both modern white Christian and Jewish theologians. Race is never questioned, rarely analyzed, and rarely considered in their analysis of the modern or postmodern condition of religious knowledge, religious communities, or theologies between the two groups. There are an increasing number of studies of Jews and race as well as classic studies on the relation of Jews and blacks and important work on Jews in the racial imagination of Europe. But the intersection of these concerns with theology, Jewish and Christian, is painfully absent. For examples of important texts on race and Jewish life, see Karen Brodkin, *How Jews Became White Folks and What That Says About Race in America* (New Brunswick: Rutgers University Press, 2000); Seth Forman, *Blacks in the Jewish Mind: A Crisis of Liberalism* (New York: New York University Press, 1998); Eric Goldstein, *The Price of Whiteness: Jews, Race, and American Identity* (Princeton: Princeton University Press, 2006).

67. By meditation upon the body, black and Jewish, I want to draw attention to the meaning of the body, black and Jewish, within the racial imagination. I am not referring to a comprehensive comparative analysis of the ways in which Africans and Jews have been treated from the beginning of the colonialist moment through slavery and the flowering of Enlightenment anti-Semitism, although such a treatment is greatly needed. Nor is my concern an archeological exploration into the relation of the primordial people groups that inhabited the worlds now referred to as the Middle East and North Africa in an effort to discern the interactions between "ancient" Hebrews and Ethiopians. Nor is my central focus the ways in which Africans and Jews have been inscribed within racial categories, although that central fact must frame any meditation. In this regard, I will use the twin notions of "black" and "Jew" in this section to indicate Africans' and Jews' appearance within the racial imagination. I will also explore the contours of the iconic space that exists between the black body and the Jewish body within racial calculus. Here I am using the concept of icon in its most basic theological sense—as an artistic rendering that helps facilitate a sense of the divine life revealed in Jesus Christ. The icon exists in the midst of a constellation of participatory nodes

within the life of the church. In their rendering of bodies, icons reach out to those looking at them, extending artistic lines into the lines of their existence that connect them to the multiple acts within the spiritual life, for example, prayer, worship, and liturgy. The inner logic of the icon is the incarnate life of God in Jesus of Nazareth. As St. John of Damascus taught, because God became flesh and was seen, touched, and heard in the flesh, humans may draw images of this God and the life he lived for us. Cf. Jim Forest, *Praying with Icons* (Maryknoll, N.Y.: Orbis, 1997).

68. Not every people in the world at a particular moment entered the racial calculus. Nor am I saying that racial calculus is the only factor in the formation of peoples from the day Prince Henry offered his first tithe of black bodies to the church in thanksgiving. Nor am I ignoring the microhistories of resistance to racial formation. This question signifies the power of placement and points toward the horror of the racial imagination. But it also suggests a presence(s) within the racial calculus that announces its potential destruction by their very presence in it. The black body and the Jewish body presented just such a danger from the very origins of the modern racial imagination.

69. Jonathan Schorsch, *Jews and Blacks in the Early Modern World* (New York: Cambridge University Press, 2004), 166–67. By Sephardic Jews he means the Jewish Portuguese Diaspora communities in Amsterdam and other places in the seventeenth century.

70. Ibid., 187.

71. Ibid., 191.

72. David Levering Lewis, "Parallels and Divergences: Assimilationist Strategies of Afro-American and Jewish Elites from 1910 to the Early 1930s," *Journal of American History* 71:3 (December 1984): 543–64.

73. As one commentator noted, reflecting on black and Jewish life in America between 1880 and 1935, blacks sought to emulate Jews in their strategically deployed assimilationism: "Black educators, ministers, writers, and orators held up the noble image of the Jews. Jews, they maintained, had succeeded because *they* banded together, *they* lived cleanly, *they* saved their money, *they* used their intellect, and *they* never abandoned those left behind. In short, several generations of Black leaders told the masses of recently emancipated slaves and their immediate descendents struggling with poverty and oppression: Be like the Jews." Hasia R. Diner, "Between Words and Deeds: Jews and Blacks in America, 1880–1935," in *Struggles in the Promised Land: Towards a History of Black-Jewish Relations in the United States*, ed. Jack Salzman and Cornel West (New York: Oxford University Press, 1997), 88. One can discern, in America at least, three motifs in relation to this trajectory that existed in black communities: an awareness of black national and cultic identity; a perception of the possibilities of the nation-state; and a tacit acknowledgment of the incredible power of racial identity.

74. Kevin Kelly Gaines, *Uplifting the Race: Black Leadership, Politics, and Culture in the Twentieth Century* (Chapel Hill: University of North Carolina Press, 1996), 68–69. Gaines states, "African Americans found the medium [of photography] well suited for trying to refute negrophobic caricatures. In addition, black painters, illustrators and sculptors, along with writers of fiction, produced antiracist narratives and iconography

featuring ideal types of bourgeois black manhood and womanhood. . . . Studio portraits of uplift and respectability—depicting black families with attributes of cleanliness, leisure, and literacy—found expression in the sitters' posture, demeanor, dress, and setting. In most portraits, whether of individual, of wedding portraits, or of groups, one sees an intense concern with projecting a serious, dignified image. And these still portraits of refinement sprang to life in performance rituals, often based in the church, of elocution, preaching, and in the jubilee and quartette singing of Negro spirituals. Anything less than stylized elegance would betray the ideals of race advancement and, indeed, hold the race back, as did the profusion of commodified, demeaning portraits taken of unsuspecting, often youthful and destitute African Americans. Many whites, however, remained unmoved by African Americans' attempts at respectful self-representation."

75. Lewis, "Parallels and Divergences," 31.

76. Racism emerged as an object of discourse within the generative processes of white identity in such a way as to name, identify, and address its effects without fundamentally challenging its most basic constitutive resource, whiteness. No American historian or historian of the civil rights movement and its effects has given an adequate account of this ability of whiteness to evade its own historic connection to racism and the need for its dissolution. See insightful analyses in this direction from the following: Eduardo Bonilla-Silva, *Racism Without Racists: Color-Blind Racism and the Persistence of Racial Inequality in the United States* (Lanham, Md.: Rowman and Littlefield, 2006); Robert Post and Michael Rogin, eds., *Race and Representation: Affirmative Action* (New York: Zone, 1998); Manning Marable, *Race, Reform, and Rebellion: The Second Reconstruction in Black America, 1945–1990* (Jackson: University Press of Mississippi, 1990); David L. Chappell, *A Stone of Hope: Prophetic Religion and the Death of Jim Crow* (Chapel Hill: University of North Carolina Press, 2004).

77. Eric J. Sundquist, *Strangers in the Land: Blacks, Jews, Post-Holocaust America* (Massachusetts: Belknap Press, 2005); Also see Jack Salzman and Cornel West, eds., *Struggles in the Promised Land: Toward a History of Black–Jewish Relations in the United States* (New York: Oxford Press, 1997)

78. The central arguments growing out of the civil rights movement have been on how to transform this fiction into truth or how to expose this fiction or how to modify this useful fiction by means of a new, more expansive reading of the civil rights movement. The central tensions between blacks and Jews since the civil rights movement flow out of these abiding arguments and whether either group has betrayed the spirit of the movement, a spirit defined now in terms of capitalist opportunity, fair and just treatment under the law, and equal access to America's resources. The sociopolitical conversation indicates a lost opportunity to question the foundations of the racial imagination.

79. There was tremendous danger in playing in the rough seas of representation. If racial representation had held Jewish and black bodies adrift, captive to the power of death, it would be very risky business to venture out onto those waters, even with superb navigational skills. But they in fact had no choice. Standing always in the background for Jewish and black bodies, generating much of the roughness of representational

sea, was racial-scientific discourse. The bodies of blacks and Jews came into view as "biological data" for gauging such things as human degeneracy, criminality, intelligence or the lack thereof, social evolution, and sexuality. Racial-scientific discourse on the body diseased the Western social imagination and informed the processes of racial representation. So it was in light of these discursive realities and occasionally in direct confrontation of them that generations of black and Jewish artists courageously engaged in self-expression. Nineteenth- and twentieth-century racial-scientific discourse on the body grew directly out of the colonialist comparative anthropological discourse. And as I noted in previous chapters, that discourse was a strange mixture of biblical-genealogical and phenological reasoning brought to focus on colonial subjects. By the end of the nineteenth century and the beginning of the twentieth century, racial-scientific discourse on the body had not only given rise to racial eugenics discussions in Europe, South Africa, and America, but had also encased racial essentialism in scientific authority executed through the language of biological determinism. Gustav Jahoda, *Images of Savages: Ancient Roots of Modern Prejudice in Western Culture* (London: Routledge, 1999); Alan E. Steinweis, *Studying the Jew: Scholarly Antisemitism in Nazi Germany* (Cambridge: Harvard University Press, 2006); Saul Dubow, *Scientific Racism in Modern South Africa* (Cambridge: Cambridge University Press, 1995); Pat Shipman, *The Evolution of Racism: Human Differences and the Use and Abuse of Science* (New York: Simon and Schuster, 1994); Stephen Jay Gould, *The Mismeasure of Man* (New York: Norton, 1981); Sander L. Gilman, *Smart Jews: The Construction of the Image of Jewish Superior Intelligence* (Lincoln: University of Nebraska Press, 1997).

80. From Ralph Ellison and Albert Murray to Henry Roth and Saul Bellow, from Cynthia Ozick and David Mamet to Toni Morrison and Ishmael Reed, from John Edgar Wideman to Philip Roth and a whole host of writers too numerous to name, they walked on the water of representation, never drowning, and drew a cadre of disciples into the water with them. See Adam Zachary Newton, *Facing Black and Jew: Literature as Public Space in Twentieth-Century America* (Cambridge: Cambridge University Press, 1999); Paul Berman, *Blacks and Jews: Alliances and Arguments* (New York: Delacorte, 1994); Emily Miller Budick, *Blacks and Jews in Literary Conversation* (Cambridge: Cambridge University Press, 1998).

81. Cited in Newton, *Facing Black and Jew*, xi.

82. Cited in Eric J. Sundquist, *Strangers in the Land: Blacks, Jews, Post-Holocaust America* (Cambridge: Belknap Press of Harvard University Press, 2005), 19.

83. Berman, *Blacks and Jews*, 40.

84. Michael Alexander, *Jazz Age Jews* (Princeton: Princeton University Press, 2001), 182.

85. M. M. Bakhtin, *The Dialogic Imagination: Four Essays* (Austin: University of Texas Press, 1981); M. M. Bakhtin, *Problems in Dostoevsky's Poetics* (Minneapolis: University of Minnesota Press, 1984); Tzvetan Todorov and Mikhail Bakhtin, *The Dialogical Principle* (Minneapolis: University of Minnesota Press, 1984).

86. Such activity must be analyzed as part of a wider social phenomenon that was deeply embedded in American social performances. See Susan Gubar, *Racechanges: White Skin, Black Face in American Culture* (New York: Oxford University Press, 1997).

87. Eric Porter, *What Is This Thing Called Jazz? African American Musicians as Artists, Critics, and Activists* (Berkeley: University of California Press, 2002); Stanley Crouch, *Considering Genius: Writings on Jazz* (New York: Basic Civitas, 2006).

88. In this regard there is Louis Armstrong's important work, "Louis Armstrong + The Jewish Family in New Orleans, La., the Year of 1907," in *Louis Armstrong: In His Own Words, Selected Writings*, ed. Thomas Brothers (Oxford: Oxford University Press, 1999), 3–36. Also see Alexander, *Jazz Age Jews*, 155; Ted Gioia, *The History of Jazz* (New York: Oxford University Press, 1997).

89. Burton W. Peretti, *The Creation of Jazz: Music, Race, and Culture in Urban America* (Urbana: University of Illinois Press, 1992); Gioia, *The History of Jazz*, 135ff; Gerald Early, "Pulp and Circumstance: The Story of Jazz in High Places," in *The Jazz Cadence of American Culture*, ed. Robert G. O'Meally (New York: Columbia University Press, 1998), 393ff.

90. Richard Cook, *Blue Note Records: The Biography* (Boston: Justin, Charles, 2003).

91. Paul Berliner, *Thinking in Jazz: The Infinite Art of Improvisation* (Chicago: University of Chicago Press, 1994); David Andrew Ake, *Jazz Cultures* (Berkeley: University of California Press, 2002); Martin T. Williams, *The Jazz Tradition* (New York: Oxford University Press, 1993).

92. Jon Cruz, *Culture on the Margins: The Black Spiritual and the Rise of American Cultural Interpretation* (Princeton: Princeton University Press, 1999); Ronald Michael Radano and Philip Vilas Bohlman, *Music and the Racial Imagination* (Chicago: University of Chicago Press, 2000); Ronald Michael Radano, *Lying Up a Nation: Race and Black Music* (Chicago: University of Chicago Press, 2003).

93. Zygmunt Bauman, "Assimilation into Exile: The Jew as a Polish Writer," in *Exile and Creativity: Signposts, Travelers, Outsiders, Backward Glances*, ed. Susan Rubin Suleiman (Durham: Duke University Press, 1998), 321–52. Bauman states, "To be in Exile means to be out of place; also, needing to be rather elsewhere; also, not having that 'elsewhere' where one would rather be. Thus, exile is a place of compulsory confinement, but also an unreal place, a place that is itself out of place in the order of things. Anything may happen here, but nothing can be done here. In exile, uncertainty meets freedom. Creation is the issue of that wedlock. What makes the exile an unreal place is the daily effort to make it real—that is, to cleanse it of all things that are out of place" (321).

94. Peter Ochs, "Recovering the God of History: Scriptural Life after Death in Judaism and Christianity," in *Jews and Christians*, ed. Dunn, 117.

95. In fact, the black theology movement inaugurated by black theologians such as James Cone, J. Deotis Roberts, Jacquelyn Grant, and Cheryl Sanders sought to do precisely that—to think Christian faith from the perspective of the horrors of slavery forward.

96. Ochs, "Recovering the God of History," 117.

97. Emmanuel Katongole, "A Different World Right Here, A World Being Gestated in the Deeds of the Everyday: The Church Within African Theological Imagination," *Missionalia* 30:2 (August 2002): 206–34. Also see his "African Renaissance and the Challenge of Narrative Theology in Africa," in *African Theology Today*, ed. Emmanuel Katongole (Scranton: University of Scranton Press, 2002), 207ff; Kwame

Bediako, *Christianity in Africa: The Renewal of a Non-Western Religion* (Maryknoll, N.Y.: Orbis, 1995); Andrew F. Walls, *The Cross-Cultural Process in Christian History* (Maryknoll, N.Y.: Orbis, 2002).

98. I am aware of the historic rationale for our social commitment to the church in terms of our ability to make proprietary claims on this sacred space. I am also aware of the important account of the multiple benefits continuously derived from life in the black church. But these disproportions suggest an ironic reciprocity in which Christian faith appears the symbiont of weakness and death. It is as though Christian faith fumbles along like an old country doctor applying quaint but ultimately ineffective homeopathic remedies to complex medical problems. I am not suggesting by this analogy that faith is irrelevant; rather, the question is how to give a healthy theological account of this situation.

99. Jonathan Boyarin, *Palestine and Jewish History: Criticism at the Borders of Ethnography* (Minneapolis: University of Minnesota Press, 1996); Anita Shapira, *Land and Power: The Zionist Resort to Force, 1881–1948* (New York: Oxford University Press, 1992).

100. Edward Soja, *Postmodern Geographies: The Reassertion of Space in Critical Social Theory* (London: Verso, 1989); Gray Gereffi and Miguel Korzeniewicz, eds. *Commodity Chains and Global Capitalism* (Westport, Conn.: Praeger, 1994).

101. Jeffrey M. Hornstein, *A Nation of Realtors: A Cultural History of the Twentieth-Century American Middle Class* (Durham: Duke University Press, 2005). Also see bell hooks, *Belonging: A Culture of Place* (New York: Routledge, 2009); W. J. T. Mitchell, ed., *Landscape and Power* (Chicago: University of Chicago Press, 2002).

INDEX

Acosta, Antonio de, 65

Acosta Porres, José de, 36; on Andean religions, 95–100; and Aristotelian-Thomas tradition, 68–72, 86, 88, 99; background, 65–66; on barbarian typologies, 102–6; on demonic activity, 98–99; *De Procuranda Indorum Salute*, 85, 92, 102–12; on discipline, 109; on doctrine of creation, 87, 89–90; and economic circuit, 89; education, 66–68; on faith, 108; health, 82; *Historia Natural y Moral de las Indias*, 85–95, 112; on *huacas*, 96; on humanism, 222; on idolatry, 96–100, 111, 113; on miners, 93–94; on native knowledge, 91; on Noah's ark animals, 91; pedagogical imperialism of, 112–16, 208, 209; and piety, 65, 66, 105, 109; supersessionism of, 97, 98; on temptation, 109–10; and Toledo, 75; ugly daughter analogy, 92–93

Adoptionism, 166–67

Agency: African, 123, 157, 159; and citizenship, 10–11; and consumption, 243; and displacement, 58–59; racial, 58, 59; and theology, 8; and translation, 155; and whiteness, 305 n. 137

Alexander, Michael: *Jazz Age Jews*, 280

Alfonso, King, 27, 28–29

Alienation, 116, 135, 156, 165, 348 n. 50

Almagro, Diego de, 73

Amo, Anton Wilhelm: *De jure Maurorum in Europa*, 187; *Tractatus de arte sobrie philosophandi*, 187

Amos (prophet), 269

Andeans, 72–76, 93–94; religious practices, 95–100

Anderson, Benedict, 222, 223–24

Andrews, William, 207–8

Anti-Semitism and racism, 278

Apaches, 54–57

Appadurai, Arjun, 243, 244–45

Aristotle, 69–71, 88, 113

Armstrong, Louis, 281

Arnold, Matthew, 152–53

Assimilation practices, 208, 230–31, 277–78

Atheism, 8

Athletes and skin color, 246

Augustine, Saint, 89–90, 92

Azurara, Gomes Eanes de. *See* Zurara, Gomes Eanes de

Baker, Houston, 186

Baker, Richard, 180–81

Baldwin, James, 279–80

Baptism of slaves, 182